EX LIBRIS

VINTAGE CLASSICS

SIMONE DE BEAUVOIR

Simone de Beauvoir was born in Paris in 1908. In 1929 she became the youngest person ever to obtain the *agrégation* in philosophy at the Sorbonne, placing second to Jean-Paul Sartre. She taught at the lycées at Marseille and Rouen from 1931 to 1937, and in Paris from 1938 to 1943. After the war she emerged as one of the leaders of the existentialist movement, working with Sartre on *Les Temps modernes*. The author of several books including *The Mandarins* (1954), which was awarded the Prix Goncourt, Beauvoir was one of the most influential thinkers of her generation. She died in 1986.

ALSO BY SIMONE DE BEAUVOIR

FICTION

She Came to Stay

The Blood of Others

All Men Are Mortal

The Mandarins

The Woman Destroyed

The Inseparables

Misunderstanding in Moscow

The Image of Her

NON-FICTION

The Ethics of Ambiguity

The Second Sex

Memoirs of a Dutiful Daughter

The Prime of Life

The Force of Circumstance

A Very Easy Death

All Said and Done

Adieux: A Farewell to Sartre

Letters to Sartre

SIMONE DE BEAUVOIR
AMERICA DAY BY DAY

TRANSLATED FROM THE FRENCH BY
Carol Cosman

WITH AN INTRODUCTION BY
Douglas Brinkley

VINTAGE CLASSICS

3 5 7 9 10 8 6 4 2

Vintage Classics is part of the Penguin Random House group of companies

Vintage, Penguin Random House UK, One Embassy Gardens,
8 Viaduct Gardens, London SW11 7BW

penguin.co.uk/vintage-classics
global.penguinrandomhouse.com

Translation copyright © The Regents of the University of California 1998
Foreword © Douglas Brinkley 1996
Translated from Simone de Beauvoir, *L'Amérique au jour le jour*
© Editions Gallimard, Paris, 1954

The moral right of the author has been asserted
This edition published in Vintage Classics in 2025
First published in Great Britain by Victor Gollancz in 1998

Penguin Random House values and supports copyright. Copyright fuels creativity, encourages diverse voices, promotes freedom of expression and supports a vibrant culture. Thank you for purchasing an authorised edition of this book and for respecting intellectual property laws by not reproducing, scanning or distributing any part of it by any means without permission. You are supporting authors and enabling Penguin Random House to continue to publish books for everyone. No part of this book may be used or reproduced in any manner for the purpose of training artificial intelligence technologies or systems. In accordance with Article 4(3) of the DSM Directive 2019/790, Penguin Random House expressly reserves this work from the text and data mining exception.

A CIP catalogue record for this book is available from the British Library

ISBN 9781784879884

Typeset in 11/13pt Bembo Book MT Pro by Six Red Marbles UK, Thetford, Norfolk
Printed and bound in Great Britain by Clays Ltd, Elcograf S.p.A.

The authorised representative in the EEA is Penguin Random House Ireland,
Morrison Chambers, 32 Nassau Street, Dublin D02 YH68

Penguin Random House is committed to a sustainable future
for our business, our readers and our planet. This book is made
from Forest Stewardship Council® certified paper.

To Ellen and Richard Wright

Contents

Foreword by Douglas Brinkley	xi
Preface	xvii
January	1
February	25
March	125
April	227
May	323
Itinerary of Simone de Beauvoir's travels (with page references)	389

Foreword

I teach an experimental course called 'American Odyssey' in which college students spend a semester reading classic works while travelling around the country on the Majic Bus to visit historical sites and meet writers. The curriculum includes fifty books, ranging from *Leaves of Grass* to *The Color Purple* to *On the Road*. Recently, I've added a new title: *America Day by Day*, a forgotten gem by Simone de Beauvoir, long out of print.

Beauvoir journeyed to America in January 1947, armed with an effusive letter of introduction from her soulmate Jean-Paul Sartre and ecstatic about experiencing four whirlwind months. Although she did not intend to write a book, she kept a detailed diary of her observations, which was published in France in 1948 as *L'Amérique au jour le jour*. At the time of her trip, two years before the publication of *The Second Sex*, Beauvoir was considered more of a café society curiosity than a feminist trailblazer. Even in 1952, when the book was translated and published in England as *America Day by Day*, it generated few sales and little notice. But with the passage of time, *America Day by Day* emerges as a supremely erudite American road book – that distinctive subgenre based on flights of fancy rather than flights from economic hardship, as in John Steinbeck's *Grapes of Wrath*. In broader sociological terms, her critique outpaces William Least Heat-Moon's *Blue Highways: A Journey into America*. In the realm of pure prose style, it easily transcends Henry Miller's *The Air-Conditioned Nightmare*. And, for my money, in the field of European highbrow loathing of the cruder aspects of our democratic experiment, it is preferable to Charles Dickens's haughty *American Notes for General Circulation*.

Raised as a bourgeois Catholic schoolgirl in Paris following World War I, Beauvoir was an intuitive sociologist, although her more poetic passages show an unexpected empathy for those afflicted with loneliness. It's these flashes of authentic compassion for the common people she meets that make *America Day by Day* so endearing. Although she regularly mounts her soapbox to denounce everything from atomic weapons to bad food, she exudes maternal kindness to everyone she meets, regardless of his or her narrow politics or jingoistic worldview. Although cynical about the hegemonic intent of the United States government, she displays a keen appreciation of 'American dynamism' and the GIs who had liberated France from the Nazis. Leaving all her preconceptions back in Montparnasse, the indefatigable explorer made the transatlantic journey ready to embrace America with her 'hands, eyes, mouth'.

Beauvoir's story begins with her 'smooth flight' from Paris to Newfoundland to New York's La Guardia Airport. Embraced upon arrival by the Condé Nast set at a gaggle of cocktail parties, cheered on at Vassar College, where she took part in a symposium called 'Women's Role in Contemporary Society', gossiped about as the 'prettiest existentialist' by Janet Flanner in the *New Yorker*'s 'Talk of the Town', Beauvoir made a significant splash. The *New York Times Magazine* even commissioned an article from her – 'An Existentialist Looks at Americans' – which appeared on 25 May 1947. Although much of her itinerary revolved around her well-arranged lecture schedule, she allowed plenty of free days for aimless explorations and journalistic pulse taking. Beauvoir, like an anxious literary traveller, wanted to pinpoint the intellectual fountainhead of the nation that produced the likes of Ernest Hemingway, F. Scott Fitzgerald and John Dos Passos. The first chapters of *America Day by Day* take place in prosperous postwar Manhattan, where Beauvoir was overwhelmed by the cult of American consumerism, disturbed by our national attraction to luxury cars and Madison Avenue come-ons, and angered at the anti-communist groupthink mentality she encountered wherever she went. She perfectly captures the alienated sensation of being a stranger in Gotham:

Between these houses that have existed without me for years, for centuries, these streets were travelled by thousands of people who were not me, who are not me. But now I'm walking here. I go down Broadway; it's really me. I'm walking in streets not yet travelled by me, streets where my life has not yet been carved, streets without any scent of the past. No one here is concerned with my presence; I'm still a ghost, and I slip through the city without disturbing anything. Yet from now on my life will embrace the contour of these streets, these houses. New York will belong to me; I will belong to it.

A reader is struck not only by the meticulous descriptive passages on American history and geography but also by Beauvoir's ability to encapsulate our national psyche ('Optimism is necessary for the country's social peace and economic prosperity') and to comment so deftly on our shortcomings ('even people of goodwill ... refuse to articulate clearly the current conflict between justice and freedom, and the necessity of devising a compromise between these two ideas; they prefer to deny injustice and the lack of freedom').

Just because Beauvoir is a refined tourist in an America that stood, in Winston Churchill's words, 'at the summit of the world' does not mean her adventure is a tame one. There is an indisputable truth to her matter-of-fact observation that 'as in all big cities, people use a lot of drugs in New York'. Her attempt to get high on a marijuana cigarette in the Plaza Hotel with a shaggy cabal of Greenwich Village idlers is a hilarious misadventure. Her radical-chic ability to embrace all aspects of shadowy bohemia without a tinge of guilt or paranoia sparkles throughout. Sexually liberated, she meets men on the road – including, in Chicago, a thinly disguised Nelson Algren, who becomes her lover – and alcohol consumption is a prominent part of her travels.

Clearly a voyeur of America's transient underbelly, Beauvoir is able, like George Orwell in *Down and Out in Paris and London*, to penetrate the haze and blue smoke of our nation's tenderloin districts deeply enough to offer detached insights into desolation row. In Chicago, with Algren as her guide, she learns first-hand about the world of morphine addicts and petty thieves, murderous gangsters and midnight cops. 'America is a box full of surprises,' she writes, intoxicated by her walks on the wild side.

As one would expect, feminism is discussed openly. Although she often compares the American women she encounters with European women, what Beauvoir finds most peculiar about feminism in America is that women disdain others of their sex, that sisterhood is just a slogan bandied about rhetorically by the enlightened few. As she explores everything from our national horror of prostitutes to mass frigidity, she sounds more like a precursor to Camille Paglia than Betty Friedan: 'Woman is much less comfortable in this masculine world, where she has only recently been admitted as an equal,' she writes. '[Their] inability to prove themselves concretely is a constant source of irritation, which, in their confusion, they readily turn against men.'

Beauvoir's peripatetic journey by automobile, train and Greyhound bus took her from coast to coast and back, and illuminating sections of the memoir are devoted to Hollywood, the Grand Canyon, Reno, New Orleans, Las Vegas and San Antonio. Always amused and exhilarated by the lapdog friendliness of urban and rural folk alike, she is also flabbergasted that these same good-natured people embody the volatile, schizophrenic mixture of 'strictness and hypocritical licence'. An eternal rebel, she has an uncanny eye for the shallow extravagances of American culture and an abolitionist's rage at the evil of segregation south of the Mason–Dixon Line. While San Francisco and Chicago are celebrated in *America Day by Day*, other cities get scorched: 'Williamsburg is one of the sorriest shams to which I've ever fallen victim,' or, 'I dearly hope I'm never fated to live in Rochester.'

Like Georgia O'Keeffe before her, who once said, 'If you ever go to New Mexico, it will itch you for the rest of your life,' Simone de Beauvoir was spiritually enveloped by the high desert terrain she encountered on the enchanted road from Santa Fe to Taos with the Sangre de Cristo Mountains hovering in constant view. To Beauvoir, the richly textured curves of the adobe walls and abandoned pueblos were national heritage sites of untold mystery more potent than all the 'discouraging' marble monuments in Washington DC that induced 'boredom'. Toward the end of her journey she lectured at Smith and Wellesley on the metaphysical novel, providing her the opportunity to sightsee around Boston and to reflect on her recent American travel discoveries. 'Emerson and Damon Runyon belong to the same world. You cannot understand Chicago, Los Angeles or Houston if you forget that they are haunted by the troublesome, propitious, irritated or complacent ghosts of the old Puritans,' Beauvoir writes. 'If you want to find a way into the difficult heart of America, it's in Concord that you will find the key to open the first gate.'

A mix of literary and sociological references and perspicacious musings, *America Day by Day* brims with philosophical speculation and memorable aphorisms. After attending a Louis Armstrong concert at Carnegie Hall, Beauvoir writes, 'The American public has more or less murdered jazz, but they still love it.' Travelling through the Mojave Desert for a hundred miles past curio shops and jackalope stands, she observes, 'Tourism has a privileged character in America: it doesn't cut you off from the country it's revealing to you; on the contrary, it's a way of entering it.' And, at last, in a line that could serve as a motto for the whole Beat Generation ethic: 'All these mass-manufactured fates are haunted by a thousand dreams of escape.'

For women, and men, who want to experience vicariously Jack Kerouac's open road with less macho romanticism and more existential savvy, *America Day by Day*, hidden from us for nearly fifty years, comes to the reader like a dusty bottle of vintage French cognac, asking only to be uncorked.

Douglas Brinkley
New Orleans, 15 October 1996

A slightly shorter version of this foreword appeared as 'The Existential Tourist' in the *New York Times Book Review* of 11 August 1996.

Preface

I spent four months in America – very little time. Furthermore, I travelled for pleasure and wherever I happened to be invited. There are vast areas of the New World I haven't even glimpsed. As a private individual, I crossed this great industrial country without visiting its factories, without seeing its technical accomplishments, without making contact with the working class. Nor did I enter the elite circle where US politics and economics are hammered out. Yet alongside the fuller pictures that more competent people have drawn, it does not seem useless to me to recount, day by day, how America revealed itself to one consciousness – mine.

In place of a serious study, which would be presumptuous for me to attempt, I can offer a faithful account [of my travels]. Because concrete experience involves both subject and object, I have not tried to eliminate myself from this narrative: it is truthful only because it includes the unique personal circumstances in which each discovery was made. That is why I have adopted the journal form. Although written in retrospect, this journal – reconstituted from notes, letters and memories that were still fresh – is scrupulously accurate. I have respected the chronological order of my amazement, my admiration, my indignation, my hesitations and my mistakes. Frequently, my first impressions become clearer only as time goes by. For the topics that seem important to me, I have noted how one passage is related to another. But I insist that no isolated piece represents a definitive judgement. Indeed, often I never arrived at a fixed viewpoint, and it is the whole collection of my indecisions, additions and corrections that constitutes my opinion. No selection has been exercised in telling the story: it is the story of what happened to me, neither more nor less. This is what I saw and how I saw it. I have not tried to say more.

January

25 January 1947

Something is about to happen. You can count the minutes in your life when something happens. Strokes of light sweep the ground, shining red and green; it's a gala evening, a late-night party – my party. Something does happen: the propellers turn faster and faster, the engines engage. My heart can't follow them. In a single movement the red beacons are crushed to the earth. In the distance, the lights of Paris flicker, sober stars rising from a dark blue abyss.

There. It's happened. I'm flying to New York. It's true. The loudspeaker called out, 'Passengers bound for New York . . .', and the voice had the familiar accent of all voices heard through loudspeakers on station platforms. Paris–Marseilles, Paris–London, Paris–New York. It's only a trip, a passage from one place to another. That's what the voice was saying; that's what is written on the steward's blasé face. Because of his job, he finds it quite natural that I'm flying to America. There is only one world, and New York is a city of the world. But no. Despite all the books I've read, the films, the photographs, the stories, New York is a legendary city in my past; there is no path from the reality to the legend. Across from old Europe, on the threshold of a continent populated by 160 million people, New York belongs to the future. How could I jump wholeheartedly over my own life? I try to reason with myself – New York is real and present – but this feeling persists. Usually, travelling is an attempt to annex a new object to my universe; this in itself is a fascinating undertaking. But today it's different: I feel I'm leaving my life behind. I don't know if it will be through anger or hope, but something is going to be revealed – a world so full, so rich and so unexpected that I'll have the extraordinary adventure of becoming a different me.

The smooth flight is already a promise: I've already escaped myself. The earth has slipped to the bottom of an alien ether. I am nowhere: I am *elsewhere*. And what time is it? What season are we in? It's summer in the Azores, in the shade of broad straw hats. The ground of Newfoundland is covered with snow and frost. It's eight o'clock in Paris and two o'clock in New York. Time and space are intertwined. My dreams are less extravagant than this great wing I'm attached to, gliding motionless between clouds and stars.

I've slept. I open my eyes. In the black sky carpeting the abyss, horizontal, stationary fireworks suddenly explode: stars, webs, circles, showers of multicoloured lights. Water trembles between the glittering chandeliers. It looks like Venice gone mad. Or some great victory being celebrated on earth . . . 'Boston,' says the stewardess. The Puritan name evokes a city of sober stone. Traced in fire and gold on the velvet of the plain, its image looks giddy. Boston. America. I look avidly. I can't yet say, 'I'm in America.' In only a minute I could crash to the ground, but I'm in a sky that belongs to no continent: *the* sky. Beneath me the night gathers again; America is sleeping. But in the distance fireworks explode from a new celebration: a city, a village. It seems that in this country the stones and bricks change at night into blazing spangles; every little village is a glowing Christmas tree.

Descending from sky to earth is a small ordeal. The limpid, weightless air thickens into an atmosphere hugging the terrestrial crust and swept by eddies. The splendid flight becomes applied navigation. My temples throb, my ears hurt; my eardrum becomes that membrane described in the natural history books: it tightens, it vibrates, it hurts. I was only a gaze, an expectation: now I have a pocket of a stomach, a bony box of a skull, a membrane of an eardrum – a whole machinery of separate and ill-fitting parts. I've closed my eyes; when I open them again, all the stars in the sky have rolled onto the earth. It's a glittering mass of gems and precious red stones, ruby fruits, topaz flowers and diamond rivers. I haven't known such splendour and such passionate desire since childhood. All the treasures of *The Thousand and One Nights* that I dreamed of back then and that I never glimpsed – here they are. All the fair booths I didn't go into, the merry-go-rounds with wooden horses, Magic City, Luna Park – here they are. And the stage sets at the Châtelet Theatre, the birthday cakes, the crystal chandeliers lighting up the night in rooms full of music – these are given back to me, given to me. That holly branch hung with necklaces, bracelets, clusters of transparent, glossy candy that I so badly coveted one Palm Sunday – here it is. I will hang these sugar jewels around my neck, my wrists; I will crack the crystal between my teeth; I will crush the shining sugary fruit against my palate and savour a taste of cassis and pineapple on my tongue.

The plane descends; it pitches. Bound to the winds, the fog, the weight of the air, it is living a turbulent life among the elements; it belongs to nature. It descends. The strings of pearls become streets, the crystal balls are streetlamps; it is a city after all, and the very words of childhood are too impoverished to name its promises. A factory smokestack sways in the sky. I make out houses along an avenue, and I think, 'I will walk down those streets.' The smokestack sways a second time; we are circling around. The woman next to me murmurs, 'The engine's making an odd noise.' We turn, leaning on one wing, and I think quickly, 'I don't want to die. Not now. I don't want the lights to go out.' The smokestack has disappeared. The red beacons draw near, and I feel the thud of the wheels touching the runway. We were just waiting our turn; an airplane lands at La Guardia every minute.

The elements are conquered, distances annihilated, but New York has vanished. To rejoin it, you have to go through the narrow tunnel of terrestrial life. Papers are passed from hand to hand; a doctor perfunctorily examines our teeth, as if we were horses for sale. We are led into an overheated hall, and we wait. My head is heavy; I'm stifling. People had warned me, 'It's always too hot in America.' This dulling heat, then, is America; and this orange juice handed to me by a young woman with shiny hair and a practised smile is also America. It will have to be discovered slowly; it will not let you devour it like a big piece of candy. The Christmas trees and luminous fountains are far away. I will not catch another glimpse of that festive face; it doesn't shine for those who bear down on the land with all their human weight. My name is called; a bureaucrat examines my fine visa made of stiff paper, decorated with red seals like a medieval charter. He nods his head. 'You come from a beautiful country,' he says, 'but you've come to an even more beautiful one.' He asks me for eight dollars. Then the customs officers rummage idly through my suitcase, and I enter the great round hall where people get bored and doze off. I'm free, and on the other side of the door, New York is waiting.

DP [Denise Perrier, from the French cultural services] has come to meet me; I don't know her. But off I go, borne away beside a young woman I've never seen, through a city that my eyes don't yet know how to see. The car drives so fluidly, the road beneath the wheels is so smooth that the earth seems as evanescent as air. We follow a river, we cross a metal bridge, and my neighbour says suddenly, 'That's Broadway.' Then, all at once, I see. I see broad, brightly lit streets where hundreds and hundreds of cars are driving, stopping and starting again with such discipline you would think they were guided from above by some magnetic providence. The regular grid of the streets, the immovable stop signs at the perpendicular intersections, the mathematical sequence of red and green traffic lights all create such an impression of order and peace that the city seems silent. The fact is, you don't hear a single honk or exhaust backfiring, and now I understand why our American visitors are surprised by the awful screeching of brakes at our street corners. Here the cars glide by on a blanketed roadway punctuated by rising geysers of steam. It's like a silent film. The shiny cars look like they've just left the showroom, and the pavement seems as clean as the tiles of a Dutch kitchen. Light has washed away all the stains; it's a supernatural light that transfigures the asphalt, that wraps a halo around the flowers, silk dresses, candies, nylon stockings, gloves, bags, shoes, furs and ribbons offered in the shop windows. I look avidly. I will probably never find this silence, this luxury, this peace again; I will never again see those ramparts of black lava around Central Park, those gigantic dominoes of stone and light. Tomorrow New York will be a city. But this evening is magical. We drive around without finding a parking space. This is an obligatory rite, and I give myself over to it with a neophyte's curiosity. In the restaurant decorated with red and gold palm trees, the dinner is a meal of initiation; the martini and lobster taste of the sacred.

DP has booked me a room in a huge hotel at Forty-fourth Street and Eighth Avenue. She asks how long I can stay. 'As long as she likes, if she behaves herself,' says the manager with a big smile. This seems to be a stroke of luck; it's not that easy to find lodging. DP leaves me, but I don't go up to my room. I walk across Broadway. The air is soft and humid, a southern winter; after all, New York is at the same latitude as Lisbon. I walk. Broadway. Times Square. Forty-second Street. My eyes have no memory; my steps, no plan. Cut off from the past and the future, a pure presence – a presence so pure, so tenuous that it doubts itself. All the world seems in limbo. I say, 'This is New York.' But I don't completely believe it. No rails, no tracks – I have not traced my path on the surface of the earth. This city and Paris are not connected like two elements of the same system. Each has its own atmosphere, and the two do not coincide, they do not exist together, and I couldn't have passed from one to the other. I'm no longer in Paris, but I'm not here either. My presence is a borrowed presence. There is no place for me on these sidewalks. This strange world where I've landed by surprise was not waiting for me. It was full without me; it *is* full without me. It is a world where I am not: I grasp it in my perfect absence. This crowd I'm jostling, I'm not part of it; I feel invisible to every gaze. I am travelling incognito, like a phantom. Will I manage to reincarnate myself?

26 January

In the middle of the night, in the depth of sleep, a wordless voice suddenly says, 'Something has happened to me.' I'm still sleeping, and I don't know if it's a great happiness or a catastrophe. Something has happened to me. Perhaps I've died, as so often happens in my dreams. Perhaps I'm going to wake up on the other side of death. As I open my eyes, I'm afraid. And then I remember: this is not quite the otherworld. It's New York.

It wasn't a mirage. New York is here; everything is real. Truth bursts in the blue sky, in the soft damp air, more triumphant than the night's unreliable charms. It's nine o'clock in the morning. It's Sunday. The streets are deserted. A few neon signs are still lit. Not a pedestrian, not a car; nothing disturbs the rectilinear grid of Eighth Avenue. Cubes, prisms, parallelograms; the houses are abstract solids and surfaces; the intersection, an abstract of two volumes – its materials have no density or structure; the space itself seems to have been set in moulds. I do not move; I look. I'm here, and New York will be mine. This joy is familiar. Fifteen years ago I was leaving the train station, and from the top of the monumental staircase I saw all the rooftops of Marseilles at my feet. I had a year or two to spend alone in an unknown city. I didn't move; I just looked, thinking: 'This strange city is my future; it will be my past.' Between these houses that have existed without me for years, for centuries, these streets were travelled by thousands of people who were not me, who are not me. But now I'm walking here. I go down Broadway; it's really me. I'm walking in streets not yet travelled by me, streets where my life has not yet been carved, streets without any scent of the past. No one here is concerned with my presence; I'm still a ghost, and I slip through the city without disturbing anything. Yet from now on my life will embrace the contour of these streets, these houses. New York will belong to me; I will belong to it.

I drink orange juice at the edge of a counter, sitting in a polished booth on one of three armchairs raised on a little dais; little by little, I take on flesh and blood, and the city grows familiar. The surfaces become façades; the solids turn into houses. On the pavement the wind stirs up dust and old papers. Beyond Washington Square, the grid begins to bend. The right angles break down; the streets are no longer numbered but have names; the lines curve and tangle together. I'm wandering through a European city. The houses have only three or four storeys and come in opaque colours somewhere between red, ochre, and black. Sheets dry on the fire escapes that zigzag against the façades. These sheets that promise sunshine, the shoe-shine boys posted on the street corners, the rooftop terraces – they vaguely evoke a southern city, yet the worn red of the houses makes one think of the London fog. The fact is, this neighbourhood is like nothing I've ever seen. But I know I will love it.

The landscape changes. The word 'landscape' suits this city that's been deserted by men and invaded by the sky. Rising above the skyscrapers, the sky surges through the straight streets; it's too vast for the city to tame, and it overflows – it's a mountain sky. I walk between the steep cliffs at the bottom of a canyon where no sun penetrates: it's filled with a salt smell. Human history is not inscribed on these carefully calibrated buildings; they are more like prehistoric caves than the houses of Paris or Rome. In Paris, in Rome, history has permeated the bowels of the ground itself; Paris reaches down into the centre of the earth. In New York, even the Battery doesn't have such deep roots. Beneath the subways, sewers and heating pipes, the rock is virgin and inhuman. Between this rock and the open sky, Wall Street and Broadway bathe in the shadows of their giant buildings; this morning they belong to nature. The little black church with its cemetery of flat paving stones is as unexpected and touching in the middle of Broadway as a crucifix on a wild ocean beach.

The sun is so beautiful, the waters of the Hudson so green that I take the boat that brings Midwestern tourists to the Statue of Liberty. But I don't get out at the little island that looks like a small fort. I just want to see a view of the Battery as I've so often seen it in the movies. I do see it. In the distance, its towers seem fragile. They rest so precisely on their vertical lines that the slightest shudder would knock them down like a house of cards. When the boat draws closer, their foundations seem firmer, but the fall line remains indelibly traced. What a field day a bomber would have!

There are hundreds of restaurants in these streets, but they are all closed on Sunday. The one I find is packed. I eat hastily, rushed by the waitress. No place to rest. Nature is kinder. Within this harshness, New York becomes more human again. Pearl Street with its elevated train, Chatham Square, Chinatown, the Bowery. I am beginning to get tired. Slogans run through my head: 'City of contrasts.' These alleys smelling of spices and packing paper at the foot of façades with thousands of windows – that is one contrast. I encounter another contrast with each step, and they are all different. 'A vertical city', 'passionate geometries'. 'thrilling geometries' – such phrases are perfect descriptions of these skyscrapers, these façades, these avenues: I see that. And I've often read, 'New York with its cathedrals.' I could have invented the phrase – all these old clichés seem so hollow. Yet in the freshness of discovery, the words 'contrasts' and 'cathedrals' also come to my lips, and I'm surprised they seem so faded when the reality they capture is unchanged. People have told me something more precise: 'On the Bowery on Sundays, the drunks sleep on the sidewalks.' Here is the Bowery; the drunks are sleeping on the sidewalks. This is just what the words meant, and their precision disconcerts me. How could they have seemed so empty when they are so true? It isn't with words that I will grasp New York. I no longer think of grasping it: I will be transformed by it. Words, images, knowledge, expectations – they won't help me at all. To pronounce them true or false makes no sense. It is not possible to confront things here; they exist in another dimension – they are simply here. And I look and look, as astonished as a blind man who has just recovered his sight.

27 January

If I want to decode New York, I must meet New Yorkers. There are names in my address book but no faces to match. I'll have to talk on the telephone, in English, to people whom I don't know and who don't know me. Going down into the hotel lobby, I'm more intimidated than if I were going to take an oral exam. This lobby stuns me with its exoticism, an unnatural exoticism. I'm the Zulu frightened by a bicycle, the peasant lost in the Paris metro. There's a newspaper stand and a cigar stand, a Western Union office, a hairdresser, a writing room where stenographers and typists take dictation from clients – it's at once a club, an office, a waiting room and a large department store. I perceive around me all the conveniences of everyday life, but I don't know what to do. The slightest action poses a problem: How do I get postage for my letters? Where do I mail them? Those flutterings near the elevator, those white flashes, I almost took them for hallucinations. Behind a glass window, letters fall from the twenty-fifth floor into the depths of the basement – the mailbox. At the newspaper stand there's a machine that spits out stamps. But I'm confused by the coins. One cent, for me, seems like both one *sou* and one *centime*; five cents is then five *centimes* but also five *sous* (that is, twenty-five *centimes*). For ten minutes I try in vain to get a telephone line; all the machines reject the nickel I stubbornly keep sliding into the slot meant for quarters. I remain sitting in one of the booths, worn out. I want to give up: I hate this malicious instrument. But in the end I can't just stay wrapped in my solitude. I ask the Western Union employee for help. This time someone answers. The faceless voice vibrates at the other end of the line: I have to talk. They weren't expecting me, and I have nothing to offer. I simply say, 'I'm here.' I have no face either; I'm just a name bandied about by mutual friends. I say again, 'I'd very much like to see you.' It's not even true, and they know it; it isn't them I want to see, because I don't know them. But the voices are almost friendly, natural. This naturalness already comforts me, as a kind of friendship. After three calls, though, I close my address book, flushed.

I go to the hairdresser; I feel less uprooted. In every city I've known, these places are much alike – the same odour, the same metal dryers. The combs, the cotton balls, the mirrors have no personality. Surrendering to the hands massaging my skull, I'm no longer a ghost: there's a real meeting between me and these hands – it's really me turning into flesh and blood. But even this moment isn't entirely routine. For example, I notice that I don't have to hand the hairpins one by one to the girl doing my hair: they're attached to a magnet she wears around her wrist, and a magnet removes them when my hair is dry. This little trick amazes me.

Everything amazes me, both the unexpected sights and those I've anticipated. I didn't know that in front of the apartment buildings in the elegant neighbourhoods there would be a greenish canvas canopy marked with a big number and extending onto the sidewalk, as if announcing some kind of wedding. A porter stands on the threshold, so every building really looks like a hotel or a bar. The entry, too, guarded by uniformed doormen, resembles the entrance hall of a palace. The elevator is staffed by an employee: it's difficult to receive clandestine visits. On the other hand, in movies I have often seen these buildings without any concierge, similar to provincial apartments in France. You step inside a glass door and find a series of bells corresponding to each tenant; each person has a mailbox. You ring the bell, and a second glass door opens. I also recognise the broad, flat doorbells I've seen in films. They make a more muffled sound than French bells do.

What disconcerts me is that those movie sets that I'd never really believed in are suddenly real.

So many small surprises give the first few days a particular grace – I could never be bored. This business lunch in a restaurant on Fortieth Street is perfectly dreary. With its carpets, its mirrors and its polished surfaces, this elegant place looks like the tearoom in a big department store, and of course it's overheated. But in my martini, in the tomato juice, I learn the taste of America. This meal is another communion.

This grace has its price. The exoticism that transfigures each of my moments also leads me into traps. It's a beautiful sunny day, and I want to walk along the East River. But the 'Drive', that broad elevated causeway spanning the river, is reserved for cars. I try to cheat, and I walk along, glued to the wall. But it's difficult to cheat in America. The gears are precise; they serve man, provided he's quietly compliant. The cars hurtling along at sixty miles per hour over this sort of highway come dangerously close to me. There's a square near the water where people are strolling, but it seems impossible to reach them. I muster my courage and cross to the centre line separating the two lanes of traffic, but I have to stand there a long time, planted like a traffic light, waiting for a brief lull so that I can cross over. I still have to jump over a metal railing to get to safety. Under my winter coat, which is too heavy for this sun, I'm more exhausted than if I'd climbed a mountain. A few moments later, I find out that there are pedestrian passageways under the Drive and that it's also spanned by bridges.

The river smells of salt and spices. Men are sitting on benches in the sun: tramps and blacks. Children on roller skates hurl themselves over the asphalt, jostling each other, shouting. Low-cost housing is under construction along the Drive; these vast buildings, which narrow as they rise, are ugly. But beyond them I glimpse the city's high towers, and across the river I see Brooklyn. I sit on a bench looking at Brooklyn amid the noise of roller skates, and I feel quite happy. Brooklyn exists, as does Manhattan with its skyscrapers and all of America on the horizon. As for me, I no longer exist. There. I understand what I've come to find – this plenitude that we rarely feel except in childhood or in early youth, when we're utterly absorbed by something outside ourselves. To be sure, on other trips I've tasted this joy, this certitude, but it was fleeting. In Greece, in Italy, in Spain, in Africa, I still felt that Paris was the heart of the world. I'd never completely left Paris; I remained inside myself.

Paris has lost its hegemony. I've landed not only in a foreign country but in another world – an autonomous, separate world. I touch this world; it's here. It will be given to me. But it's not even to me that it will be given; its existence is too dazzlingly clear for me to hope to catch it in my net. The revelation will take place somewhere beyond the limits of my own existence. In a flash I'm freed from the cares of that tedious enterprise I call my life. I'm just the charmed consciousness through which the sovereign Object will reveal itself.

I walk for a long time. When I reach the bridge, the sun is all red. The black trellis of the steel bridge bars the flaming sky. Through this iron gridwork I can glimpse the high square towers of the Battery. The bridge's horizontal thrust and the skyscrapers' vertical lift seem amplified. The light is a glorious reward for their audacity.

I have a rendezvous at six o'clock at the Plaza Hotel on Fifty-ninth Street. I climb the stairs of the elevated railway. This railway is touching, like a memory; it's scarcely bigger than a provincial miniature railway. The walls are wooden; it seems like a country station. The gate is also made of wood, but it turns automatically – no employee. To go through, all you need is a nickel, the magic coin that also activates telephones and opens the doors of toilets, which are modestly called 'restrooms'. We roll along above the Bowery at second-storey level. The stations whizz by: we're already at Fourteenth Street, then Thirty-fifth, Forty-second. I'm waiting for Fifty-ninth, but we rush past – Seventieth, Eightieth – we're not stopping any more. Below us, all the streetlamps are lit. Here is the nocturnal celebration I glimpsed from up in the sky: movie houses, drugstores, wooden houses. I'm transported through a wondrous amusement park, and this little elevated train is itself a fairground attraction. Will it ever stop? New York is so big . . .

I've gotten on an express train. At the first station I get off and take a 'local'. I wait for a long while in the Plaza's scented, overheated lobby. It's the same setting as in the restaurant this morning: too many mirrors, too many carpets, drapes, polished surfaces. I wait an amazingly long time, and suddenly I realise that I'm at the Savoy-Plaza; my rendezvous is across the street. Tired, confused, dazed after so many discoveries and mistakes, I sit down at the Plaza bar. Fortunately, everyone's waited for me. The martini revives me. The big, dark, oak-panelled room is overheated and overcrowded. I look at people. The women surprise me. In their carefully coiffed, perfectly waved hair they wear whole flower beds, aviaries. Most of the coats are mink; the intricately draped dresses are sewn with bright spangles and decorated with heavy, unimaginative costume jewellery. All these women are wearing open-toed shoes with very high heels. I'm ashamed of my Swiss shoes with the crepe soles I was so proud of. In the street, on this winter day, I haven't seen one woman with flat shoes. None have had the free and sporty look I attribute to American women. All are dressed in silk, not wool; they are covered with feathers, violets, flowers and flounces. There's too much finery, too many mirrors and drapes; the food has too many sauces and syrups; everywhere, there's too much heat. Superabundance, too, is a curse.

Yesterday I had dinner at DP's with some French people. This evening I'm having dinner at the home of more French people. And after dinner, BC, a Frenchwoman, is going to take me to some bars. When I'm with French people, I sense the same disappointment I felt when I was with my parents during my childhood that nothing was completely real. There was a glass wall between things and me, so all birds seemed to be in birdcages, all fish seemed to swim in aquariums, all chimpanzees seemed stuffed – and I so dearly wanted to see the world truly, without restraints . . . I don't like the taste of whiskey; I only like these glass sticks you stir it with. Yet until three o'clock in the morning, I drink Scotch docilely because Scotch is one of the keys to America. I want to break through the glass wall.

28 January

I have a lecture to prepare. I sit down at one of the desks in the 'writing room' amid the murmur of voices dictating reports to stenographers and the clacking of typewriters. It's quiet and subdued; you'd think you were at Bon Marché!* I decide to sit in one of the bars around Central Park. I don't much like them; they belong to the big hotels and are bathed in the same cosy and respectable atmosphere as the lobby with the luxurious display cases. Although they serve alcohol, they remind me of tearooms for old ladies; whiskey takes on the innocence of fruit juice. These are places where the street doesn't intrude: nothing can happen here. Yet they have a magic for me. Friends whose trips to America I've so envied pronounced these names – the Sherry Netherland or the Café Arnold – with the pride of the initiated. I follow in their footsteps. I have no past of my own, so I borrow theirs. New York still belongs to them. I'm only a newcomer, and it's already something for me to slip into their intimacy with the city. I have the modesty of a guest invited at the last minute.

It's not customary here to do work in places where people drink: this is the land of specialisation. In places where drinks are served, you drink. As soon as my glass is empty, the waiter comes over to enquire; if I don't empty it fast enough, he prowls around me, looking at me reproachfully. This morning the taste

---

* A popular Parisian department store.

of whiskey doesn't seem so bad. But it seems wiser to leave before the fourth glass.

I give my lecture to a French audience. I go to a cocktail party at the home of a Frenchwoman. All the guests are French, except for two French-speaking Americans. I'm not, however, in a colonised country where the local customs make it nearly impossible to mingle with the natives; on the contrary, we're the ones who form what they call here a 'colony'. I would really like to leave. I'm quite excited by the time I arrive at the house of AM [Dorothy Nordman], who has invited me for dinner; at long last I'm getting inside an American home. But apart from Richard Wright, whom I knew in Paris and whom I'm delighted to see again, everyone is French. There are even people from the embassy, and everyone is speaking the French of France in a very official tone.

All these French people I meet are pleased to explain America to me — according to their experience, of course. Nearly all of them have a strong bias: either they hate it and can think only of leaving or they shower it with excessive praise, as the collaborationists did with Germany. R, a university professor, is one of these. As soon as he shakes my hand, he asks me to 'promise' to write nothing about America: it's a such a difficult, complex country that even twenty years isn't enough to understand it; it's deplorable to criticise it superficially, as certain French people do. America is so vast that nothing anyone can say about it is true. In any case, I must 'promise' to write nothing about the blacks. This is a painful and difficult problem on which no one can have an opinion without a wealth of information that would require more than one lifetime. And besides, why are the French so determined to concern themselves with the blacks? Aren't the intellectual and artistic accomplishments of whites far superior? Even the music of modern white composers has more value than jazz.

V, who is anti-American, explains to me scornfully that this attitude is the only feasible one for a Frenchman living in this country; otherwise, he would live in a state of intolerable anger and revolt. No European values are acknowledged here, and V acknowledges no American values. The daily atmosphere seems unbreathable to him. He despises New York.

The servility of R's attitude disgusts me; besides, during the war he supported Pétain – a dyed-in-the-wool collaborationist. But I can't believe there's nothing worthwhile in this country. I'm utterly taken with New York. It's true that both camps tell me, 'New York is not America.' V irritates me when he declares, 'If you like New York, it's because it's a European city that's strayed to the edge of this continent.' It is all too clear that New York is not Europe. But I'm even more distrustful of P, another pro-American Pétain supporter, when he contrasts New York – a city of foreigners and Jews – to the idyllic villages of New England, where the inhabitants are 100 per cent American and endowed with patriarchal virtues. We have often heard 'the real France' praised this way in contrast to the corruption of Paris.

I still have nothing to say; I can only listen. But I think that America is a world, and that you can no more accept or reject *a* world than you can accept or reject *the* world. It's a matter of choosing your friends and enemies, of asserting your projects and your singular revolts. America – a piece of the planet, a political system, a civilisation; classes, races, sects and men taken one by one. There are the cops and the robbers, the engineers and the artists, the malcontents and the smug, the profiteers and the exploited. I know very well that every hatred will be the inverse of a love, every love the inverse of a hatred.

29 January

Again I slept late. But there's something in the New York air that makes sleep useless; perhaps it's because your heart beats more quickly here than elsewhere – people with heart conditions sleep less, and many New Yorkers die of heart problems. In any case, I'm enjoying this windfall: the days seem too short.

Breakfast in the corner drugstore is a celebration. Orange juice, toast, *café au lait* – an unadulterated pleasure. Sitting on my revolving stool, I participate in a moment of American life. My solitude does not separate me from my neighbours, who are also eating alone. Rather, it's the pleasure I feel that isolates me from them. They are simply eating; they're not on vacation.

The truth is that it's all a holiday for me. The drugstores especially intrigue me. I stop at one on any pretext. To me, they are the essence of American exoticism. I was not really able to imagine them. I hesitated between the tedious vision of a pharmacy and – because of the word 'soda fountain' – the image of a magical fountain spewing out billows of pink and white ice cream. The fact is, drugstores are the descendants of the old general stores in colonial towns and the encampments of the Far West, where the pioneers of past centuries found cure-alls, ointments, tools – all the necessities of life. They are at once primitive and modern – that's what gives them this specific American poetry. All the objects seem related: the same great bargains, the same unpretentious cheerfulness. The glossy paperback books, the tubes of toothpaste, and the boxes of candies have the same colours: one has the vague impression that reading these books will leave a sweet taste in your mouth, and that the candy will have stories to tell. I buy soap, creams and toothbrushes. Here the creams are creamy, the soaps are soapy: this honesty is a forgotten luxury. As soon as you stray from this norm, the quality of the products becomes more dubious. Certainly, the stores on Fifth Avenue will satisfy the most exacting tastes, but those furs, those suits of such international elegance are reserved for the international capitalist. As for the more popular shops, at first their abundance and sparkling variety are astonishing. But if the men's shirts are attractive, the ties are doubtful, the women's handbags and shoes are quite ugly, and in this profusion of dresses, blouses, skirts and coats, a

Frenchwoman would have trouble finding anything that didn't offend her taste. And then one soon perceives that beneath their multicoloured paper wrappers, all the chocolates have the same peanut taste, and all the best-sellers tell the same story. So why choose one toothpaste over another? In this useless profusion, there's an aftertaste of deception. There are a thousand possibilities, but they're all the same. A thousand choices, but all equivalent. In this way, the American citizen can squander his obligatory domestic freedom without perceiving that this life itself is not free.

I'm strolling alone, looking at the window displays. Those inspired by Dali are worth a look: those gloves flying in trees like birds, those shoes stranded among seaweed – only one or two stores in Paris could offer something similar. If one had to pay to enter, there would be a crowd to admire this fashion theatre. But the show is free, and even the women pass by without looking; everyone in the streets is striding purposefully ahead. Other, less inventive displays evoke the windows you see in big department stores at Christmas time: here's Broadway through the ages, elegant women in turn-of-the-century dress climbing into a carriage in the light of an antique streetlamp. I am certainly a tourist – everything entertains me.

I spend the afternoon and evening with old friends, Spanish communists who came to New York as refugees in 1940. I know that for many refugees, America has been a land of exile, not a place they've come to love. These Spaniards don't like it either. They say life is cruel in New York for immigrants and for the poor.

CL [Fernando Gerassi] is a painter, and like many artists he knew in Berlin, Madrid and Paris, he lives in semi-poverty. But in Europe there was nothing dishonourable about poverty: a poor artist experienced the favours and friendships of bohemian life. By lending him money, people provided one of those services that are natural between friends. Here, says CL, no one would let you die of hunger, perhaps, but offers of a dinner or a loan are alms granted grudgingly, making friendship impossible. In any case, even now that they have improved their material situation, my friends live in great isolation: there are no cafés or salons where intellectuals meet; everyone leads separate lives. And the distances are so great, SL [Stépha Gerassi] tells me, that after a day of work one hesitates to spend another hour on the subway to get together. There are people we would like to see, SL says, and with whom we have to limit ourselves to occasional telephone calls – preserved friendships that lose their fragrance like strawberries frozen in blocks of ice. Under these conditions, without peers, without competition, creative effort is particularly thankless. An unknown painter wouldn't know how to elicit the interest of other painters who are unaware of him, or that of the informed public, given that there is no informed public. Almost the only way to be discovered is to hire a publicity agent. One of them has made overtures to CL. He put forward three proposals: a little publicity, a lot of publicity, enormous publicity. With the third proposal, success is assured, claims the agent. The second plan will bring only some opportunities. In any case, even the first plan, which is worthless, is too expensive for a painter who doesn't sell his work.

Returning from a French restaurant where we ate a *duck à l'orange* worthy of Paris before the war, I'm struck by the beauty of the big boulevards under the neon sky. My friends sigh. They are thinking of forbidden Madrid, of Paris, where they neither belong nor work now. And I sense that New York can also be a prison.

30 January

I explore New York neighbourhood by neighbourhood. Yesterday I saw the banks of the Hudson and Upper Broadway. Today I walked for hours along the East River and roamed the German streets around Ninetieth Street. New York gives me all the pleasures of a walking trip through the mountains: the wind, the sky, the cold, the sun, the fatigue. When I turn back toward the hotel, around five o'clock in the afternoon, I've walked and looked so much that I'm intoxicated. My legs no longer carry me, but my eyes, tired from seeing, want to see more. Next to my hotel, they're showing *Henry V*, with Laurence Olivier. I go in.

I love the film, but when I leave the movie house, I feel unsatisfied. Those coloured images didn't speak to me of America. Looking at them, I forgot New York. This evening, more than any evening, I would like to grasp it – with my hands, my eyes, my mouth. I don't know how, but I will grasp it. I walk in the same streets where I walked like a ghost Saturday night. I've become embodied. I hear the sounds of Times Square; I see the painted cardboard smoker's round mouth blowing real smoke rings. I jostle people; they see me. And the city is organised around me. I know where my hotel is. My Spanish friends' apartment house and DP's place point me in my favourite directions. I've explored the streets from One hundred and twenty-fifth Street to the Battery . . . on Saturday I was enchanted with my perfect ignorance; this evening I'm quite proud of my expertise. We always find something to feel superior about.

I walk slowly. I want to string the lights around my neck, stroke them, eat them. Here they are – and what can I do with them? My hands, my mouth, my eyes have not taken in this night. There are bars and restaurants here; I'm not hungry or thirsty. The stores – none of the objects they're selling will give me New York. A book would tear me away from New York. But strolling around Times Square won't help either. These people seem to be walking just like me, but they're going somewhere. The night is leading them ceremoniously toward a desired encounter. My desire is nothing but a myth – New York, which is everywhere and nowhere.

I go into another movie house. The black-and-white screen is like morphine, and the actors' American accents move me. The film is entertaining – *Lady in the Lake*. But when I leave, I'm disappointed again. I've forgotten New York once more. For a long time, movies represented America for me, and I remember in August 1941, when I crossed into the unoccupied zone under false pretences, how excited I was to find American films in Marseilles. I went to see three a day. But now I'm in America, and nothing can represent it any more.

I drink orange juice in a drugstore and then whiskey in a bar. If America were far away, perhaps the taste of Scotch would restore my memory of it in one fell swoop. Here it's powerless; and how can I get back something I've never found? I return to the movies and choose a newsreel programme so that no other story deflects me from what I'm looking for. I need black-and-white images like a drug, but I would like them to fill me without distracting me completely. After an hour I'm in the street again. It's midnight; the city is bathed in that captivating and cool clarity that the summer sun sheds during the white nights of the Far North; it's impossible to go home and go to sleep. On Forty-second Street the vividly coloured posters announce mostly 'thrillings' – scary films – and 'laff movies' – funny films. I stop. On every side of the cashier's window, warped mirrors reflect the passers-by. I look at myself; for a moment I stand and make faces at myself. My head is heavy. I go in. This time, I almost reach my goal; the film is stupid enough for me to think, 'This is New York, and I'm in a New York movie house.' But I've sought this joy too intensely. It vanishes, and I'm bored. Boredom leads me nowhere. It's two o'clock in the morning; I go back to the hotel.

31 January

What makes daily life so agreeable in America is the good humour and friendliness of Americans. Of course, this quality has its reverse side. I'm irritated by those imperious invitations to 'take life easy', repeated in words and images throughout the day. On advertisements for Quaker Oats, Coca-Cola, and Lucky Strike, what displays of white teeth – the smile seems like lockjaw. The constipated girl smiles a loving smile at the lemon juice that relieves her intestines. In the subway, in the streets, on magazine pages, these smiles pursue me like obsessions. I read on a sign in a drugstore, 'Not to grin is a sin.' Everyone obeys the order, the system. 'Cheer up! Take it easy.' Optimism is necessary for the country's social peace and economic prosperity. If a banker has generously lent fifty dollars without any guarantee to some young Frenchman in financial straits, if the manager of my hotel takes a slight risk by cashing his customers' cheques, it's because this trust is required and implied by an economy based on credit and expenditure.

This amiability is disconcerting. In the afternoon I go to cash a cheque. As soon as I enter the bank, a uniformed employee comes toward me to help. I might think he is waiting for me. He directs me toward a kind of lobby lined with desks; on each desk is a sign announcing the employee's name to the public. I sit down; I show my papers to Mr John Smith. He's not some anonymous cog, and I am not an anonymous client; he does me the courtesy of addressing me by name, personally. He okays my cheque, and the cashier immediately gives me the sum I've requested. In France, the verification would have been done on the other side of the counter, without my involvement and no doubt grudgingly; then I would have been assigned a simple number. But I'm not a fool. This respect granted the citizen is completely abstract; that same polite smile that assures David Brown that he's a unique individual will also gratify John Williams, who is unique, too. Nothing is more universal than this singularity recognised with such ceremony. One suspects a hoax. Nonetheless, thanks to these considerations, the American doesn't need to strain to feel his human dignity. It may be commercial, but the cordiality of salespeople, employees, waiters and porters is never servile. They are not bitter or stiff, and though it is encouraged by self-interest, their kindness is no less real. We've held German soldiers responsible for the way they carried out orders of extreme cruelty – and, in fact, man is never passive. In obeying he gives up his freedom, and submitting to evil is a way of reclaiming it for himself. Most of the time he reclaims it through inventions and initiatives that make his responsibility apparent. Likewise, the American citizen does not submit passively to the propaganda of the smile: on a foundation of obligatory optimism, it is really he who freely presents himself as cordial, trusting and generous. His kindness is less suspect the less interested he is in the success of the system – he is more duped than duping. Whatever I think of American ideologies, I will always have a warm sympathy for taxi drivers, newspaper vendors, shoe-shine boys, and all those people whose daily gestures suggest that men could be allies. They surround themselves with a climate of trust, cheer and friendship. The next guy is not automatically an enemy; even if he is mistaken, he is not immediately presumed guilty. Such benevolence has become quite rare in France. I am a foreigner: this seems to be neither a defect nor an eccentricity here. No one laughs at my accent, which is deplorable; rather, they try to understand me. If I haven't got the change to pay the taxi driver, he doesn't suspect me of ill will; he helps me find it. Indeed, he's magnanimous enough to call it even if I'm a few cents short. Besides, I'm particularly fond of taxi drivers. During the entire ride they converse with me. It's often difficult to understand them; their accents are often disconcerting, even to New Yorkers. Many of them were in France during the war, and we talk about Paris. I'm always overcome with emotion to think that here is one of those men we welcomed with such joy and love, one of those men whose helmets and uniforms meant deliverance. It's strange to meet up with them again here, each with his name and his individual life – those anonymous soldiers who arrived from an inaccessible world, a world separated from our misery by barriers of fire and sword. They have a slightly condescending sympathy toward Paris, like the customs inspector who welcomed me by saying, 'You've come from a beautiful country to an even more beautiful country.' Toward me, their cordiality takes the form of scolding since I've caught a cold. It's the fault of the New York climate, which jumps without warning from hot to cold. But in their eyes, I'm dragging with me one of the pitiable taints of old Europe. They ask me severely, 'Do you have a cold?' They're a bit shocked. A good American citizen is not sick, and for a foreigner to catch a cold in New York is impolite. They offer me remedies; one even offers me a packet of pills out of his pocket.

Yes, the other day I distrusted both R. and V. I don't want to rush to judge America. But one thing I'm already sure of – aside from the beauty of New York – is that there is a human warmth in the American people.

February

1 February

Walks through New York, art galleries, museums. I do my duty as a tourist conscientiously. From time to time I go to see a publisher or magazine editor, and even in these activities I'm still a tourist. For instance, when I enter a large building on Lexington Avenue, I'm stopped short by the gigantic placard on the wall listing all the offices in the building. The office building is a city in itself. Moreover, as in the subways, the elevators are divided between 'locals', which serve the first seven floors, and 'express', which rise swiftly to the eighth. A business meeting is an excursion. The waiting rooms are like viewing platforms. I love to contemplate New York's houses from the sixteenth floor. The roofs are flat; they're not real roofs but asphalt and cement terraces. They often function as parking lots, and it's strange to see the shiny cars lined up on top of the sixteenth floor.

I don't pass up the chance to meet Americans. Last evening I was at AM's, where Richard Wright spoke of his French experience; apart from his talk, the gathering was rather dull. But I met RC [Lionel Abel], whose name I had carefully written down in my address book. He's a poet and essayist who translates French works into English — obviously, he speaks French very well. Today we had lunch together, and he offered to take me to a party at the home of some American intellectuals. I eagerly accepted. Around seven o'clock I arrive at a small apartment on Twentieth Street; full of books, pictures and furniture, it is more old-fashioned than many Parisian interiors. Except for RC, I know no one, and nobody speaks French. How did I land here? Again I feel like a ghost, a ghost who slips through walls and watches the human world without taking part in it. It's magical but deceptive, for can you see anything if you understand nothing?

I'm given a big manhattan. The hostess is wearing a long dress of black-and-red taffeta. Thick, black curls fall to her shoulders, and she has the dark-rimmed eyes of a sleepwalker. The female guests are less peculiar, but among nearly all of them an oddly knotted scarf, a clash of colours or heavy bangs hint at originality: this is a gathering of writers and artists. All these women are elegant. RC's wife is a waitress in a drugstore; that young brunette with the frizzy hair works in the publicity department of a big magazine; another woman is a fashion writer. Their dress and manner give no suggestion of the difficulty of their existence. As for the men, I don't know where to fix my eyes: so many faces, all different, but all devoid of meaning for me. American voices surround me with an exotic cacophony. I feel lost. Yet at this moment, everything is beginning for me, everything is promised: I cannot accept that all these people around me will remain inaccessible. I drink a second manhattan, a third. If I speak in English, I must find some common ground with these people: Americans must initiate me into America.

After my fourth manhattan, I find myself speaking English with RC and a man with a goatee, DMD [Dwight Macdonald], who edits a left-wing intellectual journal [*Politics*]. We're discussing one of the problems that currently preoccupy leftist intellectuals in France – the problem of violence. RC's attitude – shared by C [Nicola Chiaromonte], an Italian friend – is that violence must be rejected absolutely and in every case. C thinks that action is possible without violence – he cites the example of Gandhi. RC maintains instead that action isn't necessary. He's a Jew and is very critical of America; he doesn't see himself as at all responsible for its faults and doesn't see why he ought to try and rectify them. His position is purely individualistic. DMD is less passive; he's politically committed through the journal he edits and the articles he writes. But I think his effort seems very solitary to him. Giving up the theoretical discussion, I ask him for some concrete information. What should I see in New York? He smiles – nothing, there's nothing to see. What films does he recommend? None. What good books have been published recently? No good books are published any more. He explains to me that the French infatuation with American literature gets on his nerves. He concedes Faulkner, but he regards Hemingway, Dos Passos, Caldwell and Steinbeck as journalists, flat realists. And for us to translate James Cain, [Horace] McCoy and Dashiell Hammett into French means we must think Americans are a barbaric people. It's irritating that we enjoy these babblings when there has been an American literature worthy of Europe's: Melville, Thoreau, Willa Cather, Hawthorne. I say that I admire them too, and I try to discuss them, but he's talking too fast for me. I'm defeated in advance. I'm defeated especially by his graciousness; he lives in the building and goes up to his apartment, returning with an armful of books. He tells me to keep them as long as I like. And then, since among other things I've asked him about jazz, he goes into the next room to find AE [Bernard Wolfe, once Trotsky's secretary], who has written a book on the subject, and promises to take me one evening this week to hear a good band. He leaves me his telephone number, and I tuck it into my bag like a good-luck charm. Books, the promise of an evening of jazz, perhaps friends . . . I go home dizzy with pleasure. I feel I've taken a big step forward.

3 February

I continue my journey of exploration by foot, in taxis, on the top decks of buses, in the subway. The subway is fast, but I don't like it. In Paris, in Madrid, in London, a station is a tiled hall with its displays, its doors – a closed and cosy place. Here, the underground stations are all the same, indistinguishable – a combination of rails and platforms between bare walls, under a low, dark ceiling. No employees. Only at the entrance to the long corridors is there a small kiosk where you can get change and procure those ritual nickels. And almost no signs. Fortunately, within Manhattan there's only one direction, from uptown to downtown. Between the Hudson and the East River you have to take buses; they stop every two blocks. It's a pleasant mode of transportation, but slow.

I go to the top of the Empire State Building. You buy tickets on the ground floor in an office that seems like a tourist bureau. One dollar. Twice the price of a movie ticket. There are a lot of visitors, probably people from St Louis or Cincinnati. We are directed toward the express elevators that go in a single bound to the eightieth floor. There, you have to change to reach the top – a real vertical journey. Passing through a lobby where they sell miniature Empire State Buildings and different sorts of souvenirs, you reach a large glassed-in hall. There's a bar with tables and armchairs. People press their noses against the glass. In spite of the violent wind, I go out and walk around this gallery where spectacular suicides occur several times a year. I see Manhattan narrowing to the south toward the point of its peninsula [or, rather, island] and spreading northward; I see Brooklyn, Queens, Staten Island, the ocean with its islands, the continental edge lapped by the sea and penetrated by two sluggish rivers. The geographic plan is so clear; the water's luminous presence reveals the original earthly element with such clarity that the houses are forgotten, and I see New York as a piece of the virgin planet. The rivers, archipelago, curves and peninsula belong to prehistory; the sea is ageless. By contrast, the simplicity of the perpendicular streets makes them look extremely young. This city has only just been born; it covers a light crust of rocks older than the Flood. Yet when the lights come on from the Bronx to the Battery, from New Jersey to Brooklyn, the sea and the sky are merely the setting: the city confirms the rule of man, which is the truth of the world.

I go down into the city's depths. For a long time I wander on the lower level of Rockefeller Center. This is as vast as the *souk*s of Fez, and its labyrinth is hardly less confusing. There are long corridors, intersections where mechanical stairways empty out, shops, banks, offices, cafés, a post office, a central telephone office, hairdressers, restaurants. More than once I realise, turning a corner, that I've been going around in circles. Attached to one of the buildings, on the same floor below street level, there's an open ice rink. Passers-by lean over a balustrade above to watch the skaters; you can also sit in the cafeteria, which is on the same level as the rink, and watch while you eat ice cream.

I go into the galleries on Fifty-seventh Street, similar to our rue de la Boétie: antique shops, luxury boutiques, art objects. But instead of facing the street, most of the exhibition rooms open onto the tenth or twelfth floor. Many French painters: Masson, Picasso, Dubuffet. Among the Americans, abstract painting seems to have the place of honour; in the sculpture of the younger artists, surrealism survives. Its church is Peggy Guggenheim's gallery, designed by the architect Kisler. This gallery is like no other: the setting is even more important than the objects of worship themselves. Brancusi's birds and Lipschitz's women rest not on pedestals but on wooden platforms suspended from the ceiling by cords: it reminds you of riggings, topmasts, a boat. The paintings of de Chirico, Max Ernst, Dali, Tanguy and Miró are not hung on the walls but are set on easels or even on the ground amid chairs and stools that belong to the world of Dr Caligari. You might say that the art objects are meant to decorate this strange palace and not that it was conceived for their sake – this is its peculiar charm. Along with the sculptures and paintings, there are all sorts of baroque objects: bottles encrusted with shells, a large ship's wheel, which, if you turn it, sets in motion a series of copies of Duchamp. This is a scaled-down surrealist exhibition with playful ruses and marvellous offerings.

Of course, I want to get to know Harlem. It's not the only black neighbourhood in New York. There's an important black community in Brooklyn, three or four areas in the Bronx, another called

Jamaica in Queens, and a few more on the city's outskirts. In New York itself one finds neighbourhoods here and there where black families live. Until 1900, other than the one in Brooklyn, the most important black community in New York was situated near West Fifty-seventh Street. Harlem's apartment buildings were originally built for white tenants, but transportation was inadequate at the beginning of the century, and landlords had difficulty renting apartments in the eastern end of the district. At the suggestion of a black man, Philip A. Payton, who was involved in the rental business, blacks were offered the apartments on One hundred and thirty-fourth Street. Two buildings were filled this way, and soon more. At first, the whites didn't perceive this invasion of black people; when they tried to stop it, it was too late. Blacks gradually rented all the available apartments and began to buy the private houses that were going up between Lenox and Seventh Avenue. Whites then felt justified in moving; as soon as one black family was spotted in a block of buildings, all the whites fled as if they were running from the plague. The blacks soon took over the whole district. Social and civic centres were formed; a black community took shape. Harlem expanded most spectacularly after 1914.

Those among the French who get down on their knees to worship all-powerful America adopt all its prejudices even more obsequiously than Americans do. One of them says to me, 'If you like, we'll go through Harlem by car; you *can* go through Harlem by car, but you must never go on foot.' A bolder Frenchman declares, 'If you're determined to see Harlem, in any case stick to the large avenues. If something happens, you can always take shelter in the subway. But above all avoid the small side streets.' And someone else tells me with a shiver that at dawn some whites were found in the gutter with their throats cut. In the course of my life, I've already come across so many places where right-thinking people declare you *could not* go that I'm not too impressed. I deliberately walk toward Harlem.

I walk toward Harlem, but my footsteps are not quite as carefree as usual; this isn't just a walk but a kind of adventure. A force pulls me back, a force that emanates from the borders of the black city and drives me back – fear. Not mine but that of others – the fear of all those whites who never take the risk of going to Harlem, who feel the presence of a vast, mysterious and forbidden zone in the northern part of their city, where they are transformed into the enemy. I turn the corner of one avenue and I feel my heart stop; in the blink of an eye, the landscape is transformed. I was also told, 'There's nothing to see in Harlem. It's a corner of New York where people have black skin.' And on One hundred and twenty-fifth Street I indeed discover the movie houses, drugstores, stores, bars and restaurants of Forty-second or Fourteenth Street; but the atmosphere is as different as if I had crossed a chain of mountains or the sea. Suddenly, there's a swarm of black children dressed in bright shirts of red-and-green plaid, students with frizzed hair and brown legs chattering on the sidewalks. Blacks sit daydreaming on the doorsteps, and others stroll with their hands in their pockets. The open faces do not seem fixed on some invisible point in the future but reflect the world as it is given at that moment, under this sky. There is nothing frightening in all this, and I even feel a new kind of relaxed gaiety that New York hasn't yet given me. If I suddenly came upon Canebière [in south-eastern France] at the corner of rue de Lille or Lyon, I would have the same pleasure. But the shift from my usual surroundings is not the only vivid aspect. Nothing is frightening, but the fear is there; it weighs on this great popular festivity. Crossing the street is, for me, like crossing through layers and layers of fear: the fear filling those bright-eyed children, those schoolgirls, those men in light suits and those leisurely women.

One hundred and twenty-fifth Street is a border – there are still a few whites in evidence. But on Lenox Avenue, there's not a face that isn't brown or black. No one seems to pay attention to me. It's the same scenery as on the avenues of [downtown] Manhattan, and these people, with all their indolence and gaiety, seem no more unlike the inhabitants of Lexington Avenue than the people of Marseilles seem unlike the residents of Lille. Yes, one *can* walk on Lenox Avenue. I even wonder what it would take to make me flee, screaming, toward the protective entrance of the subway. It seems to me I would have as much difficulty provoking such an attack as I would provoking murder or rape in the middle of Columbus Circle in broad daylight. There must be some strange orgies going on in the heads of right-thinking people; for me, this broad, peaceful, cheerful boulevard does not encourage my imagination. I glance at the small side streets: just a few children, turning on their roller skates, disturb the lower-middle-class calm. They don't look dangerous.

I walk on the big avenues and in the small side streets; when I'm tired, I sit in the squares. The truth is, nothing can happen to me. And if I don't feel entirely secure, it's because of that fear in the hearts of people who are the same color as I am. It's natural for a wealthy bourgeois to be afraid if he ventures into neighbourhoods where people go hungry: he's strolling in a universe that rejects his and will one day defeat it. But Harlem is a whole society, with its bourgeois and its proletariat, its rich and its poor, who are not bound together in revolutionary action. They want to become part of America – they have no interest in destroying it. These blacks are not suddenly going to surge toward Wall Street, they constitute no immediate threat. The irrational fear they inspire can only be the reverse of hatred and a kind of remorse. Planted in the heart of New York, Harlem weighs on the conscience of whites like original sin on a Christian. Among men of his own race, the American embraces a dream of good humour, benevolence and friendship. He even puts his virtues into practice. But they die on the borders of Harlem. The average American, so concerned with being in harmony with the world and himself, knows that beyond these borders he takes on the hated face of the oppressor, the enemy. It's this face that frightens him. He feels hated; he knows he is hateful. This thorn in his conciliatory heart is more intolerable than a specific external danger. There are fewer crimes in

Harlem than on the Bowery; these crimes are only symbolic – not symbolic of what might happen but of what is happening, what has happened. Minute by minute the men here are the enemies of other men. And all whites who do not have the courage to desire brotherhood try to deny this rupture in the heart of their own city; they try to deny Harlem, to forget it. It's not a threat to the future; it's a wound in the present, a cursed city, the city where they are cursed. It's themselves they're afraid to meet on the street corners. And because I'm white, whatever I think and say and do, this curse weighs on me as well. I dare not smile at the children in the squares; I don't feel I have the right to stroll in the streets where the colour of my eyes signifies injustice, arrogance and hatred.

It's because of this moral discomfort, not timidity, that I'm happy to be escorted this evening to the Savoy by Richard Wright; I'll feel less suspect. He comes to fetch me at the hotel, and I observe that in the lobby he attracts untoward notice. If he asked for a room here, he would surely be refused. We go to eat in a Chinese restaurant because it's very likely that they wouldn't serve us in the uptown restaurants. Wright lives in Greenwich Village with his wife, a white woman from Brooklyn, and she tells me that every day when she walks in the neighborhood with her little girl, she hears the most unpleasant comments. And what's more, while we are looking for a taxi, men dart hostile looks at this black man with two white women. There are drivers who deliberately refuse to stop for us. After this, how could I claim to mingle peacefully in the life of Harlem? I feel myself stiffen with a bad conscience. While Wright buys tickets at the door of the Savoy, two sailors speak to Ellen and me, the way all sailors the world over speak to women at the doors of dance halls. But I'm more embarrassed than I've ever been before. I'll have to be offensive or ambiguous – my very presence here is equivocal. With a word, a smile, Wright sets everything in order. A white man couldn't have found just this word, this smile, and I know that his intervention, so simple and natural, will only aggravate my embarrassment. But I climb the stairs with a light heart: this evening Richard Wright's friendship, his presence at my side, is a kind of absolution.

The Savoy is a large American dance hall, nothing exotic. On one side, the dance floor is bounded by a wall where the orchestra sits. On the other side, there are boxes with chairs and tables, and beyond, there is a kind of great hall that looks like a hotel lobby. The floor is covered with a carpet, and people are sitting in the armchairs looking bored. These are customers who don't drink anything; they pay only the entrance price, and during the dances the women do needlepoint, as at a town ball. We sit in one of the boxes, and Wright puts a bottle of whiskey on the table. They don't sell whiskey here, but the customer has the right to bring his own. We order sodas; we drink and look around. Not a white face. Actually, this place is no more off-limits than Lenox Avenue, but only a few jazz devotees and foreigners have the gumption to venture here. Most of the women are young. They wear simple skirts and little pullovers, but their high-heeled shoes are sometimes bizarre. The light or dark tint of their skin dresses their bare legs better than nylon stockings. Many are pretty, but they all seem especially lively. What a difference from the strained coldness of white American women. And when you see these men dance, their sensual life unrestrained by an armour of Puritan virtue, you understand how much sexual jealousy can enter into the white Americans' hatred of these quick bodies. In fact, only a very small percentage of lynchings or racial incidents have a sexual pretext, yet whites stubbornly believe and say that blacks covet white women with the lust of savage beasts. Here again, they're only camouflaging another, quite different fear; they're afraid that white women are 'animalistically' attracted to blacks, and the men themselves are fascinated by their own fantasy of sexual prowess. Their envy extends even further. They readily – and bitterly – say, 'Those people are freer and happier than we are.' There's some truth to this assertion. What gaiety, what freedom, what life in that music and dancing! This is even more striking since this big dance hall has something domestic and ordinary about it. In Paris when blacks dance, mingling with whites in rue Blomet, they're too self-conscious; among the women especially, the licence of their gestures is provocative, verging on the obscene. Here they are among themselves and don't try to produce any effect; many of these young women belong to respectable families and probably go to church on Sunday mornings. They have worked all day and have come to enjoy themselves quietly with their boyfriends. They dance simply and quite naturally; you need perfect inner relaxation to allow yourself to be so utterly possessed by the music and rhythms of jazz. It's this relaxation that also allows dreaming, feeling, loafing and laughing of the sort that's unfamiliar to most white Americans. Of course, racists use this as an argument: why would you want to change the condition of blacks if they're the freer and happier ones? An old argument found on the lips of capitalist bosses and colonials – it's always the workers or the natives who are freer and happier. Indeed, the oppressed escape the power of the idols that the oppressor has chosen, but this privilege doesn't justify oppression.

I listen to the jazz, watch the dancing and drink whiskey; I am beginning to like whiskey. I feel good. The Savoy is the biggest dance hall in New York, the biggest in the world: something in this statement is soothing to the spirit. And this jazz is perhaps the best in the world; in any case, there's no other place where it can more fully express its truth – in the dancing, in the hearts and lives of the people assembled here. When I used to go to hear jazz in Paris or to see blacks dance, the moment never seemed enough in itself: it promised me something else, a more complete reality, of which it was merely a vague reflection. It was this very night that it promised me. Here I'm touching something that leads to nothing but itself; I've come out of the cave. From time to time in New York I've known this fullness that allows the surrendered soul to contemplate a pure Idea. That is the greatest miracle of this journey, and it was never more dazzling than today.

4 February

During the night, New York was covered with snow. Central Park is transformed. The children have cast aside their roller skates and taken up skis; they rush boldly down the tiny hillocks. Men remain bareheaded, but many of the young people stick fur puffs over their ears fixed to a half-circle of plastic that sits on their hair like a ribbon – it's hideous.

At five o'clock I have an appointment at the Plaza bar with the editor of a big magazine to discuss a projected article. The discussion is difficult because he's more than half-drunk. I take him to a party that JC [Jean Condit] is giving for me; she's a beautiful young American woman who works for *Vogue* and is friends with a Frenchwoman I know. For my benefit, she's brought together the editors of different magazines and other people likely to help me make my way in New York. Such kindness confounds me; I'm nothing to her, she expects nothing from me. I'm even ashamed – we're not so outgoing in France.

It's a very American party – lots of people, lots of alcohol, even more alcohol than people. Everyone continues to stand, except my hostess, who is soon reclining on a sofa. The conversational tone rises. I argue bitterly with a magazine publisher, whose air of superiority irritates me. Then I find myself violently at odds with an insistently insolent young man: Have you read the Hindu philosophers? Do you know Confucius? And Jakob Böhme? And if not, how can you dare to have philosophical opinions? Taking a good look at him, I see he's not so young: he's thirty, perhaps thirty-five. I try to explain to him that he's confusing thought and erudition, but he takes advantage of his knowledge of English to talk faster than I can. He points out one of his friends, saying, 'There's the most intelligent man in America.' I find myself surrounded by the staff of a journal [*Partisan Review*] that calls itself 'left-wing' and 'avant-garde', and their aggressiveness surprises me. In even sharper tones, they renew the reproaches I heard from DMD, who was part of the same group for a long time, then separated from them. To like the American literature we like in France is an insult to the country's intelligentsia. They, too, make an exception for Faulkner, but they tear into Hemingway, Dos Passos, Caldwell and especially Steinbeck, who seems to be their *bête noire*. I'm a little bewildered; I'm not familiar with their journal, I don't know what they're implying or what their values are, and through the virulence of their attacks, I can't make out what points we have in common or what underlying disagreements separate us. The martinis, the whiskeys and my difficulties understanding English increase my confusion. Around nine o'clock in the evening I find myself in the company of 'the most intelligent man in America' in a restaurant below street level, where they serve us magnificent steaks. But the feverish discussion dampens my appetite. Now they're after me about politics in relation to an article by Merleau-Ponty, 'The Yogi and the Proletarian'. They hate Stalinism with a passion that makes me realise they are old Stalinists. I think alcohol is making us choose our words unwisely; it seems my statements are worthy of a Soviet agent. But these free spirits might easily be taken for American imperialists. The tall, insolent young man declares in the middle of the conversation, 'Anyway, it isn't the Russians who send you food; America created UNRA [the United Nations Relief and Rehabilitation Administration].' If even so-called left-wing intellectuals are so proud of the boxes of condensed milk their government dispenses to us, how can we be surprised by the arrogance of the capitalist press, by that tone of condescension that I've observed almost everywhere when France is mentioned and that is beginning to exasperate me? I'm indignant, and we argue in earnest. The very excess of our anger gradually calms us. It's hot. GF is streaming with sweat. We're embarrassed at not really knowing, any of us, whom we're dealing with. Doubtless, a more thoughtful exchange of ideas would have been more profitable: they spoke with such fire that they weren't listening to me, and I didn't understand them very well. We leave the restaurant. It's snowing outside, and under the pure sky the cold is penetrating. Someone proposes resuming the discussion, but I'm worn out with holding my own in English for so long and with so many strangers. My mouth is dry, and I still feel a few pangs of anger in my chest. It's past midnight; we'll meet again another day.

5 February

Yesterday's conversation has shaken me. During this first week I was too enchanted by my discovery of New York to let myself be depressed by reading the daily and weekly papers, but this morning all the anger and fear I'd stifled came back with a vengeance. I'd been duly warned, and I knew the general direction of American politics, but the climate is even more intolerable than I'd been told. Above all, most of the magazines and papers – the Hearst publications leading the pack, of course – are busy creating a war psychosis. Day after day they repeat that conflict is inevitable and that it's needed to prevent Russian aggression. *Life* has even declared in a resounding article that the world is already at war; the use of arms therefore becomes legitimate. And within the country, this embryonic state of war, of cold war, authorises exceptional measures; foreign policy encroaches on domestic policy. The Communist Party, though recognised in the abstract, is no longer a party but a fifth column; it has become a national duty to fight it. Along with war psychosis, the 'red terror' is growing; every man on the Left is accused of being a communist, and every communist is a traitor. Now that Europe is transformed into a battlefield, any intervention is authorised. They speak of Europe as a pitiable but uncooperative vassal; France in particular is a highly undisciplined child. Domestically, Congress is actively preparing anti-labour legislation. Of course, in a capitalist country, freedom is always deceptive, but even the appearance of democracy itself is fading from day to day, and from day to day despotism breaks out with increasing impudence. This is the basis of everything I read, hear and see. Today it strikes me with such force that the New York sky itself is clouded: the luxury of the drugstores, the smiles, the cheery, nasal voices, the cigarettes, the orange juice, all have a sour aftertaste.

Fortunately, I'm offered a good opportunity to focus my anger. Yesterday, at JC's, a dead-drunk journalist gave me an appointment at the *New York Times* to talk about a prospective article. The paper occupies a huge building; an elevator takes me to the tenth floor. The journalist has sobered up during the night. He takes me to the office of one of the senior editors. The senior editor is swivelling in his revolving armchair. From the height of his own power and American power in general, he throws me an ironic look: So France amuses itself with existentialism? Of course, he knows nothing about existentialism; his contempt is aimed at philosophy in general and more generally still at the presumptuousness of an economically impoverished country that claims to think. Isn't it preposterous to want to think when you don't have the advantage of being one of the heads of a big American newspaper, one that moreover does away with thinking? 'Yes,' he says, 'in France you pose problems, but you don't solve them. We solve problems, we don't pose them.' The armchair swivels and creaks. In France, the powerful people of this world affect intimidating indifference; this man plays at flippancy. Perhaps his restlessness – like the gum chewing of so many Americans – is meant to mask a feeling of inner uncertainty. It seems to me that in this country, the inferiority complex is never far from the surface, even if it's carefully hidden beneath bold self-assurance.

In my brief experience, I sense that America is hard on intellectuals. Publishers and editors size up your mind in a critical and distasteful way, like an impresario asking a dancer to show her legs. They have contempt from the start for the product they're going to buy, as well as for the public on whom they'll foist the goods. Their role is to create between these two ridiculous forms of humanity – the author and the reader – a relationship that is equally preposterous, but which their skill will nonetheless convert into respectable dollars for the publisher. The very precision of their methods turns writing into a grocery store item. They say, 'I want 2,500 words. We pay so many dollars for 1,500 words.' A French editor must also count columns and lines of type, but with more flexibility. As for the contents of the articles, in France it is still accepted that certain values have meaning and that the public is capable of recognising them. Here, it's a question of concealing from stupid readers the fundamental foolishness of the pages they're offered. This stupidity, amplified by the arrogant contempt of the businessmen who exploit it, rules the day. You are not allowed to trust the public, in the hope that they will trust you. You must give them what they want; the problem is that you must surprise them at the same time, surprise being one of the recommended forms of bait. Hence, a serious dilemma – propose a subject for an unpublished article, and they tell you that Americans aren't interested in that; choose a question that concerns them, and they object that it's already hackneyed. The trick is to invent a provocative little novelty amid the commonplace.

I don't know if it's my mood this evening that's spoiled the enchantment of New York. The truth is, the nightclubs are suffering from the beginning of a depression, modestly called a 'recession' here. I first go with my Spanish friends to Fifty-second Street – the street of elegant cabarets – to Billie Holiday's place. A sparse audience is listening to a tepid band, waiting for Billie to sing. She is there; she smiles. She is very beautiful in a long, white dress, her black hair straightened by a clever permanent and falling straight and shiny around her clear brown face. Her bangs look like they've been sculpted in dark metal. She smiles, she is beautiful, but she doesn't sing. They say she's on drugs and sings only rarely now. We go down to Greenwich Village. The setting of Café Society downtown is pleasant; the attractions aren't bad, but the place is nearly empty. We go to Nick's, on the corner of

Tenth Street. Last year, apparently, the jazz was first-rate and the audience sizeable. Recession. The large room is decorated with stags' heads, giving it the look of a hunting lodge, but the band is mediocre and almost no one is there. We drink and talk, but I'm disappointed. The lights and the animation of the streets promise a thousand nocturnal enchantments. Isn't there any place these promises are kept? Perhaps we didn't know where to look. I'll keep searching.

6 February

Among all the daily walks I've taken in New York, today's is one of the most beautiful. CL [Fernando Gerassi] wants to show me the Spanish Library in Upper Manhattan. We climb to the top deck of a bus that follows the banks of the Hudson. It's a beautiful, cold day; the squares are covered with snow. The bus rolls along slowly, and the trip lasts more than an hour. Suddenly, a door opens, and I find myself in the heart of Spain. The silent rooms smell like Spain and are decorated with majolica, sculpted wood and precious leathers; on the walls of the gallery that surrounds the central hall hang Goyas, El Grecos and Zurbaráns. Some have a suspect look; a few canvases at the Metropolitan Museum also struck me as copies. Americans are probably too eager for old paintings to be very fastidious. But some pictures here are clearly authentic, and it's a forgotten joy to contemplate them in this atmosphere that reminds me of the Escorial and the churches of Toledo. On the other side of the courtyard, we find an Indian museum – masks, beaded belts and buffalo skins marked with sacred designs. A papier-mâché model shows Manhattan when it was still occupied by the Native Americans. Only three centuries ago, there were such huts and fires amid the rocks that are now outcroppings in the public gardens. The island was then called 'Manhattanick', which meant, with strange prescience, 'the island of drunkenness'. The Indians sold it to the Dutch East India Company for sixty pieces of silver. The Dutch built New Amsterdam there, and in 1653 they built the wall from which Wall Street gets its name in order to defend the town against the claims of the English. But ten years later they ceded it to King Charles II, who made a gift of it to his brother, and in his honour, the city took the name New York. All this history is not very old. At the beginning of the last century, Upper Broadway – where we're walking – was just a country road. We go up as far as the Cloisters, which Rockefeller brought from Europe piece by piece and where he assembled a collection of medieval art objects. We arrive just as they're closing the gates, but we're not sorry we came. The most striking thing is the site itself. The Cloisters stands on the hills called Washington Heights, at the end of a narrow spur. You cross a large, empty park, whose paths disappear beneath a thick layer of virgin snow, and you reach the extreme point of New York. The city suddenly stops here, coming up against a large curve of the Hudson. On the opposite bank are the high, wild cliffs of New Jersey. Ahead of you, the city is now just a strangled corridor between Washington Heights and the plateau of the Bronx. You see the strata of those hills that serve as an underpinning for the regular rows of apartment houses. This relief still looks somewhat untamed; the architecture hasn't disguised its curves. The houses have merely been planted on this bit of unspoiled territory. Beneath the snow, in the light of the setting sun, this chaotic landscape seems almost to revert to nature. You'd think you were at the edge of a frozen end of the world. We're alone, at the point of this silent headland, like two forgotten survivors. We're almost astonished to rediscover the lights, the noise and the life on the plain below.

7 February

The newspapers cover a press conference held by George Marshall, in which he declares that he's opposed to any kind of disarmament.

Furthermore, today is the start of the trial of Eisler,* the number one communist leader, accused of conspiracy against the government, contempt of Congress, tax fraud and passport falsification. Willingness to go to war is asserted; the persecution of the Reds goes on.

This evening I must give a lecture at Vassar College. For the first time I enter Grand Central Station, that huge building whose tower dominates Park Avenue. It reminds me of the lower floor of the Rockefeller Center: restaurants, cafés; lunchroom; drugstore; telephones; bookstores; vendors selling flowers, cigars and candy; hair salons; shoe-shine stands. Stairways everywhere. There are waiting rooms, a hall where they sell tickets, black porters with red caps. But nothing suggests the presence of the trains hidden underground.

It's the first time I've taken a train. I stand for a moment in front of a door that opens ten minutes before departure: a corridor descends to the lower floor. I enter a coach. The train car doesn't look like any French train car but rather like the inside of an automobile. The air is, of course, overheated. In the central corridor, vendors of magazines, ice cream, Coca-Cola, candy and sandwiches pass up and down. *Café au lait* is also served in cardboard cups. The train plunges into an underground tunnel; it emerges between New York's apartment houses at third-floor level. It follows Park Avenue, whose splendour has faded and which is now just a wretched boulevard crossing the Puerto Rican section. Then it crosses the Bronx. To my left, I glimpse the Cloisters perched on its hill. Now the train follows the Hudson. Today I can hardly believe that New York has the same latitude as Naples. The Hudson is frozen; the snow swirls in a thousand patterns on the ice. The cold has not discouraged the

---

* In 1947 the House Un-American Activities Committee looked into the alleged spying of Gerhard Eisler and, in the process, called in his brother, Hanns, a German-born film composer who had fled the Nazis. This was the start of HUAC's investigation of Hollywood, and there were international protests. Hanns Eisler was extradited in 1948.

pigeons; they gather on the frozen surface. On the other side of this vast skating rink, the empty hills surprise me — so close to one of the world's capitals, and so forsaken. Poughkeepsie is the first small American town I've seen. Under the snow, with its wooden houses and its cheerful streets, it reminds me of a winter sports resort. The houses scattered along the sides of the white roads have the artificial look of chalets in Mégève. How peaceful to leave New York! The car stops in front of a sumptuous villa; this is my hosts' house. Hall, living rooms, library, dining room, spacious rooms in a sort of medieval style that at once evokes a 'deluxe' inn and a monastery. My room is as white and peaceful as the snowy countryside. It invites illness; you might wish for a slight fever so that you could really enjoy the silence and the freshness of the walls and curtains. About a hundred metres from here, a turreted gate opens onto the campus, which is a large plot of virgin country with hills and woods. Between the medieval-style buildings, which are dormitories, libraries and laboratories, I meet college girls in ski clothes carrying skis on their shoulders. They go hesitantly down a little slope that wouldn't faze a French beginner. I'm taken to visit the gymnasium; there's a dance class going on. In blue shorts with bare legs, the students balance on their tiptoes. In the blue water of the swimming pool others swim rhythmically under the eye of a teacher who knits as she watches them. In the library they seem so comfortable and free: they read, curled up in deep armchairs or sitting cross-legged on the floor, scattered through little rooms by themselves or gathered together in large halls. Through the bay windows, you can see the trees, the snow. How I envy them. But I must have tea with the French teachers of the college, then dinner with them at my hosts' house. It's the sort of carefully prepared meal you'd eat at a well-kept family *pension* – no cocktails or wine. Two male professors are invited, but the atmosphere is clearly feminine; there's something soft and quaint about it. I discover here the same spirit of caution as in our *lycée* classrooms, but it has been aggravated among these exiled French people by their concern for their country's reputation; a critical remark about the teaching of philosophy at the Sorbonne is enough to make them raise their eyebrows.

I'm taken to the lecture hall, which has a rather large stage decorated with Greek scenery; the students will soon give a performance of *Les Mouches* [*The Flies* by Sartre]. Theatre has a central place in the life of the college and is one of the official fields of study. I sit down and begin to speak. All the college girls who know a little French have gathered; they are between sixteen and twenty years old. Their four years of study correspond more or less to our two years of *baccalauréat* and preparation for the *licence*. How pretty they look! Up close, their faces are not so special. But their hair is beautiful, like in shampoo advertisements, and their features are heightened by make-up as heavy as a woman of thirty would wear. Whatever nature lovers might say, this mixture of freshness and artifice, those heavy, painted lips half-opened over dazzlingly youthful teeth, the smiling eyes of a sixteen-year-old beneath long mascaraed lashes seem quite attractive to me. Many of them have kept on their ski clothes. Others wear that outfit that the older professors censure in vain but that is almost a uniform at Vassar – blue jeans rolled above the ankles and a man's shirt, either white or chequered in vivid colours, which they leave hanging outside their trousers and knot in front with studied carelessness. The shirts are bright, but the jeans must be worn and dirty. If need be, they roll them in the dust or sew odd patches on them, mending them with darker thread where they are torn. Dressed like boys, made up like streetwalkers, many of these young girls are knitting as they listen to me. I'm told their taste for knitting was cultivated during the war. The survival of this craft is surprising in a country of mass-produced goods. I suppose that for many of these students, knitting is an anticipation of marriage and maternity.

Vassar is one of the most aristocratic colleges in America: this means that studying here is very expensive, and those accepted are carefully selected according to their intellectual abilities, their families and their wealth. They come from all the states in

America, and from time to time one or two blacks are accepted. There are also several scholarship students, but on the whole this luxurious culture is reserved for the wealthy elite. All these college girls have a striking air of health and happiness; I'm also astonished by their off-handedness, without any insolence, by their understated ease. Their courtesy has the charm of spontaneity, and their spontaneity the tact of politeness. I would like to know if they are aware of their luck and whether such an easy life isn't harmful. The professors answer me vaguely: the girls are nice, serious and hard-working. Elsewhere, I hope to meet teachers who are more discriminating or less discreet. But in any case I'm in a bad position – I'd have to be twenty years younger to get to know the girls.

8 February

I meet more college girls on the train going back to New York. They are going to spend the weekend in the city. They are scarcely recognisable: just like their mothers and older sisters, they wear hats with feathers, flowers, violets; heavy furs; and high-heeled shoes. They are much less charming than yesterday. I see clearly that the originality of their campus garb is only another kind of conformity. Jeans or mink – two uniforms. I think that American women never dress for comfort, for themselves. Their clothing is first and foremost a declaration of a certain standard of living. That's why there's no place for any personal flair that cannot be valued in dollars (save in certain artistic or intellectual circles, but even that rests on a firm foundation of silk and fur). There is only a quantitative hierarchy: the same wealth requires the same coat. A woman's social success is closely tied to how luxurious she looks; this is a terrible burden for the poor. A working girl, a secretary, is forced to spend around 25 per cent of her salary on the beauty parlour and cosmetics. She would be looked down on if she came to the office in the same outfit two days in a row. To work at certain big women's magazines that require a sophisticated elegance, a woman needs a more expensive wardrobe than if she were a hostess in a Parisian nightclub. Many young women can't make the necessary outlays, and for this reason a great number of jobs are off-limits to those who need them most. When you arrive in New York, the brilliance and variety of hair and colours seem miraculous, but this miracle has its price. Another fact strikes me as significant: the standard clothing imposed on the American woman is not designed for her convenience; these women who keenly defend their independence on every occasion and so easily become aggressive toward men, nevertheless dress for men. Those high heels that paralyse their movement, those fragile feathers, those flowers in the dead of winter – all those showy things are clearly finery meant to emphasise their femininity and to attract masculine looks. The truth is that the garb of European women is much less servile.

I have an appointment at five o'clock in the lobby with AE [Bernard Wolfe], who promised the other day to take me to hear some good jazz. While waiting for him, I glance at the newspapers. They are all full of the speech given in Washington by Dwight Green, the Republican governor of Illinois. He said with unusual vehemence what many Republicans express rather more timidly: every foreign country is hateful, especially Great Britain and Russia, and the United States must arm itself to the teeth, intensify the production of atomic bombs, and subdue every country whose subordination is necessary to American security.

I hardly remember AE's very distinctive face; there were too many new faces around me and we barely exchanged four words. I'm somewhat surprised to find myself walking down the street next to this stranger who talks to me with the cordiality of an old friend and calls me by my first name, American-style. The ease of human relations here charms me. Perhaps friendships in France are more solid and deeper, I don't know; but in any case, with us, the first meeting never has this warmth. And these people are so ready and willing to help! I expressed a desire to hear jazz, and here I am on the way to the concert Louis Armstrong is giving at Carnegie Hall. It's a rare stroke of luck, as it's been years since Armstrong made a solo appearance in a concert hall, and all the seats were booked long in advance. AE is an aficionado – he has his contacts. But that he should allow me to benefit when he doesn't know me – such gratuitous kindness is once again so astonishing that it fills me with shame.

'We'll go by MM's [Milton ('Mezz') Mezzrow's] to get the tickets,' AE tells me. Once more, I feel a sense of wonder that I'm still not blasé about. How marvellous to see a name, an image, transformed into flesh and blood! Shortly before leaving for New York, I was listening to Don Redman's orchestra in Paris, thinking about my departure, and leafing through the black journal *Ebony*; its images seemed singularly moving in all that they promised about America. One was of MM, laughing in the streets of Harlem. A white musician, married to a black woman, he has lived for twenty years among blacks and plays in a black band. He told his story in a book [*Really the Blues*, written with Bernard Wolfe] that's recently been very successful. It is he who welcomes us to a study filled with books and records. Several people are around him, and it would be intimidating if they weren't all Americans. AE introduces me to NG [Calder Willingham], among others, who has just published a rather scandalous novel about a military school in the South [*End as a Man*]. He's a tall, red-headed fellow who looks like an adolescent, even though he's already married. He has Fred Astaire's chin and looks typically American to me, as though I'd seen him twenty times, bits of him, in Hollywood films. MM brings me a glass of whiskey; he gives me an inscribed copy of his book and several of his recordings. NG also gives me an inscribed copy of his novel. There I am, my arms full of books and records, surrounded by friends who seem like they've known me forever. I know that they passionately love jazz and that they passionately hate American capitalism, racism, puritanical moralism – everything I despise in this America to which they belong and in which they find many things to cherish. This is enough to make me feel closer to them than to the servile or hostile French, for whom this country is merely an abstract power.

Carnegie Hall, the biggest concert hall in the world, is packed. The American public has more or less murdered jazz, but they still love it. Armstrong appears to frenetic applause, and once again I'm moved by the marvel of seeing someone materialise: I recognise the face I've seen in so many photographs. But Armstrong has gotten old. Now he hardly plays except for commercial purposes, and then with one of those oversized orchestras in which the intimacy and truth of jazz are lost. It seems he wanted to appear with this kind of orchestra tonight, and they had a lot of trouble convincing him to play with only five musicians. For the last numbers, however, he has insisted on gathering his whole troupe. And the public welcomes this music for dinner dancing with as much enthusiasm as for the authentic jazz – so pure and transcendent – in the first part of the programme.

As soon as I'm outside, I jump into a taxi, my arms laden with my records and books and my head still buzzing. I am going to dinner in a Spanish restaurant in the Village with the staff of the *Partisan Review* to resume our discussion from the other evening. Today the tone of the conversation is very different; right away, GT [William Phillips] and PB [possibly Philip Rahr] apologise for their vehemence. They're afraid of having seemed rude. They're even more repentant because it's not the custom in this country to push a discussion of ideas too far. As in Madame du Deffand's salon, good form puts the brake on passions. If some antagonism threatens to burst out into the open, the discussion is cut short, and people fall back on vague, polite formulas. I, for my part, apologise; with my French habits, I was probably the one who exacerbated the dispute. We are profusely polite; to everything I suggest, they say yes. As I have trouble making myself understood, they think I've said black when I mean white. They approve, I correct – they still approve. This excessive caution makes us laugh, which relaxes the atmosphere a bit. We will try to speak frankly, without anger. Out of prudence, we sidestep the political question and confine ourselves to literature, a subject on which I'm more interested in their opinion, in any case.

First, they complain about the hard lot of American intellectuals. Their journal has scarcely ten thousand readers, which is insignificant in America. A writer who doesn't deliberately concoct best-sellers has enormous difficulty living by his pen. He is offered no compensation on the moral level: no friendship with other writers (each one is alone), no influence over the public (which pays attention only to monetary success). Even success doesn't give the literary person access to good society: his reputation is always less flashy and more fleeting than that of a Hollywood star. In these statements I find an echo of what CL was telling me about painting. In France, too, it's not easy to make a living from literature, but no one talks about the writer's position with such bitterness.

At GT's, over a bottle of whiskey, they take up their attacks against best-sellers. There is, they tell me, an authentic American literature, inherited from and closely linked to European culture. In the last century, there was Thoreau, Whitman, Melville, Hawthorne, Henry James and Crane. (They don't mention Edgar Allan Poe. They never do. I think they regard him as a French writer.) Closer to our times, there is [Thomas] Wolfe and Fitzgerald. This is a civilised literature that aims at both formal perfection and a deeper grasp of the world. Apart from Faulkner, all the writers we like in France run counter to this tradition. They have fallen into an unaesthetic and superficial realism. Description of behaviour has replaced a deeper psychology, and documentary precision has replaced invention and poetry. Hemingway and Wright compared with James Joyce, for instance, contribute nothing. They tell stories – that's all. If we like these books, it's out of a sort of condescension. In

Tortilla Flat or *Tobacco Road*, we like discovering a people whose customs astonish us like those of some barbaric tribe. In France, we wouldn't hold the equivalent of these novels in such high esteem. (I wonder if this idea of equivalence makes much sense, but never mind.) It's such condescension that makes us lump together Dashiell Hammett and James Cain (who are scorned here), McCoy (who is totally ignored) and Faulkner. We should go ahead and enjoy reading detective novels if we like, and the works of Steinbeck and Dos Passos if we can. But we should do this in the same way as we enjoy the Hollywood films that GT himself enjoys when he's tired – the ones to which no one would think of granting any aesthetic value.

I agree that realism takes on the false colours of poetry when exported from one country to another; they themselves admire *La Femme du boulanger* [*The Baker's Wife* by Marcel Pagnol]. I agree that snobbery ensures the success of any American novel and that many are translated indiscriminately – indeed even concocted. Certainly, the contribution of a Dashiell Hammett, much as I still value him, is not that of a Faulkner. But I don't agree with the premise of this discussion. This irritates them, and they blame it on the influence Steinbeck and Hemingway have had on those best-sellers, whose mindlessness is stifling an authentic American literature. A fight must be waged against them if other avenues are to open up. What avenues? They cannot name a single young writer who satisfies them; their ideals remain negative and very vague. They seem to be dreaming of a return to the psychology of analysis and a certain classicism – all things that bore us in France today. Besides, although they contrast America with France, they don't like any living French writers either.

'They despise all living writers because they themselves are neither writers nor living,' some living American writers told me. They attack their critics with as much vehemence as these critics have used to denigrate them. The *Partisan Review* folks, they explain to me, need idols because they don't have the resources to help themselves. They admired Stalin; then they shifted to Trotsky; and in the end, they bowed to the Tradition. It's their god of the moment, the justification of their hatred. They themselves are sterile; that's at the bottom of it, and that's why – having few readers, no political influence and no passion – they hate life not only as it appears in literature but wherever they find it.

There is probably a good deal of injustice in this judgement. But what is striking is the split between the intellectuals and the writers. Most of the writers began as paperboys or shoe-shine boys and have acquired their culture haphazardly. It's very rare that cultivated men write – or at least write books that strike some chord. This quarrel is almost a class quarrel. In France, we have intellectuals to spare, whereas the effort of writers to integrate life in its crudest form into literature was quite new to us and singularly enriching. I will agree with *Partisan Review* that life can become sterile if the novelist is too facile, and that indeed much of Steinbeck and the latest book by Caldwell are too contrived. But their indictment of realism has no clear meaning. We know exactly what the realist school was in France – rank prejudice masquerading as impartiality in the face of reality. It's a self-destructive attitude. But in the American novels we like, reality is described through strongly felt convictions involving love, hate and rebellion. Life is revealed in its truth, through the hero's consciousness. What, then, does the word 'realism' mean? And besides, what do we like in Stephen Crane, especially in that novella called *Maggie*, if not an audacious realism in the face of the conventions of the time?

What I felt clearly in the course of these arguments is that 'American literature', like America, is not a homogeneous, closed monolith, as we tend too often to believe from a distance. It is a living and shifting reality traversed by various currents that often collide. That the new generation should turn away from the writers (even the great ones) who preceded them is natural, even necessary, but they will not find the answer to their problems in Melville or Hawthorne. These problems are new problems, to which they must bring new solutions. If they are any good, they will become part of the Tradition themselves.*

9 February

'Sundays,' an American woman told me, 'we spend the morning in bed reading the *New York Times*.' The first time I bought the Sunday *New York Times*, I thought I'd made a mistake, that I was carrying a whole pile of papers, but this whole pile was just one paper. Even on weekdays I have difficulty managing these masses of paper. I've learned to put aside the sports section; the business section; the section on marriages, deaths and social events. My eye skips over the ads that fill pages and pages. But I still get lost, and what I find most disconcerting is that this great international newspaper is also a local paper; the problems of disarmament are given equal coverage with the miraculous cure of the Thompsons' blue baby, or the way the newly married war veteran Smith ingeniously keeps house in a trailer. Here, too, it's a matter of persuading the American that all of America is interested in the special case of each citizen: each day the press chooses at random some very concrete examples, which it offers as proof to its readers. And although they organise collections on behalf of a sick child or send cards of congratulations to happy couples, it's a small price to pay to give people the impression that they are actively participating in the life of the country. People are then all the more willing to hand over to specialists such problems as the freedom to work, the fight against the Reds, and intervention in European affairs.

It's a beautiful, frosty day. In the morning I go with Richard Wright to attend a service in a black church – the Abyssinian Baptist Church. The largest in New York, it has twelve thousand to fourteen thousand members. Its pastor is a popular

---

* This discussion, the French edition notes, is taken up again on page 260.

figure – the Reverend Adam Clayton Powell. He's a young, ambitious man with such light skin and aquiline features that I would never have taken him for black. He is engaged in intense social activity, has often helped striking workers, publishes a black paper, and is a New York City Council member. He's one of that rather rare breed of ministers who devote themselves to supporting and expressing the claims of black people. I'm struck by the social aspect of his sermon: it seems less like a religious gathering than a political meeting. He reminds blacks of their hard lot, but he says they cannot improve things through revolt or hatred. First, they must win God's love, for there are also injustices among themselves: there are rich and poor, sick and healthy, and they must learn to help each other. Let them come to church, let their morals be pure, let them live for what is good, and then the day will come when their troubles will be over. The members of the congregation listen with ardent attention and punctuate the sermon with outbursts of 'Yes! All right!' – stamping their feet and clapping their hands. But it's a very well-to-do, highly respectable, middle-class congregation, which knows how to moderate its responses. Wright tells me that to hear the best spirituals and to feel the emotional side of black religion, you must visit the churches in poorer neighbourhoods. He will take me there. The political, lay aspect of the service was striking. You have to understand, he explains to me, that there isn't a minute in a black person's life that isn't penetrated by social consciousness. From the cradle to the grave, working, eating, loving, walking, dancing, praying, he can never forget that he is black, and that makes him conscious every minute of the whole white world from which the word 'black' takes its meaning. Whatever he does, a black man is 'committed'. There is no black writer who can avoid the problem of commitment. It is resolved in advance.

We drive down Harlem's broad avenues [toward Greenwich Village], chatting as we go. A village peace reigns here; the streets are deserted like Parisian boulevards during the Occupation. On the sidewalks the children play in the snow, despite the bitter cold. Never did Greenwich Village more deserve its name. In the provincial streets bordering the two- and three-storey houses, the snow muffles all the noises; it covers the roofs, it invades the stoops, it's ankle-deep, and the cars parked along the sidewalks are literally buried. But in the evening on the Bowery, the cold has lost its country charm: under the black ceiling of the El, those men they so cruelly call 'forgotten men' or 'men alone' shiver in the cold.

The Bowery is the street of misery. Trams – I think these are the only trams in New York – pass noisily under the El. All the houses and shops are the colour of grey bread, of unwashed faces. Below, they sell luxury furs and diamonds; these jewellery stores are gloomy halls where various merchants sit side by side at their counters. Farther up, you find primarily second-hand stores, bric-a-brac shops, with used clothing and clusters of old shoes hanging around half-opened doors. There are tailors, including a tailor for fat men who exhibits photographs of the obese dressed with his help in jackets and trousers of incredible dimensions. And, of course, there are pawn-shops designated by the traditional sign – three big copper balls. They are also recognisable by the guitars leaning against the shop windows. Amid tarnished jewellery, phonographs, watches, cameras and kitchen utensils, one always sees guitars, so noble despite their mixed surroundings, as in Picasso's paintings. Trumpets and saxophones often keep them company. Squeezed between these shops are the Bowery hotels for 'men without women'. The peeling façades, the dusty windows are heartbreaking. These are shelters where, for a few cents, you can rent a mattress or just a corner of floor space swarming with cockroaches. The poorer New York tramps go to the flophouses, where they sleep sitting on benches, their arms leaning on a rope and their heads supported by their folded arms. They sleep until their time runs out; then someone pulls the cord, they fall forward, and the shock wakes them. Those who are even poorer stay on the street. The sick, the old, the failures, those down on their luck – all the outcasts of American life prowl these sidewalks. They sleep on the asphalt, regardless of the frost and rain; they cower on the steps of small stairways going down to cellars; or they remain standing, leaning against the walls, trying to sleep standing up. They have only one goal in life – to drink. In the black and cold misery of the Bowery, the profusion of neon signs announces a paradise in every bar. But drunkenness has its price, too; they try to sell you, or sell each other, their last shirt, their worn-out shoes, a stolen knife. A rag, picked that morning out of the garbage, can stir up all the passionate dealings of an auction house or the stock exchange. But usually they have nothing to sell, so they beg. My friend SL [Stépha Gerassi], who works in the neighbourhood, knows more than one of them. To beg, they clown around; that's the rule here. From the US president to a bum, people solicit by clowning. 'The bank is closed, ma'am. I cannot cash my cheque. Would you be willing to lend me twenty-five cents?' Sometimes when a woman clutches a book under her arm, she sees two shining eyes: 'Lend me the book – I'll give it back.' And they do give it back; they've borrowed it to read. S tells me that many women live on the Bowery, as well, but one sees them more in cafés than in the street. There's one called 'the queen of the Bowery' – an old woman once celebrated for her beauty. She lives in squalor but has a hoard of money.

The most famous bar on the Bowery is Sammy's. Until recently, it was just a bar like the others, a kind of flophouse where, for a few cents, you could drink and sleep the day and night away. In the afternoon its appearance hasn't changed. The only clients are tramps – men or women who drink cheap beer at the counter or sleep, sitting in the chairs with their chests on the table. But Sammy, the owner, had a brilliant idea. He got together some old actresses, singers and dancers between the ages of sixty and eighty, and he features them in the evenings, decked out in feathers, performing the dances and songs of their youth. The bar has become a cabaret – 'Sammy's

Follies' — and a big success. Outside, in front of the door, men wait in the cold for a nickel to fall from the sky and allow them to enter. The lucky ones lurch joyfully around the bar, where, painted on the wall above the magnificent arsenal of bottles, the queens of the Bowery reign. But it's respectable, middle-class people who are seated at the tables, drinking whiskey and eating hamburgers. The walls are covered with photographs, press clippings and autographs. There are also old coloured posters — advertisements for silent films featuring rape and murder. As in all the New York nightclubs, a female photographer in a clinging black silk dress circulates among the tables; with a pleasing smile, she aims her flash at couples and happy groups. We are sitting beside the platform: a man is playing a piano, and a sad young woman is playing the violin. She's out of place here — too elegant and unhappy. There is also a woman who frantically works the cash register. One by one, the singers come on. They've been chosen for their girth: Mae Wests with more than a touch of cellulite. Their hair is red or crow black; their make-up is spread with eager extravagance — orange circles on sagging cheeks, chalky powder in the folds of a double chin. Only their eyes — despite the false eyelashes, the eyeliner, the mascara, the blue eyeshadow — remain human. That fragile orb cannot be touched; it escapes all disguises. All these old gals wear huge hats with orange or green feathers and glittering jewellery; black silk dresses encase their bodies and their jutting bosoms. They sing cowboy songs, sentimental ballads, all the hits of 1900. They attempt dance steps, hopping and bouncing their heavy breasts. Many have real talent, beauty, and still enough fire, life and sleazy femininity that they receive equivocal applause. The public is fascinated. I notice a woman sitting alone at a table, still young and respectable, drinking whiskey after whiskey and staring at the stage with a hard look. Other women roll their eyes and laugh hysterically. The major attraction is an octogenarian whose doll-like face, embedded in a formless mass of flesh, still has a touch of beauty. She sings, giving her large hat a vulgar slap. She undulates, and despite her eighty-five years, she immediately evokes the Mae West she was. When she raises her silk skirts, revealing canary-yellow knickers ruffled around the knees and legs worthy of Mistinguett [a celebrated Parisian music-hall dancer of the 1920s to 1930s], the public shouts. Hysterical women hitch up their dresses and half-faint on the shoulders of their embarrassed men. The old woman tours the room, kissing men's pates as she goes. She sashays along, and from time to time starts to toss up her dress behind her; a whistle calls her to order. The public shouts more and more loudly. With a great tambourine roll, amid applause, laughter and wild cries, the star goes to sit down in the corner of the room, all alone. She looks very old and tired. She will do this again tomorrow.

To be sure, this is not a pretty sight; it makes fun of miserable old women. But what do the right-thinking people who protest against it offer them? After all, Sammy allows them to earn a living. If the Bowery exists, Sammy is not to blame. And the Bowery is the underside of Wall Street. You have to look elsewhere for reasons to be indignant.

10 February

The snow melted during the night, and the streets of New York are covered with a grey sludge. They're as dirty and neglected as the streets of Paris during a winter of the Occupation. This city isn't as clean as it first seemed. Trash cans sit a long time on the sidewalks, and sometimes in the mornings, on the poorer avenues, they burn the garbage in big tin boxes. And in the evenings, after I've walked in the streets, my face is often as black as if I'd just come out of a coal chute.

In three days I'm leaving New York. I have a lot of shopping to do and business to take care of, and all morning long I stride along the muddy streets of the better neighbourhoods. In their windows, candy stores display huge red hearts decorated with ribbons and stuffed with bonbons. Hearts are also ingeniously suspended in stationery stores and tie shops. It'll soon be Valentine's Day, the day when young girls give gifts to their boyfriends. There's always some holiday going on in America; it's distracting. Even private celebrations, especially birthdays, have the dignity of public ceremonies. It seems that the birth of every citizen is a national event. The other evening at a nightclub, the whole room began to sing, in chorus, 'Happy Birthday', while a portly gentleman, flushed and flattered, squeezed his wife's fingers. The day before yesterday I had to make a telephone call; two college girls went into the booth before me. And while I was pacing impatiently in front of the door, they unhooked the receiver and intoned 'Happy Birthday'. They sang it through to the very end. In shops they sell birthday cards with congratulations all printed out, often in verse. And you can 'telegraph' flowers on one occasion or another. All the florists advertise in large letters, 'Wire Flowers.'

This afternoon I went to the movies and saw a documentary, produced by the 'March of Time', about the pursuit of happiness as it is practised in America. First you saw bookstores where men and women were buying books with promising titles: *The Secret of Happiness*, *Happiness in Five Lessons*, etc. Then sequences about physical culture – for gymnastics, there are exercises in persuasion reminiscent of the Coué method [using self-hypnosis to promote well-being]. Others who are dissatisfied consult seers and astrologers. Others write, full of hope, to specialty papers and avidly, indiscriminately study the answers of some 'Miss Lonely Heart'. Still others listen to Mr Anthony's radio broadcasts or go to consult him themselves. Mr Anthony is famous in America, and his broadcasts are a huge success. He welcomes souls in pain, asks them to discuss their problems and gives some banal response, and the whole conversation is transmitted over the radio, including the sobs that often break the caller's voice. The hoax was so blatant that Mr Anthony was banned in the end, but he has his imitators. And the documentary didn't cover licensed psychoanalysts, many of whom are unscrupulous exploiters.

This very official little film confirms what everyone has told me – it's only on posters and advertising pages that Americans have those round cheeks, radiant smiles, calm gazes and faces glowing with good conscience. The truth is, nearly everyone has some personal trouble. Drink is one remedy for this inner malaise, whose more ordinary face is boredom. As society accepts the fact of drinking, it doesn't seem like a sign of dysfunction; it's the functional form of the dysfunction. But despite everything, alcohol is not a universal panacea, and certain individuals express this uneasiness that everyone secretly feels. That's why Mr Anthony or the psychoanalysts offer their services. If psychoanalysis is so in vogue in America and if psychology is one of the favourite topics of conversation among intellectuals and cultivated people, it isn't because Americans expect that these disciplines will help them find themselves. On the contrary, it's because these disciplines help them escape. When you feel dysfunctional, you're tempted to question the rest of the world. This revolutionary attitude is dangerous to the society it threatens and agonising for the individual who finds himself facing decisions, risks and responsibilities. It is accepted a priori that it's your dysfunction that's at fault, and you're only too happy to consider your muddle an illness as curable as a head cold. The questions you pose and your doubts and anguish are denied any inner truth: they are considered a given reality that must be studied scientifically. You are not a subject debating with yourself in a singular drama but an objectively defined case. Every individual is a case, a universal singularity. The individual most notable for his extravagances, his eccentricities, for the affirmation of his individuality is called a 'character', and again, this is a general category in which one's personal and singular freedoms are denied. The case is expressed by the 'problem'. Every American citizen has a problem, just as he has civil status. If he is normal and well informed, he knows how to define himself in terms that already indicate the solution. If he is less well informed, he defines the problem and demands a solution from competent people. And it is precisely these problems, accompanied by their solutions, that the radio and the press broadcast. If the subject is too muddled, he goes to the psychoanalyst to restore his equilibrium. Psychoanalysis is a vast enterprise of social recuperation; its sole aim is to permit each citizen to take his useful place in society. At this moment, there is a whole category of individuals they are actively trying to heal – the GIs back from Europe or the Pacific, whose experience abroad has been unsettling. DP [Denise Perrier], whose job is to test patients with psychological problems, tells me that many of the patients are veterans. It's easy to understand why, after breathing American optimism throughout their youth and living in a country that denies the existence of evil, these young men were overwhelmed by a sudden confrontation with the world at war, and their experience doesn't fit the system into which they must now reintegrate themselves. Those with the courage to continue believing in this experience represent a new force, but many simply feel lost. They are regarded as cured when they have lost their awareness of being lost. To adapt here is really to resign yourself; to be happy is to be wilfully blind. Many things would change among Americans if they were willing to accept that there is unhappiness on earth and that unhappiness is not a priori a crime.

11 *February*

I'm giving a lecture to the Cultural Relations [section], followed by a cocktail party. A Frenchwoman, at least forty years old, challenges me: 'In the name of French youth, I declare myself against everything you've said.' Another woman shakes my hand effusively: 'I thank you in the name of France.' I would certainly like to know what supernatural voices give them such mandates.

Once more, I notice how formal many French officials are; the so-called important Americans immediately know how to establish a human understanding with anybody. And when it comes to speaking in public, an American audience is not intimidating because you know they are interested not in finding fault but in listening to you.

This American benevolence attracts me and irritates me at the same time; it's so trusting. But trust is an ambiguous feeling: is it generosity or hypocrisy? And should you trust *all* people? Friendship is doomed if it isn't a choice. Benevolence is carried so far here that they refuse to believe, for example, in the German atrocities. Watching the films from Buchenwald, the American shrugs his shoulders: those corpses aren't Russian or French – they're Austrians who were killed in a bombing, and they're being passed off as Nazi victims. It's true that the clumsy propaganda of 1914–18 – those little Belgian children with slit wrists that the American Red Cross could never identify – has inclined Americans to be sceptical. And we ourselves needed time, between 1940 and 1944, to believe *everything*. But there is stubbornness in this refusal. And it's uncertain whether this stubbornness is a form of humanism. They'll believe anything of the Japanese, for example. Humanism is tempered by racism; benevolence does not extend to yellow people, whereas a lot of American citizens are of German ancestry. And then [George] Marshall's policies imply that German crimes should be forgotten.

It would certainly be false to see American moral optimism as merely a form of politics; these sons of Puritans sincerely believe in Goodness and Virtue. People have quoted to me words of the German philosopher [Max] Scheler, which seem exactly right. 'I thought,' he wrote, 'the Americans were hypocrites; I thought that when they say God, they mean "Cotton". No. When they say God, they mean "God". The miracle is that there is always cotton.' And indeed, if you begin by appending God to cotton, by identifying Virtue and Prosperity, you can invoke God and Virtue without hypocrisy or risk. Good offers as many resources as Evil – no doubt more, if you know how to channel it. American myths rest not on lies but rather on skilfully exploited truths. It is certainly true that Europe needs America; in the eyes of average Americans, imperialism takes the shape of charity. The arrogance of Americans is not the will to power; it's the will to impose Good. The miracle is that the key to Paradise is in their hands. I remember a young American in Paris last summer. His wife was suffering from the heat, and he wanted to find some salt capsules to relieve her. There were none at any pharmacy. 'There *must* be some,' he said angrily. He was determined and ran from one pharmacy to another, increasingly shocked: 'There *must* be some.' This 'must' indicated trust in the order of the world, but it was also threatening, for if this order is found to be unpredictably disturbed, it needs to be restored.

No doubt Good cannot be defined so imperiously without positing a certain Evil. The important thing is that the one should not encroach on the other and that Evil must appear merely as the distinct opposite of Good. There are bad women, but those who are virtuous are utterly virtuous. There are bad citizens; they are put in prison. The good citizen is loyal through and through. The Japanese are conveniently the devil incarnate. This way, we get a harmonious universe in which Good triumphs by the very fact of its existence. Between those great pictures of Épinal, so close to the legendary figures of childhood – John who grumbles and John who laughs, the wicked alcoholic and the good paterfamilias, Ganelon and Roland* – intermediate realities do not register. If I try to suggest them, I often feel that the person I'm speaking to cannot absorb such a nuanced image – his mind goes blank.

Several times during this cocktail party I'm struck by the

---

* The bitter feud between Roland, Charlemagne's nephew, and his stepfather, Ganelon, is detailed in the classic *Song of Roland*.

questions people ask about the Occupation in Paris. Some believe that we faced the threat of bayonets on every street corner, that we were constantly beaten and molested. They ask, 'You spent four years in Paris?' as if they were asking, 'You spent four years in Ravensbrück?' Others are surprised that we really had to do without pineapples and oranges during the war; they even hesitate to believe it. Yet they did without many things themselves. When I offer them some actual details, I feel I'm shocking them. If Americans have so little sense of nuances, it isn't that they're incapable of grasping them – after all, American reality itself is sufficiently nuanced – but that they would be troubled by them. To accept nuances is to accept ambiguity of judgement, argument and hesitation; such complex situations force you to think. They want to lead their lives by geometry, not by wisdom. Geometry is taught, whereas wisdom is discovered, and only the first offers the refreshing certainties that a conscientious person needs. So they choose to believe in a geometric world where every right angle is set against another, like their buildings and their streets.

12 February

My Spanish friends take me for a drive around New York. We leave from Greenwich Village and head toward the East River. The traffic is terribly slow in the middle of the afternoon; every two blocks there's a red light. On the [East River] Drive, though, you can go at top speed. We pass the Queensborough Bridge and drive until we get to the Triborough – a huge bridge, or rather a combination of three bridges spanning fourteen miles. Beside the broad roadway where trucks and cars go by, there's a pedestrian corridor. But of course no one attempts this long journey on foot. To the left there's a view of a plain covered with wretched little houses; to the right, Manhattan is carved out of the horizon with the splendour of its skyscrapers. In a single sweep, you can see the buildings around Central Park, the Empire State Building, the Battery. We go through the poor districts, we pass a cemetery, then another; there are lots of cemeteries around here. We are leaving New York. There's one of those famous clover-leaf intersections that avoid any crossings and seem to make any collision impossible. Yet there are many accidents in America, primarily due to speeding or drunken driving. I'm surprised to find myself so quickly in the countryside, in the woods. There's a good view from the road, and in the distance we glimpse a vast working-class city whose small houses, all identical, are relentlessly aligned in geometric rows. The children who live here have never seen New York, and the adults who work in the neighbouring factories don't go there often. Their horizon is the infinity of wooden shacks and the yards of black earth. Saint-Denis and Saint-Ouen are towns full of charm and fantasy compared to these desolate settlements.

We leave this sorry landscape behind us. Now we follow the bay – blue water, sun and seagulls. But it's only a brief escape. We come back toward Queens. Queens is a whole city, bigger than Manhattan; it includes villages and neighbourhoods. We get lost in a residential area where street upon street of cottages slumber in the snow. The broad avenues that we finally reach after many detours help me understand New York. A few days ago, in the big public library on Fifth Avenue, I saw a series of engravings representing old New York; those are the very images that materialise before our eyes. It's as though these broad roads lined with lodgings, advertising billboards and vacant lots were just recently laid out by some pioneers' rough hands; it is immigrants who live in this unfinished city. By comparison, Manhattan suddenly seems old. The memories of several generations have already accumulated there; the past, inscribed on the stones of Broadway, is a promise of the future. These avenues in Queens might be swept away tomorrow. A team of men has just constructed them; another team would be enough to dismantle them. You don't feel that a whole people has claimed them. They are there, but no one wants them as they are. The buildings have risen haphazardly, standing either isolated or clustered together. This unregulated growth doesn't make a city.

We turn into a side street that's muddy and bumpy like a bad country road. The car needs to be repaired, and we leave it at a garage. The mechanic offers us a lift in one of his cars that's going back to New York. We accept, and since we have a few minutes to wait, we go into a bowling alley next door. I've often seen the word 'bowling' glowing in big, red letters in the night. It's the old game of ninepins, like the one the dwarfs play in *Rip Van Winkle*, only modernised. Instead of a wild ravine, I find a bar with chairs and tables. The lanes lined up side by side are made of polished wood. When the big ball has knocked down the pins, they fall into a trap, and a mechanism automatically collects them again. Sitting on comfortable benches, the customers watch the game, which is also a performance. I remember a set of ninepins in the alley of a French village one afternoon on 14 July [Bastille Day]. The uneven ground provided traps for the players. Gardens, cafés with music and dancing, tables shaded by plane trees – all this is replaced in America by these large air-conditioned halls where, with no laughter or discussion, people throw standardised balls onto precisely measured lanes. Into the gears of this machinery they've inserted one human being – the pin boy. He's hidden behind a barrier while the player throws the ball. You see only his feet and hands when he sets the pins back up again, and then he quickly withdraws so as not to get hit by the heavy wooden mass. The rhythm of these appearances is regulated like the movement of a piston. The game is so popular that the lanes are booked days in advance. It's monotonous to watch.

A driver takes us back. On the avenues of Queens, he disdainfully runs all the lights, something no one ever does in Manhattan. Even at night in the most deserted streets, the cars are models of docility. Although there aren't many rules in America, it's costly to break them; the fines are very steep. But despite its size, Queens is only a suburb, and discipline is slack. We get on the huge iron bridge. Trucks roll by on the upper deck. On this deck the cars are all about the same size and the same dark colour – nearly identical. They follow each other at intervals of ten centimetres. Two lines heading toward Manhattan and two going toward Queens fill the entire roadway. They advance so uniformly, they look like they're being transported by a conveyor belt leaving the factory where they were just made. I wonder what would happen to this perfect chain if one of the cars stalled.

This is my last night in New York for two months. I go down to Greenwich Village with my friends. Near Washington Square they show me a charming café, the Jumble Shop, which looks almost European with its red-tiled floor and its quiet little tables arrayed along the walls. You can eat and drink there all night. During years of exile, French writers and painters tried to resuscitate Les Deux Magots and Le Café de Flore here, but they failed; their get-togethers were always too contrived. For one reason or another, New York doesn't have the right atmosphere for café life.

We wander into a nightclub in the Village. The room is very pretty; it's a big barn with connected wooden beams decorated with wagon wheels. Would-be cowboys, smiling and wearing make-up, sing and do lasso tricks; all the performances are appalling. There's quite a crowd, but it's an unsophisticated one. At a certain moment the master of ceremonies, introducing the show at the microphone, approaches one of the tables: 'What state?' They're from Ohio, and the orchestra plays the Ohio anthem. The next table is from Illinois; again, a local song is played. From table to table, a dozen states are mentioned; there is not a single New Yorker.

We find the New Yorkers at Café Society. There's a much larger crowd than the other day, probably because the programme has changed. This evening Josh White, currently a famous black singer, is performing; he writes the words and music to all his songs and accompanies himself on the guitar. He's handsome – almost too handsome and too magnificently dressed – and his songs are almost too touching. One is dedicated to [Franklin] Roosevelt, whom the blacks – even those on the Far Left – respect because he did a lot for their cause. In a bolder song Josh White recalls that during the war blacks and whites spilled their blood side by side, and that this blood was the same colour. The house applauds warmly; this is a rather avant-garde club where the public has liberal ideas. However, I feel uncomfortable. Several weeks ago a young black woman came here in the company of white friends to hear some black pals who'd been a great success with the public. The management refused to serve her, and there was a small scandal. People applaud a song or words. But the blacks who sing and play know very well that they don't have the right to sit in the audience. They must not have much friendship in their hearts.

Is it bad luck, or is it the 'recession'? I don't really enjoy myself in New York nightclubs. Except in Harlem, I haven't heard any good jazz. In my view, the Blue Angel, which is causing such a stir at the moment, does not (as they claim) combine the charms of Europe with those of America. I thought it was merely pretentious and bland with its mirrors, carpets, candelabra, crystal, funereal lighting and respectable shows. In many of these nightclubs, as in the elegant restaurants and the bars of big hotels, there's a 'tearoom' atmosphere I find stifling. The decor, like the public, is distinguished neither by good taste nor by real luxury; such places exude opulence, and everywhere there's the same scent of money. I liked a narrow corridor on Fifty-second Street where a black pianist plays old jazz; journalists drink and eat there till dawn. I also liked a dark little bar on Lexington around Fifty-seventh Street, with large wooden tables where men sit drinking alone. At Tony's and at the Tally Ho you can get together to talk; you can even sit quietly, writing letters or articles. But these are the exceptions. In almost all the middle-class places saccharine music plays over the radio or on a record player, filling your ears and finally clogging your brain. What's nice in New York are the little popular bars, the local bars whose clientele is like the crowds in our pool halls. These places are open to the world. People are living out real moments of their lives, and you feel a true human warmth. Only, you can't do anything but sit at the counter and drink. You can't stay too long. For the last time for two months I take a turn around Times Square, I stroll on Broadway, and I understand. No, the promises of this sky, of these lights cannot be fulfilled anywhere; nothing exists in complete harmony with the splendour of these nights. The plenitude I dream of, which would take me out of myself, will never be more than a phantom. I will never be promised anything but myself, and this is nothing if I make nothing of myself. The night is merely a setting; if I try to seize it, to make it the substance of the moments I'm living, it dissolves in my hands. Something has to happen to me – something real – and the rest will follow in abundance.

13 February

The train plunges underground and emerges above Park Avenue – I'm leaving, I've left. My heart is as torn as if I were leaving someone special. I didn't think I could love another city as much as Paris. Nearly every morning, I would set off along the streets, in buses, in taxis, on the subway, and then I would walk. I followed the banks of the Hudson; children roller-skated, and others amused themselves on the swings in little squares like the courtyards of nursery schools. Above me paraded statues, monuments and imitation castles. The water was green, ready to change into hardened ice. The wind swept over it and blew a cold scent into my face. In the distance the George Washington Bridge opened majestically onto the roads of another America. I ascended along the East River as far as the Harlem River; before me I saw the great flat archipelagoes, covered with factories, connected by iron bridges, furrowed with roads and train tracks. I crossed the Brooklyn Bridge, alone in a narrow passageway, blasted by the wind coming through the latticework. The iron girders shook as trucks and trains went by: this bridge seemed as dangerous as a mountain path in a storm. In the distance, straight and still, the towers of the Battery had the calm of medieval turrets. My solitary path led down toward the street with complicated twists and turns, just as a very steep path loses its way in a valley. In the middle of New York I also encountered unexpected hills: here and there the earth heaves up, the rock shows through, and from the height of this vantage point a whole plain is revealed. Next to the sober buildings of the university [Columbia] I abruptly reached the edge of a cliff, and I saw stretching out endlessly a chequerboard of little red and black houses with flat roofs, separated by streets of dark earth. The air seemed thick with heavy fumes; this was the Bronx, with its poverty and its tedium. In the middle of Harlem as well I came up against rocks scattered haphazardly along twisting paths. On a platform above, black people were daydreaming, while looking at the hazy silhouettes of skyscrapers on the far horizon.

I travelled through the Bronx for hours. One endless avenue followed the crest of a hill. At my feet a dark valley opened, furrowed with train tracks. I climbed down into this valley, and after getting lost in unknown streets, I suddenly found myself on a huge metal bridge crossing the Harlem River. Below me was the black water; all around, the chaos of the outlying districts; and the whole city was present in the purplish vapours that rose to the horizon. At nightfall I took a taxi along the banks of the Hudson. From the other side of the water, on a site of factories and the New Jersey shipyards, a whole riviera was lit up . . .

Now the train moves on. It crosses a northern landscape – this is how I picture Canada. From time to time you can glimpse the open sea in the distance, but the bays that cut deeply into the coast are frozen, as are the lakes and ponds. The bare woods are carpeted with snow. The sky is a hard blue above this frigid landscape.

I loved New York and I loved my life in New York: the telephone calls that woke me in the morning, the letters I read at the drugstore counter, mapping out my agenda for the day. Every week I eagerly bought the *New Yorker* and took great pleasure in its covers with their understated colours, its elliptical cartoons, and especially the tantalising list of films and exhibitions. There was always some enjoyable film to see: *Henry V, Lady in the Lake, Brief Encounter, Laura, Journey in Fear, Conflict* . . . And how easy it was to be part of New York life! People lined up at the movie houses on Broadway beginning in the morning. At any moment of the day, when you have an hour to kill, you can go and see animated films or newsreels. But especially at night, on crowded Forty-second Street, the movies have the simultaneous attraction of foreign festivals and national celebrations. At Times Square you can see the most recent Hollywood productions; on Forty-second Street they specialise in old cowboy films, 'laff movies', and those films that give you goose bumps – 'thrillings'. In a little movie house on one of the grand boulevards in Paris they used to show these horror films twenty years ago; since 'talkies' came in, they've hardly changed. I've seen those murdered mummies that had to be stopped with a stake through the heart; I've seen vampires ghoulishly drinking innocent blood and robots possessed by uncontrollable powers that wreak death and terror . . . Every time the mummy appears, the public groans – not with terror, of course, but with delight, since no one believes it any more.

The animated pictures disappointed me; they've become fixed and mechanical. And the films I saw did not give me New York as I had hoped one evening. But they helped me anchor myself in America. I was no longer looking at the screen with the same eyes as in France; the exoticism of the drugstores, streets, elevators and doorbells had disappeared; they were quite simply realistic details. But this realism was more poetic than any invention. The screen transfigured everyday objects, re-establishing that distance between the drugstore and me that seems to disappear every time I drink an orange juice and yet continues to exist. It was through these black-and-white images that I first knew America, and I still think of them as its real substance. The screen is a platonic heaven where I grasp the Idea in its purity once more, an Idea that is only approximately embodied in the stone houses and neon lights.

We are crossing New Haven – dark, gloomy docks and black water. Night is falling. Far behind me, the arrow of the Empire State Building is lit up, and I will not see it. Never again will I see New York with fresh eyes. The first stage of this trip is over.

Streets, museums, bars, movie houses. There were people, too. Never before had I seen so many new faces in so little time – Europeans in exile and Americans. The word 'European', which I never use in France, often comes to my lips here. It struck me after a discussion with some Americans that Italians, Spaniards, French and German Jews all come from the same fatherland, which is also mine – they all have the same values, the same taste for debate and discussion. However, despite these affinities, I didn't prefer their company. Too accustomed to America to feel it day by day, they weren't sufficiently rooted here to love it or hate it intelligently. Nearly all of them denigrated it too systematically to help me get to know it. The people I want to see again when I return are those free-thinking Americans who participate in the life of this great continent without being lost in it. Many of those I barely met touched me with a generosity, a ready warmth, a cordial simplicity that, for these three weeks, has never ceased to astonish me. How I regret being unable to love more unstintingly a country where the reign of man is affirmed with such magnificence, where the love of one's fellow man seems at first sight so easy to achieve. Why is it that the goodwill I often felt around me is so utterly powerless? Will it always be this way?

14 February, Washington

In New London I just had time for dinner by the sea before giving my lecture. I took the night train for Washington, where I have another lecture to give. This is the first city in America that I'll see after New York. I don't know anyone here; I'll stay only a day and a half. Just as I was beginning to feel at home in America, I've become a tourist again.

My hotel is at the upper end of town, on the edge of a park vaster than the Bois de Boulogne. From my window I see tennis courts and a large garden. You'd think you were in a resort town. My room has the quiet, dull luxury of resort hotels. There's a radio you can listen to for two hours by sliding fifty cents into a slot. I don't really know what to do with myself. I know how to wander around a European city. But in America, it's another story . . .

I must take the plunge. I go downstairs. I take a taxi. These avenues lined with peaceful houses, elegant and discreet stores, are nothing like the streets in New York. All the houses are made of brick. There are few cars, few pedestrians. It's a provincial city. The taxi turns down a broad road lined with monuments as white as marble – perhaps they are marble. In any case, the style is Greco-Roman. In the distance stands the Capitol, which I've seen so often in movies. I stop. To gain time before leaping into the unknown, I've decided to go to the museum [the National Gallery]. It's also in the Greco-Roman style, with a huge, majestic staircase. The interior does not belie the façade. With its enormous marbled columns, its colonnades, its flagstones and its green plants, this museum is a cross between a mausoleum and a Turkish bath. The richness of its collections stuns me. Yet there is something restful about finding yourself in the serene and international world of paintings: I could be at the Louvre, the Prado or the Uffizi. The new world meets the old – there is only one past. When I emerge, I'm surprised to find myself in Washington again.

I am a conscientious tourist. I lunch in the commercial centre of town – a glum and ugly area where geometry does not achieve grandeur but produces only tedium. And then I climb the Capitol's steps. Hundreds of Americans, coming from all corners of America, make this pilgrimage. As people do at all monuments, they measure with their eyes the cupola's height and stop before the statues. The boldest ones climb to the top of the dome on a series of stone stairs and iron ladders. Everyone glances timidly at the great hall of Congress, half-empty at the beginning of this afternoon's session. Official guides explain the past and the present. I'm satisfied with a superficial glance. With its corridors, halls, underground passages, terraces, stairways, monuments, colonnades and galleries, the Capitol is as boring as the Pantheon or the Chamber of Deputies. And the green esplanade that extends to the obelisk erected in memory of George Washington is more disheartening than the Champ-de-Mars. Despite the soft light and the freshness of the grass, it looks to me like a torrid desert – boredom burns. In the whiteness of their marble, the museums and embassies refract the dull heat of a relentless summer. I cross over to the left, fleeing these official splendours and going toward the docks that smell of fish and tar. The 'Potomac' – it's a word to conjure with. Part of its poetry for me is no doubt owing to the beautiful red colour of Cocteau's book [*La Fin du Potomak*] with its Mortimers and its Eugènes. And then there is the savage sound of old Indian names; this savagery is a surprise in Washington, which asserts that nature has been conquered by politics, diplomacy, and monuments to the dead. The Potomac is frozen. Boats, yachts and ferries are caught in the ice. I'm at the water's edge. Children amuse themselves by throwing heavy stones onto the shining surface, which sometimes resists the shock and sometimes cracks. Large parks and green banks border the river, which curves out and extends into a lake. It's very large, and the wooded hills on the other bank seem far away. Down below, in an island of greenery, I glimpse the whiteness of marble colonnades – the Lincoln Memorial. A little farther, to my right, at the top of a ridiculous staircase, there's more marble whiteness at the Jefferson Memorial. Such ugliness is disconcerting in the land of noble skyscrapers. But if you sit on the staircase with your back turned to this city where History is petrified into boredom, you can contemplate a site worthy of the memories it evokes. The Potomac is a great northern river that shines with frozen brightness amid spring greenery under a blue southern sky. For the people of New York, Washington is already the South, and I feel the South in that unexpected warmth after leaving the snows of Central Park. It's marvellous to be sitting in the sun beside a frozen river under a bright sky.

After my lecture an old woman tells me, 'Actually, poor Pétain was an existentialist. He was struggling mightily to choose . . .' I have the impression that Pétain had a lot of sex appeal for old French ladies in America.

15 February

It seems futile to me to set out on foot this morning to see Washington: the dimensions of these American cities are discouraging. I want to take refuge in some corner with a book and pretend I'm not travelling. But this doesn't take into account the untiring kindness of Americans. Two old ladies telephone and offer to drive me around the city. Half an hour later we're already on our way. We drive down the hill and follow the bottom of a ravine. This park is a large swathe of unspoiled countryside, wooded, ever-changing, crossed by rivers bordered by huge rocks. It reminds me of Brittany near Huelgoat. In the middle of the woods stand the graves of an old cemetery. We reach a wealthy residential area. Once more, I'm completely astonished to encounter in reality what looked to me like a studio set in the movies. Along the deserted sidewalks I recognise those white gates opening onto flower gardens, and those white wooden houses, neat and monotonous. Suddenly, I'm surprised to find myself in the heart of an old Dutch town: the tidy, narrow streets are paved with cobblestones; the old houses are covered in a coat of red or white plaster through which you can glimpse the rectangular bricks beneath. This is Georgetown, the oldest section of Washington. Dates appear on the façades – 1776, 1780. The small windows, pointed roofs, balconies and wrought-iron work remind me of the childlike houses of the villages in Zuider Zee. A few miles away we're transported to an English village with its cottages of flowering geraniums, its broad, straw-coloured roofs, its calm streets. I didn't at all expect to find the picturesque remnants of old Europe around Washington. I think joyfully that America still harbours plenty of unexpected pleasures.

We cross the Potomac and enter Arlington National Cemetery. This is a magnificent park where only highly honoured officers are buried. There is no avoiding the dreadful monument crowning the top of the hill, where the view of the Potomac and Washington is otherwise breathtaking. But nothing disfigures the green lawns and winding paths. The graves are vertically placed flat stones, bearing simply a name. No inscription, no crown, no flower. The trees and sky are enough to honour the dead. The stones are placed quite far apart, lost in the greenery: each dead man reigns over large subterranean spaces. And the general impression is that the placement of each grave was guided by personal considerations. There is no symmetry, no overall plan. Probably the shade of this tree suited this dead soldier, the open ground that one.

They do not speak willingly of death in America; you never come across a funeral in the streets. It is true that on the avenues I often glimpse the words 'Funeral Home' lit up in neon lights at night. But the name is intended to be comforting; from the outside, the places look like bars or cabarets. I've read handbills that say, 'Funeral Home: Reception rooms. Playrooms for children.

Bathroom. Cloakroom. Moderate prices.' This is where, before burial, the dead man throws his last party. His uncovered face is made up in bold colours, he wears a gardenia or an orchid in his buttonhole, and his friends come to greet him for the last time. But these pleasant homes wedged between drugstores and bars give me the creeps. I always expect to see some zombie or vampire making its escape, because in these places the truth about death is really denied. In the cemeteries, though, it is revealed, and that's what gives these gardens of mourning their unexpected charm. All of a sudden in this country, where health and happiness are guaranteed by the most modern processes, one discovers that people die, and life regains a dimension it had lost in claiming to fashion itself after the Quaker Oats ads. On Broadway, despite the weighty affirmation of the skyscrapers, in Queens, despite the desolate uniformity of the working-class districts, in Arlington, despite the marble serenity of the Capitol, the cemeteries remind us that every existence is singular and that every man is in himself an absolute. They remind us that life is carnal, that even with air conditioning the air is breathed with real lungs. Returning to the earth, man gives proof that he is not a mechanical creature; he is flesh, and real blood runs in his veins. It's the graves in America that confirm with the greatest authority that man is still human. I don't know if Americans are aware of this reminder, if they feel more tenderness than they admit for the sleep that will give them respite from their breathless lives. The fact is, they don't bury their dead in rows, and their cemeteries have more personality than their towns. Among these stones half-sunk in the earth, one finally escapes the banality of daily life.

We have no time to go to Mount Vernon; I'm sorry. I go to see a few of the paintings at the museum again and take the train to Lynchburg [Virginia], to give a lecture at Macon College [Randolph-Macon Women's College].

The sky is blue again. The earth turns red, and the shade under the pines is red as well. I think: I'm going down South.

Going down South is always fascinating; I wonder if this is still an attraction on the other side of the equator. Here the word 'south' carries more emotional resonances than anywhere else. It's the tragic earth described by Faulkner and Caldwell, the land of slavery and hunger. Now and then I glimpse a dark wooden shack on a hilltop and black men milling around it – I'm touched. Neon lights, drugstores, smiles, prosperity, ease – the world is not this cut-rate paradise. There is another truth, the truth of poverty, exhaustion, hatred, cruelty, revolt – the truth of evil. Tragic earth, human earth, where life is a drama and not a social process managed by experts. This landscape, whose warm colours evoke the Riviera, covers a dark and bloodstained canvas on which men's labour and suffering are etched. Here and there, beneath the golden slopes, the design shows through: a meagre ploughed field, a cabin lost in the forlorn countryside, a brown, unsmiling face.

Lynchburg. I won't go any farther today, but in a few weeks, after many detours, I'll go deeper into the South. Two friendly young women take me through the town whose name is laden with menace. I glimpse only that 'Main Street' described by Sinclair Lewis. In all the towns across America this is the street of shops and movie houses where, by decree, no tree grows: its shade might put this or that shop at a disadvantage, to the profit of its competitors. The streets teem with black children, peaceful residences, and here, miles from town, Macon College.

16 February

Upon waking, I wonder just why I'm staying here in this sanatorium. The room is white and fluffy, like the one at Vassar. With nurse-like attention, a woman has placed a breakfast platter beside me. Last evening, to spare me any fatigue, they brought my dinner to my room. Without leaving my bed, I drink the orange juice, eat the crusty rolls, and savour the charms of convalescence in the *café au lait*. Nothing is stranger to me than these restrained pleasures. Amid such attentive care I feel so fragile and precious I almost frighten myself. Perhaps I've undertaken a detox cure: no alcohol, no noise, no movies, no music, no fever. I draw an armchair up to the table. I've stayed here today to write an article before hurrying back to New York and going north. But I like to nurse the illusion that I'm restrained by force and working to distract myself. There's nothing more restful on a trip than to imagine you're in prison.

At noon a delegation of college girls comes to take me to lunch. The students are grouped around noisy little tables in a big dining room. It's Sunday, and they're wearing those ladylike outfits I can't stand — a raw-silk dress decorated with a scarf and a crocodile-skin belt. This is about the extent of their fantasies. Aloud and mechanically, they all say grace together with mouths painted thick with lipstick. Then they put a plate in front of me with an array of white cheese, mayonnaise, jam, fish and lettuce leaves. After Virginia-style fried chicken, some of these young girls take me for a walk through the college; we climb up a tower, from which you can see great stretches of blue pines around sunny lawns. And we continue to chat. They talk to me about their plans for the future, the most essential of which is to find a husband. Some want a husband and a career, but most would willingly forgo the career. It's fine to have a job for a year or two, they explain to me; first, it's a way of meeting young men, and then it's a way of declaring their independence. Having given this proof, they can marry without any feeling of inferiority. For this category of rich and spoiled young girls, marriage seems like the only honourable fate; remaining single is considered a defect. Sunday is the day for husband hunting. The campus lanes are invaded by shiny automobiles, and couples sit on the lawns in the sun: the college girls are entertaining their 'dates'. This name, signifying a 'rendezvous', is given to any young man who comes courting. The fact of the rendezvous is much more important than the particular partner. A college girl's prestige depends essentially on the number of dates she accumulates. It's a disaster for the girls who are at some physical disadvantage. The couples are free to stay on the lawns or to leave the campus. At Macon the students have sworn not to drink alcohol, no matter where they go. They explain to me proudly that college life depends in great part on the honour system. They take their final exams without surveillance, on their honour. On the whole, the honour system plays a large role in America. For example, in hotels illicit couples are asked to swear that they are married; by pretending to believe their words, the personnel avoid many difficult problems. If the perjury is flagrant, the culprit is severely punished. Through such strict punishment Americans show their faith in American loyalty. This faith allows them to reconcile an austere morality with a convenient freedom of mores. But this is never guaranteed; eyes that are complacently closed can always be opened.

They also talk to me, without being very specific, about the sororities, which correspond to the male fraternities. This is a kind of club prevalent in all the colleges. Only girls from particularly distinguished families or with great personal prestige are admitted. The members busy themselves doing various kinds of social work, they explain vaguely. A French student here on scholarship is sceptical. In her opinion, these sororities have only one purpose, which is to reinforce the already very aristocratic character of colleges; membership is highly prized only because of the exclusion it implies. At Macon, more than in the North, the college girls form cliques. They come from different states, but the southerners are in the majority and feel they belong to a higher caste. The old antagonism of North and South is perpetuated and expressed here, often in violent arguments. In particular, on racial questions the Yankees are liberals whereas the daughters of the South share their families' prejudices. To be sure, there would be no question of admitting a student of black ancestry to a southern college. One of the professors, who is originally from the South but who has a democratic sense of justice and equality, tells me sadly that it is impossible to eradicate such deep-seated prejudice. Persuasion, reasoning, and personal influence all fail; these young minds are already made up.

I'm taken on a driving tour. This is the first time I'm immersed in the American countryside. It's wild and beautiful here: wooded hills, tobacco fields, red earth, a mild southern climate. A river runs along the foot of the mountains. I don't quite know why it seems impossible for me to situate this temperate landscape in Europe – perhaps because its features are too emphatic. And then it appears uninhabited. You glimpse a house now and then, but it doesn't seem part of the landscape. In France, the houses are made of the same granite, the same lava, the same clay as the soil. They've aged under the same rains and the same sun. Through them, man has become as deeply rooted in the earth as a tree. Here, the houses are made of wood, as impersonal as pavilions at an exhibition, and so precarious and foreign to nature, whose solitude they destroy, but without peopling it. Yes, I miss the farms of Provence. But these vast horizons are fascinating. How I wish I could travel freely along these roads . . .

18 February, Rochester, NY

During a trip, one morning or one evening you almost always end up asking yourself in confusion, 'What am I doing here?' The moment has come; I open my eyes and find myself sitting in a leather armchair in the middle of a hotel lobby, and I think, 'Of all the places in the world, why have I landed in Rochester?' I spent two nights in trains, doing some hasty shopping in New York in between. When I arrived here at dawn, it was raining, and no room was available until ten o'clock. It might have been the beginning of a Simenon novel. I sat down in the hall among other suffering travellers and dozed. It's raining all the time. One week ago I didn't even know the name Rochester. Five hundred thousand people live here, around factories where they make photographic products and equipment. I feel lost. Once I get to my room, I fall asleep and have horrible nightmares.

Dr B, who organised my lecture for this evening, comes to take me to lunch. We travel by car across a northern city, a relentless city of right angles and standard stores crushed under a grey sky. The red earth and blue skies of Virginia are far away. However, in all the cities, the residential neighbourhoods are charming; the streets are covered with snow, and fir trees surround the wooden houses, some of which are very pretty. These places seem more like the kind of resort developments you find on the Cote d'Azur or around Arcachon than part of the city. There are sumptuous dwellings reigning over vast gardens but also identical houses in rows aligned between two more rows of identical houses. Each has its little square of grass, and these adjacent lawns become one large avenue of grass. The air is pure and pleasant to breathe. These are sensible houses, but they possess neither the pleasures of the countryside nor those of the city; life here must be adequate yet austere. Dr B, a professor, lives in one of these homes. The interior is comfortable and light, with many windows, few furnishings and few knick-knacks. Mrs B tells me that most of her friends, like herself, would prefer to live in apartments: these houses, even the modest ones, are heavy burdens. Despite American conveniences, upkeep is difficult. Almost no one has a maid in America, and housekeepers are rare; although many places deliver merchandise to the home, one cannot avoid a certain amount of shopping in town. These are major expeditions. There are very few apartments, and they are reserved for the privileged elite, so the entire middle class lives in houses far from the commercial centre. 'With two children to raise, the work is so demanding that a woman no longer has time to lead an intellectual life,' Mrs B tells me. She herself prepares an excellent meal for us. Bridge parties, teas, cocktail parties, women's clubs – these are the leisure activities of wealthy women. In the upper middle class, the American woman is as overwhelmed by household cares as a petit bourgeois Frenchwoman.

The countryside is beautiful under the snow, with its bare hills and frozen ponds. As in red-and-blue Virginia, I'm struck by the generosity of the landscape. The lines have the amplitude that I admired in New York in the sweep of the skyscrapers, bridges and avenues. We go out late in the afternoon; the sun sets slowly in a northern sky, as though the light were taking a long winter's sleep on the burnished snow.

We dine by candlelight, with all other lights extinguished, at the house of Dr B's friend; this lighting is a sign of luxury. I give my lecture in a museum hall with medieval ribbed vaulting. When I return, it's only eleven o'clock. I hesitate at the hotel door; I take a few steps, and then it hits me that despite the neon signs, the night is as deserted and desolate as in Limoges or Avallon. I dearly hope I'm never fated to live in Rochester.

19 February

'Are you going to see Niagara Falls?' Dr B's son asked me. I enquired, 'Is it beautiful?' 'Oh, yes! It's beautiful!' In New York people had told me, smiling, 'It's a honeymoon spot,' but they usually added, 'Still, it's worth seeing.' I've wanted to see the falls for a long time. Not because of Chateaubriand [and his description in *Travels in America*], but because, when I was the same age as Dr B's son, I saw them one Sunday at the Châtelet Theatre, all green and foamy. An acrobat crossed them on a high wire, carrying in his arms the heroine whom he'd so audaciously saved from dreadful dangers. I'd also read in an adventure book a description of the falls that always seemed to me a fine exercise in style. Since I have a free day, instead of travelling directly to Cleveland, I'll go by way of Buffalo.

Buffalo isn't far. The bus rolls for two hours across a meagre plain: snow, bare trees and detached wooden houses. They are sometimes scattered and sometimes clustered together, forming what they call a 'village' here. In the distance there's a glimpse of the white line of the lake. It looks like a monotonous, indistinct backdrop unfurling. Buffalo. The name is coloured red and yellow from old children's magazines, the gamy smell of Buffalo Bill's boots and huge herds of buffalo; it has the primitive crudeness of a pioneer camp on the shores of a stormy lake. We follow the tramline into a dark street lined with low houses and crossed by straight streets, whose black pavement stretches out to infinity. For twenty or twenty-five miles we continue to enter Buffalo. The bus stops in the middle of Main Street: movie houses, stores, huge bank buildings. I check my suitcases at the station, which is simultaneously a drugstore, a bookstore and a waiting room, and I take another bus to Niagara Falls.

Niagara Falls is not a set at the Châtelet Theatre. It's a miniature version of Buffalo, a town of dark and dismal factories. You arrive there by a route that follows the lake, but you don't see the lake – you see warehouses and factories; you breathe in the odour of smoke and gasoline. The bus stops in front of a tourist office, where coloured posters offer boat and car tours. A uniformed employee grabs me; because I don't have time to take a group excursion by boat, he puts me in a taxi. I pay a few dollars in exchange for a pink ticket, which I am to give to the driver when we return. He's a specialised driver, who also serves as my guide. He takes his role seriously and doesn't stop talking. We follow a route along the edge of a gorge, and he describes for me all the factories that disfigure the landscape on the opposite bank. We cross a large bridge, but then we must stop; we're entering Canada. The customs officers are used to it – all the tourists cross the river to see the falls from the Canadian side, which offers the most interesting views – yet they examine my passport for a quarter of an hour. It's not that they find anything amiss; they simply look it over carefully. Once over the bridge, we continue to follow the gorges, where the Niagara River lies hidden at the bottom; I still haven't seen the colour of its waters. The driver stops in front of a small building; there's a lunchroom, a souvenir shop and an elevator that for fifty cents takes me down to water level. I look. What else is there to do? It's water. I go back up and we leave. Another stop. This time I find myself on a terrace where I can glimpse a bend of the Niagara River and a tributary that swells it. I go down, then we leave, driving in the opposite direction toward the falls. The taxi stops for me at a lookout point, then at another in the middle of a park carpeted with snow, and I finally discover the lake. Certainly in Chateaubriand's time, before the factories and tourist lodgings were built, this landscape must have been striking. Amid the pines, the lake is vast. It's not frozen, but its green-and-white water seems just on the verge. Perhaps, as I once read in a novel by Jules Verne, you could just throw in a chunk of ice and the entire rippling surface would freeze over. The lake is beautiful, like a Jules Verne landscape, promising all sorts of adventures and wonders. The wind stirs the green waters, revealing their keen white swells – you could cut your finger on them. Water that's both liquid and hard, choppy water, all needles and blades. If the lake suddenly froze, it would give a long, tragic moan. That would be more marvellous than the Northern Lights. Compared to the vast richness of these potential wonders, the falls themselves are a wonder that is too clearly circumscribed. Perhaps when I view them from below, I'll find them more inspiring. But I'm not ready to descend. The car climbs up a hill; I'm taken to the best lookout point. This is a two-storey building with a lunchroom and souvenirs; I take a ticket from the cashier, and I'm led into a totally dark room where I go forward, groping along a ramp. Careful! A lighted torch shows me a dark well, and all around, on the walls, there are frescoes depicting missionaries in long robes. The guide throws the torch into the well, and the water blazes. It was the Indians who discovered this wonder, and the missionaries after them. The water is really ablaze. My guide fills a glass, which I empty, and when I've drunk, he lights some mineral deposits at the bottom, which produce a large flame. This flame doesn't burn; the guide puts his hand through it with impunity. Again I find myself at the Châtelet Theatre. I go out, and an elevator hoists me up into a large, glassed-in hall. In front of the windows, there are telescopes that you can activate for a nickel. Above, there's an open-air terrace. From here the lake is infinite, but the falls seem crushed, the cascades indistinguishable from many others.

It's not over. Now we descend to the water's edge. I enter a new building. The elevator goes underground. I find myself in a tiled gallery, where the air is damp. Two cloakrooms open onto this corridor – one for men, the other for women. I enter. There are hundreds of slickers hanging along the walls, hundreds of boots in various sizes sitting in rows on the shelves. An attendant takes my coat and shoes; she helps me pull on the boots and put on an enormous oilskin cape with a hood covering my head. I'm going to walk under the falls; I imagine I'll pass behind the curtain of weeping waters, as I sometimes did in the Bois de Boulogne (or was it at the Buttes-Chaumont?) in my childhood. But no. I'm in a subway corridor; at the end there's a kind of window from which, by raising my head, I can see the falls from top to bottom. They are half-frozen, but you can't even touch the sumptuous stalactites. Another corridor, another small basement window. A man dressed in waders like me looks hesitantly at the sign: 'No Passing.' He passes; I pass too. With your feet in the hard snow, you get a better view of the half-frozen waters. Like me, the man is visibly disappointed. He has a camera and asks me to photograph him. His fat red face laughs in a becoming way under his oilskin hood, against the backdrop of the waterfalls. We return wistfully along the tiled corridors. It wasn't really worth the trouble of changing clothes.

There's nothing to do but return. Apparently in the evening, multicoloured floodlights bathe the waters in enchanting colours; I can almost imagine this spectacle. Perhaps if you walk at leisure, without a guide, on guard against the advertised attractions, you might succeed, despite the factories and the organised tourism, in recapturing the beauty of this great watery landscape. As for me, I've enjoyed myself, but the way I would at a provincial circus. It's very rare in America that noteworthy sites are not classified and protected; I wonder why Niagara Falls wasn't declared a park or national monument.

At three o'clock I find myself in Buffalo once more. An icy wind is blowing. I enter a pink-and-white cafeteria where they make doughnuts as the customers watch; the pale fritters are slowly carried on a sliding sheet across a lake of boiling oil and come out golden and hot on a platter. After a quick lunch, I gather up my courage and go out for a walk. I would like to see the lake. I walk down Main Street, against the wind. The sidewalk becomes confusing terrain, the half-frozen mud slippery beneath my feet. Depots, warehouses, rails, abandoned hulls of great ships – I am walking in a no-man's-land that is neither port nor station, nor town. Far away you can see the lake, but there's no way of getting to it. The wind becomes increasingly sharp. It gets dark; against the soot-black buildings the neon lights glow red, like embers crushed by an opaque heap of cold cinders. New York must be beautiful at this hour: the windows of the buildings are a pale mica between the golden stones; the mist in the sky sweeps through Lexington Avenue . . . Here, it's Buffalo; the sky remains distant, like a regret. I look down Main Street. I have nothing to do but go to the movies. I have a choice between *The Razor's Edge* and *Sinbad the Sailor*. I opt for *The Razor's Edge*. It's five o'clock; when I leave, it's eight. Three hours of nearly intolerable boredom. But while drinking a whiskey to comfort myself, I tell myself that I haven't completely wasted my time. Somerset Maugham is English, but the film made from his novel is typically American. In it, a well-intentioned young man suffers from that slight malaise one observes today, particularly among war veterans, and cannot find satisfaction in life, love and success of the sort America provides. He decides to set off in search of his soul. Just as he would go to mineral springs in search of health, he takes off to see specialists: first to the Sorbonne, where he reads an impressive number of books; then to India, where, on a high plateau, a man with a white beard and bare feet tells him the secret of wisdom. Armed with this talisman, he comes home to do good.

This first part is already full of meaning: the hero's restlessness seems decidedly abnormal; his fiancée, unable to understand him, breaks off their engagement; and it is not a question of his living with this anguish, of searching deeply for its meaning, by himself – it is never a question of inner experience. He must go outside himself to seek a cure. The second part also deserves some thought. In short, the secret is that he must live for charity, and this charity takes on the puritanical aspect of a battle against debauchery. After curing several people of neuralgia, the hero tries to redeem a prostitute, a formerly decent woman who has become morally deranged and driven to drink by a ghastly automobile accident that killed her husband and children. He fails, and the unfortunate woman dies with her throat slit. Then, frustrated by the impotence of his good intentions, he signs on as a miner in the north of France. He was capable of renouncing his fortune and the woman he loved, of spending years looking for the answer to his problems – but this is a totally empty solution. He never gets the idea that he might really try to *act*; he confines himself to cultivating a vague soulfulness. This story certainly leaves you with the sad impression that in America even good intentions do not offer any hope.

The bar where I'm drinking a whiskey is lit in dark violet; it's so hot, so velvety, that the street outside the window is glacial by comparison. The absurdity of my presence here strikes me even more strongly than in Rochester, and I'm suddenly filled with joy. This town is a straggling village as lost beneath the sky as a hamlet on the Causses plateau. But its desolation has been multiplied on a gigantic scale; between me and this village of five hundred thousand inhabitants, there's not the slightest tie – we have nothing in common. I go out onto Main Street, and someone inside me laughs, as if one half of my personality were playing a good joke on the other. Just what am I doing on Buffalo's main street? I walk because it's cold, but I'm going absolutely nowhere; there's no place I'd want to go. I'm no longer in Paris, no longer in New York, not yet in Chicago – I'm nowhere. I've escaped the laws of space. The two halves of myself laugh together; the joke is as funny for the duped as for the duper.

This gaiety is likely to dissipate rather quickly. To end the evening, I go to see *Sinbad the Sailor* in Technicolor. This film is so typically American that there's nothing to think about. All I can do is quickly forget it and go to sleep.

20 February

To take me to the station the taxi drives for half an hour through a deserted street that is exactly the same mile after mile, intersected at right angles by streets that are exactly identical. 'It's big,' says the driver. That's just what scares me – it's big. Why did they build so many copies of the same house? What proliferation! The streets are empty in the cold morning light and yet saturated with humanity. How sad it must be inside these houses, and how sad it is to go outside. Sad to me; surely the inhabitants of Buffalo think that Buffalo is the most beautiful city in America – let alone the world. That's what all Americans think of their home towns.

The train rolls through the same countryside I drove through yesterday. It's not that I'm retracing my steps, but it's the same white plain, the same lake on the horizon. And at the end of the iron tracks I encounter the same city all over again: Main Street, dark buildings, small houses of dirty wood, great opulent thoroughfares and muddy vacant lots. To wander around on foot here is crazy – that much I understand. I entrust myself to a taxi driver. When you leave the downtown area, Cleveland becomes more distinct from Rochester and Buffalo. There are large, rather cheerful parks, and a road follows the lakeshore. I stop at the museum, which I was advised to visit. It's a small, isolated building that stands in the middle of French-style gardens with frozen ponds. I enter and feel the same soothing sensation as in Washington – what an alibi! I am escaping America, Cleveland and myself. And after those three desolate days it's a forgotten joy to find myself in front of objects that are a pleasure to look at. There is a beautiful Picasso from the blue period and also an exhibition of Degas. I feel like I've recovered a lost sense; in being given something to see, I've had my sight restored. At the corner of the paintings, there are often city names: Cincinnati, Albany. Some are full of promise: Toledo. But I know. Hundreds of cities like Buffalo and Rochester, each with its little museum, its painting by Degas . . .

So many towns! Waiting for the bus to Oberlin, Ohio, in a large station posted with timetables, I'm fascinated by the list of names: Detroit, Pittsburgh, St Louis . . . Hundreds of towns, hundreds of times the same town. You could travel day after day in the same bus, across the same plain, and you'd arrive each evening in the same town, which would have a different name every time. The idea makes me dizzy. My bus drives along the same street repeated indefinitely: it's Cleveland for miles and miles, then Cleveland's outlying districts, and always the same street. The city has changed names, yet it's the same street. Another town and the same street. There is probably no way out. I close my eyes, defeated.

Oberlin is a peaceful village built around a college, the first to open its doors to women, in 1833. The hotel where I get out has the old-fashioned charm of our provincial hotels. I dine at the Maison Française with the students, and after my lecture they take me for a drink – a glass of milk. Oberlin is 'dry', like most college and university towns. This doesn't stop either students or professors from drinking heavily in private. It's above all a matter of an old tradition: there's no country where respect for tradition is more ingrained than in America, one of the students tells me. We drink milk in a dreary cafeteria, and we chat. Most of the intellectuals I met in New York amazed me with their abstention from social and political questions, but these young people amaze me even more. I know very well that in a sense there is no political life in America, but at their age it's normal to try and create one. No. Even among themselves they don't talk about social problems;

they hardly talk about intellectual matters either, they say. 'What do you talk about?' I ask. They shrug their shoulders – nothing. More specifically, sports or college organisations. These are the chief distractions offered to the students. They elect presidents and committees; they thrash around and think they are acting. The students who talk to me are conscious of this hoax and of all the hoaxes of American democracy. They deplore the battle being waged by Congress against the AFL [American Federation of Labor] and the CIO [Congress of Industrial Organizations] – under the pretext of revising labour legislation, it is determined to destroy the workers' unions. They also deplore the fact that capitalist forces are hastening democracy's demise with dizzying speed. But it's this demise itself, they say, that makes all action impossible; the social pressure is too crushing. The Constitution even prevents the citizen from intervening in political life. An indirect intervention – on an intellectual level, for example – is forbidden by private agreements, dictated by capitalist interests: a professor soon loses his job if he teaches ideas judged to be subversive; publishers and critics ban a subversive book when it is not officially condemned. These statements offer testimony to the oppressive nature of American democracy. They agree, but they're not tempted to fight it. One of them, who is originally Hungarian and has only recently become an American, voices his criticism with particular vehemence. The only solution he sees is to return to Europe – the only place where it still means something to think.

What is most striking to me, and most discouraging, is that they are so apathetic while being neither blind nor unconscious. They know and deplore the oppression of thirteen million blacks, the terrible poverty of the South, the almost equally desperate poverty that pollutes the big cities. They witness the rise, more ominous every day, of racism and reactionary attitudes – the birth of a kind of fascism. They know that their country is responsible for the world's future. But they themselves don't feel responsible for anything, because they don't think they can do anything in this world. At the age of twenty, they are convinced that their thought is futile, their good intentions ineffective: 'America is too vast and heavy a body for one individual to move it.' And this evening I formulate what I've been thinking for days. In America, the individual is nothing. He is made into an abstract object of worship; by persuading him of his individual value, one stifles the awakening of a collective spirit in him. But reduced to himself in this way, he is robbed of any concrete power. Without collective hope or personal audacity, what can the individual do? Submit or, if by some rare chance this submission is too odious, leave the country.

21 February

Thirty-six hours to spend in Chicago – not much. I take the first morning train, but it's already two o'clock when I arrive at the station. The taxi carries me down an avenue crushed by the heavy, black metal construction of an elevated railway. They've reserved a room for me at the Palmer House, the most monstrous of all the hotels I've seen. Bar, cafeteria, lunchroom, blue room, red room, Victorian room, gypsy orchestra, Mexican orchestra, flowers, candy, all sorts of stores, travel offices, airlines – it's a whole town with its residential neighbourhoods, its quiet avenues and its noisy commercial downtown. It's hard to breathe in the lobby, which is permeated by a stifling heat and the thick scent of dollars. My room is on the sixteenth floor. An old woman with white hair guards the entrance to the hallways; she is the one who keeps my key. Every client is as closely watched as in a provincial family *pension*.

As in Washington, I first take refuge in the museum. At the Art Institute there is a magnificent collection of impressionists and contemporary paintings; for the two hours I spend looking at them, I feel solid ground beneath my feet. But as soon as I'm back on the terrace, on the lakeshore and on Michigan Avenue, which winds out of sight, I'm gripped by anxiety that verges on anguish. I love the hard line of the skyscrapers; they are more massive than in New York, and they're purer – no Renaissance windows, no Gothic bell tower. They were built at a time when the skyscraper had won the game and needed no more excuses for itself. I walk down Michigan Avenue, where an icy wind is blowing. I wander through the streets downtown, which they call the Loop. I'm happy to find myself once again in a city that seems to be a metropolis and not a straggling village indefinitely multiplied. But what can I grasp of it? Chicago. The name alone fascinates me: I remember Bancroft in *Chicago Nights* and so many other stories of gangsters. I think of *Studs Lonigan*, in which Farrell describes life in the Irish neighbourhoods; of *Black Metropolis*, that enormous study of life in the black section of the city [done by St Clair Drake and Horace R. Cayton]. There are also the slaughterhouses, the burlesque houses . . . And I'm leaving tomorrow.

My New York friends gave me two addresses: a writer and an old lady. If I don't want to waste my evening, one of them must come to my rescue. To get a taste of Chicago at night, the writer seems preferable. I pick up the telephone and ask for Mr NA [Nelson Algren].* A surly voice answers, 'You have the wrong number.' To be sure, I look it up in the phone book; it must be my pronunciation. I dial again. I've hardly opened my mouth when the voice repeats, this time with irritation, 'Wrong number.' He hangs up. What should I do? I try the old lady; she isn't home. Good. I have a melancholy supper at a drugstore counter. Yet I don't want to let this night slip through my fingers. I'm incapable of doing anything alone: New York began to open up for me only when I had guides to show me the city. In the swirl of lights, in the labyrinth of streets, I would never find the right places. I tackle the writer again; he hangs up. I'm determined. I ask the telephone operator to take the message. As soon as she hears the ring, she says with gentle authority and an

---

* This encounter was the start of a love affair between the two, which continued after Simone de Beauvoir returned to France.

accent that inspires confidence, 'Please be patient and stay on the line for a moment . . .' Upon hearing the name of our mutual friends, the stranger on the other end of the line softens up, his voice brightens; of course, he'd be delighted. He will meet me in half an hour in the lobby.

I'm beginning to get used to meeting people I don't know in public rooms or on station platforms. We recognise each other at first glance; it's surprising. But when it comes to spending a long stretch of time together, I'm always a little anxious. In Washington I hesitated a long time before calling F; he was a Frenchman, and people had asked me to bring him books and news from Paris, but did he want these books and messages? He welcomed me very cordially. We spent three hours together in a friendly way, though no doubt we would never see each other again. I didn't know how to judge what he was saying or how he was reacting to me. This obscure, one-time confrontation seemed to sum up the absurdity and deceptive illusion of travel far better than my futile walks around Times Square. Again, have I not come empty-handed? This evening I have disturbed a stranger so that I might spend an interesting evening. How indiscreet! Moreover, I am running the risk of being bored. I'm not in a good mood when I go down to the lobby, holding a book in my hand as a sign, as if I were going to an interview arranged by a marriage bureau. I console myself thinking that at least the evening's outcome is not in my hands; I've done my best, and my conscience is clear.

Every time I meet an American, I have to serve a new apprenticeship in his language. I wonder whether in France there are such individual differences in pronunciation. I easily understand RW [Richard Wright] and AE [Bernard Wolfe]. But sitting in front of NA in a quiet little bar, I lose half his sentences. And I have the impression that he has as much difficulty as I do. He hesitates about what to show me in Chicago. There is no good jazz, the nightclubs for the middle classes are no more interesting here than in New York, and the idea of seeing burlesque shows doesn't excite me. If I like, he can take me to places where I'll probably have little occasion to venture. He can give me a glimpse of Chicago's lower depths; he knows them well. I accept.

He takes me to West Madison Avenue, which is also called Chicago's Bowery. This is where you find hotels for single men, flophouses and wretched bars. It's very cold, and the pavement is almost deserted, yet there are several lost-looking men lurking in the shadows of doorways or roaming the icy sidewalks. We enter a bar that reminds me of Sammy's Follies, but there's no show and no spectators — no other tourist but me. NA is not a tourist; he comes here often and knows all these people — bums, drunks, old ruined beauties. No one would turn around if the madwoman of Chaillot came in. At the back of the room, there's a small black band. A sign says 'Absolutely No Dancing', but couples dance anyway. There's a cripple who walks with the heavy steps of a duck. Suddenly, when he begins to dance, his legs obey him. He turns and jumps; he gambols with an ecstatic, maniacal smile on his lips. Apparently, he spends his days and nights here, and all night long, every night, he dances. Sitting at the bar is a woman with long, fine, curly hair tied with a big red ribbon. Sometimes her hair is blonde, and her doll face seems to belong to a young girl; sometimes her head seems covered with white stuffing, and she's a siren well over sixty. She empties one bottle of beer after another, all the while talking to herself and shouting defiantly. From time to time she gets up and dances, hiking her skirts. A drunk asleep at a table wakes up and grabs the arm of a fat crone dressed in rags, and they caper around. They dance with a joyous abandon that verges on madness and ecstasy. So ugly, so old, so wretched — for a moment they lose themselves, and they're happy. I feel stunned; I stare at them and say, 'It is beautiful.' This epithet surprises NA; it seems so typically French. 'With us,' he says, 'beautiful and ugly, grotesque and tragic, and also good and evil — each has its place. Americans don't like to think that these extremes can mingle.' Satisfied that this place fascinates me, he says to me, 'I'm going to show you something even better.'

In a sense, really, it is better. Here there are only men – the men of West Madison Avenue with the faces of criminals or idiots. They're so dirty you'd think their very bones were grey, and they spread around them a dreadful stench of poverty. At one o'clock in the morning they begin to gather, seeking shelter against the snow and nightly freeze. Some approach the counter, squeezing a few nickels in the palms of their hands – they want a beer. Others try to sell us a pair of scissors or pencils, begging fifty cents. A peroxided blonde handles the cash register. 'Everything I know about modern French literature is thanks to her,' NA tells me. 'She is very up-to-date.' And as I hesitate to believe him, he asks F to come and join us for a glass of wine. 'How is Malraux doing on his latest novel?' she quickly asks me. 'Is there a second volume? And Sartre? Has he finished *Les Chemins de la liberté* [*Roads to Freedom*, a trilogy including *The Age of Reason*, *Troubled Sleep* and *The Reprieve*]? Is existentialism still in vogue?' I'm stupefied. This woman spends all her nights supervising this bar, which is also an overnight shelter; her favourite amusements are reading and drugs. It seems she frequently takes drugs and has escaped from prison more than once, and she's been in and out of the hospital God knows how many times. From time to time, she also has love affairs, but they rarely turn out well. She explains to me that on the upper floor there is a large room with mats where for ten cents you can stretch out till morning. But many of these wretches would rather use their ten cents to drink a glass of beer; then the blonde lets them stay for free in the hall that leads from the sleeping room to the restrooms. 'Come see!' she says to me. I see. Sitting on benches, curled up on tables, crouching in the corners, scores of men are sleeping, their jaws hanging open, in their filth and vermin. Even in sleep they aren't truly relaxed; their muscles remain tense, and they'll wake with their bodies stiff all over. Louis XI invented the torture of cages so small that a man could never lie down. With their necks twisted, their joints aching, what dreams could offer them escape? As I look at them, a red-headed woman with a heavily painted face and curled hair minces over on her high heels. With virginal hesitation, she says, 'I would like to go the restroom, but all these men . . .' The cashier shrugs her shoulders: 'They're really too sleepy to bother you!' We go back down to the bar, where I swallow a whiskey, and soon the redhead reappears, disappointed.

Going home through the cold streets, under the black ceiling of the El, I tell myself that poverty never seemed so awful as in New York and Chicago. I've seen Vallecas district in Madrid, the Côte de Grace in Lisbon, the swarming streets of Naples, and, in the Sousse [in Tunisia], children with feet turned backward and eyes blinded by twisted eyelids. This poverty of poor countries is often dreadful, but given the barrenness of the soil and the dry riverbeds, it's an animalistic sort of squalor. And, of course, a sense of injustice, as well as the stupidity of it, is always present. But the face of poverty in a rich country is closer and crueller! In Naples, in Lisbon, as poor as people are, they still have their animal pleasures: the warmth of the sun, the freshness of an orange, embraces in the darkness of their beds. You often hear them singing and laughing, and they talk with each other. They are poor together; together, they tend their sick, mourn their dead and honour their saints. Around their afflicted bodies, at least they feel some human warmth. Here, the poor are cursed with the great curse of loneliness. They have no homes, no families, no friends, no place on earth; they are just refuse, useless flotsam, regarded with indifference. *Why* have they come to this? Universal optimism renders them suspect; it must be their fault. The police harass them, and in fact everything pushes them toward becoming guilty; they're all potential criminals. This social misery relegates men to a level below dumb animals. They make their way in a hostile world where their enemies have human faces; they have no friend but alcohol, and it's a costly friendship. In solitude, need and drunkenness, their minds wander; beyond hunger, there are strange beasts inside them who eat them alive.

22 February

I'm awakened by a telephone call: a Frenchman from the consulate [called JL below] informs me that he has organised a lunch and a dinner for me. I'm so sorry that I haven't seen anything of Chicago yet and there's so little time. But there's nothing I can do. My host is probably no happier than I, but it's his job to greet his countrymen – neither of us can help it.

I revisit the museum, the Loop and Michigan Avenue. The morning passes in a flash. At noon I'm at the hotel again with JL and a rich, cultivated American [V], who is a friend to France. They are very kind, and the old francophile women whom they take me to visit are very kind, too. Only, I have the distressing feeling that I'm wasting precious time. We lunch at a club with sumptuous rooms at the top of a large building. Through the bay windows I look at the canal [river] and the skyscrapers, and I try to convince myself that I'm really seeing Chicago. But the city is separated from me; it's been framed like a window display, or rather I'm the one who's been framed in a display window. Across from me sits a blonde Frenchwoman, who has been introduced as a baroness and journalist; she gives lectures across America on 'French cheerfulness during the Resistance'. And throughout the meal she recites patriotic slogans. JL and his American friend quickly whisk me away. They propose a drive, which consoles me. We make a grand tour of the city: the lakeside, gardens, fine hotels, luxurious residences. This Chicago is a city of wealth and festivities. But the American shakes his head. 'It's all a façade!' he says. In fact, as we drive toward the Polish section, where I met NA, the scenery changes: warehouses, factories, vacant lots, hovels. Trains circulate through the avenues and bar the way; the streets are much dirtier than those of New York; everywhere there is chaos and poverty. The beautiful dark automobile seems highly out of place on Wabansia Avenue, a long, indistinct area bordered by wooden shacks.

When we find ourselves in the Polish section, where NA lives, we stay there. It's too cold for a long walk, and moreover, this section is a city in itself. There are more Irish in Chicago than in Dublin, and more Poles than there ever were in Warsaw. We spend the afternoon walking in these streets and entering bars, where we drink vodka. Some of these places are also groceries that smell of dried fish; others are restaurants where they sell pink and yellow cakes coated with sour cream. The waitress doesn't even speak English. The place we choose has the bare, impersonal and neutral quality of truly American places. For a long time, evidently, it was the meeting place of a famous gang. I'm a little disappointed; I imagined that the gangster bars were recognisable by some sign, by a mysterious quality in the atmosphere, but of course the gangsters gathered on street corners like everyone else. I ask NA about this period, and he tells me that except in unusual circumstances, one didn't see anything particular in the streets, but one had a vague sense of insecurity, and there were areas where you avoided walking at night. As for Prohibition, there was hardly any difference between then and now. What were called 'speakeasies' were the same bars that sell alcohol today, only one paid a little more for the whiskey, and the beer wasn't as good. In certain places, they still take precautions before opening the door to customers.

I enjoy myself in these bars, in these little streets where the biting wind blows; I don't feel like such a tourist. It seems to me that I'm living a real Chicago afternoon in the company of an authentic native. NA spent his childhood and most of his adult life here. It's a classic American writer's life, similar to many I've read about. The surprise is to discover in an individual case that these stereotypical stories are true. He spent his early years roaming around Chicago: here the children, like their elders, formed gangs and readily banded together to rob some grocery store. The raid was so quick that the shopkeepers could barely defend themselves. By the time they called the police, the looters were already far away and difficult to identify with any certainty. Baseball games played in the vacant lots also occupied an important part of their leisure time. NA was an adolescent during the Great Depression. He looked for work throughout America, stowing away in freight trucks, eating and sleeping at the expense of the Salvation Army. In New Orleans he was a pedlar; the job paid little, and for weeks he lived exclusively on bananas. To facilitate sales, he promised all the women who bought five dollars' worth of merchandise a permanent wave at a certain hairdresser's salon – the clients soon inundated the hairdresser's shop, forcefully claiming their due. When the ruse was discovered, NA left for Mexico and eventually re-entered the United States, doing odd jobs: hot dog and hamburger vendor, masseur, pin boy in a bowling alley. He says that this job, which consists of endlessly setting up the pins that players constantly knock down, is one of the most tiring. Working steadily at a gas station with a friend, he began to write, at first for pleasure, then with the hope of earning some money. His first novel met with some success, and he obtained contracts with a publisher, which allowed him to undertake new books. He became friends with Richard Wright and James T. Farrell, and people often refer to them collectively as 'the Chicago School', although there are no great literary affinities between them. During the war, he was in Germany and Marseilles; he stopped in New York on his way there and back, but it's not a city he knows. He never leaves Chicago. He almost never visits any other writer. His friends are the people of the Bowery or his neighbours in the Polish section. He seems to me one of the most striking examples of that great intellectual solitude in which American writers live today.

When I find myself with JL and V in a large, elegant restaurant in the Loop where they serve martinis and grilled lobster, I have trouble believing I'm still in the same town. Before driving me to the station, they show me the illuminated skyline, nearly as beautiful as New York's. But I think with retrospective fear that had I not been so persistent last evening, I would have known nothing of Chicago except a stage set with lights and stone, a deceptively opulent and orderly façade. At least I had a glance behind the painted set. I saw a real city, tragic and ordinary, fascinating like all cities where men of flesh and blood live and struggle by the millions.

The station where I embark for Los Angeles makes a surprising contrast to the one where I arrived yesterday: it's only a large, half-demolished wooden shack. V fills my arms with magazines and books, and JL settles me solicitously in the train. I'm so sorry to leave. I must arrange somehow to come back to Chicago.

23 February

I pull the rough green curtains, fix them in place, hang my dress in the closet, and arrange my things in the mesh bags. The window is covered with a blind, and I switch on the little light above my head. On the other side of the thin partition, people come and go in the corridor; yet no room with thick walls has ever given me this feeling of relaxation and calm. This sleeping berth I'm stretched out on is more than a bed; it's a whole dwelling reduced to the dimensions of a bed. There are childhood memories associated with this pleasure. I remember a weeping willow in which I made a house, a large, canopied country bed with heavy curtains, and that dark compartment where I loved to hide under my father's desk. Psychoanalysts see in that a desire to return to the maternal womb, but this language is too symbolic and doesn't clarify anything. My berth is not the recollection of lost happiness; it gives me a satisfaction sufficient unto itself: it is refuge, solitude, separation. The tension and fatigue entailed in every existence originate in other, larger forms of existence; in these berths stacked on either side of the corridor, like tombs in the galleries of the Catacombs, each person achieves an absolute solitude. This nocturnal dwelling evokes the peace of the funeral chambers of Mycenae and Cerveteri; no appeal from the outside world can penetrate here. My life is no longer pulled in different directions or tied to anyone or anything; it has closed in on itself in the silence of death. I turn off the light and shut my eyes. I feel the rhythmic movement of the train as it rolls into the unknown; this movement also brings me peace – the peace of an alibi. Not only am I separated from everything, but I am not situated at any particular spot in the universe: I'm just passing through. I have no more ties to the earth, no more desire or curiosity. The sleep that pulls me from this world is in harmony with the rolling of the train, which minute by minute denies me any unique place in it. That's probably why my sleep is always so refreshing on trains.

When I awake, the train car's appearance has changed. Nearly all the travellers have risen, and the sleeping berths have been replaced with comfortable seats. In the overheated lavatories, women and children are washing. Wedged into my upholstered cubicle among my books and baggage, I'm enchanted with the prospect of two long, empty days before me. After these past weeks in which I've constantly been straining toward some kind of conquest, it's really relaxing to allow myself to be borne along – captive, passive – to the rhythm of the wheels. I open a book. I'm going to have a good long read, like those Vassar students I envied. The countryside is so ugly it won't distract me. The reading that will charm these hours is also the pretext that will allow me to savour indolent leisure. The words 'Orient Express' and 'Trans-Siberian Railway' have always set me dreaming. I used to wish I could travel by train for many days; then, as in Jules Verne's *La Maison à vapeur* [*Steam House*], the train truly becomes a dwelling place, and it's such a strange dwelling that life escapes its usual routine of days and nights and unfolds with marvelous freedom. It's probably not accidental that the memory of Jules Verne, whom I haven't thought of in twenty years, pursues me through America: this is a country of mechanical wonders where, on an adult scale, the childish imaginings of travel literature are realised.

As I enter the dining car for lunch, a tall, greying American accosts me with that abrupt familiarity you find among taxi drivers and university professors alike. He questions me, 'Am I French? Am I giving lectures?' He is, too. He sits down across from me, looks at me mischievously, then asks me point-blank, 'What do you think of Russia?' I return the question. He laughs. 'There's good there, as well,' he says. This is the first time I've heard this view expressed. Assured of my sympathy, he tells me that he was a professor at Harvard, that he spent several years in Russia as a newspaper correspondent, and that he then took up his professorship again but was fired after publishing a book that was too sympathetic to Stalin. Since then, he has written several works in which he criticises American capitalism, and travels the lecture circuit, speaking out in favour of Russia. At the moment he is on his way to speak in Emporia [Kansas]. He seems to know everyone on the train and doesn't stop shaking hands as we make our way back to our car. In that half-serious, half-kidding tone that is the rule among Americans of this generation, he tells me that he's going to Europe this winter to gather information about European problems; they seem to him to be essentially problems of supplying food. As he questions me about the future of France with that air of a lenient judge they so readily adopt here, I answer him that it would be difficult to distinguish our future from that of the world and that it partly depends, therefore, on American politics. He exclaims, 'But what can we do for you? Don't we send you enough condensed milk?' It's as if they think they can determine the fate of Europe with the ammunition of canned goods. Is this a pretext to ignore their real responsibilities and to forget, among other things, that decisions about war and peace are in their hands?

This man is certainly well intentioned, but his optimism is scarcely more reassuring to me than the Oberlin students' apathy. 'If everyone had good intentions, all would be well!' he says cheerfully. He adds forcefully, 'All would be well!' What worries me most is that he seems so ill informed about France, ignorant even of the names of its political leaders and writers, and, moreover, he does not know a word of French. This is not a good start for a fact-finding mission. I would even be sure he was pulling my leg somehow, if I hadn't already learned that many Americans have a breathtaking confidence either in the simplicity of the world or in their own capacities. They will claim to investigate a situation as complex as that of Europe in a week, starting with nothing and with almost no method. Good intentions are the universal panacea for everything. I would like to inform myself more specifically about his projects, but we're already at Emporia. He gets off. From a thick leather folder he takes a book and gives it to me as a present. It is a conciliatory work, with a preface by Ambassador Davies, which attempts to prove that Russia is a country like any other, neither imperialistic nor revolutionary – a moral and conservative country with whom an understanding is possible. Russia is basically another America, as idyllic and paradisical as its sister. This is discouraging reading, doubly so. I reject this gentle pastoral with an enormous portrait of Stalin on its cover. A moment later the black porter in the sleeping car stops. His face lights up, and he laughs with all his teeth. 'A good guy!' he says, pointing to Stalin. 'A good guy!' Henceforth I am a friend, and he showers me with attention.

25 February

When I awoke yesterday morning, it was in an endless desert of pink stones. I spent the whole day in the bar with magnificent bay windows that allowed the desert to invade the train. In Albuquerque, the afternoon sun was burning-hot. On the platform, Indians with braids were selling rugs and little multicoloured moccasins. In the garden of the beautiful Mexican-style hotel, tourists sitting in rocking chairs watched the train travellers, who watched them back. I knew I would return at leisure to these regions in a few weeks, so I felt no regret as I saw the great plateaus of flaming colour and the Indian shacks disappear. It was still desert while I slept. But at dawn, when I pull back the curtain, the scenery has changed. A grey fog fills the damp prairies and the trees; in the distance the hills are a blur against a muggy sky. This is how I've entered California. The name is almost as magical as 'New York'. It's the land of streets paved with gold, of pioneers and cowboys. Through history and movies it's become a legendary country that, like all legends, belongs to my own past.

I'm burning with impatience. This time I'm not arriving as a tourist in a land where nothing is meant for me; I'm coming to see a woman friend who happens to be living in a land everyone says is marvellous. It's perhaps even stranger to feel expected in an unknown place than to prepare yourself to disembark without help. I don't know what awaits me, but someone knows. The sea, orange juice, mountains, flowers, whiskeys – I'm not going to encounter them and try to possess them; they will be given to me. Someone is waiting for the right moment to present them to me as a gift. They already are a gift; and in my heart I feel the anxiety and greed of childhood Christmas Eves.

The fog lifts a little. I see long, shady avenues of palm trees and quiet houses surrounded by fresh lawns. The train stops at a little suburban station – Pasadena. For another half-hour, we roll through the outlying suburbs cut out of the shapeless countryside, and the train goes underground. Los Angeles. A black employee unfolds three folding steps, which connect the train car to the ground. I am on the deserted platform, then in a corridor, and finally in the hall where N [Nathalie ('Natasha') Sorokine Moffatt, a close friend] is waiting for me.

A year ago N married a GI [Ivan Moffatt], who is now a scriptwriter in Hollywood. When she came to join him, they hadn't a penny between them, and M was earning very little money. N was expecting a baby. Thanks to the credit system they practise here, they could rent a kind of barn and transform it into a liveable house and also buy a car, something absolutely necessary in this city of vast distances. Now M's situation has improved, but his salary is almost entirely consigned to paying off his debts. Besides, a law requires parents to take their children to the doctor once a week during their first year; this is very costly. It's hard to balance the budget every month. I know all that and also that M's car is red. So I am utterly astonished to see a little yellow car standing in front of the station. N tells me, 'It's ours. M bought it last week just so we could drive around.' 'Nothing simpler,' adds N, 'since you buy without paying!' Obviously. But I'm stunned by such ease. Los Angeles also stuns me. This city is unlike any other. Below me, the downtown looks just like the downtowns of Rochester, Buffalo and Cleveland, which themselves evoke New York's downtown and Chicago's Loop. It's the tall buildings housing banks, stores and movie theatres; the monotonous chequerboard of streets and avenues. But then, all the neighbourhoods we drive through are either disorganised outlying districts or huge developments where identical wooden houses multiply as far as the eye can see, each one surrounded by a little garden. The traffic is terrifying; the broad roadways are divided into six lanes, three in each direction, marked off by white lines, and you are allowed to pass to either the right or the left. You can turn to the right only from the right lane, to the left only from the left; this last manoeuvre is often prohibited, which complicates one's itinerary. At intersections the car that has arrived first has priority, a rule that provokes thousands of disputes. The experts manage marvellously, and the cars move along at a disquieting speed. N must also go as fast, or the car will be rear-ended; I understand why she might be a little tense behind the wheel. She relaxes when we arrive at the hills, where the most elegant part of the city rises in tiers. Here the avenues thread their way between golf courses, gardens and parks, which conceal luxurious residences. We make our way slowly through Beverly Hills, where the Hollywood stars live. We take a broad, almost rustic road bordered by fields and gardens, and the car stops in front of a hedge, which is cut through by a gravel drive. We've been travelling for one hour, often at more than forty miles per hour.

The house is at the back of a garden blooming with roses and bordered by tall eucalyptus trees; it's a wooden house with an outside staircase, and it doesn't look American. The ground floor is a huge studio belonging to a painter whose own wooden house stands in another corner of the garden. N lives only on the upper floor. The rooms are nearly bare, furnished with beds and stools that N and M made with boards painted in bright colours. There are a few Indian rugs, a few beautiful Mexican objects, a cock in shiny metal, wax oranges. The bathroom is already installed, but there is no refrigerator – they expect to have one next year. From the terrace at the top of the stairs, beyond the indistinct vastness of the city, you glimpse the sea. At the back of the garden there are three horses that belong to rich neighbours. N has taken the horses on as boarders; she also raised ducks, but a coyote climbed up from the depths of the canyon and ate them all. The mountains in the distance look wild: one feels that the most sophisticated city in the world is surrounded by indomitable nature. If human pressure were relaxed for even a moment, the wild animals and the giant grasses would soon reclaim possession of their domain.

After a short stop, we leave again in the little car. It's a damp, foggy day; the sky is grey – such days are rare in California. I understand how M has helped us by buying this car: there's no subway in this city at ground level, the bus and tram routes are interminable, and taxis are rare and expensive. As for walking, that's out of the question; there's not a single pedestrian on these endless roadways. Those who don't have a car hitch rides at the street corners. Los Angeles is almost as big as the Cote d'Azur; in fact, it isn't a city at all but a collection of villages, residential neighbourhoods, and encampments separated by woods and parks. Brentwood, Westwood, Beverly Hills and Hollywood are each autonomous areas. The area closest to our house is Westwood, which is five or six miles away. It's a real 'village', in the American sense of the word. It has its main street, stores, banks and drugstores, and around this commercial centre it has its residential neighbourhoods. One peculiar aspect of Westwood is that because of its proximity to a university, the consumption and sale of alcohol are prohibited – there's no bar, no liquor store. You have to go as far as Brentwood if you want to buy a bottle of wine.

Hollywood, as everyone knows, is where the studios are. The stars live in Beverly Hills. To see their houses, you have to enter an artificial park humming with neither the muffled life of the countryside nor the feverish life of the city; the luxurious villas are surrounded by a false solitude. Avenues lined with garages and with flat-roofed boutiques, barely one-storey high; a blue coastal road above the sea; vast camps of parked trailers, those caravans in which many homeless Americans live on the outskirts of towns; working-class sections filled with monotonous shacks – all this is spinning in my head. Along the roads, large billboards suggest, 'To visit the houses of the stars, call the Smith Agency.' The fog has dissipated. Against the hard blue of the sky, airplanes write advertising announcements in trailing white letters. In the sun, the dust, the noise, Los Angeles has the ugliness of a Parisian fair.

We lunch at the seaside at the counter of a restaurant-bar whose walls are lined with photographs of stars. At the end of the afternoon I give a lecture, an activity that seems out of place today. At dusk we meet M in a Hollywood bar. I am amazed to see him in civilian clothes. Perhaps because the soldiers wore the American uniform in such a non-military fashion in Paris, it seemed to me like a form of national dress. When I arrived in New York, I was vaguely surprised to find men dressed in business suits. In the twilight the harshness of the city is softened. Hollywood Boulevard follows the contours of a hill; sitting at the bar, we look through a large bay window and see at our feet the spread of houses where the first lights are coming on. Little by little Los Angeles is transformed into a large, glittering lake. The window that frames the night and my friends' presence make this vision a performance meant for me. Los Angeles has prepared a triumphant welcome for me: all evening I am going to walk through a celebration given in my honour.

The back fins on M's big red car bear the traces of many misadventures: life is hard here for automobiles. It carries us toward the Mexican part of town. There are few blacks in Los Angeles; instead, there are many Mexicans, who are more or less despised, and sometimes boycotted, but for whom the whites feel no racial hatred. On the East Coast, California seems like an exotic land; in California, exoticism means Mexico, which is so close geographically and historically, since a hundred years ago this coast belonged to Mexico. We drive for half an hour, and when we stop, I'm dazzled by an extravagant riot of colours: it's the energy, the life, the gaiety of Spanish markets and Moroccan *souk*s. The street is a large bazaar: small kiosks lit by candles are set up on the esplanade, where you can buy wonderful objects – yellow or red jackets embroidered with palm trees and birds, colourful dresses, cowboy boots decorated with red or green leather, sandals, dolls, pottery, rugs, fabrics, necklaces and beaded bracelets. They sell miniature skulls and little jointed skeletons, favourite fetishes of a people in love with death. One of the most seductive novelties is a garland of pinecones and dried foliage painted in crude blue, yellow and red; it's a decoration to be hung from the ceiling, and it has the rustic splendour of strings of onions and garlic, dried mushrooms, and hams hung from the wooden beams of French farmhouses. On both sides of the street, stores sell the same sparkling merchandise. Of all the shops, the most beautiful is the one where they make candles. It's a palace of colours. In a penetrating odour of wax and resin, enormous tapers rise up from the floor, hang from the ceiling and decorate the walls. There are fat ones, thin ones, red ones, yellow ones, blue ones, green ones; they are decorated with hearts, tears and scrolls. Scarlet wax pinecones, oranges and pineapples sit in cut metal candleholders. And the wax boils in large vats. In the *souk*s of Marrakech the dyers brew the same blue, yellow and blood red dye in similar vats. But here the colours melting together are dangerous to touch; they burn. Once cooled, they form enormous pedestals, where they are jumbled together in a rococo confusion.

All the jumbled wonders of the bazaar have found their place in the restaurant we enter. The tables are lit by tapers for which the most amazing chandeliers have been devised: stuck in an empty bottle, the candles weep multicoloured tears night after night, and the glass is drowned in the thickness of a rainbow formed by wax stalactites. These candleholders seem fashioned by the whim of some petrifying fountain, but also conceived by a slightly delirious mind – at once natural wonder and surrealist fantasy. The waiters and waitresses wear Mexican dress. We order some tequila, and the waiter hesitates: N looks very young, and they cannot serve liquor to minors. She shows them her identity card. In any case, since adult consumption is unlimited, we could easily have tricked them, but this way she has the right to her own glass. I watch the Mexican dances and eat chilli con carne, which takes the roof off my mouth. I drink the tequila, and I'm utterly dazed with pleasure. In New York I knew the keen joy of discovery; here, I receive gifts – it's another kind of happiness.

26 February

None of the Americans I knew in the East had ever set foot in California. When they have free time, they're more drawn to Europe, which is almost as close. And there are many people in this part of the country who have never seen New York. It's impossible to find the New York papers here, except in rare, specialised shops; everyone in Los Angeles reads the Los Angeles papers. All the states have their local press and a vivid sense of their own uniqueness. But California is, I'm told, the only state – along with Texas, perhaps – that thinks of itself as California before feeling it's part of the USA. Its attitude is explained by its history, its geographic situation and especially its economic autonomy. If I think about New York or Chicago here, in Los Angeles, I have the impression of being altogether elsewhere and yet still part of the same world. Through its radio, its magazines and its manufactured products, America is utterly present in each of its parts – but these are more or less strangers to one another. There is no direct communication between the different states, yet they all participate in the unity that transcends them. The result is a mixture of uniformity and regionalism that is often disconcerting.

N takes me for another day-long tour through a Los Angeles that is both familiar and utterly unexpected. Near Westwood I see a veterans' hospital that is like a village unto itself. Here they rehabilitate the wounded, the amputees, the disturbed; they shelter the invalids and the incurables and provisionally lodge certain veterans who have not yet found either work or housing. There are living quarters, libraries, drugstores and cafeterias, where the sale of alcohol is prohibited, of course. In front of the doors, men sit sadly warming themselves on benches in the sun, and others walk around looking bored.

We cross one suburb after another – nothing but suburbs. The city slips away like a phantom city. The streets thrown down any which way on the sides of hills, in the hollows of valleys, have been laid down at random as needed without any general plan. We drive a long time before arriving at our destination – the 'optimistic' cemetery called Forest Lawn Mortuary. It covers a vast hill where, as at Arlington, broad roads wind their way. It's a verdant park shaded by luxurious trees. Here and there on the damp lawns stands a flat plate with just a name. It looks like the dead are buried beneath the grass with rural simplicity, as in Corsican cemeteries: there's no monumental tomb, no mortuary chapel; one imagines simple wooden coffins ingenuously entrusted to the earth. We find an open grave with men gathered around it. We approach without qualms, since no one has accompanied the dead to his grave – it's not the custom in this cheerful land. In fact, the grass is merely a light crust covering a vast network of masonry. The graves are built of concrete; the coffin is lowered by a system of ropes and pulleys. The grave diggers are not gardeners but mechanics. And as for the grass that disguises the cement architecture, it comes in large strips that are rolled out like linoleum. It must be mass-produced somewhere. N tells me that the coffins themselves are airtight so that worms cannot live in them; the bodies are mummified with greater or lesser perfection, depending on the cost of the plan. In any case, the insides have been removed, the faces made-up and painted; they are on view for a day or two to relatives and friends in the funeral home. At the top of the hill there is a panoramic view of Los Angeles, the sea, and the mountains behind. A chapel stands there, but the most astonishing monument is the 'Book of David', a simulacrum of a book that is at least as tall as a man and open in the middle. On the open pages, written in large printed letters, one reads an inscription that says in effect, 'How beautiful it is, from the height of this majestic cliff, to look down upon the city of the living and the city of the dead. This is one of the summits of the world. But what you do not see is that in the sides of this hill are the largest reservoirs of water in Los Angeles. They contain x gallons of water, and it is thanks to them that our lawns are always green. Such is the greatness of man!'

Again, suburbs, developments and intersections, and here we are in Pasadena. Softly sloping avenues loll between orange trees and thickset palms. The big oil families live in these sumptuous homes; compared with the stars of Beverly Hills, they represent an old aristocracy. Suddenly we come out into wild nature; hairy vegetation covers the sides of a steep canyon, and stark mountains are outlined on the horizon. The little road jumps from one side to the other with turns so complicated that we get lost. Not a car, not a house, not a pedestrian – you'd think you were hours from civilisation. We drive a long time without finding anyone to tell us which way to go.

I'm utterly astonished to see that the place where I'm supposed to give my lecture is a little house lost on the edge of the canyon. It looks like a hunting lodge. To get back to Westwood, we follow a broad drive where cars whizz by at deafening speed. From time to time, we're passed by one of those little cars called 'hot rods', which young men make themselves from old models. They take off the frame, the bumper, the doors – anything that isn't absolutely necessary – and they attach an instrument to the engine that boosts its power and makes a terrible racket. The wild young people squeeze into it in bunches; their favourite sport is to jump from one lane to another, leaving all the other cars in the dust. It's a dangerous game that often causes accidents.

Back in town, I'm surprised by the number of pedestrians hitchhiking at the street corners. N tells me that drivers no longer stop as readily as before. In America, the car is a familiar machine. Whereas in France one hesitates to entrust the wheel to a friend, here they even hand it over to strangers. Launched on the endless American roadways, a traveller used to welcome the company of someone who could relieve him; when they had a long way to go, they often advertised for a companion who knew how to drive. But in recent times so many drivers have been robbed or killed and so many cars have been stolen that people are now afraid. They're especially mistrustful in the evening. However, Americans are obliging, and these young men [who are hitchhiking] aren't risking much should a car break down – there are so many cars! Again this evening, the traffic is maddening. I admire the boldness and skill of those children, ten to fifteen years old, who hawk newspapers at the intersections, weaving between the cars, jumping onto the kerbs.

This evening we're dining in a canyon that opens onto the sea and where a whole colony of artists or would-be artists lives.

There are little cafés vaguely reminiscent of old Montparnasse, among them a charming café-restaurant. It has a kind of half-dome decorated with hangings in green, white and red stripes with a semicircular bar in the middle and only five or six tables against the walls. The owner is a homosexual and sleeps with the cook; the cook makes the rules and accepts only clients he remembers. He serves us magnificent steaks dripping with the beautiful red blood that usually scares off puritanical Americans. Where shall we go from here? M hesitates. He says that nights in Los Angeles are not much fun. Bars and nightclubs must close at midnight. It's a very moralistic town. Children don't have the right to walk around freely after nine in the evening. In many districts, alcohol is prohibited. No 'burlesque' houses – the shows are censored. Besides, the recession is being felt here, as in New York, and the clubs are half-empty. Of course, the moralism in which Hollywood encases itself doesn't stop the papers from announcing some sensational new crime every day. At the moment, Los Angeles is haunted by the ghost of Black Dahlia. Around a month ago, a beautiful young brunette called 'Black Dahlia' was found dismembered in a vacant lot. Since then, two or three young women who live in the same neighbourhood have been murdered in approximately the same way, and as in a cheap crime novel, a card was found near the cadaver with the words 'Black Dahlia'. That's what they now call the murderer himself. He hasn't been found. The interesting thing is that these crimes have provoked hysterical attacks of denunciation and self-accusation. Women have written to or called the police to turn in unfaithful lovers; men have turned themselves in, recounting their crimes in great detail, and serious interrogations were needed to convince them of their innocence. They were released, and in the night the real Black Dahlia may lie in wait for a new victim. Women are afraid to walk alone after midnight. If they venture out, the next day many say they were followed, accosted or even assaulted by a man who was surely the Black Dahlia – they give different descriptions. Each day, the local papers devote long columns to this story, which is also the main topic covered by *Time*, *Life* and all the big magazines.

I think N and M have decided to give me a taste of how sinister Los Angeles nights are, because they take me to Venice. This is a deserted seaside amusement park. No one is riding the carousels, no one is laughing in the fun house. The streets are brightly lit but deserted. Among the satin cushions and dolls, the vendors look like they are keeping a vigil over the dead. In the hopes of cheering ourselves up, we climb onto the 'Scenic Railway' [a roller coaster], but from below we hadn't gauged the terrifying turns. Carried into a ghastly vertical drop, N and I close our eyes while a firm and sepulchral voice intones behind us, 'Oh, boy, am I sorry we did this!'

As we drive back toward Westwood, the bars close one by one. And on the heels of the Black Dahlia, terror slips through the deserted streets.

27 February

The house is open day and night, and when we leave, no one thinks of locking up; I'm not even sure there are locks. In France, people always bolt the doors of houses in the country or suburbs when they leave them. I love this trusting unconcern. Delivery people come in quite calmly and deposit the milk, bread, eggs and bills on the kitchen table. To tell the truth, at N's house, there isn't much to steal. In general, though, the idea of theft is not an obsession in America. Objects are not sacred; they can always be replaced.

This morning I'm awakened at eight o'clock by a car stopping in front of the house. Someone climbs the stairs and pushes open the door; this morning visit intrigues me. When I get up, I meet a rather elegant young woman in the dining room, who greets me guardedly. This is the housekeeper. She, too, has a car; it would be impossible for her to earn a living if every hour of work were doubled by an hour in transit. Gasoline and auto maintenance cost nothing here. The purchase is on credit; it's to her advantage to save her time, which is worth around a dollar an hour.

Today I am going to visit the Hollywood studios. M made a lunch date with us. We cruise along for a good fifteen minutes around Gower Street without finding any place to park the little yellow car. From time to time we see a free place: we rush over, but there's always a red line that means no parking. Opposite RKO Studios there's a parking lot reserved for employees; N decides to try it, but the guard fiercely defends the little rectangle of asphalt where she manages to slip in. 'It's my husband's car.' 'IM's car is red,' the guard protests. But in the end, he admits defeat.

We are invited to lunch by S [George Stevens, co-founder of Liberty Films], the director M works with. He has reserved a table at Lucy's, a restaurant situated between the three big studios: Warner, RKO and Paramount. It would be impossible to get a table without this precaution; it's the fashionable spot where all the beautiful movie people congregate. The elegance of the patrons is rather flamboyant; the platinum blondes are dressed in soft pink and pale blue, and as in New York, they're decorated with feathers. Of course, they suffer here from the bane of all wealthy America – superabundance. Too much noise, too much perfume, too much heat, too much luxury. But after martinis – which are to martinis in Paris what the ideal circle is to circles drawn on a blackboard – the meal is delicious. S has asked two scriptwriters to join us, a man and a woman who are friends of M. The work of these 'writers' does not exactly correspond to that of the French scenario or dialogue writer. They work for the studio, where they spend eight hours a day in an office. They must find ideas for films, either in their imagination or preferably in the latest published books, and sketch out the structure of a script. They must also collaborate on the editing and dialogue of films that are already in the works. All these are thankless tasks, due to a division of labour so extreme that no one has a hold on the complete work. They repeat to me that censorship has become increasingly harsh in the past two years, which makes coming up with a subject more and more difficult. They think of making a film from the latest Steinbeck book, *Wayward Bus*, but there's a respectable young woman in it who sleeps with the driver, purely for pleasure. It is impossible to include such an episode in a movie, yet it's essential to the story. It will have to be replaced by a sentimental drama of the usual moral and touching sort, which would distort the characters and remake the plot so drastically that nothing would be left of the original novel. They hesitate. They tell me that they constantly find themselves hamstrung in this way. The scripts are becoming increasingly stupid and monotonous, and the public is beginning to notice. Being served their favourite dish day after day, they are finally fed up with it. Hence the success, particularly in New York, of English and Italian films, and even French films, which are poorly distributed and always distorted by arbitrary cuts. And Hollywood is in decline. Many films made in the studios during the last ten years have never been sold. Apparently, the directors lack the enthusiasm needed to undertake important work. S, for example, who was once very successful, today limits himself to routine work.

S is around forty-five years old, with a big, friendly face. He has always lived in California, where he was born, and his father worked in the movies, too. S is as accomplished a man as anyone could be; he's had stunning successes, he's had affairs with the most beautiful stars in Hollywood, and he's got an enormous fortune. Yet he is usually ill at ease in company and hardly speaks. Today he seems relaxed. He loves N and M, and the story of our evening in Venice puts him in a good mood. He tells me emotionally how he entered Paris several days after the Liberation. I can just imagine him in uniform, under a helmet. As he describes his campaign, he repeats earnestly several times: 'It was a moment of truth.' Yes. A moment of truth; he's right to speak of it nostalgically.

We change the subject. We say that N and I are going to take a car trip for several days through California. S perks up. We are planning to go through Lone Pine, where he spent his childhood and where, ten years ago now, he made his greatest film [*Gunga Din*]. He hasn't been back since, although the place is only four hours from Los Angeles. It would be wonderful to go back. He suggests joining us there with M and showing us the area. The date is set, and S is as happy as a child. He has four cars, he's the master of his time and his life, and he has only a little work at the moment; why hasn't he ever done this four-hour trip he's so taken with? I have already noticed among several Americans this lack of initiative and inventiveness, but this case is the most surprising of all. M, who is half-English and who spent his youth in London, tells me that he was also stunned to learn how many Americans were entangled in their freedom. This trait is particularly striking in California, especially in Hollywood. S, who is bored at the studio from morning to night without much to do, knows no better diversion than alcohol. It's from a lack of imagination that so many Americans obstinately drink themselves into a stupor. Yet S is intelligent, curious, full of overflowing vitality. He takes us to his office. His secretary brings us one of those tasteless coffees they drink here. She's blonde, around forty years old, ravaged by drink. She's legendary at the studio because she often has terrible hangovers in the mornings. Since she lives on the other side of the valley, she telephones to declare with aplomb that she can't come because the valley is flooded. S questions me with passionate interest about France, its intellectual life, its literature, its philosophy, and makes me promise that at Lone Pine I will give him a serious explanation of the Cartesian cogito.

The Hollywood studios don't seem so different from their French counterparts. To be sure, these are cities. But I'm beginning to get the idea: a college, a hospital, a warehouse – here, right away, it's a city. In a large hall they're in the process of taking publicity stills. Aspiring pin-ups in fanciful bras and panties show their sumptuous legs. They are photographed in the most complicated poses, perched precariously on the steps of stools and ladders, which will, of course, be invisible on the posters. They'll appear natural and relaxed. How exhausting it must be to produce one of those smiles, broadcasting in every direction that life is fun! It's a pitiful job that doesn't pay much. I see them shoot an interior scene; there are the same hesitations, the same delays as at Joinville or Epinay [French film lots]. And you encounter the same De Chirico-like miracles: a tree planted in the middle of a bedroom, a Louis Philippe dining room that's open to the sky. On the whole, this fairground of wonders exudes fatigue and boredom; everyone works indolently, without great ambition, not even financial. Outside in front of one of the gates, three men are sitting on folding chairs at the edge of the sidewalk: it is a cool day, and they are burning bits of wood to warm themselves. They stretch their hands toward the flames in the classic gesture of tramps. They are strikers. It's been three months since the carpenters went on strike for more pay; by now, it's a lost cause, and this symbolic picket line is heartbreaking.

Los Angeles is far from possessing the beauty of New York or the depth of Chicago, and I understand why some French people spoke to me about it with such distaste: without friends, I'd be lost. But it can be as enjoyable as a kaleidoscope — with a shake of the wrist, the pieces of coloured glass give you the illusion of a new rosette. I surrender to this hall of mirrors. After visiting Mexico the day before yesterday, this evening I'm going to Hawaii. The French consul has invited me to dinner with N and M. In the entrance hall there is an exhibition of Hawaiian jewellery, shell necklaces, leis and softly coloured seeds. I have never seen such an enchanting restaurant: it's as beautiful as the Palais des Mirages in the Musée Grevin. Greenhouses with luxuriant plants, aquariums, aviaries where birds coloured like butterflies swoop, all bathed in a murky, submarine light. The tables are glass pedestals in which the gleaming ceiling is reflected; the prismatic pillars are faceted mirrors in which space is infinitely multiplied. We dine under a straw hut at the end of a lake, in a forest, in the middle of an enormous diamond. The waitresses' costumes are a modest version of Hawaiian dress. In cylindrical glasses, which hold nearly a pint, we are served zombies (cocktails made from seven kinds of rum poured on top of each other: the amber liquid is layered from dark brown to light yellow). The meal transports us, unexpectedly, to China. The dishes don't have that overly visual impact that often discourages the palate in America; instead, they look very appealing. And if French cooking is 'thoughtful', as Colette says, this cuisine seems the fruit of a thousand years of meditation.

At midnight we are alone on top of a hill. We sit on the ground and smoke in silence. Los Angeles is beneath us, a huge, silent fairyland. The lights glitter as far as the eye can see. Between the red, green and white clusters, big glow-worms slither noiselessly. Now I am not taken in by the mirage: I know that these are merely streetlamps along the avenues, neon signs and headlights. But mirage or no mirage, the lights keep glittering; they, too, are a truth. And perhaps they are even more moving when they express nothing but the naked presence of men. Men live here, and so the earth revolves in the quiet of the night with this shining wound in its side.

28 February

Congress's campaign against union workers is growing daily. Senator Taft, followed by other Republican senators, accuses the CIO leaders of being affiliated with the Communist Party – the usual manoeuvre. M is indignant. When I ask him, 'Isn't there anything one can do? What are you doing?' he looks quite disconcerted, like everyone to whom I've put this question.

This morning I'm leaving with N for our trip through California. The first stop is Ojai, a mountain town where M's parents live. They will join us this evening. Right away, the road starts off across the hills; it is deserted and primitive, with wonderful vistas of the sea. Now and then there's an inn; all of them are picturesque, built in the Western style, like log cabins. Sometimes they have, as a sign, an old covered wagon with green canvas; more often, one or two wagon wheels leaning against the wall. Next to one of these places, a large elephant, in the flesh, is displayed behind bars. Farther on, a live lion catches the eyes of passers-by. The country inn we stop at would have promised a fine meal in France. There's a huge chimney, wooden benches, leaded windows, beamed ceilings — but they serve us drugstore food. We leave the main road and drive down toward the valley on a narrow, winding, bumpy path. In a shady corner near a river, there's a campground for tourists, with tables, benches, fireplaces, swings and seesaws. Campers only have to pitch their tents. Of course, they'll come by car; everything is on too grand a scale for walking or biking. People also gladly camp in those trailers I've seen parked on the outskirts of Los Angeles. They're really houses on wheels outfitted with every American comfort. But they are allowed to park only in specially designated areas, and the side roads, such as the one we're on, are closed to them.

The valley we've entered offers just the kind of landscape you'd expect to find in California: enclosed by mountains on three sides, it opens wide on the fourth and descends toward the sea, which can be seen in the distance. This whole amphitheatre is planted with orange trees, lined up as regularly as the trees in orchards on old tapestries. What I didn't foresee are those little brown metal stoves placed all along the furrows. The valley is rather high up, and on some winter nights the temperature can drop to freezing; the entire harvest would be lost. Like the minutemen during the Revolutionary War, certain designated men must drop everything when the alarm is given and run to light and stoke the protective fires. The little yellow car jolts along across the fields; it rolls through the loose earth and gets stuck, then scales the hills covered with rocks and brush where N loves to ride horseback. We rejoin the road to Ojai. In this delightful spot Ojai is as desolate as a Midwestern town — there's a dull white street lined with banks and stores and intersected at right angles by other white streets.

We go shopping for dinner. This is the first time I've entered one of these big stores. It looks like an agricultural fair: oversized, smooth and polished, the fruits and vegetables all have the slightly false lustre of perfect greenhouse products, unmarked by the vagaries of rain and sun. N grabs a little metal cart from a corner and pushes it in front of her; we walk down the aisles and gather up whatever we like. There is such a profusion of meat, fish and especially canned goods that the choice is very difficult; our needs and even our desires are not up to such magnificent abundance.

E [Iris Tree], M's mother, is an Englishwoman who married an American, divorced and remarried fifteen years ago. She was extremely beautiful, as I can see in a photograph taken by Man Ray. She travelled widely and always moved in artistic and literary circles; she was friends with Frieda Lawrence and [Lady] Bret. N tells me that the life E leads today with V is typical of the life of many West Coast artists and intellectuals, who come in large numbers, attracted by the land's climate and beauty. E is particularly interested in theatre. In an obscure corner of the valley N shows me a little isolated pavilion that they've made into a theatre. There, a troupe of amateurs puts on modern or classic plays from time to time under E's direction. E takes the female leads; the rest of the troupe is made up partly of actors from Los Angeles, partly of Ojai residents. Among others, there is a carpenter whom E is patiently training. At the moment they are preparing for a performance of *Macbeth*.

The house, hidden among orange groves, is surrounded by an overgrown garden full of trees and flowers – no hedges or walls; no bolt on the gate, although no one would be there. The garden, on something of a height, looks out over the valley and the sea and imperceptibly blends into the countryside. The large bay windows of the studio let in the garden and the sky; its walls seem as light as tent canvas and don't feel at all confining. Yet this is not a camping set-up; it's a real interior, and one of the most attractive I've ever seen. The Mexican style is predominant. Rugs, hangings, old Indian pottery – only rare pieces. I especially love the big, proud cocks of cut metal. I lounge around. Again, this is an old childhood dream: walk through the woods and miraculously find a little house that wasn't waiting for you but was prepared for you, that isn't yours but belongs to you. Walk from room to room, touching objects, tasting different dishes, both unexpected and expected . . . The telephone rings. M and his mother tell us that they'll be late because of a forest fire that's closed the road between Los Angeles and Ojai.

F is the first to arrive in a big convertible. I've often heard about him; he's what they call here a 'character'. The most striking thing about him is his beauty: dark hair with very blue eyes, a large, bony and cheerful face. Then you notice his clothes. He is magnificently dressed in luxurious cowboy garb: hand-tooled leather boots, corduroy trousers, a buckskin jacket, a checked shirt, a wide belt encrusted with turquoise, a silk scarf held by a turquoise pin, and silver rings on his fingers. Perhaps he wears a bit too much jewellery, but it's Native jewellery that goes with the leather boots and jacket. Such an outfit isn't a masquerade in California. F takes us into his room and shows us a collection of leather and silver belts, buckskin jackets, scarves and boots with red-and-green designs that would be the envy of any woman alive. He rides horseback like a real cowboy and earns his living playing small roles from time to time in Hollywood films. The rest of the time he's bored, like everyone in America with too much leisure time. He goes off in his big car to meet other people who are also bored, he takes them to other people's homes, and when he's managed to get a large enough group together, he thinks he's really having a good time.

M and his mother arrive at last. E is very thin and still looks young in an orange dress cinched in at the waist by a gold-studded belt. We eat the dinner N prepared; we drink whiskey and listen to records. E has a remarkable collection of cowboy songs and songs that the pioneers sang on their difficult journey west. I also hear the old medieval English songs that were revived in the eighteenth century by popular musicians in America. Some are very similar in theme to old French ballads. 'Randall, My Son' is the story of a knight who has been poisoned by his sweetheart and comes back to die in his mother's arms – almost the same tale we sing of King Renaud. I listen. And perhaps America has never seemed so insistently present as in these refrains from its past. At this very moment Times Square is lit up, blacks are dancing with abandon at the Savoy, the old belles of the Bowery are hitching up their skirts, lonely men are shivering on West Madison Avenue and begging in flophouse doorways, balls are rolling on the waxed lanes of bowling alleys and on the green felt of billiard tables, students at Vassar and Macon are sleeping in their white beds, bodies pickled in alcohol are sprawled at the corner of a counter and in distinguished salons, crowds are silently watching a drama painted in black and white, and in lonely rooms men are typing and old ladies are knitting. My memories already make me dizzy: America is nowhere. But music escapes the limitations of time and space. It can capture something out of thin air and give it to me. At least that's what I think tonight.

March

1 March

Through the wide open door I see E dressed in an exotic silk negligee sitting in her huge bed; two enormous dogs are lying on fur throws, and two strangers are speaking, sitting at her bedside. In the garden a man is walking back and forth with a book in his hand, clearly quite agitated. N is busy in the kitchen. The cupboards and the refrigerator are empty, in the best bohemian tradition. Fortunately, we bought enough yesterday to prepare an adequate breakfast.

I feel regret at leaving this house that I may never see again. Another small death; there have been so many on this trip. But tomorrow I have to be in San Francisco, and we don't want to rush. N and I settle into the big red car, which M is lending us because it's faster than the other one. N drives through a hedge, exits successfully, and we leave the garden in a cloud of dust; it's been scarcely a week since she got her driver's licence after two fruitless attempts.

Leaving Ojai, we have a little trouble finding the way. It's amazing, but in America there are no signposts or mileage indicators; even at intersections there are no directions. A garage owner gives us directions; blue plaques with the number 1 and a bear, the California symbol, must guide us, but they appear only now and then, and never, it seems, when you come to a crossroads. The weather is fine; the wind smells of orange blossoms. We drive along the contours of the coastal hills, and in the distance we glimpse the sea and the fashionable beaches. Sometimes we pass through residential neighbourhoods, and the road, running between gardens, becomes a carefully groomed avenue lined with trimmed shrubs and shaded by beautiful trees. Sometimes we thread our way through the deserted mountains. Not a single car on this narrow, winding road. It gets increasingly primitive, and N and I say to each other that Georges Duhamel must have had very little first-hand experience of America to have claimed that the countryside was hidden by advertising billboards. Despite its sprawling cities, its factories, its mechanical civilisation, this country remains one of the most unspoiled in the world. Man with all his works is a new and sporadic phenomenon here, whose laborious efforts merely scratch the surface of the earth's crust. This, at any rate, is the feeling you get as soon as you go any distance from the great metropolitan centres.

In a relentlessly ugly little town we eat hamburgers with onions squeezed between the two halves of a bun. And we continue on our way until nightfall. We stop around seven o'clock in a straggling village on a bay that surrounds an enormous rock. I have often looked longingly from the window of a train or bus at places like the one we're going to sleep in, which are called 'courts' or 'motels'. It looks like a modern-style convent. The wooden cottages with attached garages are set around an enclosure; they are rented for one or several nights by motorists in transit. When no room is available, a large notice announces: No Vacancy. But this evening there is no such notice, and we head toward the first cabin, which a neon sign in a good, hopeful green colour indicates is the office. For one night we're the owners of a tiny seaside villa; we have a big room, a bathroom, a gas ring, and a balcony where we can sit and watch the first stars. We've paid, we've been given the key, and we are free to come and go. The restaurant we eat in is as pleasant as our lodging. It's a veranda built on pilings above the water. The little tables are lit by multicoloured candles whose flames flicker in the darkness. The candles have been set in the necks of those bottles covered with dripping wax that I'm so fond of. The fish they serve us tastes delicious. Outside, there's only one street, with no movie house or drugstore. I will go to sleep soon — I need it.

2 March

We leave at seven o'clock to travel the three hundred miles from here to San Francisco. The road is hollowed out of rock along the sides of the mountains that drop straight down to the sea; it winds dizzyingly above the abyss. Not a house, not a car, not a plant or domesticated animal; men are far away. In the car that shelters us and carries us along, we're as lost as if we were crossing the Causses or the Corsican scrub on foot. It's the perfect place for Humphrey Bogart to murder his wife and claim it was an accident. We are dazed when after two hours we suddenly discover, suspended at the edge of the coastal road, an inn built of logs and surrounded by flower-filled verandas. So people really do come this way occasionally. We eat eggs and bacon. The countryside sparkles around us. This site and this solitude have their price: the breakfast costs as much as a dinner. The proprietor is surprised to see us leave. One doesn't often see women travelling alone through California. American women drive in the cities, but they rarely take a trip without a masculine escort — this is about the extent of their independence.

Nature doesn't get any tamer; we continue following a big, primitive rock wall above the sea. We come into Monterey at eleven o'clock. This was the site of the battle in which Southern California was taken from Mexico, a famous battle in which, I believe, four men died. Monterey is an old port that has piously preserved the vestiges of its Mexican past. A notice enjoins motorists to follow the red dotted line marked on the pavement: according to the most rational itinerary, it leads you to the town's chief points of interest. In front of flamboyant, decrepit old wooden houses there are signs that tell their history; the residences of honourable governors and of notorious outlaws are labelled with the same care. Here, you find a century-old theatre and an antique *posada*; there, you find the shacks where the gold seekers deposited their sacks of precious powder. There are many picturesque spots, orange or apricot walls, arbours and painted inns, but the effect is a little like part of a museum, and you still feel you're in the USA. It's in the port, on the other side of the central, purely American part of town, that we are happily uprooted. A vast wooden pier stretches out into the sea between Mediterranean-coloured fishing boats. In booths on every side they are selling enormous fish – pink, teal, silver, smooth or scaly – resting on mounds of ice. On the ground they have spread large abalone shells that are still damp with algae and coated with iridescent mother-of-pearl. They cost five cents apiece. The smell of the market is as fresh as the sea. At the end of the pier there are restaurants built on pilings, all built of wood, all with balconies and sunny terraces. We choose one in the Mexican style: yellow walls, painted wooden furniture in lively colours with simple designs, everything fresh and bright. In the evening they light candles set in wax chandeliers. We lunch on the balcony, above the fishing boats; it's very sunny but tempered by the wind. The cuisine is Italian. We eat fresh fish and a pizza. We ordered a 'small', not a giant, or a large, or even a medium; they bring us a crust stuffed with tomatoes and anchovies that would cover two plates. We sit there, imagining. The 'giant' pizzas must be as big as wagon wheels.

The countryside becomes gentler. We walk through Carmel, one of the most famous places on this coast; it's a pretty village full of gardens, trees and flowers.* We don't have the time to visit the Spanish mission, but we do walk through the park. This word doesn't have the same meaning in America as it does in Europe – it designates a site that has been given

---

* Simone de Beauvoir must have misremembered the sequence of towns en route. She probably went through Big Sur to Carmel to Monterey.

government protection. Sometimes you have to pay to enter, but it's a slice of unspoiled nature; here the park is nothing but part of the coast. For a dollar we can continue to follow the seashore instead of taking the highway. The rocks and the violence of the waves are reminiscent of Quiberon. It's very beautiful, but we miss the solitude of the morning: hundreds of motorists come from San Francisco to spend Sunday here. Soon we leave Carmel and find ourselves in the desert. We pass through huge pine forests. In the hollow of a valley, in a clearing, or at the opening of gorge, we occasionally come upon an isolated inn or a lodge made of cabins grouped together or a camp of huts built around a spring. We'd like to stop for a few days in these places, as secluded as the places where monks used to build their hermitages. Even when the sign indicates a population, we see only the rare house half-hidden by trees and separated by vast zones of silence. I squint my eyes to see Big Sur, where Henry Miller lives, and I see nothing but a little log inn flanked by a gas station. Scarcely anything on this harsh and magnificent coast has been touched by the hand of man.

As you approach San Francisco, the beaches become more numerous and they are swarming with people. It's the end of a Sunday afternoon, and people are beginning to return to the city. The cars follow the narrow, winding road, where passing becomes a problem, but they go forward at different speeds. There are the arrogant racing cars and the wretched old rattletraps that puff along, up the coast. The traffic increases. Now there's a long line snaking in front of us with shining tail lights, and we have to resign ourselves to following. Once, N passed two cars by accelerating hard, but it took her a long time to regain her place in the line on the right side of the road.

Still, we're horribly impatient. Leaving such solitude, the idea of a big city is fascinating – its life, its lights – and we're dazed with all the fresh air and fatigue. We want walls around us, a steady armchair, a whiskey and some sophisticated warmth. At an intersection of major highways the traffic jam breaks up, and the cars fan out in different directions, but what will we do with this new-found freedom? Where is the city? We see hills where white cubes rise in tiers, one above the other. It looks like an Arab town or a group of cemeteries. Is that the city? To try and orient ourselves, we climb one of these cliffs, but from the top we see nothing but the same road stretching in front and behind, making a dizzying descent. The car's brakes are not very good, and we are more terrified than we were on the 'Scenic Railway'. We plunge down and would like to avoid hills from now on, but that's impossible; these suburbs are built like switchbacks. We must have taken the wrong road, for here we are in an endless park. Where is the city? It's as though someone had conjured it away. Suddenly, we come out on a great, red-gold bridge – the Golden Gate Bridge – and to our right, we discover the splendour of San Francisco, tiered on its hills around a magnificent bay. The city is all white and golden in the setting sun. It's heart-stopping. Something so new in America – a city whose form is visible, a city that hasn't just capriciously risen from the ground but that has been built and whose architecture is part of a great natural design. I would like to get out of the car and look, now that we've finally got something human to look at, but a sign flashes the words: No Stopping. No stopping, and what is even more serious, no turning around: we're not allowed to drive to the city. Without knowing it, we are caught up in the flow of traffic, and all we can do is cross the bridge. The idea of a detour of at least thirty miles depresses us. The employee who collects the toll declares, 'You must cross over.' Clearly, American mechanisms are of awesome perfection; they don't allow for error or the means to correct it. On the roads, as in life, success is everything. We negotiate; in the end, the employee takes pity on us and shows us a complicated manoeuvre involving turns and underground detours by which we'll pick up the road to the city. N simplifies; she heads into a tunnel with a sign saying, 'No Entry', and behind us we hear the sound of a plank dropping into the sea. But when we come out into the light, San Francisco lies before us.

An American doesn't travel without carefully reserving hotel rooms in advance; ten times I was told that without this precaution I wouldn't find any place to sleep. I had no trouble in Buffalo. Here, too, we find something after what seems like a rather brief search: I must say that in France we often have worse things to contend with. We leave our car in a garage and take a taxi that unflinchingly toboggans down the hills and up again to the Mark Hopkins. This is San Francisco's 'Empire State Building'. On the top floor the bar, with its muffled light, its carpets, its leather armchairs, the gentle murmur of voices and the clink of glasses gleaming with whiskey, is just the haven we were dreaming of. But they stop N at the entrance: they serve liquor here and the place is off-limits to minors. She shows her ID card, and we go in. The walls of the room are glass, and we walk around slowly, watching the bed of lights beneath us. It's much more beautiful than the night-time view of Los Angeles, or even New York, because of the large design of the bay traced in bright lines on the background of the dark waters, and because of those fiery ladders rising from the sea. Looking at this artificial sky unfolding at the gates of this great wilderness, I feel more than ever what I've so often felt in America – there is no distance between the human realm and that of nature. It was with brute hands that human colonies created these landscapes of stone and light, and man conquers the earth only because he is part of it. Perhaps it's because these cities lack the mediation of a long history that they seem so abruptly hewn from the earth's crust; deprived of a human past, they plunge their roots directly into the depths of the planet, which is hundreds of thousands of years old.

We look for a long time. On trips, there are moments that are promises and others that are souvenirs. This is enough. This will serve as a measure of future moments; its design is delicately imprinted on the future. We look for a long time, and then we go down to mingle with the night.

3 March

I've seen many cities built above the sea. As different as Marseilles, Algiers, Lisbon and Naples are, they all have a common feature: their hills are used as architectural elements. The streets marry their curves; they climb in spirals so artfully that the sea can be glimpsed from almost anywhere. What looks so complicated on a map seems simple and natural in reality. But it's quite the opposite here: San Francisco is a shockingly stubborn abstraction, a geometric delirium. The plan was traced on paper without the architect even glancing at the site. It's a chequerboard pattern of straight lines and right angles, just as in New York or Buffalo. The hills, those very material obstructions, are simply denied; the streets scale them and hurry down without deviating from their rigid design. As a result, you hardly ever see the ocean. Enclosed between successive barriers that cut off the horizon, the streets have a provincial calm; they are paved with red bricks that evoke the fresh tiling of Dutch kitchens and lined with white houses three or four storeys high. San Francisco does not have the warm, cosmopolitan colours of Barcelona or Marseilles. The memory of the gold miners, their camps and their brawls seems far away. You can walk a long time in its peaceful, bourgeois neighbourhoods without suspecting that you're in the heart of a city of eight hundred thousand inhabitants.

Suddenly, at the top of an avenue much like the others, we find ourselves on the edge of a cliff with a view of the sea. The road leading down to the plain spread out at our feet is so dizzying that it seems mad to risk it by car. That's another consequence of this abstract city planning – the slopes are so steep that some are closed to cars, and they discourage trams. They are accessible only by little cable cars, heirs of the old horse-drawn streetcars.

At the top the horse would make a semicircle and set off again; today, the conductor simply goes from one end of the car to the other. Sometimes accidents happen, and they hold a referendum to see whether the public wants to eliminate these obsolete vehicles. The public is divided. The sentimental souls, women in particular, want to preserve them out of love of tradition. It's likely they'll keep a line going for that reason.

We do not see much of San Francisco because we stay only four days and don't know anyone, but we have some happy times. We walk on foot. We stroll in front of the display windows in Chinatown, admiring the silks, the jades and the goslings hanging naked and shining behind the windows of the food shops. Telegraph Hill is a little Montmartre, where you find artists' studios, little cafés and tiny villas. We climb to the top and, from its summit, contemplate the blue-and-gold bay. To the left, the Golden Gate Bridge glows red in the sun. It was also by referendum that such a warm, copper colour was chosen for this great metal bridge; all the flames of the Mediterranean are cast in its girders. Every year, three or four desperate people jump from the top of this dizzying platform. To the right, the Bay Bridge is made of two sections resting on an island. It connects San Francisco to the industrial cities on the other side of the bay: Oakland, Berkeley and Richmond. San Francisco no longer seems like a placid provincial town but like the heart of a vast network of three million inhabitants. Downtown, there's the same animation as in New York or Chicago. Market Street is another Broadway. From the centre, the roads lead to outlying districts, where you find the infinite desolation of big cities: unfinished avenues like those in Queens or Los Angeles, stations, warehouses, garages and deserted intersections. But even surrounded by factories, housing projects, work and poverty, the bay is a luxurious paradise. A little island floating on these happy waters looks like a peaceful Eden; it turns out to be the prison where men on death row await the gas chamber.

We go down to Fisherman's Wharf. The boats rock in the narrow basins between the wooden piers. The little square is surrounded by restaurants with big transparent bay windows where you eat lobster and fish. At the doors they sell doughnuts as well as shellfish, crayfish and big shrimp stiffened on blocks of ice. The smell of boiling fat mingles with the smell of seaweed. But if you think of the old port of Marseilles with its songs and its sea urchins, this picturesque scene seems too tame.

We've explored the suburbs and the surrounding countryside by car. We've followed the coast, crossed the parks, climbed the hills. At the beach there's a sad little amusement park like Venice in Los Angeles; two miles farther on there are wild coves among the rocks. We've crossed the Golden Gate Bridge, going as slowly as possible, since you're not allowed to stop there. We've crossed the Bay Bridge. It penetrates quite far into the city, and we wandered around for a time before finding the approach; we saw it high above our heads and didn't know where it began. There's an entrance toll and a notice that warns of a five-dollar fine if you run out of gas in the middle of the bridge. At the beginning, a small device discharges the cars of any electricity they've accumulated. In New York or Washington I often felt electric shocks when I touched metallic objects; people even claim that you can sometimes see sparks fly when people shake hands.

Oakland, all factories and developments, is hideous. But it's always the same surprise: five minutes after passing the last building we're on hills covered with woods and lakes, where for miles and hours we don't meet another human being. The little road winds above the contours of the bay, through woods and shrubland, pines and flowering trees. This landscape might evoke certain unspoiled, temperate corners of France, but it's very different: no houses, no animals, no fields, no orchards, no gardens. The French countryside is made up of 'estates'; every piece of land has some legal status, even swamps and marshlands. This earth, on the other hand, has escaped annexation; men may have fixed settlements, but they cross the land like nomads.

A vast industrial area extends to the south-east of San Francisco along a flat, marshy coast. Trucks smelling of gasoline surge down the highway. I know few places that are less attractive. But here, too, you can take a little road to the right, and in a few miles you leave the twentieth century behind. Almost the entire peninsula is covered by an ancient stand of sequoia trees. 'Sequoia' is still a beautiful, legendary word. This forest is less imposing than those I loved in the Technicolor films, but the colours are more subtle; the reddish trunks have the muted beauty of old Persian carpets, of faded silks, of tarnished gold. From the coastal route one can see the ocean on both sides: the forest unfurls in dark green masses, as it has for millions of years, toward the open sea on the left, toward the bay on the right. We are closer to San Francisco than Meudon is to Paris. It's difficult to believe.

Returning from our wanderings as night falls, we feel lost. We roam around Market Street, entering bars, newsreel cinemas and restaurants, letting ourselves drift along with the crowd. And I have the same feeling I often had around Times Square: How can I become one with the night? What's the way in? In Los Angeles, someone told us about a nightclub – the Dawn Club – where they used to play good jazz, but it's closed. Surely there are other places that could give us something of this city, but those are just the places we wouldn't know how to find. There are people who know them, who could take us there – but we don't know those people. We remain on the surface of the lights, the noise, all the promises that throb in the night in a big city. We won't manage to plunge in.

American cities are too big. At night their dimensions proliferate; they become jungles where it's easy to lose your way. The second evening we wanted to see *The Killers*, the film based on the new Hemingway novel, which was playing in an outlying district. We set out on foot in the evening, thinking that after a short walk we'd catch a tram, bus or taxi. Suddenly, we were on a dark road lined with tracks, unmoving trains and hangars, crossed now and then by other deserted streets. We were in the heart of town yet in a desert. It began to rain violently, and in the wind and rain, we felt as forlorn as on a treeless plain – no shelter, no cars in sight. At last we saw a light and rang the bell at the gate of a kind of depot – something that we would never dare to do in France but seemed natural here. Men busy with boxes and bales of merchandise led us to the telephone so that we could call a taxi, and we waited a good quarter of an hour under their roof. After two miles we were again in a district full of lights and drugstores. We even arrived in time to see *The Killers*.

Tuesday, after my lecture at Mills College, the French consul took us to a nightclub in Chinatown. Most of the customers were Chinese. The waitresses, the hostesses and the dancers all pretended to be Chinese, though in fact, many were Filipino and one or two were probably Japanese. The great attraction was to see those pretty girls with slanted eyes dancing the French cancan. The room was decorated with cabaret chinoiserie. The authentic, everyday picturesqueness of the audience and the tainted exoticism of the setting and attractions created an artificial atmosphere that I found charming. This outing helped us to get a better sense of San Francisco by night. And N and I decide that we've spent a thoroughly enjoyable evening.

It seems obvious that we should go to the Chinese theatre. We tried yesterday, but we were stopped at the door: the show was reserved for Chinese. This evening we're allowed in. There are no other whites in the hall. It's already ten o'clock when we arrive, and the show started some time ago. The audience – men, women and children – looks very unassuming. A seat costs only fifty cents, and the hall is swarming. It's bare and full of smoke, like a Belleville movie house. Most of the spectators are sitting, but some wander through the aisles, coming and going, standing a moment and watching, then going away again. Nearly everyone is busy eating something: sausages, ice cream, candy. The luxury of the stage contrasts with the poverty of the auditorium: it's decorated with enormous baskets of flowers with silk streamers and looks like an altar. Embroidered with gold and silver, bursting with colour, the actors' costumes are a royal feast. The silk panels and decorative streamers are also extraordinarily rich. Dark red make-up transforms the actors' faces into rigid masks: I know that these have a symbolic language, but I don't understand it. Nor do I know the meaning of the accessories, in particular those large beribboned batons the actors are playing with. The story, of course, isn't clear to me. My consolation is that my neighbours don't understand it much better: they speak colloquial Chinese, and the drama unfolds in classic Cantonese. But like them, I am caught up in the beauty of the mime, the rhythm of the music, and the voices. If I don't follow the plot, I grasp the situations one by one. Love, challenge, anger, vengeance, betrayal and despair are expressed through pantomime and dance that are highly stylised and poignant. The musicians sit on one side of the stage, and the stagehands circulate quietly around the stage, changing sets, placing and removing furniture, in front of the audience's eyes. Paul Claudel [a French poet and playwright] wanted to imitate this freedom in *Le Soulier de satin* [*The Satin Slipper*], but his effort seemed too forced; at best, he could hope for intelligent compliance from his spectators. The charm here is that the assistants are automatically invisible. The hero lost one of the huge feathers on his helmet during a battle, so one of the helpers picked it up and readjusted it without interrupting the actor. No one saw it. The spectator's gaze, attuned to this imaginary world, no longer perceives the real world.

We were just going to take a quick look and leave, and we have stayed two hours. We go to eat in a little Chinese place like the one we enjoyed so much yesterday. When we leave, we don't feel like going to sleep. We walk down toward the wharf; a banner announces quite pompously: 'International Concession'. We've been told that it's not a good neighbourhood, but it seems quite dead. A few half-drunk sailors are not enough to create the bustle of a port town. The bars with Hawaiian or Mexican decor are empty; a pianist or guitarist plays mournfully in the gloom. There's no one at the box office at the 'Variety Show', which advertises luscious pin-ups. There's only one place the public pours into – a nightclub called To Joyful 1900, which aims to re-create a turn-of-the-century cabaret. People drink whiskey or beer sitting around little tables on pink plush armchairs, while comics in chequered suits, moustaches and straw hats, as well as dancers in black silk stockings, cavort on stage. The attractions are amusing to us because they're just the kind of show featured in the classic Western. At one point the stage empties and everyone turns toward a screen, where they project sentimental old songs. The orchestra joins in, and the whole room picks up the chorus. In this instant, past and present truly merge. Half a century ago it was customary to sing such charming refrains. Today, the audience not only evokes an old-fashioned tradition, but it also throws itself into this with real energy. On screen, the printed couplets have the poetry of images projected by a magic lantern in the days when movies and the phonograph had not yet been invented.

Did San Francisco have something better to offer us? Or were the secrets that we were annoyed not to have discovered simply a mirage? We'll never know.

6 March

On Tuesday I gave a lecture at Mills College. The campus is a luxuriant park, perched on a hillside that's pungent with the smell of eucalyptus. As in the East, the buildings are in a medieval style with panelled halls, tapestries, blue-and-gold coats of arms and varnished beams. Only the cafeteria and the post office are out of keeping with this solemn past. I saw the college girls' rooms, which are like all comfortable student digs: sofas, shelves, family photographs, and personal touches in the choice of knick-knacks and reproductions hung on the walls. In the corridors the girls go around freely in pyjamas or bathrobes. The professors' houses are scattered throughout the park. I spent part of the evening at the home of Darius Milhaud, who teaches music here.

Today I must speak at the University of California at Berkeley. A young writer who runs a bookstore across from the campus comes to get me with a car. He edits an avant-garde review influenced by surrealism and Henry Miller. There's an intellectual regionalism in America; Henry Miller isn't very important in New York, but on the West Coast, where he lives, he's thought of as a genius. Many of his books are censored, but copies are passed around under the table; there are even excerpts recorded on albums. The bookstore V takes me to reminds me of Adrienne Monnier's 'Maison des amis des livres' [a Parisian salon and bookstore]; it's quite small with a tiny picture gallery in the back. Many of the names I read on the shelves are unfamiliar. I would very much like to inform myself about the new generation of writers, and I ask for advice, but the recommendations I get don't match any of the ones I got in New York. No one seems to agree, even about the older writers – with the exception of Melville and Faulkner. Of course, in France, too, we have our factions, our prejudices, our preferences, but the indecision here indicates a certain disarray. Writers turn their backs on the past without having a sense of the future. Nearly everyone agrees, however, that there's a great poetry revival going on.

While we're discussing these things, V, who is a poet himself, brings me armloads of reviews and books. He gives me a record, a fragment from *Tropic of Cancer* [banned in the United States at the time]. My books and records are out of place in the Faculty Club dining room, an austere, terribly dark dining room with a big family dining table in the middle and a group of serious old gentlemen around the table. As in France, and even more so here, most of the university people are cut off from avant-garde literary or artistic movements. They also seem cut off from life. They will surely not be the ones to spark a bit of discomfort, a concern about responsibility, among the young people they are entrusted to teach; they will merely endorse the students' conformity and apathy. The day before yesterday Congress began to discuss a project of intervention in Greece, called a project to 'aid' Greece, and George Marshall forcefully declared that he was ready to combat communism in Greece. Meanwhile, Truman is preparing a proposal to Congress, asking that any person judged to be 'disloyal' be eliminated from government service. Obviously, the communists are their target once again, as well as all the liberals of the Left. I look at the sporty young people, the laughing girls in my audience, and I think that surely, like the students in Los Angeles, there are only one or two who are concerned with this news. It's sometimes said that America is the country of youth. I'm not so sure. Real young people are engaged in moving toward the future of mankind, not enclosing themselves in the complacent resignation that's been assigned to them.

7 March

In the morning we cross the Golden Gate Bridge without any hope of returning. We've left San Francisco and we're headed off to an adventure on unknown routes. N takes the wheel, I the map. And we're full of the joy of beginning a new journey. On the road in our car, these wild regions will offer us the risks and solitude of wandering in the mountains on foot.

We go around the bay. The sun is already hot as day breaks. Our first stop is Sacramento, where we arrive at around ten o'clock. In this capital of California, I taste for the first time in America the poetry of dead cities. The Capitol, a smaller version of the one in Washington, stands at the back of a park, amid lawns and trees. In modern cities, trees are confined to gardens, but here they invade the avenues, where the smell of plants and the silence are surprising; they form a thick vault above the central boulevard, which is lined with beautiful old wooden houses.

I love their elaborate architecture – the gables, the porches, the verandas. I love their dusty colours. One expects to see old gentlemen in silk hats and women in crinolines descending the steps. We've left San Francisco behind, and here we are in Bruges or Aigues-Mortes. In Europe, the defunct capitals are eight centuries old; here, the capital is scarcely one century old. But it feels just as embalmed.

From Sacramento to Reno I've chosen the route on the map that seems the most direct and the least travelled. It passes Lake Tahoe, which I've heard so much about. It crosses a bare plain and then enters pine forests. Now and then we encounter a logging village – finally, human constructions that match the landscape. They are hewn from trees with reddish trunks, made of those logs we saw piled in clearings. The wood is no longer an impersonal material but has its own colour, odour and texture – it's a living thing. Sometimes the houses form an encampment, and sometimes they're arranged along twisting streets. We go through a gold mining town that's now called Placerville, but its real name is Hangtown, and the inn has a sign depicting a tree where they used to hang murderers and thieves. This town is only half-dead, but others are entirely abandoned and are called ghost towns. The long-deserted houses are falling into ruins; you can still see the half-effaced inscriptions announcing a tavern, a theatre, and sometimes the shreds of posters. The forest becomes increasingly lonely. On an old marker I read: Placer, 1½ Miles, and I'm almost as moved as if I'd discovered Sleeping Beauty's castle at a bend in the road. This is really where those men lived whose legends enchanted my childhood, whose stories set me dreaming. Here – or in a nearby forest, but it amounts to the same thing – Charlie Chaplin made *The Gold Rush*. These landscapes – which I imagined through the screen and books and which existed on the fringes of the world, just like fairy-tale palaces or the painted heavens of Fra Angelico – now I've seen them with my own eyes.

We haven't seen a house in a long time. Suddenly there's a

sign: '6,000 feet'. I look at it, incredulous: we've barely been climbing since Sacramento. Seven thousand feet. I'd been told that the Rocky Mountains [she's actually in the Sierra Nevada] rise so gently that you climb without realising it, but people say so many things . . . Eight thousand feet. We need proof. The ground is gradually covered with snow, and there's an icy wind blowing in our faces. We discover high mountains all around us – you'd think you were in Switzerland. I also think of the snow in *The Gold Rush*. We are at a pass; a sign tells us: 'Slippery Surface' – in other words, the road is icy. Then we remember that the garage attendant shrugged his shoulders as he watched us drive off. 'The car will hold steady or it won't,' he said; and we thought, naturally, that it would. But what if it were to break down right here? It would take at least a day's walk to reach human habitation, and we haven't seen a single car. N descends slowly. Below, there's still the cold and snow. Despite our breakfast in Sacramento, we're hungry and we're beginning to imagine a warm, comfortable resting place on the shores of Lake Tahoe. The lake lies in a circle of snowy mountains; its waters are steel blue. We walk toward it to get a better view; the earth is hard and cold beneath our feet, and the wind is blowing in our faces. The lovely, gracious inns are closed. We set off again. The map indicates several stopping places, and it isn't lying, but all the houses are buried in snow; there's no one around. We'll have to go all the way to Reno on our empty stomachs. According to the map, a little road will take us there in twenty miles – not so far. We find the road, and we also find a barrier with a sign: this is a mountain road, impassable in winter. The tarmac disappears beneath the snow.

I'm angry at myself. So many times I've felt that at the city gates nature lies in wait, harsh and untamed, and in San Francisco's temperate zone I forgot the opposing forces of climates, mountains and seasons. I looked at the map as if it reflected a world submissive to the reign of man, with distances convertible to hours and exact gallons of gas. This morning we were in

San Francisco, it's true, and police officers directed traffic. No more officers, no more direction. We no longer need to obey, but nothing obeys us either. The needle on our gasoline gauge is dangerously close to zero.

Retracing our steps and rejoining the road to Carson City would mean sixty miles with no help in sight. We'd certainly run out of gas. If we go on, we'll find a village twenty miles away – perhaps it won't be abandoned. We decide to take this chance and continue following the contours of the beautiful, frozen grey lake. The village is inhabited. We fill up our gas tank and eat; hamburgers never seemed so delicious.

Still eighty miles to Reno. We cross the state line and enter Nevada. Night has fallen, and nothing interrupts the monotony of the mountain road. At last, the first motels are lit up. Motels, courts and lodges line the roadway for miles and miles. There's the greatest variety in these artificial villages: some are Mexican-style, others are like igloos, others like English cottages. With their neon lights, lawns and shrubs, they seem like amusement parks or dance halls. It's disappointing to think that there are only rooms and beds. 'No Vacancy'. 'No Vacancy'. Everything is full. In these cottages people who want divorces come to stay for the required six weeks' residence. This industry, which accounts for Reno's wealth, never comes to a standstill. Before finding a place to stay, we wander for a long time in the city. At last, we're offered a room 'for five people', where we spend the night in luxury.

America is a box full of surprises, but Reno is one of the greatest astonishments for me. Associating this name with Hollywood, I imagined a luxurious Monte Carlo populated with glittering movie stars. And I fall into a crude Western town. Two illuminated avenues cut across each other at right angles. A sign hung above the pavement announces in neon letters: 'The Biggest Little City in the World'. Around these two central arteries, the streets are dark and deserted. The cafeterias and restaurants are wretched, the bars empty. All of life is concentrated in the 'clubs'. Outside they glow with lights; their large animated signs evoke in fiery flashes the heroic gold rush era: a man strikes the ground with a pick; a mule loaded with ingots jerkily climbs a hill; a covered wagon gallops toward the promised land. To enter, you push on those swinging doors cut knee-high that I've seen so often in Westerns; then you find yourself in the heart of a gigantic fair. The walls are decorated with the same legendary pictures as the façade, but they can hardly be distinguished through the thick fumes. Pressed around the gambling tables, at the bar and in the aisles, there's such a picturesque crowd that you'd think they were movie extras. Yet even an ingenious film director wouldn't have been able to invent them. The heavy odour of whiskey and gin, the big, dirty cowboy hats, and the soiled checked shirts are simply too authentic. These are workers from the silver mines, cowboys from their ranches, and tramps – derelicts ruined by gambling who still come to inhale the smell of dollars. The women look as wretched as those on the Bowery. Even the dealers have a down-at-the-heels and unhealthy look. These places are off-limits to minors (once again, they want to stop N), but they stay open all night. We buy some chips, multi-coloured pieces of cardboard worth a quarter, a nickel or even a penny. Card games, dice games – there are God knows how many different games that I don't understand anything about. We'll take a chance only at the roulette table. Next to the dealer stand piles of magnificent silver dollars – the first I've seen. They despise paper money here, favouring only silver that you can weigh in your hand. Besides, it's rare that someone bets a whole dollar. With an intent, maniacal air, a woman scatters one-cent chips on the four corners of the tablecloth. Most people play tiny sums this way, with scientific seriousness. Above the bar, enormous notice boards announce the horse races going on across America; bookmakers take bets. And in order to keep their clients in suspense, they distribute lottery tickets; they draw numbers at all hours, and the winners receive chips that they play in the slot machines.

It's a surprise to leave these sleazy dives and find ourselves once more on the dingy streets. The stores don't have the luxury of Hollywood, but they're meant for a well-heeled, respectable clientele. There are posters of rosy, smiling young women in bridal gowns: 'All arrangements for marriages. Quick divorces. Get married at Chapel X, the Little Chapel of the Stars.' The display windows are full of dresses in frothy white tulle, shiny satins, wedding rings, engagement rings, jewellery and wedding gifts of all sorts.

These appeals to domestic life on the threshold of gambling dens populated with lone men and lost women, the glittering lights and bursts of sound enveloping this wretchedness – these provide such vivid contrasts that I'm left speechless. But N explains to me the paradoxical logic involved. Nevada is the least populous and poorest state in the USA. It has only three cities: Reno, Las Vegas and Carson City. It's inhabited by mine workers and especially by cowboys, who live hard lives on solitary ranches. These ranches are still ruled by the law of the jungle; people settle herd or land disputes and personal quarrels with guns, not in the courts. No bourgeoisie, so no bourgeois morality. Nevada was never burdened with the puritanical prohibitions that weigh on the other states: gambling, the sale of liquor, nightlife and divorce are all authorised here, as is prostitution – at least on the outskirts of town. This licentiousness, a result of the land's poverty, has become the source of its wealth. By contrast, opulent California is stifling in its rigid armour of morality. Difficulty getting a divorce, repression of prostitution and gambling, strict regulation of alcohol consumption, a limited nightlife – I felt these constraints in Hollywood. So Californians joyfully, avidly, cross the state line to taste all the pleasures freely, and in exchange they bring their good money to Nevada. Hence the prosperity of Reno and Las Vegas. But first these towns have a local clientele: the cowboys' and miners' only amusement is to come and risk their hard-earned wages in the clubs. If silver money is the medium of exchange here, it's partly because the people of Nevada have a primitive attachment to the metal extracted within its borders. It's also because they're too poor to buy anything in the other states – so much so that coins forged in this area don't leave it. Some are found in other parts of America, but in small quantities.

Now I understand. And Reno in its glittering, sordid truth fascinates me even more than the artificial casino its name evokes. I have trouble going to sleep in this town, where hope and despair never sleep.

8 March

In the same way other newspapers announce prizewinners, marriages, birthdays and births, every morning the Reno newspapers proudly list the divorces granted the day before. It's a long list that sometimes includes the name of some well-known star.

We leave for Lone Pine, where M and S are going to join us tomorrow. Up to Carson City, the road crosses a desert – a desert of stones and red grasses at the foot of snowcapped mountains. The little town, the capital of Nevada, is still asleep; not a car or pedestrian to be seen. It's nine o'clock in the morning – perhaps it never wakes up. A little museum displays old relics: a century-old locomotive, gold diggers' carts. Sacramento, Hangtown, Carson City. The past is so moving here because it's so recent; it's hardly a century old, and yet it's as distant as our Middle Ages. It has the sheer inevitability of epics and illuminations, and yet life still pulses under the veneer of something dead and buried. That rusting locomotive with its wood-filled tender is as old-fashioned as a horse-drawn carriage, but it holds the promise of all the trains that circle the earth today. Cut off from the future that it heralded and that was its meaning, the past is dried, like a pressed flower. In the Far West the break isn't yet complete. And in France we probably have these souvenirs of the recent past as well, but they are located in our history; they belong to the past. Here, the last century measures the entire past. Before that, nothing had begun. Looking at these carts, crossing these ghost towns, you dream of a world on a human scale where you might reach a hand across time and space and pull secure borders around yourself.

Yesterday we entered Nevada almost without realising it. But to re-enter California is another matter. It's a closed and distrustful state. The customs officers carefully examine our papers, and N would have incurred a serious fine if she'd picked me up as a hitchhiker along the road. They open our suitcases. Large notices warn that it is forbidden to bring seeds, flowers or plants from another state into California. They take these precautions against parasites that can destroy the harvests. In principle, all vegetable merchandise is subjected to a vigorous disinfection upon arrival. A few years ago the emperor of Japan gave the USA a cargo of seeds as a present, and out of courtesy, they dispensed with this formality. The result was a huge epidemic that ruined all the farmers. It costs an enormous amount each year to prevent a recurrence. Surveillance is rigorous in the ports, in the train stations and on the highways. These measures are aimed especially at Mexico, where hygienic conditions are dubious. Tourists often try to smuggle in seeds or plants – the Mexican flora is so beautiful – so they are carefully searched. The customs officers ask us to empty out our pockets, and N tries to shorten the ordeal by protesting, 'We spent only one night in Nevada!' Then the employee winks maliciously: 'Ah, one night is enough!' He lets a young divorcee pass, giving her the tender smile you'd bestow on a newly-wed.

The landscape is stunningly beautiful. It's a sun-drenched desert, as arid as Andalusia or Africa, but with a veil of snow filtering the burning colours. The white mountains belie the menace of a scorching earth. The road climbs; today, too, its ascent is imperceptible, but we believe the signs: '7,000 feet', '8,000 feet'. Winter has triumphed; all around us is the bare whiteness of the Alps. The pass we reach is the highest point on any route, from Canada to Mexico. Skiers awkwardly negotiate the slopes from the summit. We go into a chalet where they serve food and drinks; we buy postcards and a few groceries. This is one of the charms of the trip – these rustic shelters where all the security of civilisation asserts itself against cold, wind and solitude. One shelter is suspended at the edge of a cliff, and another is lost amid tall sequoias and covered with snow. In all of them we find the same rough, comfortable wooden furniture, piles of magazines on the tables, phonographs with records, hamburgers and hot coffee. Black-and-white photographs, black letters on white pages, provide a rest for eyes grown weary from too many natural wonders and from the wind. Eating, drinking and reading, we solidly anchor ourselves in the human world before setting off across the wilderness again.

Down we go. The snow disappears, and the sun takes its rightful place. The earth is golden, the grass yellow, the stones bare around the large lakes that spread out between plateaus. At every turn, at every bend in the road, the landscape changes, and yet it's always the same. We're crossing a single desert and can see it all in every glimpse. We are even more lost than on the coast, where at least the sea defined the limits of the land. Here, all around us, lines stretch to infinity and the horizon is so vast it's dizzying. Not a trace of anything human. Not another person on the road or another car. We cross a mountain pass called Devil's Gate, and just as I ask N, 'Are we going to meet the devil?' a big black car surges out of the ground, behind us; it passes us and stops. And here is the most famous character in all Westerns, who has come down, off the screen, and is approaching us, with a big, light felt cowboy hat on his head and a star pinned to his silk shirt – it's the sheriff. He looks at N reproachfully: 'You touched the white line. That's very dangerous. What if a car had wanted to pass you at that moment?' Our gaze travels to the far end of the empty road, and he changes the subject. Sceptically examining our damaged fenders, he asks, 'You've already had some accidents? And whose car is this? Your parents'?' He obviously thinks she's a college girl on the loose. He was following us a for long time, well before the wheel touched the white line. This red car, these two women alone intrigued him, and he was probably bored as well. The papers are in order. He confines himself to giving N a warning. He goes off. We do, too. What we'd like to know is where he came from; for a hundred miles we have seen neither a wall nor a stand of trees where he could have hidden.

The first village we drive through is as impersonal and ugly as any I've encountered here. The second, too. Now we're at the foot of the plateau, amid limitless prairies, where herds of buffalo roam and bands of wild horses gallop, pursued by cowboys across the plain. Lone Pine, where we arrive at around seven o'clock, is just one long, disreputable street, but it's built on a privileged site. Across from our hotel, in the middle of a mountain range, stands Mount Whitney, the highest peak in America. Twenty miles away is Death Valley, which goes below sea level, so here we are between the highest and lowest points in the New World [or at least the forty-eight states]. It would take four hours on mules to reach the snows of the Rockies [the Sierra]; in one hour by car tomorrow we'll find the salty heat of the desert. And we're two hundred miles from Los Angeles. I understand what S told us so intently: 'At Lone Pine, you'll touch California.'

9 March

In the morning there's a lovely, gentle sun. Toward noon, sitting on the veranda in front of the door, we start looking down the road expectantly: the message we received last night set our meeting for noon. In the restaurant across the way we lunch on thick Virginia ham with pineapple, a combination as harmonious as *duck à l'orange*. Two o'clock, three o'clock – we're still waiting. It's four o'clock when a big car appears at the end of the road. At first I don't recognise these two cowboys: they're wearing big, light felt cowboy hats, red-and-black checked shirts, and neckerchiefs. But it's really M and S. They apologise – they had a few accidents. We've reserved rooms at the Lone Pine Hotel, where N and I already spent the night, but S immediately declares that he wants to stay at the Whitney Hotel, for old times' sake. The Whitney has no rooms. And the Lone Pine doesn't want to cancel the reservation. S is determined. He insists on the beds they refuse him and just as insistently refuses the beds they want to give him. Suddenly, we realise that he's been drinking. M also doesn't seem quite sure of himself. He tells us exultantly that this morning, at five, after each left a different party following the opening of Chaplin's latest film, he and S happened to run into each other on Hollywood Boulevard. S was so overcome with joy at the idea of spending two days' vacation that he began to celebrate at dawn. They continued to celebrate until eight o'clock in the morning, delighted at the coincidence that had brought them together. Once on the road, S began to worry: 'I think something's not working!' he kept saying. They stopped at the first village and, before making any decisions, went to console themselves with a good whiskey. S vaguely examined the car: 'Oh, it's nothing serious, after all.' So from one alarm to another, from whiskey to whiskey, they were four hours late on a drive that was supposed to take four hours altogether. 'S is so happy!' M tells us, taking us aside. You'd think he was talking about a schoolboy who was kept strictly in check by his parents and had just ventured on his first escapade.

More whiskeys. S reminds me that I must explain the Cartesian cogito to him. It's agreed – we'll do it this evening, if he likes. And he does, passionately. Meanwhile, he'll show us the place where he made his last great film ten years ago. We all climb into the car, and he starts off on a winding side road on the way to Mount Whitney. Suddenly, he stops. 'I'm going to put you to shame,' he says solemnly. He points to the white peaks: 'These are the youngest mountains in America.' Then he indicates the plateau covered with enormous rocks: 'And these are the oldest!'

I don't feel shamed because no competition is really possible, but the fact is that the contrast of the two landscapes is striking. In S's film the yellow plateaus were convincing stand-ins for the worn mountains of India; they are often used to represent Tibet as well. The Mount Whitney range provides Hollywood with images of Switzerland, the Himalayas and the Caucasus. A few steps away there's Africa with its sand dunes and the Australian bush. Miraculously, this false Tibet and this illusory Switzerland are authentic parts of the planet. And since art is made of lies, I don't see why you can't create views of Asia in Lone Pine. Of all the reproaches levelled at Hollywood, this one seems quite stupid. I jump; a sharp jolt has knocked me out of my seat. The path S is following between the yellow rocks is full of enormous holes. S doesn't see them or doesn't care. I recall this site quite precisely. But at the end of the film there was a vast plain on which a victorious army approached; I don't see it. S points out a square of ground the size of a kitchen garden: 'That's it!' He explains to me that they could obtain that magnificent perspective by mounting the camera on top of a certain rock and filming it from a certain angle. The car turns around as well as it can, and we return. Someone's in the middle of building a wood and plaster hangar for shooting a new film here. This site is used often, probably in half the Westerns. S tells me that he's gone to the top of Mount Whitney on the back of a mule. This mountain is higher than Mont Blanc, but its latitude is more southerly than that of the Atlas Mountains. There's no snow on the peak, which can be reached by a mule track.

During dinner S makes a long, sentimental speech about France, America and the world in general. He is softened by the whiskey, but his proposals are not much different from those of the sober Emporia lecturer in the train from Chicago. Why wars? Why hatred? Wouldn't a little goodwill solve our problems and facilitate understanding? Many Americans continue to delude themselves with this optimistic idealism, while the Hearst press declares that war with Russia has already begun.

Leaving the table, S repeats once or twice, 'You must explain to me Descartes's cogito.' We walk him to his room, and he falls into bed.

10 March

The next morning S is quite fresh and dignified. He's a sensitive, shy man, and he basically drinks out of shyness – it must be devastating for him. I climb into the car next to him. N and M follow us, and we leave for Death Valley. Dangerous for men, it's also hard on cars, for obscure reasons having to do with air pressure, and N and I congratulate each other that we're not venturing there alone.

After we leave Lone Pine, the desert begins again – miles of desert and suddenly, on the shores of a half-dried lake, a handful of wooden shacks. Salt is extracted from these dead waters; pyramids of white crystals gleam in the sun. No grass grows in this salty soil. At ten o'clock in the morning, not a breath of air stirs. The railroad tracks take half-rusted freight cars to Lone Pine, but there's no train in the vicinity. And it's not entirely true, as benign legend has it, that every American worker has a car; the workers here don't have any. They're shut in between the implacable sky and a petrified earth. Heat, salt and boredom: this place, so picturesque to pass through, must be a regular little hell on earth.

We see no more houses for a long time. The road winds across the mountain, where ochres mingle with bright purples. We discover a valley, deeply hollowed between two rock walls. A dry, bluish grass covers the bottom, which is cut in two by a road. Straight and stubborn, the road penetrates the large depression, then climbs in stages to the crest ahead. In this place that is so hostile to man, the road is a moving affirmation of humanness, giving meaning to a land that's long been a place of difficult and dangerous travel. All the tragic migrations of the old pioneers are embodied in this rigid white ribbon of road. Many adventurers who made their way to California hoped to shorten their trip by avoiding the detour over the high peaks and by cutting through Death Valley and Panamint Valley. Many perished in these salt deserts, where water is scarce and the heat unbearable. Today, at the entrance to Death Valley, there's a police notice: travellers must sign a register; and it is recommended that they stick to the main road, especially in summer. To get lost or break down on one of the small side roads can be a fatal adventure. Not long ago Scott – the old Death Valley hero, whose 'castle' is still on display – rode through the valley on horseback, and in an isolated spot he met an old couple whose car had broken down. He gave them a little water and promised to bring help, but in the time it would take to go and return, the unfortunate pair would die horribly of thirst and sunstroke. Scott reflected, pulled his revolver, and quickly finished them off. Scott's castle stands amid sand dunes reminiscent of the Sahara. We leave it on our left and thread our way through rocky ground rimmed with salt. This vast depression is an ancient lake dried up by the sun. Even in this season the heat is overwhelming; we are all sweating. In about two hours we arrive at the place called the Furnace, which the pioneers considered the very heart of hell. It's a tiny oasis with several springs and scrawny trees. In the last century, when the springs ran dry, the pioneers could do nothing but wait for death. Today, things have been arranged so that there's no lack of water; there's a luxurious hotel with a terrace, where people sprawled on deckchairs sunbathe, and a more modest 'court' of cabins grouped around a cafeteria.

We have lunch. Then we visit a kind of esplanade with a display of the old relics: the covered wagons with their green canvas, implements for extracting and purifying gold, carts used to transport borax once the gold mines were exhausted. At that time, all they could manage was a painful fifteen miles per day. Here we see the first public vehicles – old coaches bearing the inscription 'Death Valley Stage' in large letters. The old epics have never seemed more unreal to me than in this place where they really happened. I feel the sun's barbarous intensity; I see the difficult ridges; I measure the vastness of spaces. How are we to believe that entire families managed to cross these empty lands without the aid of a road? Some people waited for months in these parts until the most vigorous members of the wagon train could reach the coast and return to rescue them. They were rescued; they tasted the fruits of California. Can this really have happened? And scarcely a hundred years ago? Never have I felt as strongly as I do here the childish emotion excited by the Far West's recent past.

Beyond the modest oasis, the valley descends below sea level. This is where von Stroheim made the final scenes of *Greed*. Just as we see Holland through its old painters, finding a tree from Ruysdael here, a windmill from Hobbema there, a wall from Vermeer elsewhere, so we discover California through movie images. Cowboys, sheriffs, herds of buffalo, galloping horses, wild mountain passes, villages with wooden houses – I find them so enchanting only because I recognise them. But no landscape ever seemed to me as overwhelming on screen as these plates of salty earth, cut by deep crevasses and stretching to infinity between walls of fire. I never even dared to dream of touching them, yet I am touching them, and in the startling truth of the setting, the drama itself becomes real: I believe in the agony of von Stroheim's heroes. The depth of this valley frightens me.

We halt our descent and turn left to escape over the crest above. S's car suddenly comes to a stop, spitting water. This time it's really true – something's not working. It limps pitifully along to the garage. A mechanic hoses it down sceptically as it keeps spitting. S hesitates, then decides to try his luck. The car climbs two or three miles and the motor gives out. S tells us to continue the trip without him: he'll have himself driven from the garage to the nearest airfield and go home to Los Angeles. M helps him turn around and pushes the car, which slowly navigates the slope. S is understandably distressed, but I think that secretly he wanted this mishap to occur: two days of freedom was more than he could bear.

At the top of the crest we find the Mojave Desert, a vast plateau covered with stones and dried grass. It extends to the horizon. More than the subtleties of green and blue vegetation, more than the majestic outline of the mountains, it is this vastness that gives the desert its beauty. The rocky outcroppings are more inhuman than the peaks of the Alps: no one lives in their shadow or grazes herds here; no tourists venture by. Behind this first barrier there are ranges and ranges of mountains that no eye has ever beheld. They are so alien that they seem hostile; their presence is gratuitous, obstinate, like that of the moon in the sky. And all the earth is suddenly revealed as a planet similarly dedicated to the horrors of eternal peace.

We re-enter Nevada. Billboards appear along the way: 'Come see the Wild Animal Farm. Snakes. Monkeys. Coyotes.' For several miles the billboards keep repeating, 'Monkeys. Snakes. Coyotes.' At the crossing of two endless, empty roads stands a gas station flanked by restrooms and a kind of combination bar and grocery store. In the bar there's a green table for roulette. The animals' cages are outside: there are two monkeys, several snakes coiled up, a barn owl, a miserable vulture and one of those coyotes who ate N's ducks. What a strange menagerie, lost in an ocean of stones and silence! But a little farther on, at another turn-off, a new billboard invites us: 'Three Springs Ranch, 15 miles. Buffalo. Wild animals.' I suppose that the Nevada cowboys have a passion for wild animals and are proud to exhibit what they've caught.

Night falls as we approach Las Vegas. These days, Las Vegas is more fashionable than Reno. Enormous posters throughout California feature a cowboy chomping down on a big cigar and winking playfully – and below this: 'For fun . . . Las Vegas.' There's also a girl telephoning her boyfriend, showing her terrific legs, and saying: 'Yes . . . if it's at the Last Frontier Hotel in Las Vegas.' And there are the same advertisements as you see for

Reno: 'Get married in the Chapel of the Stars. All arrangements for marriages. Quick divorces.' Here we see festive gardens, which are only 'courts' or 'lodges'. And here's Las Vegas, all glittering with lights. It's difficult to find rooms, but we finally discover some in a motel that smells of tamarinds and mimosa. They rent us a whole cottage: two bedrooms, a bathroom and a kitchen. I notice that in these places, they never ask us for identification; no one knows when you come or go or whether you bring visitors. There are many ways of eluding American thoroughness.

A taxi driver shows us a restaurant whose cooking makes up for the glaring lights, the heat and the brouhaha. The clubs are much like those in Reno: the same lit-up signs evoking the gold rush period, the same games, the same lotteries all marinating in the stench of alcohol and tobacco. But the wretched clientele of cowboys and bums mingles with a more respectable public. I notice, among others, women who look distinctly lower middle class, sitting on stools on both sides of a long counter. They each have a mug of beer beside them and a bingo card in front of them. I assumed bingo was a quiet diversion played in the family, and these women are as old as the mothers and grandmothers who would play this game to amuse the children on a quiet evening. But as the lottery wheel turns above the counter, they follow it with maniacal intensity. A voice over a loudspeaker announces the number chosen, and they place their numbered chips on the corresponding spaces. They are each as alone as the old Frenchwomen who kill their evenings at the fireside. But they are alone all together by the hundreds. And in this innocent pastime they risk real money.

One of the clubs seems particularly charming to us, with a luxurious red-and-gold bar whose lights and velvet hangings date from the last century. You can imagine an Edward G. Robinson [a movie actor known for gangster roles] with sideburns sitting in these armchairs, drinking whiskey with his cronies while surveying the whole smoke-filled dive where gold seekers were ruining themselves. We, too, drink whiskeys and ruin ourselves sparingly. But we would like to see other aspects of Las Vegas. We ask advice from a taxi driver, and he proposes taking us to the black section. In Nevada, as in California, relations between blacks and whites are less tense than in New York; our intrusion will not seem arrogant. So we put ourselves in the driver's hands. He takes us outside the city. On the outskirts there are brothels; they have been closed for several days by a local initiative – it's probably temporary. Then we follow a muddy, bumpy road that crosses an undeveloped area. The little bar we go into feels like a country inn. They welcome us kindly, especially when N and I say that we are French. But it's already late; the musicians have left. We have only one drink with the driver and the owner and leave again.

This time our guide drives us to an elegant dance hall. Such as it is. He has taken us across the city to the famous 'Last Frontier Hotel'. This hotel is a whole village built of dark, polished logs. The huge hall is decorated with souvenirs from the Old West: there are wagons hanging from the ceiling, wheels propped against the walls, animal skins, stag heads, stuffed bears, revolvers, rifles. But you leave the picturesque behind when you enter the dance hall: it's one of those respectable places where nothing ever happens. The public is strictly bourgeois, provincial and common. Couples dance awkwardly to the sound of watered-down jazz. Many women wear long dresses, salmon pink or pistachio green, with tulle and spangles. The waitress brings us whiskeys. She has a hard, tired face under her dyed blonde hair. In an abrupt tone she says, 'I'd like to know what you're talking about.' Looking at N and me, she adds, 'Because I've seen you in the paper, so I'm interested.' It was a very small photograph with a short paragraph in a Los Angeles paper from a week or so ago. To have noticed it, she must scrupulously and passionately inform herself about everything that's going on in the world. And if she remembers this image, it must have seemed to her the sign of a success whose secret she would like to know. She examines us now with avid and suspicious curiosity. All these mass-manufactured fates are haunted by a thousand dreams of escape, and this woman is probably groping, beyond her ordinary routines, for the keys to the world and to life. The people of America do ask themselves questions after all.

The waitress goes off, bustling and haughty, to attend to other customers. On the dance floor the master of ceremonies claps his hands: 'Is there a lady from Texas in the audience? Would she kindly come up onto the stage?' The women at a neighbouring table begin chortling; after some laughter and whispering, one of them, dressed in pale blue silk, stands up in the middle of the room. The master of ceremonies asks for a woman from Ohio, and one from Illinois. It's the same ritual every time. When ten or so matrons are assembled in a semicircle on the dance floor, they are asked to choose a partner. New chortlings. A blonde in a cyclamen-coloured dress blushingly points to a middle-aged gentleman; the others are encouraged. Now there are ten men swaying with embarrassment under everyone's gaze. The master of ceremonies sends the women back to their places, admitting that they were only decoys to attract the men. The gentlemen don't seem too pleased. Then they're told what is expected of them – they are going to parade in front of the audience like pin-up girls sashaying in their bathing suits on the beach, and the public will confer prizes. The master of ceremonies rolls up his trousers and wiggles, with his hands on his hips, in the classic pose of beauty contests. The gentlemen still don't seem pleased. Paper hats are placed on their heads. They laugh mockingly and hesitate. Finally, a little dark-haired man decides to go ahead. He walks, posing to his advantage, swinging his behind. The whole room explodes in laughter and applause. His neighbour copies him, parading by in turn, and he, too, is applauded. Then all the men are caught up in the game, passionately trying to outdo each other's efforts. They display themselves frenetically, shaking their hips, and the public chokes with laughter. Miss Texas and Miss Wisconsin receive the most applause. They put on a new show, and this time each man is ready to kill the other for the prize. The Texan wins amid clamorous applause. He laughs and bows; as he leaves the stage, he turns and has a word with the master of ceremonies, who nods and asks for silence: 'Ladies and gentlemen, the prizewinner asks me to tell you that he represents the great chocolate manufacturer so-and-so. The best chocolates under the best conditions.'

This scene — which would be inconceivable in New York or Paris — seems to us a high point. Nothing else as fascinating is going to happen here. We go look elsewhere. The hotel is quite far from the centre of town, and when we leave, we find ourselves on a dark and deserted highway. This is where most of the nightclubs are located, but they're scattered over long distances. It's three a.m. and all the clubs are open, so we have an abundant choice. We choose several, one after the other. To finish up, we return to the club we liked most. Nothing has changed. The old ladies continue to play bingo in the breaking dawn. The dealers collect the dollars with a slightly hesitant hand, readily committing those tiny errors that would put a decisive end to their careers at Monte Carlo. The serious players are trying complicated manoeuvres with one-cent chips — two of them leave the table, happily carrying off a pile of dollars. It's fascinating to think that this feverish life never stops. Soon, no doubt, it will slow down a little. Cleaning women will come to wash down the floor, open the windows and chase off a few sleeping drunks. But the clicking of the slot machines will never stop.

11 March

In the mornings at the drugstores in New York I often saw pale young people ask the waitress for a glass of bromo seltzer and eagerly swallow the whitish liquid. I admired this lack of human dignity. This morning, N and I wonder why we should be so restrained. We can count the hours we slept on one hand; as for the whiskeys we drank, two hands are barely enough. It's nine o'clock. In the grocery store we stop in, women are doing their shopping. But the passion for gambling has already overtaken them. Two of them have their arms full of groceries and flowered hats on their heads – good middle-aged housewives. They stop in front of the slot machines and play with a quiet frenzy.

An hour later we're threading our way along the straight, ugly road from Las Vegas to Boulder Dam [now Hoover Dam], the great dyke built across the Colorado River, thanks to which the region is starting to be properly irrigated. We arrived in Las Vegas through a desert, and we leave it through a desert as well – Las Vegas is merely an isolated oasis. Twenty miles away, however, we pass a camp as miserable as the one near Lone Pine where they were extracting salt. Here they are repairing airplanes. Hundreds of planes are lined up on the ground, along with neat and dreary wooden shacks. Blue sky and stones as far as the eye can see. Sun throughout the day. At night the lights of Las Vegas must have the dangerous colours of hope. It's difficult for a young man coming from out here to become president of the United States or a Rockefeller.

In the little town of Boulder City, various signs advise us: before going to the dam, go to the information office. We compliantly follow the arrows. At the office we're given brochures that explain at great length when, why and how the dam was built. In a projection room, a film reconstructs the hard work of fifteen years. As conscientious tourists, we watch it, but we quickly tire of the sight of dump trucks and cranes. We leave to see the dam with our own eyes. The road winds through the red mountains that border the Colorado River. Around a bend we discover the artificial lake, a large sheet of fake blue water that clashes sharply with the pink rocks. This water is as out of place in the desert as a grove of orange trees on a moor, as a fresh stand of birch trees in reddish sand dunes. It's an unreal landscape of the sort painted by the naive painters of the past, and it has the deceptive colours of Gauguin. Even though it's man-made, it's a real lake that we can see with our own eyes. The dam is at the end of the lake. You don't need engineers' explanations to be struck by it; you need only look at the water level in the lake and at the bottom of the narrow canyon – and the nearly vertical drop of this high, convex wall. It extends more than two miles and contains hollowed-out galleries to which one can descend by elevators. A great number of tourists who've parked their cars at the entrance to the bridge are preparing to descend with licensed guides. Should we make the descent? In the photographs, the galleries look like the corridors in the metro; all the numbers that the guide recites are in the brochures. Besides, we'll forget them. M has to be at the studio tomorrow morning, and we're hungry. We turn around.

We go back through Las Vegas and make our way between the pines and cacti. To the south as well as to the north, Las Vegas is more than a hundred miles from the closest town. Without industry, without commerce, in the heart of a land that produces nothing, this town is a triumph of artifice. It exists only to exploit the licentiousness that is the fruitful flip side of its poverty. The plateau is carpeted with a shifting velvet of softly modulated yellows and greens; very small cacti grow squeezed together like prairie grasses. We drive through this solitude as monotonous and varied as the sea, at the foot of great, unspoiled mountains. At the gas station where we stop after two hours on the road, there are no live animals, but – even more bizarre – there is a dusty museum: stuffed animals, buffalo horns, bird skeletons, fish, skulls, human remains, foetuses in jars, and above all snakes, particularly mummified rattlesnakes. All these dead things are in the process of dying a second death, crumbling to dust. What are they doing here? We have a drink and leave.

After a hundred miles there's another gas station, with a bar decorated with colourful posters that have joking inscriptions: 'We do not answer for lost husbands.' 'Alcohol kills, but if you don't drink, you'll die anyway.' What charms us about these places is that they were meant for us. Tourism has a privileged character in America: it doesn't cut you off from the country it's revealing to you; on the contrary, it's a way of entering it. So often in Italy, in Greece, in Spain, I've felt such regret that my condition as a traveller separated me from the inhabitants, who hardly travel at all. In contrast, the average American devotes a great part of his leisure time to driving along the highways. The gas stations, roads, hotels and solitary inns exist only for the tourist and because of the tourist, and these things are profoundly part of America. These landscapes of the Far West we're travelling through exist essentially for the sake of tourists. Almost no one lives here, and their only human significance is that they welcome people who pass through without stopping. By travelling in America, I'm not distanced from it. No dream of rootedness challenges the giddy exhilaration of the car and the wind. We've left Las Vegas with no regrets. The night we spent there had value only because it had no tomorrow, and we drive on without regrets through this desert where a fixed camp, however temporary, is frightening.

Night is falling; it has fallen. A luminous wheel turns in the darkened sky: a hotel sign. A martini and a hearty dinner restore our strength – we were beginning to get tired. But we would like to reach Los Angeles sometime tonight. We've still got four hours on the road. We leave, drive around twenty miles, and the car stops. M doesn't manage to get it started again.

We look around us. Again, we're in luck. There's a house only a few metres away. We push open the gate and follow a path. Cows moo in the night. There's a large herd of cows behind wooden fences. A man in blue overalls is milking them. We ask him if we can call a garage. Amazingly, he has no telephone. But he has a car. He'll drive us to town when he's done with his work, and tomorrow morning we'll have the car repaired. In the meantime we can park it in his garden. We leave him to his cows and push the red car toward the house. It's a large, ugly wooden house with a veranda and cushioned rocking chairs. The farmer finishes his milking and cleans the dairy. He's a Dutchman who has lived here for twenty years. He has almost sole responsibility for this large herd, working from five in the morning until night. It's ten o'clock now, and he's just finished his day. We're ashamed to steal a moment of his rest, but he seems to think nothing of it. It's his duty to drive us to town, just as it was his duty to milk his cows; he does one thing after the other with the same quiet simplicity. He drives the latest-model luxury sedan out of the garage and seems to have exchanged his overalls for a fine suit with gleaming leather shoes. He takes us to town and doesn't leave us until we've found rooms. We sleep in a motel with pretty cabins made of a light wood.

12 March

Early in the morning the garage owner takes us to the Dutchman's farm. He's at work among his cows, and we wave to him from a distance. His wife greets us; she's an elderly woman with fluffy white hair, fragile and distinguished in a light blue suit. She climbs into her own car to go to town and pay her taxes. She's surely never touched a cow with her own hands or set foot in the dairy. Her husband is the one who does all the work.

Apparently, there's not much wrong with the red car. It's repaired quickly and costs nothing because M belongs to an automobile touring club that guarantees free towing and the mechanic's labour in case of a breakdown. The driver pays only for spare parts. Again, we thread our way through the cacti. But we stop at a solitary lunchroom to eat breakfast, and when we're ready to set off again, the car won't start. The owner of the place obligingly gets into his own car and, using a technique I've seen several times in Los Angeles, pushes us for a few miles. This may not be very good for the chassis, but no one minds. Once the car starts, it continues to go forward, but we'll have to be careful not to stop before we reach Los Angeles.

The landscape changes at last. We spiral down through mountains covered with brush, and in the distance we see the ocean. This place is so beautiful that it's been classified as a national park. These parks are sometimes as large as whole provinces [in France] and are under the federal government's protection. 'Monuments' are distinguished from 'parks' by being under the jurisdiction of the state they're in.* Death Valley is a monument. The Grand Canyon is a park. Often, nothing indicates a park's borders to tourists. We descend, and the landscape changes again; neighbourhoods appear, and between these clusters, houses line the road. There are trailer camps, subdivisions, motor courts, bars and taverns. The heat becomes unbearable amid the orange groves. This is the valley of Los Angeles [the San Fernando Valley], where summers are particularly scorching because the mountains block the wind on every side. There are markets and roadside stalls laden with oranges and pineapples, the only colourful, cheerful note in this dusty valley where the sun gives the white of the walls the intensity of torture and the green of the plants the anguish of death throes. The aridity of the deserts is placid and simple, like death, but these yellow grasses, these thirsty palm trees, these stunted, lustreless shrubs are the pitiful efforts of a life that refuses to die and that endures a living death. It's here that the horror begins.

The entrance into Los Angeles is a long, burning agony. In the hills of Hollywood and Beverly Hills a little fresh air revives us. Above the valley the heat is almost always temperate and bearable, even in summer. I greet the house fondly; it's wonderful just to sit and do nothing on the sunny terrace, with the blue sea in the distance and the nearby odour of eucalyptus. But how harsh work must seem in this indolent climate! Now that summer weather

---

* She's got this wrong.

has swept down on the city, I understand why, in Hollywood, ambitions weaken, minds grow dull, and only the immediate seems real. The intense blue of this sky is at once too easy and too hard.

13 March

Even though my personal life is pleasant, I have a better sense than when I arrived of just how depressing the atmosphere of Los Angeles is. We no longer walk much after driving around all morning long. It takes an effort to go down to the city. Yet N courageously takes me to the movies to see *The Best Years of Our Lives* and *Lost Weekend*. At the RKO Studios they gave us a special showing of *The Oxbow Incident*, the classic masterpiece that Americans refused to export because it tells of a lynching that occurred in the last century. Through these three films, I rediscover on screen the elevated trains and pawn shops of New York, the garages, the drugstores, the parking lots of all those cities, large and small, the airplane repair stations we encountered on the outskirts of Las Vegas, the rugged landscapes of Nevada – and this rediscovery is an even greater pleasure than that of seeing the images themselves.

We often have lunch in one of those comfortable restaurants found in every corner of Los Angeles: fake log cabins, fake cottages, fake manor houses whose bargain basement decor is often charming. Or we eat hamburgers and complimentary ice cream in drive-ins, which are large bars that cars park around in a circle; the waitresses bring the meals to the cars. After Las Vegas, the nightlife here seems quite disappointing. In one of the clubs there were men in heavy make-up and silk dresses who sang rather obscene songs half-heartedly to a meagre audience of mostly masculine-looking women. This was sad and old-fashioned. At midnight, when all the bars close, Hollywood seems like a Puritan village, not a huge, noisy, glamorous city.

Today I got a dose of the harshness of Los Angeles. I had an appointment on La Cienega with PC, a specialist on Indian matters whom I wanted to consult about Santa Fe, where I'll soon be going. As a matter of fact, he was about to go touring with his wife, and he showed me the inside of the trailer he had set up. It was a triumph of ingenuity, with a bed, chairs, a stove, a refrigerator – all folding and easily removable. They sometimes camp for weeks in this moving house on the outskirts of Indian villages. I admired it and left in search of a taxi. It was one o'clock and the asphalt was red-hot. No one ventured out into the sun on foot. With my legs and my entire body, I understood what I had only sensed – one does not walk, one cannot walk in Los Angeles, particularly on La Cienega. It is an activity so rare that scarcely a narrow band of sidewalk is reserved for pedestrians alongside the miraculously cool front lawns. Now and then, two women chat at the edge of the grass, or a man waters the lawn, but they stay put and don't move. Only the cars move, hurtling with blinding speed on broad tracks, the living and noisy artery of a large, dozing body. To move along on my feet is as futile and desperate an enterprise as if I'd found myself in the heart of the Sahara. Where are the taxis? I ask a mechanic at a gas station, and he points vaguely toward the horizon. I keep walking. I ask a young man who is nonchalantly mowing a square of green grass. He looks astonished, and right away, with that sense of mutual aid you find everywhere, in all circumstances, from one end of the USA to the other, he asks, 'Would you like me to drive you?' I say no, out of discretion. But I regret it. I drag myself another half-hour along this avenue that vaguely begins all over again, with its identical houses amid their squares of grass and gravel, before I find a yellow cab, whose driver talks to me enthusiastically about Paris.

But more depressing than the tarred roadways, the puritanical nights, and the white billboards that soil the blue sky, it's the people I meet in Los Angeles who make me feel sad – the students, film-makers and journalists. Thursday and Friday morning I give lectures at the two universities, one up in Westwood [University of California at Los Angeles], the other down in Los Angeles [University of Southern California]. The first is rich and luxurious. Spread out on a magnificent hilltop site, it seems less like a workplace than a pleasure garden. The male students lying on the grass read the newspaper and smoke; the female students tan themselves in the sun. The other university is less aristocratic, but the students sprawling on the lawns also seem to be attending a picnic.* Actually, it would be doing them an injustice to think that their lives are too easy; at the University of Southern California they're not all rich and they work at different jobs, often menial ones, to pay for their studies. The French professor who walks me through the large buildings tells me that many of them work in a serious and very scholarly way, but strictly within their specialty. In the French department they speak French very well, but these young people are no more cultured than others elsewhere, because they have no intellectual curiosity. B [a professor in the French department] takes me to the cafeteria. Students and professors jostle each other, greeting each other with a mutual ease that would stupefy our old professors. Even such congenial contact around the café tables would be inconceivable in Paris. This easy camaraderie – the politeness of students and colleagues – makes a professor's life very pleasant, B tells me, and it's also an infinitely broader life than the one he would lead in France. But the students' indifference confounds him. Just this morning President Truman made an important speech in which he explained more imperiously than before that it was necessary to send aid to Greece and Turkey, and, in terms that call to mind recent events, he announced the beginning of an anti-communist crusade. He is supported by the secretary of labour, among others, who asked that the Communist Party be

---

* Her impressions of UCLA (a state university) and USC (a private one) seem confused, or perhaps based solely on their geographical sites.

outlawed on the pretext that it is attempting to overthrow the government, and by the Chamber of Commerce, which regards the Reds as a fifth column and demands that they be outlawed and denied admission to the labour unions. Of course, these ideas have been in the air for a long time; it's also been a while since the fight against the Reds and against workers began and since the intervention in Greece was announced. But the president's speech is still an event of some importance. 'Look at these young people,' B says to me. 'Not one of them is talking about the speech. They're discussing sports news, as usual. They have absolutely no interest in politics.' He adds that this inertia is not exclusive to students. 'This morning I spoke with about ten people,' he tells me. 'Café waiters, tramway employees, newspaper vendors. Only my shoemaker, who's Jewish, said to me, "So? Have you seen Truman's speech?" The others quite simply never thought about it.'

'Of course we don't think,' Elsa Maxwell arrogantly tells me that afternoon. She's a famous journalist who writes well-informed columns for the reactionary press — I mean for the national press. There was an immediate antipathy between me and this American Clement Vautel. A heavy, voluble old lady, her bulk none too well hidden in black satin, she embodies all the faults of America with none of its virtues. She is almost a caricature. She smugly makes me read the malicious stupidities she's sold to her readers on intellectual life in France today. One by one I bring up the authors and books she mentions: 'Have you read it? And this author — have you read him?' No, she's read nothing and is proud of it. 'In America,' she says, 'no one needs to read because no one thinks. Look at me — hundreds of thousands of people think nothing but what I tell them to think in my daily column, and I myself don't think. It's fine this way. People who think are wasting their time — it's anarchy. We don't think, but we don't need to because we have instinct. Look at Truman: it's not that he thinks, but he has instinct. His politics are supremely successful because he has good instincts.' She recites this speech exactly as I have reported it, but with many more words, speaking non-stop for five minutes, barely pausing to take a breath. Then she continues: 'I have good instincts, too, and that's why I've always known how to behave and why I love life. Life is marvellous if you know how to grasp it. The only thing is to know how to find the good side of things — everything has its good side.' In a cowardly way I take advantage of the half-second in which she catches her breath. To test her optimism, I allude to the war, the bombings and the camps. She quickly interrupts me. 'Yes, the deportation camps,' she says vaguely, laughing boldly. 'Everything has a good side if you have good instincts.' And she concludes, 'In France, you think too much.' Naturally, she has chosen to tell me these truths in a joking tone, but this clowning manner, which is *de rigueur* here when you're dealing with important subjects, is still a way of gaining the upper hand. You don't even give your adversary a chance for a serious discussion; you elude criticism by being ironic yourself. All the same, I tripped her up and had the pleasure of seeing that, merely by holding my own, I disconcerted her. She soon regained her composure, though. Her optimism brings her a great deal of money and prestige. Even the sight of Buchenwald would not have shaken such a comfortable faith.

At the parties N and M take me to, it is another story. The atmosphere is congenial over glasses of whiskey. I don't see many stars. Annabella welcomes me to her charming house, where I also meet J.-P. Aumont. Charles Boyer, who is recruited every time a French intellectual stops in Los Angeles and who defends himself with a thousand ruses, doesn't show up. Most of the people I meet are screenwriters. The sad thing about their conversation is their disgust for the current state of American cinema. Everything they say, I already know: censorship allows a glimpse of eroticism, but through a camouflage of nonsense, as in *Gilda*. There are precise and childish rules governing the measurements of brassieres and slips. In the land of pin-up girls they sometimes begin a film all over again because of a plunging neckline. The screenplays are spoiled by a ready optimism that disfigures, for example, the end of *The Best Years of Our Lives*, a film that is otherwise courageously truthful. The taste for easy success leads to endless repetition and tedious clichés. For every successful film, they make twenty imitations. The actors are fixed like marionettes, their roles now defined as rigidly as those of Punch and Judy show characters. Claude Rains, Bette Davis and Humphrey Bogart, who were great actors, are more stereotyped now than Pierrot or Harlequin.

I'm struck by how, in this field – as in all others – these bitter complaints are never accompanied by any hope of change. On the contrary, everyone thinks the situation will get even worse. And it seems to me, in fact, that Hollywood isn't suffering only from an economic crisis or from an overly extreme division of labour and other contingencies; its ills are deeper – America no longer knows how to express itself or dares to admit anything. Neither the living, picturesque tragedies of the streets in New York and Chicago nor the true daily dramas of the 160 million people who inhabit this great land are brought to the screen. Movies show a conventional, papier-mâché America in which only the landscapes and the material details have some reality. From this point of view, *Lost Weekend* (with its images of Third Avenue) and *The Best Years of Our Lives* are almost unique exceptions. Literature hasn't yet been strangled, but the cinema, which is more directly tied to the forces of capitalism, has already learned to hold its tongue. This silence is the silence of death.

Tomorrow morning I'm leaving with N on a bus tour of about three weeks, which will bring me back to New York by way of the South. This evening we're saying our farewells to Los Angeles. A screenwriter friend of M's has organised a party. Another friend, who sells records and is a jazz aficionado, has brought the most interesting things in his collection: old New Orleans blues, funeral songs, Bessie Smith, Louis Armstrong. In the course of the evening we're treated to the living history of jazz. They explain to me the difference between the New Orleans style and the Chicago style. The explanation is never quite the same, but then, of course, it's analytical. How can you put into words the difference between Leonardo da Vinci and Luini, between Vermeer and Pieter de Hooch? Anyway, you'd need a lot of time. When you hear the records, however, the two schools are clearly distinguishable, even to a novice. As we listen, we eat dinner, we chat, we drink. At the end of the meal S arrives; I haven't seen him since Death Valley. Today he is no longer dressed like a cowboy but is wearing a dark suit with a big carnation in his lapel, which makes him look like a village mayor. As soon as he sees us, he hugs N and me passionately: What fun we had! How grateful he is to me for giving him an excuse to see Lone Pine again! I must return to Los Angeles so that we can climb to the top of Mount Whitney. I'm quite pleased — I thought he'd come away with a miserable memory of this excursion. But he'd felt a taste of freedom. That was enough.

I also meet William Wyler, the director of *The Viper* and *The Best Years of Our Lives*. He's Austrian by birth and speaks French very well; he seems much more European than American. He tells me interesting details about the way his last film was made. There's a wonderful moment, among others, in which Dana Andrews is sitting in the cockpit of an old, half-demolished airplane and remembers his past as a pilot. Wyler at first evoked these memories by superimposing images, but then he suppressed the images and kept only the soundtrack that went with them. Finally, he rejected even this device. He asked for a few simple images — the nape of Andrews's neck, a window, the sky — to express both past and present at the same time. And he managed this singularly successful effect, photographing the past in the present.

Afterward I chat with Man Ray, whose films and photographs I have liked so much recently. He, too, seems utterly disgusted with Hollywood, where the poetic investigations that interest him are, of course, impossible. He is married to a young brunette who looks Arabian; she wears black silk trousers with an embroidered jacket and dances magnificently. I think she's danced professionally. There are some other very pretty women. The time passes so quickly that I'm quite taken aback to discover that it's two o'clock in the morning. But N tells me that Hollywood parties are not all like this one: generally, no one talks to anyone else, and everyone drinks while waiting for the right moment to leave.

16 March

In the early light of dawn, Los Angeles is grey and clammy. These streets, which are more crowded during the day than a department store on a sale afternoon, are now deserted, and the car moves through the silence smoothly, without stops and starts. Here night, like daylight, is merely stage scenery. Pull the curtain and the scenery changes – that's all. But suddenly, this hesitant grey light that bathes the city connects it to the surrounding deserts and mountains. It, too, is subject to the cycle of hours and seasons; it rests on the base of the original planet. This is an odd moment. The stage is empty. The night has been swept away, and the day is still in the wings. At the street corners a few silhouettes appear, belonging neither to night nor to day. They raise their thumbs in the classic hitchhiking gesture and seem to be vagabonds. Where did they come from? A car has broken down at a crosswalk; we push it a few hundred metres. In my head, too, everything is grey and foggy. I've hardly slept, and I'm sad to be leaving. When will I return? In the heart of downtown, the bus station is dreary, like a subway stop in the early morning. It's a real station, with a buffet, a cigarette kiosk, newspaper vendors, a luggage room, a ticket office and numbered doors that open onto different platforms alongside the Greyhounds. On the road we often envied the swiftness of these large grey buses, which passed us easily, despite our sixty miles per hour. We thought it would be relaxing to entrust ourselves to them while travelling thousands of miles through the deserts. We settle in the front of the bus with our books and cigarettes, and we feel quite comfortable. M is sad that he can't go with us.

The bus is nearly empty. Americans never use buses for touring, only for transport, and again, only if they are people of modest means. They consider it a slow and tiring way of travelling. This relative slowness will allow me the leisure to really see the regions we cross, and I, at least, find this day most relaxing. I read, I look, and it's a pleasure to give myself over from morning to night to a long novel while the landscape slowly unfolds on the other side of the window. Once outside Los Angeles, we drive across the deserts, but there are a thousand varieties of desert. This one is red and covered with little velvety cacti the colours of autumn. The road goes along one of those ancient trails that the pioneers followed, and we enter Arizona, whose beautiful, adventurous name makes me dream of Mayne Reid and Gustave Aymard. Now and then we encounter a solitary ghost town, and I'm always moved by their mouldy wooden shacks, their old theatres with faded posters. The road climbs easily among the red stones up to a pass, where a vast horizon of arid land is revealed. It seems incredible that entire families with women and children climbed this range in heavy covered wagons.

Every three or four hours we stop at a gas station. You can eat and drink there. Sometimes, as in Nevada, the lunchroom doubles as a strange curiosity shop where live or stuffed coyotes, snakes, animal skins, stones and dried plants are on exhibit. You can find the Los Angeles newspapers nearly everywhere, as well as vividly coloured brochures recounting the adventures of the Far West. These stops are brief celebrations, allowing us to get out of the bus and leave the desert behind. I'm especially enchanted by the jukeboxes, which I hardly noticed in the big city bars; they embody all the splendours of Times Square for the cowboy lost in Arizona. Day and night, neon lights circle around the glass cage where the records are stacked; the record titles are written on the belly of the machine. You press a button corresponding to the piece you've chosen, you slip a nickel into a slot, and a metal claw discerningly seizes one of the black wafers and deposits it on the turntable. For a quarter, you can repeat the operation five times in a row. In the Far West there are few jazz tunes and few Sinatra songs – mostly it's the old nostalgic songs of cowboys and pioneers. I love listening to them. The word 'jukebox' is of somewhat uncertain origin. The Jukes are a famous family in the annals of criminology and psychiatry, because all the men were criminals and all the women prostitutes. The jukebox craze was born in a brothel owned by one of the Juke women, who would have been the first to purchase this great musical buffet.

We left this morning at seven. Night has long since fallen when we arrive at Williams, where we'll take the road to the Grand Canyon. The bus deposits us in the middle of the silent street and goes on its way to Kansas City. We have no time to feel lost: we find a hotel room immediately and go to sleep.

17 March

In California, the exotic is Mexican. Here it takes another form – it's Indian. We noticed yesterday, at the end of the afternoon, that on the billboards we encountered en route there were Indians with feathers in their hair advertising the smoothest cigarettes or the tastiest Quaker Oats. Between the usual stores on the main street, there are curio shops, where they sell moccasins, silver jewellery, real and fake turquoise, feathered headdresses, rugs, blankets, hand-woven Indian jackets and all sorts of trinkets.

At ten a.m. we get on a bus for the Grand Canyon. We drive through dark pine forests on a plateau that seems to stretch unbroken to the horizon. We pass a small airport. You find such places everywhere in America – on the outskirts of cities and villages, as well as in the desert. Here, there are barely a half-dozen little red, blue and yellow planes, which take off and land with the lightness of a bird. They are so small and so brightly painted that they seem like children's toys. We drive two hours across an entirely flat landscape. And suddenly we spot an enormous geological fault – the Grand Canyon.

The site is classified as a national park and cannot be altered. There is a train station, but it's hidden among the trees, fairly far away. There's only one hotel and some distance away, at the edge of the cliff, two small houses, which are curio shops managed by Indians. On the path along the overhang, there are a few benches. That's all. The hotel is built of dark logs and decorated with Indian rugs. Indians in costume, their long black hair tied up in red ribbons, work as porters and room servants. I love the dark and colourful hall, which doesn't isolate me from the landscape but instead offers it to me, invites me to discover it. I approach the precipice and look at the rock walls of rose and red, ochre and yellow, which enclose the Colorado River. Because of that lovely word, 'Colorado', because of images perceived long ago, I've dreamed of this place for years. I don't really know why it seemed so out of reach, but it embodied the mystery of all the landscapes I would never discover, the painful challenge of the impossible. Later, it seemed more accessible to me. People described this hotel to me, this chasm, and I no longer merely dreamed of coming – I wanted to do it. And here I am! I'm quite confused. It happens every time: the shock of reality stuns me. My imagination was incapable of inventing such splendour – specifically, *this* splendour. But what shall I do with all this beauty that's been offered?

It's too late to go down to the river today; the mule trains left in the morning. But there's a coach this afternoon that goes along the road above the gorges. The route winds through pine forests, veers away from the canyon at the most capricious turns, and then rejoins it. At every meeting point there's an overlook where tourists piously stop to view the scenery. At the last bend, which can be considered the end of the actual canyon, there's a round tower. Here, I find the same atmosphere as at Niagara Falls: the most ingenious efforts have been made to transform a natural marvel into a kind of amusement park. The tourist is plied with various attractions. In the great round hall of the ground floor, the panes of glass are arranged so as to reflect the landscape. I don't know exactly how they've been made to absorb the overly intense light; a 'conditioned' vision in filtered, softened colours has been substituted for a direct view, which would be raw and violent. Visitors crowd around these unsilvered mirrors and consciously manipulate them, one after the other. On the terrace another amusement is offered: you put your eye to a slit in a kind of box and see the world upside down. The effect is dizzying – your gaze is swallowed up in a vertical plunge into the sky, and you feel like you're falling. In the room on the first floor, the guide comments on the Indian paintings. We climb the spiral stairway. From the upper terrace, the view is vast. You can see in the distance a vast violet-and-red plateau, colours so decisive that they seem to have been painted by a megalomaniac Gauguin. This is called the Painted Desert. Ten or so telescopes, each oriented differently, offer you whichever bit of landscape you want for a nickel. When we return to the hotel around five o'clock, we're told that at a neighbouring pavilion, also equipped with telescopes, there's an evening lecture and film programme on the Grand Canyon. The tourist is offered every possible artificial means of taming this exuberantly natural spectacle. In the same way, people in America consume 'conditioned' air, frozen meat and fish, homogenised milk, canned fruits and vegetables; they even put artificial chocolate flavour into real chocolate. Americans are nature lovers, but they accept only a nature inspected and corrected by man.

The curio shop across from the hotel is called Hopi House. The Indians who live there wear American-style clothes all day, but around six p.m. they don their usual costume of leather pants, buffalo-skin jackets and feathered headdresses, and perform a number of dances. Actually, it's always the same dance, but it's called, in turn, the dance of the bear, the dance of the eagle, the dance of the buffalo. A small child in a costume hops around with a smile that's already commercial, and the audience melts. I go and sit down a few hundred feet away on one of the benches, and I watch the performance. I wanted to come here, and here I am. I look at the massive rock walls in front of me. Cut in half, like a cookie filled with cream and jam, it's the earth with its superimposed layers, its shells, its fish, its ferns encrusted in the stones of successive ages. You can follow the development of the earthly crust from bottom to top. The sun is setting, bathing the rocks in a reddish light so their minerals liquefy, then evaporate. I look. I understand the reverse mirrors and the moving windows, all those awkward attempts to grasp this scenery and harness it. It's here; I'm here: I'd like something to happen. I look – that's all – and nothing happens. It's the same story every time. Last year, there were waves of apricot-coloured dunes and palm trees touched by moonlight – nothing happened. Sand, stone, moon, setting sun; things are here, and I am here, and we come face-to-face. But in the end, I'm always the one who gets up and goes away.

18 March

The best thing to do is to make the descent to the bottom of the canyon – to no longer just look at it but to touch it and live in it for a day. At the hotel we rent blue slacks, jackets and gloves. The mules are held in a little enclosure under the watch of two cowboys in rather garish costumes. They choose appropriate mounts for us and help us climb into the saddle. About a dozen of us are making this excursion. One of the cowboys takes the lead, and the other brings up the rear. They photograph us lined up at the top of the trail; the photos will be waiting for us when we return. Below us, a train of four mules loaded with hay is descending the path cut into the side of the cliff. We begin our descent. A sign warns us: 'No Dogs Allowed.' The mules walk steadily; at every turn they lurch blindly toward the precipice, then turn away at the last minute and calmly regain their foothold in the middle of the trail. After an hour we get used to it. Now and then a placard tells us what geological period we've reached; fossilised shells and ferns are also noted. There are telephone booths all along the trail, from top to bottom, and you can amuse yourself by calling New York.

We descend very slowly, much more slowly than we would on foot. Little by little the landscape changes, becoming more real. We've left the cliff; we cross a plateau covered with spiny blue clusters. From above, it looked like one uniformly coloured surface, but now it has a thickness, an odour. Every cluster of grass exists individually, and the blues are ever-changing. After three hours we stop at the edge of some flat rocks that plummet straight down to the river. From above, it was only a bright, thin thread; from here, it's a torrent of rushing waters – cool, tempting and dangerous. If I were bathing in it, it would change again. But we are not going that far down. We stop just above, near some running water. The mules eat hay and we eat sandwiches that the cowboys give us. I doze for a moment in the sun. I don't have time, I know, but instead of this caravan on muleback, we might have walked for a long time all alone on these trails, sleeping at the water's edge, following the river night after night on foot or in a canoe. We might have lived intimately with the Grand Canyon. This is an intimacy that must be singularly difficult to establish: the beauty of the site is at first glance all too obvious to everyone. Its rare secrets surely cannot be easily prised out, but I envy those to whom they are revealed. I hoist myself up on my mule, and we ascend the cliff. I could not hope for more. Landscapes give as much of themselves as you give in return.

In the train that takes us to Williams in the evening, I hesitate between feelings of triumph and regret. It's over – I've seen the Grand Canyon. The sparkling hope I nursed so long has changed into the definite past. For all my expectations, I've been given one more memory, only a memory. I think with satisfaction, 'I've done what I wanted to do.' But it's an ambiguous satisfaction, the kind that the wise man feels on his deathbed when he consoles himself for dying by telling himself, 'I've lived a good life.'

19 March

We depart from Williams for Albuquerque at nine o'clock in the morning. We leave the pine forests behind and enter a barren desert whose reds and ochres look like the cliffs of the Grand Canyon – this is the only landscape we see all day. I love this lavish monotony. Too often in Europe the landscapes are merely obvious; often, as well, their variety and gaiety make them rather servile – they too easily reflect one's desires. In contrast, these blind plateaus gently baked by the sun exist, with a splendid stubbornness, for themselves. The bus goes within a few miles of the Petrified Forest. I wished I could have seen it because of the film by that name that I liked so much, but I especially liked it because it introduced me to this countryside, and now I'm here. Its magic is no longer invested in a word, in a place – it's invested in me. As for the fossils, I'm not very interested in them. Now and then there is a shack along the road where they sell petrified wood. Big billboards announce solemnly: 'In 5 miles, petrified wood.' 'In 4 miles, authentic petrified wood.' 'In 3 miles, your last chance for petrified wood.' And indeed, the bus stops. Outside the store's entrance there's a staircase made of great round slices of petrified wood, in which the centuries are concentrically inscribed and mineralised. It looks like some peculiar kind of marble. Inside, they sell trinkets, rings and necklaces made from this ambiguous material. They also sell Coca-Cola, chewing gum and artificially flavoured chocolate, and there are stuffed rattlesnakes, scorpions, trap-door spiders, antlers, skulls and dusty lizards all jumbled together in the window. Behind the gas station, there is a raised platform made of natural wood onto which you can climb 'at your own risk' to contemplate the Painted Desert. From that height it looks as if an enormous palette loaded with reds and violets had been crushed into the earth. The colours do not have the gentle blend of natural tones; they are discrete, as if they came from labelled tubes. The terrain's surface, which is bumpy and crevassed, contrasts sharply in its disorder with the forcefulness of the pinks, mauves and reds. In the distance we can see, already as vague as a memory, the dark hole of the Grand Canyon.

All along the way feathered Indians smile on advertising billboards, their teeth gleaming, and from time to time a real, flesh-and-blood Indian appears out of the blue and stops the bus. He usually gets off after about twenty miles and decisively walks away across the stones, toward some invisible destination. More numerous than gas stations, booths displaying Navajo rugs appear one after another. 'In 3 miles, Navajo rugs.' 'Motorists, don't miss the Navajo rugs 6 miles ahead.' A solitary Indian watches over brightly coloured weavings hanging from wires. Are there enough people in all of America to buy so many rugs? We don't pass a single car on the road.

It's only six o'clock when we arrive in Albuquerque. The beautiful Mexican hotel I'd observed from the train with such pleasure is full. We have only one drink at the bar, where we are served by young women in wide yellow skirts. There are other pretty Mexican- or Indian-style hotels – all full. We end up in a lodging house that smells of insecticide and is cluttered with old furniture and knick-knacks. We're at the top of a wretched staircase; there's no sink, but a bathroom opens onto the hallway. Since we're spending only one night, it doesn't matter. We go down to the main street, which is rather similar to those of other towns. The only things that tell us we've entered New Mexico are the curio shops full of beautiful Indian objects and two movie houses where they play Mexican films and American films dubbed in Spanish.

The people in line outside the door have tanned faces and very black hair. This state belonged to Mexico, and the Spanish occupied it for centuries, so nearly all its residents speak Spanish. There are many people in this part of the country who don't know a word of English.

In a little Mexican restaurant we eat chilli con carne that takes the roof off our mouths; we're tired of eating before we're satisfied. As in San Francisco, we feel rather lost; there must be places where the whiskey tastes of the desert and the music would give us the keys to this land with its rich past – but how to find them? Surely those in the know must appreciate them, because they're not readily available to tourists. I know that egoistic pleasure too well not to feel vexed this evening at belonging to the herd of the excluded. We leaf through a little guide to the town; it mentions only a single nightclub. The waitress knows it and speaks of it approvingly. Let's try it. The taxi makes its way down a broad, brightly lit avenue whose festive air dissipates as we move along. Now there are only garages and dreary houses. We're almost in the country when we stop, but hundreds of cars are parked in front of the gaily lit building. We push the door open: it's a concert hall, and a violinist in formal dress is in the midst of playing a sonata. We're not in the mood for classical music. We wander for a moment along the road, where a cold wind is blowing hard, and we enter the first place we find. The front room is an American bar; above the bottles, a placard reads: 'Off-limits to Indians.' The room at the back is nearly empty. A black band is playing mechanically at the edge of a dance floor where no one is dancing. We sit down in a booth. We've scarcely emptied our glasses of whiskey when the waitress smiles at us: 'Do you want anything else?' 'Okay.' We drink slowly this time, and she hovers around us, finally asking, 'Another?' We decline, but her discontented look makes us uncomfortable; in all these places, you have to drink non-stop. We leave. Outside, the wind is glacial, and we realise we're on a high plateau; once again, the ascent was undetectable. No taxi or bus, but we can go to a gas station and use the phone. We return to the hotel. Just across the street they're showing *Deception* with Claude Rains and Bette Davis. The names attract us and we go in. A disappointing deception.

20 March

It's so easy to travel in this part of the country! The buses are always empty. When you get to the station, there's a cloakroom that's open day and night with little lockers stacked on top of each other like boxes in a columbarium. You pile your bags inside, and when you've slipped twenty-five cents into a slot, you can lock the door. You take the numbered key, which allows you to recover your things without additional expense or delay. We didn't need more than a quarter of an hour to find a room in a good hotel in Santa Fe.

Santa Fe rises at one end of a plateau, at an elevation of six thousand feet. At eleven in the morning, in bright sunshine, there's a marvellous freshness to the air. From the first look, we're seduced by this little Spanish town where you can walk around on foot, the way you can in Europe. And it's not a straggling village but a real city. After New York and Chicago, after Los Angeles and San Francisco, what an enchanting and novel experience! The streets are winding – not a right angle in sight. Most of the houses are built in the Mexican style, with heavy earthen walls and no windows. There are arcades around the central square, as in Madrid or Avila. The big La Fonda Hotel – which is full, alas – resembles an African village with its earthen walls and crenellations. There are few cars; dark-haired people walk in the cool sunshine, speaking Spanish. The women don't have the long legs of the tall mannequins on the coast, but their eyes shine and their bodies are warm and alive. On the square, people chat and stroll around, as they used to do on the *ramblas* in Barcelona. Indians in elegant costumes sell embossed silver and turquoise. The beautiful objects in the curio shops are a bit reminiscent of the street market, but this makes them no less picturesque.

We have only three days to spend here — no time to lose. I consult the list of addresses PC gave me that broiling afternoon on La Cienega. This is how earlier travellers went from town to town across Europe — armed with letters of introduction. First we enter the museum to see Mrs G, who is the administrator. It's a charming provincial museum where, among other things, there's an exhibit of the memorabilia of Kit Carson, the man who fought the Indians so fiercely at the beginning of the nineteenth century. You can see his boots, his hat and his revolvers. A diorama displays the Spanish Trail, which the Spaniards took into New Mexico in the seventeenth century and which wagon trains coming from the East Coast later followed. Still later, it was crossed by stagecoach, and now it's used by Greyhound buses; trains don't climb up this far. Near Mrs G's office I recognise a young French architect, RC, whom I'd met in San Francisco. He, too, travelled by Greyhound and arrived two days ahead of us; here, he has met PB, another Frenchman, who is travelling by Greyhound from New York to Los Angeles. Thanks to this chance meeting, Santa Fe seems singularly accessible. Mrs G has invited us all to a party this afternoon, and N and I are going to lunch at La Fonda with our two countrymen. RC tells me that they were immediately given a warm welcome by people here: there's a whole colony of intellectuals and artists in this town who are attracted by the climate, the site and the proximity of the Indians, but who find local life a little tedious and are eager for any diversion.

The La Fonda is the most beautiful hotel in America, perhaps the most beautiful I've ever seen in my life. Around the patio there are cool galleries paved with mosaics and furnished in the Spanish style. In the lobby an Indian has, for years, been selling fake turquoise and petrified wood to the tourists. This small-time tradesman has a noble face sculpted with deep wrinkles, like an old chief in James Fenimore Cooper. The dining room is Mexican-style in decor, dress and varied cuisine. And here we are, four French people gathered together by chance, fraternising around a table, just as travellers fraternised at roadside inns in old adventure novels. RC is visiting America as an architect, PB as an economist, N and I without any definite point of view, and we compare our impressions with an entirely French volubility. Around us, the Americans eat in silence, as usual, and finish quickly. We're the last to leave our table. We prolong the conversation in the bar and agree to meet that evening.

Meanwhile, N and I continue to explore the town, the only town in America you might explore entirely on foot. We see houses made of wood and earth that are said to be the oldest in the New World, and a church that's one of the oldest Spanish missions. It is simple and spare like a French village church. We climb as far as the little ethnography museum, which is situated on a small hill two miles from the plaza. From there, the view is striking. During these last weeks I've seen so many landscapes, but this one touches me – I'd like to live here. It has the generous spaces and virgin freshness of the mountains and deserts of the Far West, and yet it's as orderly as a landscape in Spain or Italy; its vastness is harmonious and measured. I'd like to return here each evening, and each evening make more discoveries and grow even fonder of it. In the distance there's a smokestack – Los Alamos, where there's an atomic plant in the middle of an industrial city of eighty thousand people. It's in this area, in the heart of these deserts, that the first atomic bomb was invented.

The museum has a fine collection of Indian objects, especially pottery. But N correctly observes that if one is not a professional ethnographer, there's something irritating about contemplating charming objects that don't have the distant beauty of works of art, that are made to be possessed and handled with familiarity, and that one still cannot grasp any better than the cliffs of Colorado. We get tired of this pottery, which is so seductive, so varied, so similar in its diversity, and so useless in its attraction. What can we grasp on this journey? What can we carry away with us that we can truly call our own? What good is it to look at these pots, or at anything for that matter?

We turn our backs on these depressing displays and ask to see the director of the museum. He receives us with all the kindness in the world and points out on a map the major Indian villages we ought to try and see around Santa Fe. He quickly explains to us the Indians' situation on the reservations. (He glosses over the fact, as is his job, that all the fertile lands have been taken away from them under the pretext that they wouldn't know how to cultivate them, and that they've been left with a land of broken stones and no water, where growing crops is nearly impossible.) They earn a living primarily through their weaving, which is no longer done so much by hand but in factories. Apart from a few privileges, they are poor, and their standard of living is very low. But they can vegetate rather peacefully within their designated territories. They have neither the status of American citizens nor the rights that status confers. Furthermore, they have only some of the corresponding responsibilities [of citizenship], and under the paternalistic protection of whites they enjoy a semblance of autonomy. For example, they carry out their own system of justice, according to their own laws, as long as it's only a minor transgression. A murder or a burglary, even within the reservations, is handled by the American justice system. Yet such cases rarely come up, for these are very gentle people. They live a life rather like that of carefully kept animals in a zoo. Yet they have the right to leave this enclosure, to become citizens, and to try their luck in the vastness of America. They do not excite the hostility provoked by blacks; they are the descendants of peoples who never experienced slavery, and certainly, neither their numbers nor their ambitions and their vitality represent a racial threat. But because of their education, or perhaps their temperament, they are poorly equipped for the struggle for life, and when they get away from their usual situation, they rarely achieve a satisfying position.

We come back by car and, failing to find another restaurant

that seems appealing, we dine again at the La Fonda. The musicians languidly play vaguely Spanish tunes. We take the taxi to Canyon Road. It's a small street at the foot of Santa Fe that seems like a cross between Montparnasse and Greenwich Village. Painters, musicians, poets — often all at the same time — live there in little, wooden, artistically furnished houses. Mrs G's house is tiny and charming. The Indians have remained rather impervious to the influence of whites, but the whites who live here have been profoundly susceptible to the Indian influence. They've adopted the taste for vivid colours, for hand weaving, for the lost past — the taste for quality. Whereas the average American knows no other measure of value than the abstract yardstick of money, the aesthetes of Santa Fe suspect subtler gradations, living as they do in intimate contact with these masks, these dolls, all these familiar and magical objects for which there is no monetary equivalent. The influence is palpable first of all in the furnishings; everyone tries to acquire the rarest rugs, blankets and knick-knacks. Acquiring dolls is a delicate matter. They belong to the children, and Indians have a respect for childhood; none of them would deprive his daughter of her favourite toy. For this reason, you have to negotiate a deal with the children themselves, offering them candy, American toys or money, and there are some who resist all temptation. The way these men and women dress is also remarkable; it is a bit reminiscent of the summer residents of St Tropez. In fact, Santa Fe makes me think of St Tropez, with the Indians playing (somewhat more mysteriously) the role of the native fishermen, whose trousers and rain slickers are imitated by tourists. The women are striking in their pallor, the men in their emaciated look. Because of the altitude and climate, many pulmonary patients are sent here, but this look of ill health is certainly also cultivated. If no make-up disguises those white cheeks, it's because these ghostly faces are in fashion. And it's the fashion for the men to let their beards and moustaches grow wild.

Our French friends have come with us, as well, and the other guests assail us with questions. They ask us for the news from Paris, and we talk a lot about Henry Miller, whose trial fascinates his admirers. Santa Fe is not very far from the West Coast and belongs to Miller's zone of influence; here, they seem to think he's America's most important writer. At his instigation they are circulating a petition to free Céline [a French novelist who was a collaborator and wrote several racist, pro-Nazi diatribes] from his Danish prison. They speak to me passionately about the defence argument that Céline composed on his own behalf, in which he claimed that the Germans wrote *Guignol's Band* to destroy him. We try to tell them a little about Céline, but we're outnumbered. Americans have so much mistrust for what the French tell them about the Resistance, the Collaboration, the Occupation and the camps that the petition for Céline will certainly continue to circulate.

Before we part, they give me a sheaf of poems, articles, brochures, catalogues of exhibitions and reviews, all meant to inform me about the literary and artistic production of Canyon Road. And we're invited to another party the following day.

21 March

Again, I'm seized by a sudden inclination, wondering if we should rent a car and tour the Indian villages. We call a neighbouring garage at eight o'clock: we can leave immediately – there's a car at our disposal for the day. The cost is ten dollars for the first seventy miles and fifteen cents per additional mile.

N takes the wheel, and we leave Santa Fe by the Rio Grande road to go up to Taos, where D. H. Lawrence lived, near the most beautiful pueblo in the region. The road rises and falls majestically through the gently sloping mountains. Again, we're moved by the grandeur and beauty of the landscape. I understand why on the licence plates here, instead of the dry word 'California' or 'Nevada', you read the proud slogan

'New Mexico, Land of Dreams'. Signs in red and yellow, the colours of the old Spanish monarchy, tell us the history of the ancient trail, now converted into a magnificent road. It was along this trail that the conquistadors set forth. Here the Indians attacked a wagon train; here Kit Carson fought them; here a famous outlaw was killed. Another inscription informs us that there's a pueblo a mile away. We take a side road. It's the first Indian village we visit – charming but not surprising. Quite the contrary. The little adobe houses, the barns, the stacks of hay and straw, and the enclosures where livestock stamp around in their pens are much closer to what you find in a French hamlet than to Lone Pine or Ojai. What we rediscover here is a rural civilisation thousands of years old, which has persisted in the European countryside as it has in these privileged territories where Americans have not murdered the past. In contrast, American towns have, in our view, the repellent exoticism of things that are too new. We rejoin the road. We follow the Rio Grande. On the riverbank, the wind rustles the flowering fruit trees. After the heavy California summer weather, this dry and tender springtime is delicious.

Built in the middle of a plateau at the foot of a mountain chain, just as Santa Fe is, Taos seems to be a faithful, scaled-down replica of the little capital. Similarly, there's a plaza with arcades that shelter the grocery stores and curio shops, twisting streets, wooden and adobe houses, and flowering gardens with peach and almond trees. In the distance is an identical panorama of treeless plateaus and wooded mountains. The hotel is adobe and crenellated like La Fonda. The interior is decorated with Indian and Mexican objects; suspended from the ceiling are bunches of pine cones in bright colours. Again, this is a place we'd like to stop and live. We have a light meal at the bar and leave for the pueblo. It's hard to believe that three miles from this charming but modern little town, you find a real Indian village. Yet the Taos pueblo is the most characteristic of all the reservations. We're immediately struck by its beauty. On both sides of an open space, which is divided down the middle by a stream, rise two enormous irregular blocks, nearly as high as they are wide, where earthen houses are superimposed and overlap. There are also isolated cabins around the square, but they are crushed by the windowless walls of the citadels with their mud terraces rising in tiers. The dominant colour is dull yellow, but red and purple fabrics are drying on the flat roofs and stand out brightly against the ochre background. We've left the car at the gate to the village, and we read the inscription: it is forbidden for any white person to walk around this enclosure after five in the evening; you have to pay fifty cents if you want to park your car on the square; and you cannot take photographs without the authorisation of the governor, to whom you must introduce yourself on arrival. Arrows point the way to his residence. On the square, near the river, we find a tall Indian draped in a piece of bright pink terry cloth. He declares, 'I am standing in for the governor.' He is negotiating with a group of tourists who are parking their cars; he asks us where we've left ours. He seems unhappy that we've left it outside and claims that that was imprudent of us. We will not prevent him from earning his fifty cents; he's already disappointed enough that we have no photographic equipment. The other tourists have some and are paying a fee. The governor guides them toward the most interesting views.

We separate from the group and cross a little stone wall. The adobe houses resemble French farmhouses; there are haystacks, bales of straw and peaceful cows. The tiny children with straight black hair who are playing along the paths have the look of flourishing, free animals. We come across a group of schoolchildren, ten to twelve years old, dressed in the American style; the boys and girls are beautiful, with lively, mischievous eyes. We'd like to know if they will come to terms with the fate reserved for them in this pueblo, which is artificially cut off from the world, yet beleaguered by modern civilisation. In the schools they're taught their traditions and the fine old Indian crafts – painting, pottery, weaving – but they're also initiated into the language and the life of the larger country that shelters them. It's difficult to make out what's going on behind those young brown foreheads.

We sit down on the edge of a well from which two long poles protrude. Some women wave their arms in our direction and shake their heads with disapproval. One of them approaches: 'Go away. The governor will expel you.' We stand up and discover that the well is a kiva, a supremely sacred place where no European, even the Indians' best friend, has the right to go. As we hurry away, the governor comes running, his terrycloth cape flying behind him. We have violated the boundaries assigned to whites. He leads us back toward the little stone wall, where a fat Indian in braids is sitting, fussing over a watercolour. He asks us, 'Aren't you afraid of walking all alone? Indian women would be afraid!' We ask, 'Of what?' He laughs: 'They would be afraid.' He takes us into his house, which is light and cool, and shows us paintings in which the traditions of Indian art have been purposely forgotten. We flee without buying anything and cross the river. As we're walking back up a winding street, a man from the top of a terrace signals to us to retrace our steps. Here comes the governor again, running toward us and out of breath. It's forbidden to walk here, too. It seems that only the large, open plaza is authorised. I've heard that in many villages the Indians surround themselves with prohibitions to preserve the mystery and allure that are their chief economic resources, as they largely live on money extracted from tourists. But perhaps they sincerely respect certain taboos. The most experienced Indian observers here say that no one can claim to know them. Whether they're commercial ruses or religious prejudices, all these restrictions annoy us. To be polite, we visit a house where they're selling pottery, necklaces of colored beads, and dreadful paintings. We buy a few postcards and leave. What's needed is to be invisible and come back after five p.m., when the pueblo returns to its solitude and life there is simple and ordinary, the way it is in a French village. But even its simultaneously commercial and primitive welcome could not spoil its beauty for us.

On the way back we make a detour to see San Ildefonso. Its architecture is even simpler: houses with flat roofs grouped around two squares. In every pueblo there are two squares, one facing east, the other west, with a kiva in the centre. What surprises us here is that, although we can't figure out why, all the doors of the houses are closed, and not a soul is outside. It looks like a village struck by the plague or some secret curse.

On our return we go and drink tea, or rather whiskey and soda, in one of the Canyon Road studios. We're told in hushed tones that there will certainly be dances next Sunday at one of the neighbouring pueblos; they still don't know where or when. The Indians are very secretive because they don't like whites to come to their ceremonies, but those in the know make it their business to be informed when the time comes. Nearly all the people of Canyon Road have something to do with archaeology, ethnography or anthropology, or they are affiliated with some society for the protection of the Indians. None of them will miss the dances, and they beg us to stay until Monday to see them. They touch on many subjects, but I notice that they don't devote a minute to politics. We wait until we're at the La Fonda among our compatriots to comment on the news of the day: the government has demanded that the miners' strike end by 31 March, and John Lewis has accepted this ultimatum. Four leaders have been identified as communists at the big Allis strike that broke out in the automobile factories. I wonder if the aesthetes of Santa Fe sometimes look at the smoke rising from Los Alamos.

22 March

The workers demand that the frequently rather long period of time between their arrival at the factory and their entrance into the shops be counted as work time. The Senate votes against this proposal. Yet Truman decides on a purge of government employees: if they're 'disloyal' – meaning, in essence, if they are sympathetic to communism – they're fired. People are beginning to draw up blacklists. To be sure, the civil servants thanked in this way are free to seek work elsewhere; whether they'll find any is highly doubtful.

RC left this morning for New York. In the afternoon PB, N and I go for a drive. The road follows the edge of the plateau on which Santa Fe is built; beyond the bushes and little pine trees, the desert is as infinite as the sea. After forty miles we pass through an American-style village whose population is Spanish, and soon one of those now-familiar red-and-yellow signs points the way to an old, abandoned pueblo. It stands atop a grassy hill, dominating a vast horizon that is surrounded by wooded, gently sloping mountains. We find the remains of adobe houses surrounding a large reddish ruin – perhaps a fortress or a block of houses like those we saw at Taos, or perhaps a church built by the Spaniards, who planted a cross at the summit of the hill. Whether it's a fortress or church, what is moving is the affirmation of a human presence in the heart of these solitary mountains. Deserted but harmonious, they still, in all their desolation, seem made to welcome man, like those sites where the old Carthusians settled – sites whose savagery spoke to the soul. This is a place that makes us muse about the mysterious marriage binding our species to this planet. We muse, too, about those men who raised the cross on the ruins of villages that they themselves destroyed. How can we judge those extravagant and atrocious escapades? We can judge an act only by actively taking sides for or against it, and this past is over; we cannot join it to the present with feelings of pride or regret. That very silence in my heart makes me feel uneasy when I look at the red earthen walls and the cross.

On the way back we stop at the battlefield of Glorieta. This is a site noteworthy for the different layers of memory superimposed on it. To the left of the road, a placard points out old Indian wells. A deliberate barricade made of an iron trellis, climbing plants and grey canvas surrounds it with the mystery of carnival booths. After we pay fifty cents each, the guard opens the door for us, and we drink a glass of water that's several thousand years old. This well is the oldest in all America, made of large stones stacked on top of each other, and it's very deep. Facing it, at the foot of a rocky outcropping that dominates the gorge where the road winds its way, there's a wooden shack. This was first a fort where the Spaniards entrenched themselves against the Indians. We can easily imagine the lookouts hidden among the rocks and surveying the narrow gorges. Later, it was here that the great battle of Glorieta was waged during the Civil War, when New Mexico and Texas faced off and the southerners' spirit was broken. Although New Mexico is among the southernmost states, it did not have plantations or slaves, and its interests, like those of California, were tied to the Yankees. The Texans, who tried to push through toward the north, were defeated, at the price of a terrible slaughter – two to three hundred died on each side. The bodies remained unburied for several days and were finally interred without identification; no one even knows the location of their graves. The mumbling old man who serves as our guide claims that this battle turned the tide of victory away from the Rebels. He leads us on a rocky path that climbs to the summit of the outcropping. Again, it is a site from the movies or from the illustrated weeklies: I've seen images of a flag planted among these blocks of stone and men in blue uniforms falling heroically on this soil. In a shrub perched at the top of a rise, a dozen invisible bells tinkle in the wind. What is their meaning? We concoct a number of unconvincing hypotheses and end by asking the guard. 'I'm the one who hung them there,' he says. 'Why?' 'So they would ring.'

We come down. At the foot of the hill there are old cannons, cannonballs, fragments of wagons and stagecoaches, wheels, boards and scraps of iron. We enter a shack where we find all the paraphernalia of general stores in the Far West: an enormous boa constrictor wrapped around the ceiling beams, the skins of wild beasts, stuffed animals, skulls, skeletons, foetuses, leather belts, saddles, bridles, cowbells, revolvers, rifles, old mailbags and the remains of a stagecoach stripped by outlaws. It's here, they say, that the Robin Hood of New Mexico, Billy the Kid, the most famous outlaw, lived. Born in New York in 1850, he was twelve years old when he killed a man in New Mexico who had insulted his mother. He went to Arizona, then to Mexico and Texas, took part in the Lincoln County [cattle] war on the side of the Murphy faction, was taken prisoner, escaped his jailers in a sensational breakout, and then, while paying a visit to his sweetheart in Fort Sumner, was killed in the night by Sheriff Pat Garrett. Legend has made him a hero who killed twenty-one men in twenty-one years, who distributed the property of the rich to the poor, avenged injustice, and, with a price on his head, danced gaily in Gallisteo Street in Santa Fe. He's considered the most famous desperado of the South-West. The walls are covered with his photos, with newspaper clippings telling of his heinous crimes and posters promising rewards to anyone who will bring him in, dead or alive. The guard shows us his pistols, his daggers and his boots. All this memorabilia is rather dizzying; what's assembled here are all the props for a Western of the golden age. Even after an hour we hadn't completed the tour. And as we follow the legendary Spanish Trail that takes us back to Santa Fe, Indians and Spaniards, Rebels and Confederates [or, rather, Yankees], bad guys and sheriffs dance wildly in our heads.

We have dinner at Mrs G's. She makes me a gift then and there of a beautiful book on Santa Fe and an old silver bracelet with real turquoise, the kind you don't find in the tourist shops. Again, one of those acts of American generosity that make me feel ashamed. We cross some open land and arrive at a small cottage that's all lit up. The painter W, who is also a poet and writer, is giving a party. The house has only two small rooms: the studio serves as a cloakroom, and in the tiny living space there are already around ten people crammed together. The smell of oil paint mingles with the odour of tobacco and whiskey. From ten until two in the morning, the door to the house opens every two minutes with the arrival of new guests – it's like a comedy routine. I'm reminded of that minuscule cabin in the Marx Brothers' *Night at the Opera* where everyone crowds in. The men make every effort to re-create the old Café du Dôme [a Left Bank café frequented by international expatriates as well as French existentialists] from before the war; they wear beards, brightly coloured shirts, espadrilles and long scarves. The women seem to have escaped from the macabre tales of Edgar Allan Poe: chalk-coloured powder accentuates their pallor; their hair falls onto their shoulders in weeping sheets; their eyes are startling. They are vampire wives who will climb back into their coffins at dawn. Yet their dresses have a touch of Mardi Gras about them – although often poorly cut, they're tailored from marvellous fabrics that come from the Indian reservations or from Guatemala or Mexico. And the women wear savage and splendid jewellery: heavy silver brooches, bracelets studded with jade and turquoise, and worked leather. One of the women is quite pregnant under a green-and-red Mexican dress; another is hunchbacked and nearly a dwarf; and there's also a sad-looking, paralysed young man in a wheelchair pushed by a toothless old black man. As there is no race or class prejudice here, the black domestic is invited to sit with us; he seems quite bored. Whiskey. Vodka. A painter plays gypsy tunes on the violin while a young poet plays cowboy songs on a guitar. The guitarist holds his drink pretty well, but the violinist sways more and more dangerously as the night goes on, and the sharp notes become completely discordant. From time to time, a prostrate body is carried out to the cloakroom, which also serves as the infirmary. It's always a masculine body. The women laugh hysterically but stay on their feet. The violinist drops his violin, and the guitarist, who plays very pleasantly, tries a jazz tune. The toothless old black man suddenly wakes up and begins to sing softly, tapping his feet, clapping his hands to indicate the rhythm – faster, faster! The white man's playing isn't 'hot' enough, and the black man puts his hand on his arm and rolls his eyes beseechingly – faster! The guitarist disengages himself with some irritation, and the black man looks around him, but the faces are no longer so friendly – he's making too much noise; he's calling too much attention to himself. He goes back to sit in his corner, and suddenly he's all alone. People begin to leave. The bottles are empty; dawn is breaking. The music stops. They carry out the drunks, and everyone goes off to sleep.

23 March

We receive a call in the morning: there will be dances this afternoon at San Ildefonso; someone will come to pick us up. While waiting, we wander around Santa Fe, where the stores are closed. Not a bar or a restaurant is open, even in the hotels. It's Sunday, and the Catholic clergy who rule this Spanish town are stricter than the Protestant sects. With some difficulty, we find a drugstore where we can have lunch.

The elderly women who pick us up are not at all the 'Canyon Road' sort; they're like classic moms. They are part of the Society for the Protection of Indians (this is not the exact name of the association, but that's the idea), and they speak in the same gentle tones about the noble savages and about poor Pétain. They drive us to the village of San Ildefonso, which was so deserted two days before. Today, the place is crawling with people. There are no tourists from Santa Fe, but the whole Canyon Road crowd is gathered there. There are several women in men's clothing, flaunting their mannish looks; even those who do not deny their sex wear slacks and sandals or flat shoes. The men wear shirts with large checks and bright red or blue trousers. One has created a costume for himself out of yellow-and-green parachute material and looks like he's masquerading as a tree. All the children seem equally disguised, though it's unclear as what. The artists have brought their drawing pads and are sketching. Others have cameras, and the Indian governor makes a profitable collection. He is the only one soberly dressed, in a classic American suit. He's not the village religious chief but only the administrator; he shows us his house, where he sells terracotta wares and postcards. We see other interiors furnished with every American comfort. The studios on Canyon Road are more exotic. Among various modern knick-knacks, there's a photograph of a smiling young Indian: he's wearing a GI uniform; he fought the Japanese during the war.

The dances, which had already begun this morning, start again. Actually, there's only a single dance, which is repeated throughout the entire day. Addressed to the powers of fertility, it summons the rain and good harvests; it is performed by women who have been chosen to dress in masculine garb. Personally, I wouldn't attribute any gender to this costume: the arms, feet, neck and face are plastered white; the cheeks are streaked with red; the body is stuffed into a leather jacket and leather pants covered with ferns; and a long foxtail beats against the dancers' legs. No one is able to explain the symbolism of the various accessories. Sixteen women are lined up single file by age, from the youngest, who's three or four years old, to the matriarch, who's easily sixty, and then back down again in stages to a tiny little girl. Without moving from their assigned places, they all stamp the ground together and sing a refrain, which they repeat again and again without pausing. The rhythm is monotonous but very fast, and this exercise seems exhausting. When they finish, they form a ninety-degree angle and begin again. They dance this way four times in each corner of the square, honouring the four key directions, but between two series, they go into one of the houses to rest. They exert themselves with the passion of some deep faith; if this were not so, they would drop with fatigue. The natives watch them approvingly and encourage them with cries and gestures. The village elder seems especially enchanted. He's a fat man in blue overalls and a large straw hat, who would look like a fisherman from Marseilles if not for his two black braids. According to his age and rank, he ought to be the high priest of his tribe, but he is refused this title because he insists on getting drunk. His eyes are pink with alcohol while he hoots at the dancers, making everyone laugh.

We return by a stony trail that follows a dry riverbed, and the road curves around a big flat rock, a mesa, which towers above the plain. Several times a year the Indians gather here for sacrifices and secret ceremonies; it is the most sacred of all their places. We drive through Santa Clara [another pueblo]. From a distance the inhabitants see the dust raised by our car, and when we arrive at the square, there are half a dozen squatting women undoing their bales of merchandise. On blankets, they spread out platters, pots and terracotta animals. We buy a few of their objects. On the way back the elderly women assert that despite the inscription we saw in an Albuquerque bar, 'Off-limits to Indians', there is no racial discrimination against them. I suppose that in practice it amounts to the same thing. The whites go only out of curiosity to the reservations, which the Indians leave only for brief commercial visits to the neighbouring towns. Because they have no social power, one can allow oneself to respect them as the descendants of a conquered but once great race that never submitted to slavery. So it is true that the Indians are viewed with a benign eye and that having Indian blood in your veins is not a taint. But it is also true that this benevolence and tolerance do not carry any concrete benefits.

24 March

All the deserts we've crossed since Los Angeles were like the green countryside of Normandy compared to the one we're driving through today, from eight o'clock in the morning until night. For twelve hours the road follows a straight line that neither breaks nor curves but runs indefinitely into the heart of a stony plateau. The only interruption is a sharply pointed cactus as tall as a palm tree. The bus is nearly empty. Even the gas stations contribute to the monotony of the landscape; we know all the songs on the jukeboxes by heart, and the stuffed animals are no longer amusing. We read. But when evening falls, reading becomes impossible, since there's no light inside the buses. We're relieved to see the lights of Pecos [in Texas]. Some passengers are already settled for the night, their heads on their pillows; we wouldn't like to be in their places.

Even after seeing the Far West, when we disembark in the middle of Pecos, it seems to us that our peaceful Greyhound is really a time machine: here we are, transported a hundred years into the past. It's the village of the old Westerns. In the middle of the desert, close to the Mexican border, two streets lined with wooden shacks cross at right angles. We push open the door of a lunchroom: there are only men sitting at the counter and around the tables – cowboys with tanned faces under their big, light hats. They wear luxurious leather pants and rough leather boots cut with red or green designs, and they're all young, manly and handsome, like Tom Mix. Once again, we think we're in the movies, while we eat ham with pineapple.

The great attraction in Pecos is the house of Judge Roy Bean, 'the law west of the Pecos'. He is the most famous of those judges who specialised in misdemeanours punishable by fines and who fleeced their fellow citizens. After an eventful career as an adventurer, he became a bartender, following the construction crews of the Southern Pacific Railway. He set himself up at Langtry, a place where the two ends of the railroad line were joined in 1883, and he was entrusted with enforcing the law among the eight thousand railroad workers. Later, he settled in Pecos, where he became a legendary figure. He was at once judge, jury and executioner. He knew only one law book – the *Revised Statutes of Texas for 1876* – and he observed it in his own way. He invented ingenious punishments. He had a bear named Bruno, and when he caught a drunk, he would attach the bear and the delinquent to the same chain, sometimes for an entire day. But ordinarily he levelled fines, and he handled his revolver in such a way that his decisions were always respected. It's said that one day on the road he found a corpse with a well-padded wallet; the dead man was also carrying a revolver. Roy sentenced him for illegally bearing arms and put the wallet in his pocket. He died respected in 1903, after twenty years in service. He'd never stopped bartending, and it was in his saloon that he meted out justice. I've often seen the popular image on posters – Roy Bean seated in front of a beer barrel on the porch of his house. Today, I see the house itself with its porch and beer barrel. This wooden structure is a historical monument. Inside are the offices of the judge who presides today in Pecos and a large empty room that serves as a kind of museum. The walls are hung with revolvers that belonged to Roy, and there are newspaper clippings about him. The papers are yellowed and the weapons rusty. But in the remote corners of New Mexico and Texas, there is more than one sheriff who continues in the tradition of Roy Bean and who imposes his law and his terror on his fellow citizens.

25 March

Twelve hours by bus through deserts and cacti. You'd think America is one vast desert, scattered with a few prefabricated houses and littered with a truckload of canned goods. We go [farther] into Texas, where the cacti are no different from the cacti in New Mexico. It's night when we reach San Antonio's outskirts, which stretch for miles and miles so that you never seem to arrive. Liquor stores glitter in the night – so many that we're quite astonished. Do they drink more in Texas than in other states?

In the middle of the desert, the state line was invisible. But when we leave the bus, we understand that we've crossed a frontier. On the doors of the restrooms, we read on one side, 'White

Ladies' and 'White Gentlemen', and on the other, 'Colored Women' and 'Colored Men'. There are only whites in the large hall that serves as a waiting room; blacks are parked in a wretched little alcove. Next to the spacious restaurant reserved for whites, the minuscule lunchroom for 'colored people' can accommodate only four customers at a time. This is the first time we see with our own eyes the segregation that we've heard so much about. And although we'd been warned, something fell onto our shoulders that would not lift all through the South; it was our own skin that became heavy and stifling, its colour making us burn.

26 March

Separated from Mexico by a war, Texas had eight years of independence before becoming part of the United States. From this past, it has preserved a lively sense of its autonomy. Texans are proud to be Texans. They have the reputation of being the greatest braggarts in America, and they even brag about this. In their vast territory they've gathered all the world capitals: Paris, London, Madrid, Toledo, St Petersburg, Moscow . . . and some can even be found more than once. A type of giant rabbit with thick fur, called a jackrabbit, swarms in the bush, and they've made him their emblem. You see plush jackrabbits as big as calves used as advertisements in all the stores in San Antonio.

San Antonio is an old town [relatively] close to the Mexican border. It's lively and modern in the American way, with large stores and skyscrapers, but it also has the joyful colours of Mexico and remnants of old Spain. The heart of town is the charming Alamo Square: in a garden of blossoming roses stand an old library and an old Spanish chapel, which has been transformed into a museum. Ancient stones surrounded by flowers – here is something America hasn't yet offered me. In the vaulted chapel are the glorious relics of the period of Texan independence: cannons, revolvers, portraits of the heroes of the independence movement and a facsimile of the constitution.

It was in this old Spanish mission, which includes a chapel, a cloister and a convent protected by thick walls, that 180 Texans held out for thirteen days against 4,000 Mexicans commanded by General Antonio López de Santa Anna. When the mission was taken, there were only five survivors, and the general had them executed. But General Sam Houston took revenge at San Jacinto. With the cry of 'Remember the Alamo', the Texans were victorious, took Santa Anna prisoner, and formed a republic with Houston as president. Their flag bore a star that indicated their desire to become part of the United States, which they did in February 1845.

A little river winds through town and meanders around it. Its lower banks are lush gardens. They are joined by rustic bridges, under which lovers embrace, and over which are superimposed large city bridges carrying the streets and their traffic. An open-air theatre is set into a curve of the river, and an old house built above around a patio serves as the wings, backstage and actors' dressing rooms. The seats for the audience rise in tiers from below, while the semicircular stage is on the other side of the water. The street on which this theatre is located is lined with old wood and adobe houses painted pink and bright green. A little farther on, at the end of an eccentric and abandoned square, stands the former governor's palace. It's protected by high, grey, windowless walls. Once through the gate, however, you find yourself transported into a Spanish interior from the sixteenth century. The whitewashed rooms and the drawing rooms with their beamed ceilings are as ascetic as a monastery; the furniture is valuable, although in a crude style. No window looks onto the street, but only onto the large garden enclosed by high walls. There are stone benches under the flowering trees, an old well and a cloister on one side. The palace has a Castilian sobriety, but the red and violet bushes, the languor of the climbing vines and the perfumed trees evoke Andalusia. America is far away.

America is just next door, but she's gay under the blue sky amid the laughter of a black-haired, brown-skinned population. The curio shops break the monotony of the drugstores and the dollar shops. The most amazing thing is the famous shop called the Shop of Ten Thousand Horns. This is an extraordinary apotheosis of all the tourist shops of the Far West. The store's walls, its ceiling and its extension in the large entry hall are a forest of horns: stags, buffalo, reindeer, antelope, gazelle, fallow deer, wild goats, bulls, bison, elk, chamois – all kinds of hoofed animals have been stripped of their horns. These trophies seem both proud and humbled, like the worn flags hanging in the hall of l'Hôtel des Invalides [the French War Memorial Museum in Paris]. In the shadow of this foliage are all the beautiful Mexican objects I saw in Los Angeles, the Indian jewellery and trinkets from Santa Fe, the leather boots and belts of the Far West. It's as though a mad burglar had pillaged a museum and dumped his bag in the display window: stones and shells, scorpions, snakes, skeletons and foetuses. Then another, more discriminating burglar must have robbed an ethnographic museum: you can buy a whole cowboy outfit, an Indian costume, an Eskimo outfit or Mexican clothing. There's always something else to look at, and our heads begin to spin. At the back you can drink at a bar and eat at little tables. We order whiskey. The waitress glowers at us. 'This here is Texas!' she says proudly. And she serves us beer.

We see some pretty Mexican restaurants near the water. We choose one that attracts us with its white walls, its canary-yellow roof and its green shutters. The interior is gaily painted in yellow and green, with a red-tiled floor. It's cool inside, as though we were in the woods on a beautiful summer day. We're served by authentic Mexicans, who, despite our appeals, bring us tough steaks. They sprinkle them with spicy sauces, but this doesn't make them more tender.

Taxis are a costly luxury in California; here, the fare is negligible. We hire one for several hours. The driver takes us through some of the residential neighbourhoods. Many of these dwellings are very old, and their coloured wooden walls look dusty and mouldy, but the architecture is extravagant. I love their columns, the romantic verandas, the porches with rocking chairs and a sort of swing whose back is strewn with comfortable cushions. What an indolent, self-absorbed, civilised existence! Here, intact, is the house where O. Henry lived and wrote. Now we cross a park and vacant lots. We pass a cart covered with bunches of golden bananas. Children with beautiful black eyes throng around, urging us to buy some. For a few cents, they fill a large bag for us. The bananas are very small, soft and deliciously fragrant – not hothouse produce but real fruit grown in the earth.

The taxi stops in front of a Spanish mission. It's a church built in a beautiful baroque style, set in an overgrown garden. More vividly than at the chapel in the Alamo – after seeing so many buildings made of wood, earth, brick and adobe – I savour the surprise of touching real stone and contemplating a building that's not only picturesque but also beautiful. We go on to another mission a few miles from here that is even more striking. The pure stone church stands at the edge of a flowering meadow, surrounded on three sides by long buildings scarcely taller than a man. These were once the missionaries' cells. On the fourth side is a neglected and charming park. A path descends into a valley, climbs to a terrace, and crosses over a small bridge. On the river there's an old mill, with its wooden walls and even its wheel intact, as well as the millstones and the mechanism of winches and pulleys. At a turn in the path there's an unexpected streetlamp and everywhere a riot of flowers. In the mill, in the meadow and in front of the church, you'd think you were far from America. But when we cross the threshold of the church, we jump. A loud nasal voice resounds through the solitary vaults and begins to tell us the history of the mission. A bishop is speaking: his voice has been recorded, and an ingenious system makes the record start when a visitor opens the door. There are few things to see inside the chapel, and this voice sends us fleeing. In the distance we still hear it pursuing its insistent story in the empty church.

There are two other missions on the road, which is called Mission Road for this reason. But the driver declares that they are less interesting. He takes us to the other side of town to see a garden that was called 'Japanese' before the war and has now become 'Chinese'. We cross a large park, and the car climbs up a rise that is linked by a wooden passageway to an oriental-style pavilion. From this height we glimpse in the distance a small cluster of skyscrapers, and at our feet there's a rock garden with tiny ponds where goldfish swim, as well as the kind of bridges you see on lacquered screens, and dwarf trees that seem painted by hand. The whole is as charming as it is unexpected here and absurd. Farther on in the woods, there's a zoo. The cranes and flamingos are so brightly coloured that they, too, look like they have escaped from a children's book; these sleek, well-fed beasts did not suffer from the war. Ignoring the ethnographic museum and the museum of natural history, we go and take a quick look at the snake house. In the middle of a pit surrounded by a low wall, twenty kinds of snakes are coiled up or indolently slithering along. Corpses of chicks and baby birds litter the cement. The guard who strolls around nonchalantly in this poisonous air confirms that these snakes have not been incapacitated: their fangs are venomous, but it seems they never bite. To illustrate, he teases the rattlesnakes, who angrily shake the rattles on their tails but seem satisfied with this demonstration.

We return to our hotel on Alamo Square, and we leave on foot to explore the neighbourhoods behind it. Suddenly, without realising it, we find ourselves in the black section. Peeling wooden houses stand amid lots overgrown with weeds and crossed by cracked alleyways. In two spots, black ashes and half-burned boards tell us of recent fires. The streets are empty. Here and there we see an old black man or a fat matron swinging on one of those moving veranda chairs. Children are gathered around a kiosk selling Coca-Cola, bananas and candy. A voice from an invisible phonograph drifts out and is lost among the weeds, the ashes and the silence. Two or three blacks pass by without acknowledging us.

On the big commercial street in the centre of town they're showing Walt Disney's *Song of the South*. The white public smiles smugly at the image of Uncle Remus, the old black retainer with the innocent, childlike soul. In fact, the author of the charming tales in which Brer Rabbit pits himself against the fox's wiles is a red-headed white man. The animated drawings inserted into the film do not compensate for the irritation and disgust provoked by this insipid story in Technicolor: the greens and russets of the idyllic countryside hardly conceal the hatred, injustice and fear in which they are rooted.

This evening we will not eat at a Mexican restaurant. We choose a kind of rustic, ranch-style place along the river. There's a band, and probably people do dance when there are people – the room is nearly empty. Two couples dine at a neighbouring table, and I note that they put an enormous bottle of whiskey on the table. They order sodas, and in the course of the meal, they easily empty the bottle. Now I understand the waitress's arrogance this morning: 'This is Texas!' – meaning that you must buy your whiskey in one of those numerous liquor stores we noticed upon entering San Antonio. Indeed, you can even buy it here – it's only the sale of individual glasses that's prohibited. All the customers order their bottles when they sit down for dinner. 'This is Texas!'

It seems that a few months earlier, a cow was tied to one of the gates all evening; at midnight they let it loose on the dance floor, and some cowboys had to lasso it. But now the place has nothing as lively to offer, so we leave. We stroll in the festive streets, and we dream – as we did in Albuquerque, where we didn't find it, or where perhaps it didn't exist – of that privileged place, off-limits to the naive tourist, about which connoisseurs will tell you: 'Here, this is the real Madrid, this is the authentic Italy, this is the essence of the Orient.' But these places are distinguished by their absence of local colour, by an apparent banality: it's impossible to discover these places without a knowledgeable guide. Does such a place exist in San Antonio? It isn't certain that this town, at once reminiscent of New York, Mexico, Santa Fe and New Orleans, possesses a personal soul to which one might find the key. In any case, we don't find it. We end up in a dull nightclub, decorated with palm trees and braided straw. Two black boys about ten or twelve years old are tap-dancing in high style. The customers, sitting at tables with hefty bottles of whiskey, toss them nickels as they dance. At midnight, as in Los Angeles, all the bars and cabarets close and the town goes to sleep.

27 March

In the afternoon we take the bus to Houston. We finally leave the deserts and enter the South I've so wanted to know. Here, we find huge fields of black earth where, in a few months, the fleecy cotton – so hard on the hands of the pickers – will flower. There are lavish trees on which I see that strange parasite, Spanish moss, hanging from the branches like soft stalactites. The hard, pure ground of the deserts has soaked up water, and now the earth speaks a suspect language of growth and fertility. Plants and blights, harvests and parasites – there are no longer just naked stones without promises or lies; the clay and loam have become carriers of hope as well as despair. This is the land of wealth and misery, a luxuriant and cruel human land. Here and there, amid fecund solitude, stands a hut or a group of dilapidated huts; on the threshold, sometimes black faces, sometimes white ones – the poor whites of the South whose wretched lives are described by Steinbeck and Caldwell. And indeed, while these dwellings that I won't enter pass before our eyes, I read the fascinating report written by a North American who lived for a few months with the cotton slaves. This is Agee's book *Let Us Now Praise Famous*

Men. It's had great critical acclaim but no commercial success. He describes in minute detail how the inhabitants of these hovels live, eat, dress and work. The photographs [by Walker Evans] that illustrate the work help us understand: rickety chairs, mattresses swarming with lice, open roofs, ragged cotton dresses – no French peasant suffers such lamentable conditions. The faces are emaciated; even the children seem old. I read and I look without making up my mind whether the book is going to explain the landscape to me or whether these sights are merely concrete illustrations of the heart-rending document I'm studying.

This book is devoted to whites. But the vast majority of cotton workers are blacks, and the system to which they submit is a legacy of slavery. It's a strange paradox – and to American eyes even a scandal – this survival of a paternalistic economy in the midst of a modern capitalist society. There are very few small- or medium-sized properties here; most are vast plantations. And of those who work these lands, only one-tenth are farmers who, by being paid a fixed fee in cotton or dollars, acquire the status of relatively independent entrepreneurs. The other nine-tenths are merely agricultural workers provided with tools and wages. What makes their situation unique is that these wages are not a specific sum of money but a share, of greater or lesser proportions, in the annual cotton harvest. The worker himself, then, is put in the position of assuming the risks that are always assumed by the owners in a normal capitalist system. These risks are enormous because not only does the harvest depend on rain and wind, but the cotton market is invariably subject to speculation and to considerable fluctuation from one year to the next. To top it off, the owner gets to sell the entire harvest himself, including the tenant's share, and he declares whatever profits it suits him to declare. Under any circumstances, such freedom invites fraud, but this is especially true when men who are otherwise honourable and true to their word take a malicious pleasure in duping blacks. This form of stealing is not forbidden by their moral code. When you realise that a black man in the South has no recourse against whites, you see that his living depends exclusively on his master's goodwill. What makes this dependence even greater is that when the worker starts out, he's forced to borrow money from the owner for food and clothing during the year preceding the first harvest; he then lives on credit at enormous interest rates (up to 37 per cent). It is this situation that gives the boss the authority to seize the harvest and sell it himself. If he's not reimbursed, he has the right to sell the furniture, the farm animals — all his tenant's possessions. In principle, the tenant has one way of being released from his debt, which is to go and work on another plantation. But, by common agreement, the planters refuse to hire these defectors, who therefore find themselves bound to the soil and to a master nearly as tightly as slaves of former times.

These conditions have become even harsher since the South's agricultural situation has become less and less prosperous. There is terrible overpopulation, especially in the Old South, the region of the delta that we're now crossing. Since 1860 the population has doubled, without any increase in the amount of land being cultivated. More than half of the rural population of the United States lives in the South, which produces only 28 per cent of the country's total agricultural wealth. This beautiful black earth is naturally fertile and lends itself to a variety of crops, but the soil is light and must endure heavy rains; the concentration on cotton, without any preventive measures, has exhausted the soil. In the era of slavery, the land itself was regarded as having no value, and the only precious capital was the human chattel charged with exploiting it; the planters were not concerned with managing their wealth. Today, the exclusive cultivation of cotton ensures its ruin. Yet it is almost impossible to institute a wiser agricultural economy. In the beginning, cotton cultivation demands rather large outlays of capital, which the farmers and owners are forced to borrow because their profits are too weak to provide it. The South has always lived on credit. Loans are at high interest rates, because of the risks that result from market fluctuations, and debts can never be cleared — to repay them, people need new harvests. Hence, there is a vicious circle, since in this struggle for survival, the land becomes increasingly impoverished. Add these facts – that foreign competition has led to overproduction and a steep fall in prices; that the policies of the AAA [Agricultural Adjustment Administration] have decreased the area under cultivation, causing a terrible reduction of manual labour since 1935; that mechanisation, which could not be established until now (the techniques are still very primitive and have hardly changed since slavery), is gaining a foothold and further reducing manual labour – and one sees that the situation of the blacks and the 'poor whites' who have mingled with them is quite tragic. They live not only in poverty but in uncertainty, ignorance, passivity and poor hygiene. Their children die as easily as they are born, and those who survive are soon subjected to the harsh work of the harvest. There is no European country where agricultural workers constitute such a vast and wretched herd; you would only find such conditions in their colonies. Here, the colony is within the United States itself. This does not make the situation any more shocking, but it does make it more striking, more paradoxical and more complex.

After the vegetative fertility of the cotton fields, we find the mineral wealth of the oil wells. You can smell them from a distance. In the great desert of bare fields, this smell of factories and machines, this city smell, is the natural smell of the earth – the smell of the soil, of the sky, of the air. You can't even dream of being rid of it and recovering some lost purity: it's the fundamental truth. Infants in their cradles are already breathing it in those prefabricated houses lined up in rows on the stony ground, under the aegis of the tall iron towers. For many of the men who live here, life has had no other taste.

The rich city of Houston has its roots deep in these oil wells. Twenty years ago, it was merely a straggling village; on the lands where great buildings rise today, there were only weeds and stones. But no unseemly odour drifts through the streets. We reserve rooms in a large hotel, which, like all large American hotels, includes bars, cafeterias, lunchrooms, restaurants and dance clubs. We dine in the 'red room', which is an exact replica of Chicago's 'Victorian room' and Washington's 'blue room', with mirrors, draperies, and crystal chandeliers. There's a band, a waxed dance floor and polished waiters; yet regionalism asserts itself, and you feel you're in Texas. The diners have put bottles of whiskey in the middle of their tables. And next to us, there's a noisy party of women who look flushed under their flowered hats and men who are laughing loudly. They all stare at us steadily: How can we be foreigners? How is it that we're not Texans?

For the tourist, Houston at night is as gloomy as Buffalo. At the heart of this urban sprawl we find the same street that we walk along in every town and village where the Greyhound stops; we know its lights and displays by heart. Fortunately, a movie house advertises sensational 'thrillings'. We go in. We see Victor Francen in the role of a brilliant pianist who is paralysed in one hand and who dies pathetically at the beginning of the film [*The Beast with Five Fingers*]. His adoptive son, Peter Lorre, who devotes himself to mysterious scholarly works, is threatened with expulsion from the mansion's library by a band of self-centred heirs. Death is unleashed; a mysterious hand strangles brothers, nephews and cousins and threatens a pretty niece. It is Francen's hand, which Peter Lorre has cut off and put in a box, but we see it leaving its box by itself to go off and play concertos on the piano. In the end it attacks Peter Lorre himself, just as he's about to murder the gentle heroine. He throws the hand into the fire; it writhes about in the flames, escapes and slowly reaches for the throat of the unfortunate man. Despite the stupidity of the plot, that enormous spidery hand lifting the lid of a dish or creeping along a table is as disturbing as the opening scenes of *Un Chien andalou* [by Luis Buñuel and Salvador Dali].*

---

* Buñuel actually did some preproduction work on *The Beast with Five Fingers*, although he did not end up directing it.

28 March

MA [Marcel Morand], who has been a professor in America for twenty years, takes me to Rice University. The buildings stand amid lush lawns flowering with camellias and azaleas. We have lunch at the faculty club. These clubs are reserved for men, which gives the meal a touch of austerity; but in the universities, as elsewhere, men's clubs passionately refuse to open their doors to women. Women demand too much attention and consideration; the men prefer to be bored – at least there are no constraints. After the meal MA takes me for a drive. On the outskirts of town we cross large parks that are extensions of the unspoiled woods. The trees, entangled with vines and veiled with Spanish moss, have a tropical lushness. Idling in their shade are those lazy, languid rivers called bayous. On the edge of the forests are the luxurious houses of the oil barons; they're built in the old plantation style, in wood with porches and verandas, but they're fresh and shining. In front, tall, placid black men mow the sunny lawns. Azaleas, camellias, golden grass, well-trained servants – all is peace, order and beauty. In this limpid world, only the Spanish moss recalls the mysterious disturbances of growth and the impermanence of all prosperity.

MA is a mischievous old man, a rare sort who judges America without either hostility or complacency. Among other things, he's amused by the mixture of strictness and hypocritical licence that one encounters here, as in the rest of the country. For example, it's forbidden to bring alcohol to Rice University. If you want to enter the campus carrying a bottle under your arm, you won't be allowed to pass, but if you're just careful to put it in a bag, no one would dream of searching you. In fact, students and professors are hard drinkers, and there are some faculty members who are never seen except in a state of inebriation. Free love is frowned on, but the marriages are highly elastic. A certain professor intrigued his colleagues by coming back one autumn with a young wife who was totally different from the fiancée he'd taken to Mexico at the beginning of summer vacation. He'd had time to be married, divorced and remarried. He admitted to having precipitated matters in the hopes that his first wife's face would be forgotten and that the second one would be welcomed unquestioningly as the only Mrs Z. His first marriage had been merely a trial marriage: he'd ended it after a week.

MA tells me many other anecdotes, proving that French universities don't have a monopoly on jealousies and rivalries. Then he talks a little about the race question. Tension is greater than ever, with the blacks indignant at being given no reward for the services they rendered during the war, and the whites dreading that they might claim certain privileges and treating them even more arrogantly than in the past. The blacks look for any opportunity to avenge these insults. If a white person hires a black cook or an extra servant for a dinner party, the blacks will make formal promises, then fail to show up at the last minute – and it just so happens that no one can be found to replace them, that all the cooks and extra servants are busy that evening. Since leaving the army, blacks have demonstrated a sense of racial solidarity and a will to revolt. MA also tells me that last year, while visiting a nearby black university, he was welcomed with special warmth as a Frenchman. But when the moment came for lunch, they led him to a little room where they'd set a table just for him. 'You cannot eat with us,' the black professors said apologetically. 'We would run into terrible trouble if it were known that we allowed a white man to sit at our table.'

In most towns the elegant restaurants, like the nightclubs, are situated in the suburbs. We have dinner far from the centre of town, in a place typical of Houston – a large, startlingly white wooden inn. The South is the only region in America where food is not just consumed but cooked according to time-honoured traditions. We have an excellent regional meal. I'm told that it's a shame that I can't see a cockfight in Texas. They're illegal, but that only makes them more attractive. On the Mexican border a rough group of cowboys gathers in more or less secret spots to bet passionately on the winner. They have to be careful to keep a straight face and never lift a finger, because the bookmakers interpret the slightest blink as a wager and always turn that to one's disadvantage.

In the absence of cockfights, a professor takes me to a wrestling match after my lecture; this may not be especially Texan, but at least it's typically American. We arrive toward the end of the match in a huge sports arena filled with a delirious crowd. The women shout, 'Kill him! Kill him!' in raucous voices. In the ring the wrestlers confront each other with looks of bestial hatred, studiously imitating the stance and snarl of King Kong. It's instantly clear that this is a performance and not a real fight. One of the wrestlers throws the referee over the ropes; another hurls his adversary onto the floor of the hall. At the end of one match the loser suddenly pretends to be furious, grinding his teeth and throwing himself on the winner, who abruptly flees, terrified. They chase each other through the stands, reunite and fight while the spectators shout hysterically. They must know that it's just a show, but they refuse to believe it. Besides, they're getting their money's worth: hard knocks are exchanged, and blood flows. We leave after half an hour. L takes me for a drink on one of Houston's main streets. Here no one drinks whiskey; instead, they drink beer in large jugs. The walls are covered from floor to ceiling with huge photographs of prize bulls and cows. In one corner stands a pioneer's covered wagon with its green canvas, and giant bulls' horns hang almost everywhere. It seems that most of the cafés are decorated in this style. This evening I'll go to sleep with no regrets. I don't think that any of Houston's seductions remain hidden from me.

29 March

Black earth, tropical forests, Spanish moss, bayous – this is the last stop before New Orleans, where we'll spend four days. I'm raptly reading Mark Twain's *Life on the Mississippi* as the bus speeds along, and at every river I ask, 'Is this the Mississippi?' It's always part of it but never the whole river, just a branch of this endlessly branching delta.

Hearing me speak French, a woman approaches me at one of the stops: 'Aren't you speaking French?' She invites me to sit beside her on the bus. She's from Brittany but has been living for twenty years on a farm in Louisiana. She likes the life here and proudly shows me a photo of her daughter, who is a college student. A little farther on, a man speaks to me in a lingo I don't understand, in which the word *gare* keeps cropping up. I finally realise that he, too, is speaking French – the French that Louisiana inherited in the eighteenth century – and that he is asking me if I had brothers killed in the war [*guerre*].

Our Greyhound is certainly different from the nearly empty one that crossed the deserts of Arizona and New Mexico. Now there are lines at the bus stations, which are all situated in the heart of town. The blacks, for whom there is often no sheltered waiting area, wait outside, sometimes on benches but usually standing, until the superior race is settled in the bus; four or eight places on the back seat are reserved for them. Often, they make only short trips; they are country people travelling from one village to the other. When they ring to stop the bus, the driver and other travellers watch with a mixture of ill humor and irony as they file through the central aisle. The whites, of course, would rather travel standing up than sit next to black people if there are no other vacant seats. Several more of these whites speak an old French that is more incomprehensible to me than English. In the villages we pass through, we read above the grocery stores, candy stores and hair salons the names Malthieu, Debureau, Lefevre, Boucher, Robert – almost all French names. At dusk the bus stops for dinner in a little town on the banks of the Mississippi. We are beginning to hate these bus stations where you eat charred meat, where the jukebox plays Frank Sinatra and Bing Crosby, where the restrooms have stalls without doors for privacy, where the blacks are parked in windowless alcoves. A gentle rain is falling, but we go for a walk along a rain-soaked lane by the river. To the right and the left are tall, lonely forests that imprison its waters. It's dark, melancholy and mysterious under the damp sky.

I look at the river and think about La Salle, who died, murdered by his men, for being confused by the many branches of this monotonous delta. He came from France with four ships to found Louisiana in a blaze of glory, but failed to recognise the real outlet of this 'Father of All Waters' – a river he'd taken one perilous trip down already, going astray with his men on its unwelcoming shore. It was an agent of the Compagnie des Indes, Monsieur de Bienville, who founded the city in 1718, and in honour of the regent [Philippe II, duc d'Orléans], it was called New Orleans. The regent's namesake was raided on his behalf; archers under orders from John Law and his gang abducted loose women from the streets and probably carried off honourable citizens in their wagons as well. In 1763 Louisiana, which then included a large part of the Mississippi Valley, was ceded to Spain, which granted Americans the right to store their merchandise in New Orleans. In 1802 the colony was returned to France in exchange for Tuscany. Jefferson then offered Talleyrand fifty million francs for New Orleans and Florida, and Talleyrand sold all of Louisiana for sixty million. This guaranteed America unimpeded navigation of the Mississippi and allowed the country to extend westward in total security.

We travel long into the night. Lights appear here and there, but they're only from a gas station lost in the middle of the delta. Miles and miles of humid night, bridges, dark waters, more bridges, more waters, the same night. At last the lights cluster together. Now there are avenues, intersections, more avenues and more intersections, suburbs and more suburbs. And finally, here is Broadway, here is Market Street – the brightly lit main road, swarming with people, named Canal Street. Tomorrow morning, this city will be New Orleans.

30 March

I always feel crushed by the ghastly opulence of big American hotels. You could live a whole life without ever going out: florists, candy vendors, booksellers, hairdressers, manicurists, stenographers and typists are at your service. There are four different restaurants, bars, cafés and dance floors. It's a neutral zone, like the international boutiques in the middle of colonial capitals.

But we only have to cross the street and we're in the heart of New Orleans, in the French Quarter. The old colonial city was built in a chequerboard pattern, like modern cities, but its narrow streets are lined with one- or two-storey houses that are reminiscent of both Spain and France. They have the serenity of Anjou and Touraine, but the lovely, lacy wrought-iron balconies make me think of the balconies in Cordoba and the wrought-iron grilles on the windows of Arab palaces. An Andalusian warmth infuses the provincial silence. Exoticism here is no longer Mexican or Indian; it's French. On the gravestones in the old cemetery, on the street corners, above the shops, the French names have an antique sound. And here in the curio shops, instead of tomahawks and Indian masks, they sell oil lamps and Sèvres vases, remnants of a civilisation as remote as those of the Hopi and Navajo: pearl fringes turn out to be barbarous headbands; chandeliers and porcelain vases, strange idols. Many of the old dwellings have inscriptions: here is the house of a blacksmith, the house of the pirate Jean Laffite, the house that Napoleon did not live in, although it was meant for him and has appropriated his name; not far off is the Absinthe House. All have been transformed into bars, now quiet and empty in the morning sun.

There are several streets where every second door is a bar or nightclub. In this area they sell only books: new, used, bargains. The shops are tiny and spill out onto the sidewalk, offering the passer-by boxes full of old, damaged volumes. More curio shops, as well as pastry shops with trays of pralines and, in front of the door, a large cardboard Negress, a kerchief tied around her head, who smiles while pointing avidly to this Creole specialty. We visit a little theatre that has remained unchanged since the eighteenth century and where they perform a French play from time to time. Then we come out onto a square as pure and simple as the Place des Vosges in Paris. All the luxury of these austere old houses lies in the rich tracery of wrought iron, a warm and tender green, which runs the length of the terraces. A little museum recreates colonial life of centuries past: there are miniature houses with tiny furniture, dolls wearing ceremonial dress, and closer to our times, old photographs of groups and individuals. You can also see the jewellery, silver, dresses and porcelain of the finest families of the past. We continue to follow the silent streets and come to the fish market. Here, the present reclaims its rights; life reappears. The small shops are noisy bazaars; hordes of people jostle each other on the sidewalks; the café where we eat doughnuts is swarming with people. The fruit-and-vegetable stall with its dusty awnings, its overripe bananas, its limp lettuce and its half-rotten pears seems imported from rue Mouffetard. No more of the uniform splendour of hothouse produce: the pears, the grapes, the merchant and his customers share the same difficult and precarious life. Crossing the docks, we go as far as the waters of the Mississippi. It's a rather ordinary river flowing between the houses and factories.

The French Quarter in the heart of New Orleans is like a hard white almond, but the generous, bruised pulp that expands around this pit has a headier taste. All afternoon we go on foot and by taxi along the broad, concentric avenues, by the canal, in the cemeteries, in the parks and on the lakeshore. I would like to walk for days along these lanes. They're lined with those romantic houses whose gables, columns, porches and verandas I liked so much in San Antonio. Many of these homes are a hundred years old, and time has covered their wooden architecture with a persistent plant life, turning them the colour of lichen and moss. They're often surrounded by gardens with capricious foliage; yet in none of these private Edens is spring as magnificently exalted as it is on the public avenues, where the beds of azaleas seem endless. In France these are the boring flowers that one sees in pots at florist shops; they're gifts for your grandmother on her birthday or, bound with pink ribbons, they serve as decoration in banquet halls. Yet here they are real flowers. As luxurious bushes, growing wild like brambles in the woods or like honeysuckle hedges, they spread throughout the city in the lavish displays of banquet halls, hothouses and wayside altars. They have no scent; it's as if their overly bright colour had absorbed all their perfume. The penetrating scent that drifts through the festive lanes is the smell of autumn. The trees, whose buds have just burst forth, are already losing their leaves; they fall like golden rain on the azaleas, covering the sidewalks with a damp, scented mulch, like a forest in October. A stormy summer sky, damp and luminous grey, weighs on the springtime silk of the flowers and the autumnal decay of dead leaves.

We don't want to miss New Orleans and the secret of its nights. In the street of the Old Quarter, where we're strolling toward evening, we see announcements for Mexican and Hawaiian bands, nude dancers and showgirls, but what we want is to hear real jazz played by black musicians. Or is there any real jazz left in America? I decide to call some people whose names I was given in Los Angeles. I open the telephone book and discover twenty John Browns, twelve G. Davids and an equal number of B. Smiths. I try one at random and hear surprised, mistrustful voices at the other end of the line. I try four or five times unsuccessfully. I give up. We'll have to go it alone. With all the wisdom we can muster, we consult the little tourist guide they've given us at the hotel office. Our first choice is a good one. We're charmed by the restaurant in the Old Quarter where we go to dine. The room is decorated with naive paintings depicting boats rocking on an embossed sea, and hanging from the ceiling, there are miniature frigates with their sails and riggings. In the back the restaurant opens onto a dim patio where the tables are hidden among trees and discreetly lit by individual lamps. We're served Creole cuisine in the grand style. From time to time we see the blue flame of a brandy dessert flickering in the night, the ice cream slowly melting in the vapours from the burned alcohol, which tastes of cherries.

The French Quarter starts to liven up. Bellboys in braided uniforms are posted at the doors of nightclubs; bar doors are open, and we see whiskey shining on the counters; we can hear glasses clinking and phonographs playing from the street. Where should we go? We enter Napoleon's House, where we like the dark wood decor, but there's no jazz. The owner is very friendly because we're French, and we explain to him that we want to hear some good black jazz. His face darkens for a moment. The situation has been very tense between blacks and whites for some time now, and the blacks no longer want to perform for whites. However, he suggests that we try Absinthe House. This is supposedly one of the residences of the pirate Jean Laffite. The first room is a little bar whose wooden walls and ceiling are entirely covered with old calling cards and banknotes from countries around the world. In the second room, there are several tables and a platform with three black musicians on piano, guitar and bass.

Suddenly, we're transported. This music is nothing like the music at Café Society or even the music in Harlem – the three blacks are playing passionately, for themselves. The audience is small and not very elegant. Actually, there isn't really an audience, just a few old couples and a few families who are probably travelling through New Orleans and are so out of place here that no one takes any notice of them. The band doesn't try to please or dazzle anyone; it plays the way it feels like playing. If the bass player – a young black who's only eighteen, despite his girth – sometimes closes his eyes in a trance, this isn't servile mimicry: he's just giving himself over to the music and the promptings of his heart. Right next to the band, there are two very young white men with black hair who are listening with religious attention and laughing amicably with the musicians between pieces. They're very different from the other customers and remind us of Dorothy Baker's 'young man with a trumpet' [in a popular Jazz Age novel]. They're probably young people who are stifled by American civilisation and for whom black music is an escape. They look at us as much as we look at them, for our presence must also be somewhat unusual.

Meanwhile, we take great pleasure in drinking big zombies. This formidable cocktail was invented in New Orleans and was named for those living dead who are the heroes of so many thrillers and legends born in the South. I'm told that more than one civilised and cultivated adult in Louisiana or Georgia still believes in the existence of these tormented phantoms – the corpse must be stabbed in the chest with a sword to ensure that it goes to its eternal rest. The zombie cocktail is considered so potent that in many places they'll serve only one per customer. In reality, it doesn't live up to its reputation, and we don't feel its effects any more than we did in Los Angeles.

Our friendship with the dark-haired young men is progressing; we applaud together with the same enthusiasm, we exchange a few words, and they come to sit at our table. R is of Italian origin, C of Spanish. And the miracle is that R is precisely the young man with the trumpet that we imagined him to be. He's from a poor family and five years ago he joined the navy, where he plays the trumpet in a military band. He still has one year to go, and he ardently wishes to become a musician. He's studied a little at the conservatory in Philadelphia, which, for this reason, seems to him the most wonderful city in America. He speaks passionately not only about jazz but also about Stravinsky, Ravel and Béla Bartók. He's read only a little, but his favourite book is James Joyce's *Ulysses*. He's twenty-two years old. Of all the young people I've met in America, he's the first one who really seems young.

In New York he could bring his trumpet and play with his black friends; here, it's out of the question. And it's equally out of the question to invite the musicians to have a drink at our table. We talk to them from our seats. They smile warmly at us because we're French. Two of them have French wives, who are descendants of black families from French Louisiana and speak an archaic French. We chat with the musicians and ask them to play some old songs. We stay a long time, but we'd like to discover other places, too. The blacks beg us not to take R and C with us; they're so happy to play for people who really love jazz and understand it. We're given some addresses, and our new friends promise to be our guides the following evening.

We're dazzled by our good luck: this boisterous night no longer intimidates us; we've won it over — this time, we are part of it, not members of the sad herd of the excluded. Absinthe Barn is almost identical to Absinthe House: the same calling cards and banknotes on the walls of the bar, the same banal room with the same transient clientele. But instead of a band, there's only a pianist, who plays well, though a bit too smoothly. At the neighbouring table there's a half-drunk customer, whose hand meanders to the backs of our chairs. Such incidents never happen in America, and no sooner has N moved her chair away than the proprietor rushes over and throws the drunk out. When we leave, he apologises profusely, urging us to believe that his customers are respectable and that we can feel completely safe in returning. We look into another bar, which seems to be a meeting place for the town's artists and bohemians; we're especially struck by the great number of homosexuals staggering up to the counter. There's a sly one who has singled out a young couple, pretending to flirt with the wife but always managing to lean on the husband's shoulder. A young black woman, half-drunk, is at the piano, and she plays some old jazz very movingly. There's a swarm of people who all seem drenched in alcohol, but drunkenness and vice are worn lightly here; the atmosphere isn't heavy but seems fresh and gay — or is this gaiety in us? The night is warm in the streets under a luminous grey sky. Gradually, the nightclubs close, but we have no desire to sleep when we're still feeling so alive. We sit at the counter of a wretched bar that's wide open to the night, where a dwarf with a *café au lait* complexion is pounding frenetically on an old piano. Two tramps are dancing on the sidewalk. When they leave and the piano falls silent, we no longer have anything to do; we resign ourselves to returning to the hotel.

31 March

In the morning we walk through the same places we saw the day before. At noon we eat Creole cooking in an old French restaurant. And we take a boat that goes a few miles up and down the Mississippi. There are four decks, and each has a bar, a cafeteria or a dance floor. At night there's a band and people dance on the large polished floor, but during the day they simply sit in the leather armchairs, drinking and looking. To tell the truth, there isn't much to see. The excursion is pleasant because of the sunshine, the sky, the sound and smell of the water, but the river flows between ordinary factories and warehouses. The captain relentlessly points out the landscape over a microphone. As at Niagara Falls and the Grand Canyon, it's a matter of giving the tourists a 'conditioned', 'homogenised' version of nature through a human intermediary.

We dine on a different patio than yesterday, but it's equally charming. The colour of the sky above our heads surprises us: it's pearl grey, as luminous as dawn, and looks like it's lit by some mysterious beacon. Back in the street, we understand: a gentle fog has enveloped the city; the tall buildings on the other side of Canal Street have retreated several miles, looking ghostly and far away. The mist dulls the neon signs, but above the roofs it forms a screen on which the lights of New Orleans are reflected. The sky is nearly white in the damp air. It has a suffocating softness, almost like a storm or tears.

We find our friends again at Absinthe House. We're proud to have these friends and to feel like allies, not of the people who listen, stupefied, but of the musicians. There's a crowd this evening: a group of attentive students, male and female; bored couples; and lively parties. At one of the tables an old gentleman begins to sing. With his fresh pink face and beautiful white hair, his gold-rimmed glasses, and a self-assurance that comes from a well-stuffed wallet, he's a common and particularly loathsome type. The band accompanies him complacently. He intones another song, and I get angry. The little Italian smiles; he explains to me that a member of the audience has the right to sing, as long as he pays – the money goes to the musicians. And, indeed, I see that the tiresome singer places some dollar bills on the piano. He has an odd way of loving music.

R and C want to take us to a dance hall reserved for blacks where they have an entrée, but it's Holy Week: New Orleans is a pious Catholic town, and this evening the place is closed. They lead us to another bar in the Old Quarter where there's an excellent black jazz group with a saxophonist and trumpet player. The trumpet player is quite young and plays with all his youth, giving of himself so completely that his whole life seems committed to every note. It's here in these modest clubs, among these unknown musicians, rather than in Carnegie Hall or even at the Savoy, that jazz achieves its true dignity: there's no entertainment, no exhibitionism, no commercialism – for certain men, it's a way of life and a reason for being. Compared with art, poetry and printed music, jazz has the privileged emotional impact of a communication that is immediate and fleeting, like the very moments it transfigures. If these men's lives are often tormented, it's because instead of keeping death at a distance, like other artists, they are always mindful of the marriage of existence and death. It's against this background – the background of death – that the young trumpeter plays his inspired refrains, and you can't listen only with your ears and your mind: he offers an experience in which you must immerse your whole self. And he offers it in such a desert! People here don't even have the respectful enthusiasm of concert-goers; they're amused by jazz and scorn it from the height of their dignity as white men smugly entrenched in their money and morality. It's with the same arrogance that the great lords of the past were amused by buffoons and jesters. R asks the trumpeter a question; they exchange a few words; and the young black man beams. As he plays, he looks at us, smiling. Like the musicians at Absinthe House, he feels the need to play for someone, and it's a chance he seldom gets.

The jazz is over. A beautiful young woman with black hair comes onto the little platform. She begins to dance and slowly removes her clothes, following the classic rites of burlesque. In a corner a middle-aged woman surveys her indifferently. She looks as if she might be her mother, and we're told that she is. We're also told that the dancer is from a good family, that she's had a good education, that she's intelligent and cultivated, but in New Orleans, nude dancers readily take on legendary auras. Certainly, she is beautiful and seductive. The more clothing she removes, the more austere the faces become, expressing a detached, polite, almost bored curiosity. When she takes off her panties, leaving nothing but a little spangled triangle on a silk cord around her hips, the atmosphere is so moralistic that you'd think you were in a church on a Sunday morning.

Our friends want to try and take us to the black section. A taxi ferries us from one end of town to the other. We enter a little dance hall where the owner knows R and welcomes us amicably, but there's no band today because of Holy Week. The blacks seated at the bar give us hostile looks. We don't want to impose ourselves on them, so we leave; as we go out the door, we hear unfriendly laughter behind us. In the street, taxis refuse to stop for us. Some say no in an ironic tone, others make excuses: 'We'd get in trouble if we took white people.' And it's true that in New Orleans, black drivers have the right to work only for clients of colour. So we go by foot across this enemy territory, this part of town where we are the enemy despite ourselves, responsible for the colour of our skin and all that it implies. R tells us that despite the enormous charm of New Orleans, he couldn't bear to live here because of the hateful racial discrimination and that he'll go north again as soon as possible.

We walk for a long time. The pink of the azaleas gleams dully through the pearl-coloured fog; the sky sheds a white light, and the streets are only half-visible. The damp air clings to the skin, and the smell of dead leaves is oppressive. We stop in a little bar and drink whiskeys, talking till dawn. R is drunk with words; he says that it's so rare in America to be able to talk. He accompanies us to the hotel. The lobby, so splendid during the day, is now just a shabby waiting room; a man is washing down the tiled floor, spreading an odour of soap. It's gloomy. In an armchair, an old man is sleeping, his mouth half-open. We say goodbye to the little Italian, whose fate we will probably never know, and he tells us approvingly, 'It's rare to find people to talk with in this country.' We reply, 'It's rare to find an American like you.' He smiles, 'Oh, I know! I'm a "character".' I would like to meet him ten years from now.

April

1 April

This morning I take a taxi, travelling at random far from the centre of town, and I walk for hours through the peaceful suburbs. A harsh wind is blowing with a vengeance through the palm trees, pink azaleas and baskets of large red flowers, and from time to time the rain comes down in brief bursts. The romantic old houses seem as fragile as the flowers; the water is seeping into their wooden walls, the shade of verdigris, and the rotting boards seem about to crumble to dust, like tree trunks eaten by the elements in tropical forests. This afternoon, while Professor S and his wife are taking me for a drive, there is a deluge. I've never seen such rain. It is a revolt in the heavens, a mortal convulsion of the earth. The world is sobbing in desperation, sobbing to death, knowing that it cannot die and that there will always be more tears to shed. We stop at the sidewalk in front of an old house we want to visit, but it's impossible for us to get out and walk the two metres to the threshold. It is equally impossible to drive on. The windshield wipers work madly back and forth, in vain: the windows are streaming; the landscape is cracking and trembling as in a movie when the hero is about to die. We await the cloudburst of that final night when the world will be engulfed. But the night does not come. Abruptly, around five o'clock, the rain stops, as though the tears themselves and the revolt had become useless. In the depths of the yellow sky, the last hope has died. The flowers, trees and houses are bathed in a bright, other-worldly light.

Later, night falls as usual. I visit the inside of several old houses and touch the green lace of wrought iron. In the evening, after my lecture, Professor S has invited several colleagues to his place.

His daughter, aged fifteen and carefully made up to look something like Bette Davis, walks around the living room in slacks and bare feet. She is dressed to go to the movies with her date, and her naively sophisticated freshness, her lively and uninhibited grace make her very different from the daughters of our professors! But even in this cheerful home, among these once liberal intellectuals, the Red peril has penetrated. 'Only a few months ago,' S and his friends say, 'we thought that a democracy should respect all opinions. But now we understand that it must repress those that are detrimental to democracy itself.' The propaganda is well done. Just four days ago, the head of the FBI declared that the Reds ought to be considered a fifth column. And the word 'Red' is highly elastic. Among the workers and the middle classes, among intellectuals and politicians, freedom loses its meaning from day to day.

2 April

Through its storms, its sun, its humid nights, its pearl-grey spring smelling of autumn, New Orleans seems worthy of its most fabulous legends. I know it's also one of the poorest cities in America, where life is extremely harsh; its stagnant luxury already seems ambiguous to us, and we would have liked to penetrate further into its heart, to live here in the reality of its daily life. On leaving, I resolve: 'I will return.'

Today, we're undertaking a long journey. The bus leaves at nine in the morning and will reach Jacksonville at two at night. This is an 'express' that makes only two or three stops. They sell sandwiches and Coca-Cola on board; the seats have movable backs, and at night everyone lights a little individual lamp, as in airplanes. And the steward encourages us, plotting our position from time to time, announcing the next stop and explaining the landscape. We're travelling through Louisiana, Mississippi, Alabama and Florida. The branches of the delta are as vast as lakes;

they glisten in the sun, and the Gulf of Mexico is as blue as a honeymoon dream. Palm trees, cacti, azaleas, flowering cities, tropical forests with thick vegetation, romantic houses emerging amid peaceful lawns, solitary, dilapidated shacks in the woods, the dazzling sea, languid lagoons, Spanish moss, luxurious and sordid – throughout the day the whole South reveals itself to us with its wrenching contrasts.

And throughout the day the great tragedy of the South pursues us like an obsession. Even the traveller confined to a bus and waiting rooms cannot escape it. From the time we entered Texas, everywhere we go there's the smell of hatred in the air – the arrogant hatred of whites, the silent hatred of blacks. At the stations the respectable, badly dressed lower-middle-class matrons stare with envious anger at the pretty black girls in bright dresses and joyful jewellery, and the men resent the nonchalant beauty of the young black men in light suits. American niceness has no place here. In the crowded line outside the bus, the blacks are jostled. 'You aren't going to let that Negress go in front of you,' a woman says to a man in a voice trembling with fury.

The blacks humbly crowd onto the seat at the rear of the bus, trying to make themselves inconspicuous. During the middle of the afternoon, in the heat and jolting of the bus, which are particularly rough in the back, a pregnant woman faints. Her lolling head knocks against the window at every jolt. We hear a college girl's shocked and jeering voice crying, 'The Negress is crazy!' The driver stops the bus and goes to see what's happened; it's only a Negress who has fainted, and everyone jeers – these women are always making trouble . . . Someone shakes the woman a little and wakes her up, and the bus starts off again. We dare not offer her our seats in the front; the whole bus would oppose it, and she would be the first victim of their indignation. The bus continues on; the young woman continues to suffer; and when we stop in town, she has fainted again. People go and drink Coca-Cola without paying any attention to her; only one elderly American woman comes with N and me to try and help her. She thanks us, but she seems worried and goes away quickly without accepting further aid: she feels guilty in the eyes of the whites, and she's afraid. This is only a small incident, but it helps me understand why, when we're travelling through the overcrowded black districts, the placid Greyhound gets such hostile looks.

3 April

Between Jacksonville and Savannah this morning, N sat beside a young black man, since there was no other place. As soon as a seat among the whites became free, he pointed it out to her: 'I imagine you would rather not stay here,' he said drily. She answered that she was quite comfortable where she was, and that she was French. Then he opened up and began to talk to her. He said that he'd entered the war as a volunteer in order to have the right, on his return, to the years of free study granted to veterans; now he's a scholarship student at a black university, where he's studying to become a lawyer. With bitter passion, he explained why he so ardently wants to earn the right to plead cases in court: this is one of the only concrete ways to fight for the black cause. Behind all these docile faces – through discouragement, fear or, more rarely, hope – revolt is always imminent. And the whites know it.

Savannah is sleeping amid its baskets of azaleas. From north to south, from east to west, the city consists of peaceful squares connected by flowering lanes. Each square is surrounded by old dwellings, sometimes with a colonial church rising in their midst. In the middle of the square there's a large bed planted with azaleas, which are beginning to unfurl their leaves, and in the centre of the flower bed there's a tarnished bronze statue: some general or hero from the Revolutionary War or Civil War. The large figure of Oglethorpe, the founder of the colony, appears most often. General James Edward Oglethorpe, after visiting a friend interned for debt in a prison near London, was appalled by the prisoners' condition and demanded a parliamentary inquiry. Ten thousand prisoners were released following this investigation and were sent by him to America; a charter from King George II in 1732 granted them the territory called Georgia. The virtuous philanthropists who financed the operation forbade the sale of alcohol in the colony, which encouraged nearly all of the colonists to emigrate; more humane legislation convinced them to return. General Oglethorpe's elevated moral sense did not prevent him from possessing a number of slaves.

One of the squares is a cemetery. The flat, vertical headstones are bare and half-broken; they bear just a name and a very old date. People stroll cheerfully along the paths that wind between the graves, and children play beside them. A large park is set aside for them a little farther on, at the foot of a bronze soldier. There are swings, trapezes, merry-go-rounds, and slides on which they venture timidly, as well as all kinds of mechanical toys that frighten and delight them. Black servants survey this miniature village fair. We walk slowly from square to square, suffused by the quiet perfume of the past. I've made this journey in reverse, from the west to the east. When San Francisco was first rising up amid the rough gold seekers, Savannah was languishing in the luxury of an already old civilisation. This is the first time I have found myself transported to the early days of colonisation, into young America's most distant past. Even more than in the Far West, the time frame here is disconcerting; these men of green metal seem as antique as Caesar or Vercingetorix [leader of the Gauls], and the oldest is not even two centuries old. Savannah is deader than Sacramento and seems older than the Middle Ages, yet three hundred years ago it didn't even exist. As I know that History extends over much vaster periods, I feel, a bit uneasily, that I'm not at the end but at the beginning of an era: this pink-and-blue day, with its smell of autumn, belongs to the past – but in the eyes of what future?

In the middle of the flowering azaleas, the dormant old houses and the playing children, the statues of the great slave owners who created the city and fought for it are fixed in glory. But around this dead Savannah, there's another, living city where the grandchildren of slaves live inglorious lives of poverty and hatred: a black belt around the white city. For miles and miles, the bus followed avenues lined with wretched shacks, where unfriendly dark faces turned toward us; we felt the bite of those looks. But the black belt fascinates us; we decide to try to walk in these hostile streets. Children playing in the road look at us with surprise; the men standing on the porches, the women leaning out of the windows and staring at us, are frighteningly impassive. This is not Lenox Avenue or Harlem; there is hatred and rage in the air. Brightly coloured wash is drying in yards behind wooden or rusty iron fences. The houses are very small, squeezed up against one another, brown like the earth. The streets and squares are merely vacant lots. With every step, our discomfort grows. As we go by, voices drop, gestures stop, smiles die: all life is suspended in the depths of those angry eyes. The silence is so stifling, the menace so oppressive that it's almost a relief when something finally explodes. An old woman glares at us in disgust and spits twice, majestically, once for N, once for me. At the same moment, a tiny girl runs off crying, 'Enemies! Enemies!' It seems a long way back to the squares with flowering baskets.

I remember that on the first evening of my stay in New York, a Frenchman asked me not to write anything about the black question, on the pretext that I couldn't understand anything in only three months. I agree that my experience is meagre for such a vast subject; yet it would be unnatural not to talk about a set of facts that I've often run up against and that have such great importance in American life. So I'll take advantage here of an experience whose extent, depth and value are officially recognised in America – the experience Myrdal describes in his authoritative work *An American Dilemma*. The Carnegie Foundation decided to finance a broad inquiry into the black problem in America, and they wanted to ensure the study's impartiality, so they entrusted it to a foreigner, Dr Gunnar Myrdal, a famous economist at the University of Stockholm, an economic adviser to the Swedish government, and a member of the Senate. From 1938 to 1942 Myrdal assembled a large team of American economists and sociologists, and with their help he examined different aspects of the question. I will not attempt an exhaustive account of this lengthy survey. I will repeat only what seems crucial for accurately interpreting the impressions gathered during a journey like mine.

The black problem, says Myrdal, is first of all a white problem. To understand it, you must start there. It was whites who brought black slaves to America (around four hundred thousand of them in 1802, when the slave trade was legal, and nearly as many – illegally – between 1808 and 1860). It was whites who fought each other to decide whether to maintain or abolish slavery. Today, there are thirteen million blacks, but they possess only a tiny portion of the country's economic wealth, and they have almost no political influence. It is whites who assign them their place: their way of life is a secondary reaction to the situation created by the white majority.

This problem, moreover, should not be viewed in isolation, for it depends on the whole complex of problems posed by American civilisation. It has an impact on the whole structure of society, which is to a great extent conditioned by the presence of thirteen million black citizens. This is a white problem in an even more obvious sense, for it makes itself felt in the heart of every American, where interracial conflict is most intense and where the decisive battle is fought. Many white people feel a sense of danger when they touch on this question, and many have a vague feeling of individual or collective guilt; it creates discomfort in everyone. And the American is not cynical; he hates having a bad conscience. Hence, the great 'American dilemma'.

America is idealistic. In its schools, its churches, its courts, its newspapers, its politicians' speeches, in the text of its laws as well as in private conversations, throughout every region, among all classes, the same credo is affirmed: the one inscribed in the Declaration of Independence and in the preamble to the constitution. It posits the essential dignity of human beings, the basic equality of all men, and certain inalienable rights to liberty, justice and concrete opportunities for success. This credo was a political tool during the Revolutionary War, but it is noteworthy that it continued to be alive and effective afterward. Even conservatives in America fight in the name of liberal principles. These principles have their roots in the philosophy of the Enlightenment, Puritan Christianity, English law and especially in the early history of America. 'Let us not forget that we are the descendants of revolutionaries and immigrants,' [Franklin] Roosevelt said, appealing to the democratic conscience of the country.

Now, this credo, so deeply embedded in the heart of all whites, even those in the South, is flagrantly contradicted by the situation of blacks. No one claims that their conditions or opportunities are equal to those of whites. The very fact that blacks sense the injustice done to them and express that with growing strength prevents whites from forgetting it easily. Southerners readily say that there is no black problem, that it's a myth invented by northerners: in fact, they're obsessed with it. The bad faith they bring to discussions is proof itself of the conflict of values going on inside them. Their ignorance helps them; they claim to 'know' the black man, just as French colonials believe they 'know' the native, because their servants are blacks. In fact, their relations with them are utterly false, and they don't try to inform themselves about the real conditions of their servants' lives. But this ignorance could never be great enough to allow them peace of mind. They need other defences. There's an entire system of rationalisation engendered in the South, which is also more or less widespread in the North, and its whole purpose is to escape the American dilemma.

The surest way to succeed is to convince oneself that the

inequality between blacks and whites is not created by human will but merely confirms a given fact. It is asserted that certain racial characteristics exist that give blacks a lower rank than whites on the biological scale. But it is noteworthy that the idea of 'race' in the scientific sense is never applied precisely to 'racial' questions. Initially of African origin, American blacks are a highly mixed group. More than 70 per cent of them have white blood, and about 20 per cent have Indian blood. A black person in the USA is an individual with a percentage, however small, of black blood in his veins. That's why sociologists use the word 'caste' rather than 'race' to designate this category of citizens. Usually, certain specific physiological features distinguish blacks from whites. That's clear. But that these features imply inferiority is an unfounded assumption. The cranial capacity of blacks is a little smaller than that of whites, but science has established no connection between cranial capacity and mental capacity. The current prejudice about the supposedly gigantic size of blacks' genital organs — a sign of their bestiality — is absolutely contradicted by precise statistics. As for the 'goatish' odour of black people, whites who were asked to identify sweat samples taken from black bodies and white bodies admitted that they were incapable of distinguishing between the two. Generally, social and biological sciences today tend to view physiological and psychological variations as depending on the setting in which the individual develops, not on fixed hereditary factors. In the last twenty years there hasn't been a single serious work that dared to defend the prejudice, however convenient, of biological inferiority.

But many racists, ignoring the rigours of science, insist on declaring that even if the physiological reasons haven't been established, the fact is that blacks *are* inferior to whites. You only have to travel through America to be convinced of it. But what does the verb 'to be' mean? Does it define an immutable substance, like oxygen? Or does it describe a moment in a situation that *has evolved*, like every human situation? That is the question. And to fresh eyes it's clear that the second meaning is the correct one: 'Blacks are uncultured.' The best answer to this accusation was provided by Jefferson, speaking of white Americans, who had been put down by Old World Europeans for lacking a historical past or any constructive force, for not having produced any outstanding figures in the arts or sciences. 'We have not yet had our opportunities,' he essentially said. 'First let us exist; then we can be asked to prove ourselves.'

People also say, 'Blacks are dirty.' Here we can see evidence of southerners' ambivalence toward black people. If it's a matter of sitting with them at the same table, they judge them to be dirty – but they readily eat the food blacks have prepared, and they entrust their children and their houses to their care. In fact, when their lives are compared, blacks are just as clean and fastidious as whites. 'They are lazy, lying, thieving . . .' I note in the margins of Myrdal's book that it is striking how these stereotypes are found in the mouths of all oppressors with regard to all oppressed people: African blacks, Arabs, Indo-Chinese, Hindus, Indians seen through the eyes of the Spanish conquistadors, white workers back when the working class was defenceless. These 'racial' defects are curiously universal. 'Laziness' means that work doesn't have the same significance for the person who profits from it as for the person who executes it. Lying and theft are the defences of the weak, a silent and clumsy protest against unjust power. Furthermore (as Richard Wright points out in *Black Boy*), the white man encourages the black man to engage in petty larceny, because in that way he can prove that he doesn't aspire to the moral level reserved for whites. Generally, southern racists encourage immorality in blacks by showing extreme indulgence for all profligate behaviour *within* the black community. A black man who kills another black man is only lightly punished by the courts. Yet any transgression against whites is punished severely. For example, theft – outside the petty larceny that's paternalistically encouraged – is regarded as a crime. This is one of the reasons blacks are so often regarded as a dangerous element in society. Their crime rate is a little higher than that of whites in part because they are treated with unequal severity, in part because their poverty allows them neither legal nor illegal defence against the arbitrariness of the police, and in part because they almost all have a wretched standard of living and a social status that makes them view the white legal system merely as a detested constraint.

With even more flagrant bad faith, whites see all black women as loose and corrupt. But in the South it's impossible for these women to defend themselves against the sexual advances of white men, and it is impossible for black men to protect their families; the women are simply prey. Finally, if in the big cities so many blacks are found in the lower depths of society, it's because there are so few economic outlets open to them that they're forced to live by their wits. The faults and defects attributed to blacks are really created by the terrible handicaps of segregation and discrimination; they are the effect and not the cause of the white attitude toward black people. This is a vicious circle that George Bernard Shaw, among others, denounced in this witticism: 'The haughty American nation . . . compels the coloured man to shine its shoes and then demonstrates his physical and mental inferiority by the fact that he is a shoe shiner.'

Racists will admit for the most part that the black person is not a priori tainted as an individual; it's when he leaves his station that he becomes a danger. If he stays in *his* place, he can be a 'good Negro', full of useful and admirable qualities. But if you no longer accept that this place is dictated by the black person's own nature, if you consider that there are possibilities open to him, it becomes clear that he might adapt to situations other than the one imposed on him. The white person, however, has recourse to another argument: what proves that the place we've assigned to him is good for the black person is that he's happy in it. First of all: 'These people live on nothing.' (This, too, is a stereotype that colonists in all colonised countries apply to native populations, and it was used to speak of workers and peasants until the genesis of the other stereotype: 'Those people live better than we do.') The bad faith of such an assertion is flagrant. Clearly, the poor spend less than the rich; they do without luxuries and often necessities, and all those who don't die do survive. But the most superficial inquiry demonstrates that the cost of living is equally high for blacks and whites. Rentals in the black slums are sometimes a little less than they are for the more respectable houses of whites in similar conditions; on the other hand, in Harlem, for example, food is more expensive than in the white part of town. And in the middle class, a black man has much greater standing in his community than a white man with an equivalent salary in the eyes of other whites. Such a middle-class black is expected to maintain a higher standard of living and to be much more generous. As for blacks' famous laughter – the good humour that makes their fate so enviable – first of all, white people purposely exaggerate it. It's often just a mask that the black person dons in the presence of whites because he knows it's expected of him. (Richard Wright in *Black Boy* and John Dollard in *Caste and Class in a Southern Town* both strongly insist on the black person's double face, one side of which is expressly meant for whites.) And to the extent that this trait is authentic, it shows a moral health, a richness of spirit that should incite Americans to make a large place for blacks in a civilisation that doesn't err on the side of gaiety.

Finally, if the racist is pushed to the wall, he will have recourse to this crushing argument: 'Would you like your daughter or your sister to marry a black man?' (I've heard this objection, among others, stated in the presence of the beautiful Rita Hayworth, who replied reproachfully, 'But would you stop your daughter from marrying as she likes?' Furthermore, the questioner had no daughter. I was struck then by the outdated form of the question in a country where young girls marry without asking anyone's advice. Despite the seemingly concrete nature of the question, it is absolutely theoretical. It expresses the abstract repugnance that the average American feels at the idea of a white woman's having sexual relations with a black man.) Myrdal remarks that in the hierarchy of discriminations called for by whites, this one is the first and the most important of all. It is presented as the 'key' discrimination by which the creation of a host of taboos and interdictions is explained and justified: 'The white race must maintain its purity.' White men are not embarrassed to mix their blood with that of black women, but it is true that their children then belong to the black caste and the white race is not altered. Paternity is cost-free. For the woman, having a child is a lot of work, and apart from mystical reasons, one does not want this labour to be used for the profit of an alien caste. But this refusal to mix blood is explained only if segregation is already in effect, not otherwise. An attempt is made to justify it by positing the inferiority of mulattoes in relation to pure Negroes; but the myth of the 'bad mulatto' or the 'poor mulatto' is meaningless because 80 per cent of black citizens are mulattoes. Moreover, this myth has never prevented white men from sleeping with Negro women. Indeed, quite the contrary, among blacks themselves there's a prejudice in favour of individuals with light skin, which offers them more opportunities and greater success. Almost all important black men are mulattoes. Whites do not reject assimilation to avoid the mixing of blood; they repudiate this mixing because their hearts are set on segregation.

It is very important to note that the possibility of mixed marriages comes last on the list of claims made by blacks. Most aren't concerned about this issue. What they do call for is equality on the economic level, under the law, in the political arena, as well as in the schools, churches, hospitals and social life in general. That the entire system of discrimination should be built only as a defence against the danger of intermarriage, which is only of secondary interest to blacks, is a rationalisation that doesn't hold up.

In fact, the reasons for the white man's attitude must be sought not among blacks but among whites. (I knew an anti-Semite who used to say, 'There must be something about the Jews, because I can't stand them.' Many white racists have a similar conviction – there must be something about blacks, because I'm instinctively repelled by them.) The basic reason [for the whites' attitude] is that the present-day South has reclaimed the legacy of slavery since the trauma of the Civil War. Slavery was acceptable to democratic and Christian consciences only if God Himself made the black race inferior to the white one, and every form of social organisation tended to prevent this belief from being called into question. Later, the southern states accepted their defeat with hatred and anger; the constitutional amendments that declared blacks to be American citizens equal to whites were resented as a humiliating insult inflicted by the Yankees. The memory of this insult was kept so vividly alive that the period of Reconstruction and black domination was regarded in the South as a time of terror. Northerners did not altogether deny this tale, which justified the compromise of 1876 [when a disputed election was settled by naming Republican Rutherford B. Hayes as president in return for the effective end of Reconstruction]. But a serious historical study demonstrates that the tale involves enormous exaggerations. What remains true is that southerners were horrified by the revolution that the Yankees brought to the heart of their civilisation. Slavery had taught them to despise blacks. The trauma of the war, defeat and Reconstruction engendered a phobia that often turned into real hatred. Nowadays, economic rivalries regularly reinforce this attitude. Because there has been no political education to make oppressed groups conscious of their solidarity in the face of oppression, they are induced to hate one another. In the South, where the economic situation of the cotton workers is among the most precarious and where there is great poverty, enmity between lower-class whites and blacks is intense. It began to develop among white northerners when the migrations brought a significant black population from the South to the large northern cities. Black competition is dreaded even in the middle classes. Finally – something that southern whites never openly admit – racial discrimination gives them great economic advantages; by dividing the state and county resources unequally, they make enormous profits on the backs of black people.

The idea of segregation, as it was formulated in the 1870s [actually, the 1880s] by 'Jim Crow' legislation, is not a flagrant contradiction of the American credo; it rests on the slogan 'Separate *but equal*.' We know that the idea of 'separate but equal' in fact always means a denial of equality. Segregation soon led to discrimination. Northerners, liberals and even certain black leaders tried, at least in the beginning, to instil respect for the formula 'separate but equal'. This policy was doomed to failure because, unless segregation meant discrimination, it would impose a heavy burden on the South. For example, it would be much more expensive for a community to have two school buildings, two groups of teachers and two bus lines for rural children rather than a single school if the blacks' building, teaching staff and bus were not laughably cheap; instead, the white institutions benefit. A comparison of the budget for schools, churches, hospitals, roads, sewers, hygiene and public service in black and white neighbourhoods shows the obvious profit that whites derive from the misery in which blacks are kept.

On top of these material interests, there are psychological motives. The whites who occupy the lower ranks of the social hierarchy are happy to have people beneath them to whom they are automatically superior. The other classes are happy to see 'poor whites' using their energies against the blacks instead of against them. This situation, moreover, is unfortunate for the 'poor whites', who are so busy 'keeping blacks in their place' that they don't try in any positive way to win a better place for themselves. Whites can mask their responsibility, thanks to the vicious circle just mentioned: in the condition of blacks, they find an apparent confirmation of their behaviour toward them. One of the reasons that allows them to believe, sometimes with a large dose of good faith, in the inferiority of blacks is that that inferiority exists – but it exists because they've created it, because they are still creating it, and this they refuse to acknowledge.

They have kept up this pressure from the 1870s until the present day. The failure of Reconstruction, the establishment of 'Jim Crow' laws, and the illegal existence of political, economic and social discrimination can be explained only by a tradition of illegality that is as important in America as respect for the Constitution and for the democratic credo. The curious thing here is that illegality was once the tool of conservatives, used by the ruling caste to maintain the status quo. The current situation in the South is the outcome of revolutionary movements that ensured the failure of Reconstruction and that are symbolised by the activities of the Ku Klux Klan. In 1877, when all the southern states found themselves in the hands of southerners once more, it became easy for them to impose their rule illegally.

The US Constitution stipulates that 'the right of citizens of the United States to vote shall not be denied or abridged by the United States or by any state on account of race, color, or previous condition of servitude'. But the South prohibits blacks from voting. The entire history of the vote in the South is an effort to reconcile these two incompatible requirements. The 'grandfather clause' was instituted, requiring that a voter have ancestors who had exercised the right to vote before 1861; the Supreme Court declared it illegal. Blacks have been excluded from the party primaries, in which candidates proposed by the party are chosen – on the pretext that these assemblies are private. The question of whether the Supreme Court regards them as public or private is still undecided. A 'poll tax', or ballot tax – one too high for most blacks – is required, as is evidence of education, culture and morality, thereby allowing any black person to be arbitrarily challenged. Finally, there is the use of violence and intimidation. The black man knows that he will be 'viewed unfavourably', to say the least, if he tries to vote, and to be 'viewed unfavourably' is a serious danger. The result of all these manoeuvres is that, on the whole, southern blacks no longer attempt to claim their voting rights, which allows whites to say that blacks *can* vote but *don't care to*. The political apathy attributed to most blacks is actually just resignation. Not voting has dire consequences for them. Blacks in the North vote, which procures them some direct political advantages. In 1942 they had *one* congressman in the House of Representatives (and no senator), but it is this participation in political life that has allowed them to obtain something approximating equality with whites in relation to the courts, police protection, civil service jobs, schools, hospitals, sewers, etc.

The tragic thing about the situation of blacks in the South – aside from their wretched standard of living, which results from the South's general economic poverty – is that nothing, absolutely nothing is guaranteed them. The democratic character of the American judicial system, in which judges and the police are often elected, can be a good thing in a homogeneous society, but it becomes a grave danger to democracy in a society in which political participation is restrained and in which one caste traditionally oppresses another. The minority without political power finds itself defenceless in the face of the courts and the police. The result is that the black man is constantly in danger from whites. Only once since Reconstruction has a white man been condemned to death for murdering a black man. Even imprisonment is rarely imposed in such cases, as the jury returns a verdict of 'self-defence'. This means that the black man has no recourse against the violence and theft exercised by whites. Conversely, we know how severely the slightest audacity by a black man toward a white man is punished. Here, too, the inadequacy of the courts and the partiality of the police create a vicious circle; the black man cannot even try to struggle against the state of things that crushes him, because any such attempt will be treated as a crime. And since his fate depends entirely on the goodwill of whites, it isn't surprising that personal, residential and institutional segregation are all practised to his detriment. In discrimination, whites find both material advantages and the surest means of preventing the black person from raising himself to a status that would allow him to make his claims heard.

As for the attitude of black people, it is of course basically one of protest and refusal, but they must also adapt themselves to the conditions they've been given, so their conduct necessarily oscillates between submission and revolt. Those who can do so emigrate from the South and go north, but they need money for the trip, as well as the hope of finding work. Since the massive migrations that began in 1915, the 'Negro problem' is also posed in the North, although in a less forceful way. Here one finds, in somewhat softened form, the schema that prevails in the South. For blacks, adaptation consists in modelling their behaviour on whatever whites demand of them – an attitude that is widespread in the South, where they are more defenceless. Their most aggressive revolt is a kind of desperate anarchism that easily gives rise to crime (as with the hero of Richard Wright's *Native Son*). Between these two extremes, which are both unfortunate for the black cause, the black leaders try to invent a policy that is 'adaptive' (therefore, partially submissive to white rules) and at the same time 'progressive' (that is, capable of ignoring these rules). The differing mix of these two tendencies leads to very different tactics and strong disagreements among blacks themselves. The attitude of liberal whites is essentially to make an appeal to America, against America; to the law, against illegality; to the federal government, against the state government. They strive in particular to make the courts respect the great principles of the American credo and, in the absence of assimilation, to practise equality. Others think that no result can be obtained except by an overthrow of the entire US economy. Everyone, even the racist conservative, recognises that this is one of the most difficult problems America must face, whatever goals it has in mind.

4 April

I'd been told, 'You must see Charleston and its gardens.' We arrived there late last evening and had a lot of trouble finding a place to stay. This morning we ask a taxi driver to take us twenty miles outside of town to the great plantations that date from the eighteenth century. These aristocratic Edens are now commercial ventures: it costs two dollars at the gate, and white arrows direct visitors to the classic promenades. Yet they're deserted in the sunny freshness of the morning. Young black women, dressed in bright cotton dresses and large sun bonnets, are sweeping away the dead leaves of the autumnal spring; in the hidden lanes, black gardeners trim the hedges; but there are no other visitors strolling around. The gardens of the Alhambra, the Borromean Islands, the flower beds at Kew, the Florentine terraces, the fragrant groves of Sintra – what gardens there are in the world! But I believe these are the most enchanting. The riot of azaleas and camellias is as passionate as the New Orleans storms. Little wooden bridges, romantically curved, link mysterious lakes; furtive paths wind among the flowering shrubs; and above the waters, lawns and flowers, the dishevelled triumph of Spanish moss hangs from the large, still trees. A strange parasite, whose splendour and abjection symbolise the contradictions of a sumptuous and sordid land. It echoes the name of a disease, the name of that plague the French call 'Spanish flu'. In the forests bordering the Mississippi it hangs from the trees, rumpled, grey and dirty, like spiderwebs in attics. In these gardens it is precious and delicate, like those spiderwebs pearled with dew that hold the rainbow captive. It adorns the arching greenery of the avenues with hazy stalactites, and its magic changes these paths into caverns haunted by elves. It's the colour of smoke, the colour of amber and twilight, the elusive colour of the gowns of Peau d'Ane [a French Cinderella]. It recalls the gauze veils, scarves and flounces of those fortunate young women who admired themselves in these pools – fragile, useless, subtle and disquieting, like the lustre of pearls, like the vivid blue of turquoise. A breeze is enough to turn it into dust, resembling those dust balls you find under old furniture. It becomes just refuse, summoning to the tops of the trees the dampness of the swamps in which they take root. Beneath probing fingers, it loses its magic and is merely a little piece of growing matter, shapeless, odourless and nearly colourless, like cellulose.

But in these gardens nothing suggests the confused alchemy of life that blooms in indolent and perfect forms. Here, luxury achieves beauty. To sit on one of these benches, to look around, to breathe is a joy so complete that you understand how these curves and lights, how this harmonious affirmation of man through the riches of nature, could have seemed a supreme value to some people. Men fought passionately to preserve on earth a civilisation in which these gardens had a central place, embodying exquisite refinement: if I look only at these lawns and lakes, I understand them. But it's no accident that on returning to Charleston, before discovering any other traces of the past, we come across the old slave market. It has been preserved nearly the way it appears in the engravings of *Uncle Tom's Cabin*. In one wing, vendors have put up stands between the posts, selling Coca-Cola, bananas and ice cream. But the other part is deserted, consisting of a long rectangular hall ready to receive human chattel. Creating those private Edens which are as extravagant as the Alhambra required the vast wealth of the planters and the hell of slavery; the delicate petals of the azaleas and camellias are stained with blood.

However, old Charleston evokes neither the splendors nor the horrors of southern civilisation. Despite the floods that carried off the houses near the sea, a large part of the old city has remained intact. It was the middle-class commercial life of the small British ports that drew the first immigrants from abroad. Little houses in creamy colours – pink red, white, bright yellow – look like the toys of wealthy children. They have tiny windows and doors, and the walls are as bright as cartoon drawings. Antique shops, inns, old theatres and small shops have kept their signs from long ago, and we are walking through an eighteenth-century provincial town. At the seaside several cannons and cannonballs are reminders that a battle was fought here against the English at the beginning of the Revolutionary War. And you can visit one of Washington's many houses: he spent several nights in Charleston, and the memory of this sojourn is still piously preserved.

We eat savoury Virginia dishes in an old English inn and then take the bus again. We're going north, and the landscape becomes drier. No more forests, no more Spanish moss or bayous. Only huge fields with dark furrows, where even the promises of cotton are still invisible. Here and there, a wooden shack stands alone on the bare earth, against the red clouds of the setting sun.

5 April

We slept in Raleigh and are now heading toward Richmond, the capital of Virginia and formerly the capital of the southern confederation during the Civil War. The road was once a military route and, like the trails in the Far West, it tells us its history; but the signs designating battlefields, camps and headquarters no longer have the wonderful reds and yellows of those in New Mexico: they are an austere grey, and the inscriptions stand out in black letters.

We'll spend Sunday in Williamsburg, which everyone advised us to see, and then we'll take the evening train to New York. We're dying to get back to New York, and the bus is no longer so pleasant: there are too many travellers, too many stops and frequent delays. The bus stops are like drab railroad station buffets, overheated and smelly, where they serve inedible stews. At least we've always been lucky enough to find hotel rooms. On the bus there's a whole family returning sadly from Miami, where they were unable to find lodging. They spent three days going down to Florida and immediately turned back; they're not very happy with their vacation. Their lack of foresight amazes me, since Americans almost never go anywhere without carefully working out every mile of their itinerary and reserving a room at every stop along the way.

Richmond was the capital of the Confederacy. I keep thinking of two lines from 'John Brown's Body' that the Yankee soldiers sang as they marched from Washington:

> We'll hang Jeff Davis on a sour apple tree!
> On to Richmond! On to Richmond! On to Richmond!

In the bloody battle fought at Richmond's gates, Lee lost twenty thousand men and McClellan lost sixteen thousand; this was the Seven Days' Battle that ended in the retreat of the Union soldiers. The town we tour on foot and by taxi is gloomy and ugly. We see the capitol, where the Rebel congress met in 1861, and the 'White House', from which Jefferson Davis had to flee at the end of March 1865, a few days before Lincoln's men entered the city. In the parks and along the avenues, the trees are not yet budding; after summer and spring, we're sorry to find winter again. In vain, the driver tries to communicate some of his enthusiasm. Even the relics of the Civil War seem to leave us cold. We decide to leave that evening for Williamsburg, which is only an hour away by bus.

6 April

Williamsburg is one of the sorriest shams to which I've ever fallen victim. By comparison, Carcassonne and the castle of Hoch Königsberg have a stirring flavour of authenticity. When we arrived at night, we already feared it might be a tourist trap. For mile after mile there were lodges, motels and tourist courts, as in Reno and Las Vegas. When we began to look for rooms with the help of a kind cab driver, we realised that all the residents rent rooms to visitors. Nevertheless, on this Easter eve we wandered around for a good hour before finding something far from the centre of town. We had dinner at a fine hotel, bright and polished, which stands in the middle of a park; it was swarming with people.

In the absence of intimacy, we hope at least to find something charmingly picturesque in a place with such a reputation. And in the morning, after a long walk, we arrive at a pathetic papier-mâché stage set. The old photographs exhibited in the museum show that Williamsburg once possessed some authentic relics of its past; the ruins mingled with the life of a modern town, giving it a tepid charm. [John D.] Rockefeller decided to reconstruct a colonial city from these remnants. All the new buildings were transported to the suburbs; walls were knocked down; all vestiges of the present were suppressed, as well as those of the past that didn't fit in with the reconstruction. Then, following a plan that dated from the eighteenth century, they built 'old' taverns and 'antique' houses with new boards, as well as a palace and a prison. Williamsburg couldn't help reeking of the fair and the movie studio, but after all, there is often poetry in fairs and movie studios. I don't know what cruel chance denied it any charm. The avenues are so broad, so long, the grounds alongside so deserted, that the town never appears as a whole. You come upon one isolated house after the other, all patently inauthentic. The prison guard, for example, acknowledges that the building never looked the way it does today. There was a time when offenders were locked in filthy little cells, and another period when they were lodged in two large, nearly clean rooms, but never in these pretty cells of polished wood furnished with fresh straw. You sense similar inaccuracies everywhere. To top it off, a ridiculous masquerade is unfolding in the streets. Carriages driven by black lackeys in gleaming livery take enchanted families for rides throughout this Easter morning. On the thresholds of the little shops, in the taverns, the women who greet us wear powdered wigs and dresses with crinolines. This lifeless carnival annoys us. Only a small museum catches our attention for a moment: there, you can see naive paintings from the last century and beautiful copper birds that were used as lightning rods. But after we've looked at these things, after we've gotten lost in the labyrinth of the dreary French garden surrounding the palace and have finally escaped through a hedge, we have only one wish, and that is to get out of here. The Americans who flock here on holidays display a touching love for their past. But here this past – so raw, so real in Savannah and Charleston – is a 'conditioned' past, like the nature offered to newly-weds on the Mississippi Show Boat. It's really just a commercial enterprise, and it must be admitted that it's as successful as Lourdes in France. Pilgrims must have the same taste on every continent.

7 April

New York. A black porter in a red cap takes our luggage and gives us a numbered tag in exchange. Through a system of carts and elevators, the bags are taken down into a kind of tunnel where the yellow taxis stand ready to pick up new arrivals and swiftly disperse them throughout the city. It's seven o'clock in the morning, and I feel the same joy in my heart that I feel when I return to Paris – I'm back in my city.

When I pick up the telephone, it's not to launch calls into the void, as I did two months ago. Voices ring familiarly in my ears, and in my pleasure at hearing them, I recognise that I have real friends here. This separation has domesticated New York. All its exoticism has vanished. There is no longer another world on the horizon, against which these houses, these advertisements and window displays stand out as strange shapes; Europe is forgotten and it's this world that is the backdrop to my life. I show N the streets, avenues and skyscrapers with as much pride as if I were showing a friend from the provinces around Paris. I know that when you get on the bus, you have to slip a dime into a kind of change box near the driver and that foot pressure automatically releases the exit door. I know how to disobey the red lights and thread my way between the cars as I walk, and the idea of walking down stairs would no longer occur to me. And above all, everywhere I go, I know where I am and what's around me.

We have lunch at the top of the Penthouse. On the eighteenth floor, overlooking Central Park, the restaurant is one long terrace with a glassed-in roof. For diners who don't have the privilege of a table near the window, they've installed large mirrors that permit a view, if not of the park itself, then of its perfectly arranged reflection. Beneath me, the trees with their new spring leaves are not just a vague tangle of vegetation: this park is as familiar to me as the Jardin du Luxembourg. Fat grey squirrels run over these grassy slopes; here and there a statue rises above a green mound. I've walked around the big reservoir enclosed by iron fencing; and farther on, to the north, beside a small fountain, young black men in pastel suits stroll in the lanes, and black women sit on the benches minding woolly-haired children. All of this is present for me, beyond what I actually see.

In the afternoon we go downtown. I love those jumbled neighbourhoods that stretch between Greenwich Village and the Battery. Amid an odour of packing cases, vendors sell small items wholesale and retail, items that you find in Paris around rue Reaumur: nails, screws, springs and all kinds of hardware; cotton fabrics, string, cardboard boxes, sockets, light bulbs, door knobs and oilcloth. In the old-fashioned streets, where the houses are only two storeys high, and in the more modern streets, where the apartment houses are as high as those in Paris, you find strange objects by the ton that never exist by themselves in contemporary life. Small trucks come and go on the street littered with packing paper. By contrast, the business district is utterly tranquil. I've never seen Wall Street before at five o'clock in the afternoon. The tall, shady canyons are nearly deserted; the little church sleeps at the foot of the cliffs, surrounded by its cemetery. Suddenly, the doors of the buildings release dark waves, a rising tide of humanity submerges the streets, and we're carried off in a whirl. We passively allow ourselves to be swept along as far as the New Jersey ferry. Many of these employees, these accountants, secretaries and stenographers, have to catch a train to the other side of the Hudson; they are in a hurry to get home as soon as possible, not to stretch out the long workday another minute. At this hour it is impossible to force pedestrians to respect the traffic lights, so to intimidate the women, who are the most agitated, they've chosen handsome policemen with coaxing smiles. But the women are intractable, and the other day a cop who was trying to impose a fine on wayward pedestrians was nearly lynched. Every morning and every evening, the subway, bus or train steals an hour or more from the workers. It's understandable why they would so passionately demand that they at least be paid for minutes lost in hallways and cloakrooms – a claim that has not been met.

You reach the ferryboat through a kind of railway station where you can buy tickets for the New Jersey trains. We take only a one-way ticket for the crossing. The enormous ferry is full of people who are all rushing to the front so they can disembark more quickly; upon arrival, they stream toward the trains. We are the last to disembark, and we find ourselves lost among the trains and warehouses that stretch out of sight. There's a bus waiting, so we get on at random. It drives through dilapidated neighbourhoods. In these streets lined with hovels and filthy yards, blacks and whites live side by side, mingling in common misery. By twists and turns, the bus takes us to another ferryboat, a little higher up the Hudson. Evening is coming, and while we're crossing the river, leaning on the railing of the empty boat, we see the lights of the Battery come on. The red beam that shines at the top of the Empire State Building is as dear to me as the lights on the Eiffel Tower. And while I watch it, I feel at last what I was looking for in vain on those nights in Times Square – I belong to New York, and New York belongs to me.

9 April

It's true that what you find in New York is something other than America. Only small towns and small countries are self-satisfied; a real capital goes beyond its borders. In a strange way it's to love America to say that New York is un-American because it's open to the rest of the world.

Life here takes on an exalted dimension, because you feel you're at one of the crossroads of the world. At our friends' home, I've spent a Spanish afternoon in the company of architects and painters. Miró had come from Baleares [Majorca], where he lived for several years in semi-seclusion. By contrast, American freedom enchants him. By chance, I rediscovered a friend who had arrived from Argentina and whom I hadn't seen for ten years. I learned that the painter and writer Carlo Levi, whom I knew in Rome, had just arrived. Last evening I acted as his guide to the night spots in the Bowery and Greenwich Village. His first impressions were similar to mine. He's struck by the beauty of New York (inversely symmetrical to that of Rome), and he's surprised to find such humanity in a city often described as hard and mechanical. He, too, is struck by the silence of the nights – in Rome it's much noisier. In the calm of the little streets, a sleeper is awakened by sudden bursts of laughter, songs, shouts or even voices talking nearby, while the traffic on the main avenues forms a monotonous background noise that isn't really audible and in which individual sounds are lost. Besides, if you live above the sixth floor, you enjoy the silence of the skies.

Two months ago I met the German anti-fascist director Piscator. After working in Berlin and Paris, he now has two theatres in New York. One of them offers popular shows to which the public is invited free of charge. Way down on Second Avenue, next to a Yiddish theatre, there's an eight-storey building that looks enormous among the poor houses on the East Side. It bears Yiddish inscriptions and is the headquarters of a kind of Jewish Freemasonry, with lodges on every floor. Behind these doors, in a smoke-filled atmosphere, the merchants of the district discuss business matters with an air of almost religious mystery. On the top floor there's a huge attic that has been converted into a theatre, with a stage, an orchestra pit and, beneath the large beams of the rustic ceiling, a balcony. When I was there, they were performing a Russian play. The sets were indicated by props and panels bearing light projections. Piscator's students played the roles, and the audience applauded enthusiastically. The school itself is situated in the heart of New York, on Forty-eighth Street; there, young actors receive training, and in a small room they perform good plays, which would be unlikely to succeed on Broadway. This evening they're giving the first performance of *The Flies* [by Sartre]. For the last few days I have attended final rehearsals and found the same excitement as in Paris in similar circumstances. A French play, American actors, a German director – a good example of New York cosmopolitanism. But the existence of an experimental theatre is much more unusual here than in France. Many young people are interested in the theatre; in colleges, courses in the dramatic arts are very popular, and performances are regarded as major events, but there's not much place for individual initiative in this domain, and it's very difficult to start anything. A play is a commercial venture that cannot be launched without a large amount of capital. No one offers such sums to unknown playwrights and inexperienced actors. Piscator's attempt to mount art house drama is nearly ignored; only a very small number of devotees buy tickets regularly. Although so close to Broadway, this little theatre is as anomalous as the attic space on the East Side; its productions have almost no impact. In America such efforts always take place in austere solitude: there's no niche in between obscurity and success. The artist's work is either ignored or loudly praised by the crowd. It takes luck to make the jump and a lot of strength to survive intact.

10 April

Yesterday, after lengthy debates and negotiations, the telephone operators went on strike. To tell the truth, it's hardly noticeable: within the city the automatic phones work; long-distance calls are suspended, but you can reach Miami or Los Angeles by claiming it's an emergency. Meanwhile the Eisler story is being repeated; another communist leader, Dennis, has been taken to court for using false passports. The persecution is becoming more and more systematic, and there's scarcely any protest from the public.

It rains a lot these days. When I don't see my friends, N and I visit art galleries and museums. Yesterday we spent hours at the Museum of Natural History. It has neither the antiquated charm of our old museums nor the gaiety of the Neuilly fair, but its collections are so rich that even though we don't enjoy it, we cannot tear ourselves away from this 'naturalised' world. Not only are the animals magnificently displayed, but also the landscapes in which they were captured. Costly expeditions have been undertaken to search for animals throughout the world. On hunts that were often long and difficult, *the* lion or *the* gorilla that seemed the purest embodiment of its species was chosen from among heaps of corpses. Then, the surrounding site was recorded in detail through photographs and drawings, and samples of stones and plants were collected. In the displays they've reconstructed the whole tableau against a painted *trompe-l'œil* backdrop. The set is at once so exact and so false, the movement of the animal fixed in such definitive immobility, that we feel uncomfortable. When, in a neighbouring hall, we catch sight of life-sized Indians camped around a wigwam, our first thought is that they have been stuffed as well.

At Radio City, in the largest music hall in the world, we saw a performance of the Rockettes, but music halls are all the same and girls are girls. Today we go to the circus that's just opened in Madison Square Garden. American intellectuals have contempt for this childish and barbarous entertainment. Well-meaning French people told me about it, marvelling at it as a sociological phenomenon of the greatest importance. But if you like the circus, there's no need for excuses or justifications to sit in these stands, for here again is one of those shadows glimpsed in the cave of childhood that has now become a reality. It isn't only a circus; it's the Circus, the greatest show on earth, offering the most extraordinary, varied acts. There are three rings in which clowns, jugglers and acrobats work at the same time. There's such overabundance – you can't follow the exploits of three teams of trapeze artists with just two eyes – but in the riot of lights, colours and noise, this generosity achieves a dazzling magnificence. Even more than the boldness of the tightrope walkers and the docility of the seals, it's the setting itself – the three rings, the trapezes, the tightropes, the rigging, the bright bursts of light, the spangled costumes, the assorted props, the smell of the animals, the antics of the clowns – that's fascinating. Despite their ingenuity and perfection, the attractions are only a pretext. From time to time there's a monstrous procession of gold, silk and brocade: it's Cinderella's wedding, a reception at the English court in the time of Queen Victoria. Not a moment of respite – in between the parades, the acrobats and the wild animals, an army of clowns, dwarfs and giants turn somersaults, dance, strut and jostle one another. Yet this profusion is not enough to satisfy the spectators. Vendors circulate between the stands selling not only ice cream and candy but also whistles, trumpets, whips and all sorts of gadgets. While the girls suspended from the rigging dance a horizontal French cancan, children blow their trumpets and strike at each other with their whips, and parents amuse themselves with little mechanical toys. I don't know whether the avidity with which they devour everything offered to their eyes and ears is a measure of the tedium of their everyday lives; if so, it's a dizzying abyss.

The audience is silent at the end of the show, when a man

attempts to jump rope on a wire thirty metres above the ground. There's no net, and the spectators hold their breath. As for me, I find this anxiety unbearable, and I'm indignant that nets are not mandatory, either in France or in America. I do know that it's the risk of death that gives this exercise the reality of an event; something is happening in earnest — that's what the acrobat wants and that's what fascinates the audience and me. Only the presence of death can give a moment of life such poignant authenticity. But who is worthy of such truth here? It's offered at a moment devoted to the shallowest amusements, and it is itself untruthful. Bullfights can be defended by their sacred character; the audience solemnly participates, and the blood spilled by the animal justifies, even demands, that the blood of its killer might run as well. But here the acrobat has no living adversary; he could defy gravity six metres above the ground, without endangering his own life. Since there's no one threatening him and since the laws of physics will not kill him, it's the public itself that seems to be the murderer. Yet it refuses to assume this role: it watches; that's all. When the spectacle is real, not imaginary, its relation to the spectator becomes a difficult problem. What is clearly shocking here is that death is invited for reasons of pure spectacle; hence, its tragic aspect is compromised. Emotion is not elicited by a situation that is dramatic in itself, as when man and beast confront each other; the situation is made dramatic by eliciting emotion. Because it must be viewed in a circus, this acrobatic exercise is spiced with mortal danger. The result is a challenge to its truth that degrades the truth of death itself and places money higher than life on the scale of values. Besides, in a bullfight, the death of the toreador is only a vague possibility — necessary to the beauty of the drama but remote. The audience is not haunted by it. Here, the tightrope walker is constantly catapulted to the top of the rigging and miraculously saved. What is stirring is not that his foot touches the wire but that it hasn't missed. This is a negative achievement; whereas a juggling act is inherently charming, this exercise is just one long, prearranged horror.

After the placid parade of elephants, the circus tumultuously empties out. We go off to McCarthy's restaurant on Second Avenue to meet AE [Bernard Wolfe] and NG [Calder Willingham], the young twenty-two-year-old writer who looks like Fred Astaire. His book has caused a scandal, because it deals openly with homosexuality and vehemently attacks military schools. He is being sued by the 'League for the Suppression of Vice', but this scandal itself has promoted his success. They've done a large printing of the book, and it's even the pretext for this dinner. We eat succulent T-bone steaks, so named because the meat is cut around a bone in the shape of a T. We buy a bottle of whiskey and go up to NG's place.

Such feasts are unusual; I'm beginning to know many young writers, and I know the difficulties of their material lives. After a first successful book they're often guaranteed a retainer for one or two years by the publisher, which gives them time to write a new work. This is the case with NA [Nelson Algren], AE and NG. The advantage is that, for the time being, they're freed of practical concerns; the inconvenient part is that they're obliged to produce a second successful book in a limited amount of time. If they don't have strong talent, great ambition or rigorous honesty, they're tempted to repeat themselves rather than reinvent themselves. Instead of seeking to express themselves, they'll try to concoct a best-seller. Others make a living from translations, journalism or criticism. But journalism is consuming – many writers are swallowed up by it – and criticism pays badly, except in the major magazines. On the whole, retainers or small jobs provide rather meagre incomes. Nearly all these writers live with their wives (legitimate or not – free love is much more common than I thought), and in all these households, the woman also works. One is a waitress in a drugstore, another a saleswoman in a department store, a third is a teacher. Food and clothing are easily acquired, but of course a car is out of the question, meals in restaurants and evenings out are very rare, and travel is rarer still. They don't leave the city from one year to the next – I know the landscapes of America better than any of my friends. Their homes are as modest as those of modest French intellectuals: one or two rooms, lots of books, not much furniture. Only the comforts of a bathroom and a refrigerator indicate the higher standard of living in America. Without exception, they all have typewriters: writing by hand would seem as absurd to them as weaving the fabric for their clothes. But their real luxury is the magnificent phonograph I find in every home, even at RC's [Lionel Abel's], where there's neither a bathroom nor a refrigerator. Jazz is as much a necessity to them as bread – their only diversion in the course of the workday, their only antidote to American conformism and its attendant boredom, their only connection with life.

To grasp what jazz means to a young American writer, you have to understand the stifling routine and deadly solitude of his days. In France, in Spain, in Italy, in Central Europe, café life offers the intellectual and the artist the relaxation of comradery, emulation and exciting conversation after his daily work. There's nothing like that here. Even gatherings like the one this evening are very rare. Parties represent a social obligation to which they bow from time to time, but these are occasions for distraction more than for discussion, and it's very rare that writers meet each other at such get-togethers. In Paris, literary life sometimes takes precedence over literature itself, which isn't a good thing, but the absence of all literary life is still more debilitating. It is understandable that Hollywood and all the illusions of ease are dangerous temptations to the gifted writer, and it's understandable that those who have difficulty creating become discouraged. It takes a great deal of asceticism and energy to 'hold out' over the long haul. This is what explains a phenomenon that has long puzzled me – that after one very good book, or at least one that's full of promise, so many writers are silent forevermore. One could cite long lists of these gifted children. They are among the most striking proofs of the possibilities you can find in this country when you consider individuals one by one, as well as of the way American civilisation kills them off.

We listen to some old jazz: some Louis Armstrong from his best period, some tunes by Bessie Smith, the black singer who died after a car accident because they refused to admit her to a white hospital. We also hear some folk music that's older than jazz: funeral songs sung in New Orleans, work songs chanted by slaves on the plantations. Between two pieces, we discuss American literature. Many problems present themselves to young novelists. The previous generation forged a fine working tool and used it happily. By substituting behaviourism for analysis, it didn't impoverish psychology, as is sometimes claimed. Man's inner life is nothing but his apprehension of the world, and it is by turning toward the world and leaving the hero's subjectivity in the background that a writer manages to express that inner life with the greatest truth and depth. Subjectivity is implied through silences much more intelligently than through the babblings of inferior disciples of Proust, and this stance of objectivity highlights the dramatic character of human existence. Yet not all the authors of this school offer such a wealth of implications. Among mediocre writers, this method becomes mechanical, and all that's implied is emptiness. In any case, these techniques cannot express everything, any more than other techniques could. It is understandable that young writers don't want to imitate Hemingway and Dos Passos. They're searching. NG, an admirer and disciple of James T. Farrell, has written an entirely objective narrative, and he doesn't understand why we reproach him for often being more documentary than novelistic. In our opinion, the behaviour of his characters also sometimes seems unjustified; moreover, with his chosen point of view, he gives himself permission to dodge the problem of psychological motivation. He defends himself passionately and defends his chosen aesthetic. In contrast, AE feels the need for another art form; he is one of those to whom a well-constructed, well-written novel is no longer satisfying. He thinks it impossible to render the totality of a human being in his immanence and transcendence, in his surroundings and his solitude, without inventing new methods. Because they sense the deficiencies of the novel as it was created by their elders, many of the young writers today choose poetry. And there are prose writers who try to integrate poetry into their works; the influence of surrealism and internal monologue in the style of James Joyce is very important. The discussion goes on until two a.m., and we continue it still as we walk along Central Park toward our hotel through a soft spring night.

11 April

I show N the Bowery, the Jewish section and Chinatown. We are going to a cocktail party at the house of our friends, the Ls [Gerassis], and afterward to dinner in a French restaurant. AE takes us to hear the trumpeter Sidney Bechet on Fifty-second Street. He's one of the last musicians playing in the pure New Orleans style. He used to be famous in America. He has played in France, too, and in Paris he killed another black musician in a brawl. He spent a year in prison, during which all his hair turned white. Today he's an old man with a deeply lined face. A pianist accompanies him. This isn't enough of an attraction: the little nightclub is empty. There are only three young people listening passionately at a neighbouring table; they are probably the same sort as the little Italian in New Orleans, listening the way others pray. But Bechet could not dream of having a public worthier of his genius than the dark-faced woman in the white apron who appears from time to time at a little door behind the platform. She's probably the cook, a stout woman in her forties with a tired face but big, avid eyes. With her hands resting flat on her stomach, she leans toward the music with a religious ardour. Gradually, her worn face is transfigured, her body moves to a dance rhythm; she dances while standing still, and peace and joy have descended on her. She has cares, and she's had troubles, but she forgets those cares and troubles, she forgets her dishcloths, her children, her ailments. Without a past or future, she is completely happy: the music justifies her difficult life, and the world is justified for her. She dances standing still, with a smile in her eyes that's unseen on white faces, in which only the mouth expresses gaiety. And looking at her, we understand the greatness of jazz even better than by hearing Bechet himself.

It's clear that white Americans understand jazz less and less. It's not, as I thought, their daily bread. There's a dreadful institution here called Music by Muzak, which delivers music to whoever orders it at any hour of the day. They have several kinds of programmes: for funeral homes, for engagement parties and weddings, for cocktail parties, for bars and restaurants. In factories, too, music is broadcast throughout the plant as the workers work. And every public place possesses a jukebox. When he eats, works, rests – at every moment of the day and even in a taxi, thanks to the radio – the American is bathed in music. Some even go so far as to carry cheap portable radios. But what he is served is never jazz; instead, it's Sinatra or Bing Crosby, those saccharine melodies they call 'sweet music', which are as sugary as sweet potatoes. Most often, it's 'sweet music' that's offered in the successful clubs, or a 'sweet jazz' that's a bastardisation of jazz. The public loves big, spectacular orchestras, which can't possibly play anything but written music. What is even more serious is that even those who claim to love real jazz distort it. Since blacks can earn their living only through a white clientele, they are necessarily complicit in this perversion. When one compares Bechet or the little New Orleans bands or the old Armstrong and Bessie Smith records to the jazz that's in vogue today, you realise that Americans have gradually emptied this passionate music of all its human and sympathetic content. Mourning, work, sensuality, eroticism, joy, sadness, revolt, hope – black music always expressed something, and 'hot' jazz was the feverish and passionate form of this expression. The present was exalted in its concrete truth; it was given gravity by the weight of a feeling, a situation, tied to a past and a future. Americans turn away contemptuously from the past. ('What? You're still interested in old Faulkner?' a shocked publisher asked me.) The collective future is in the hands of a privileged class, the Pullman class, which has a monopoly on the joy of starting ventures and creating on a grand scale. The others don't know how to invent a unique future for themselves in the steel world in which they are merely cogs in the machine. They have no project, passion, nostalgia or hope that engages them beyond the present; they know only the indefinite repetition of the cycle of hours and seasons. But cut off from the past and future, the present no longer has any substance; it's nothing, just a pure, empty now. And because it is empty, it can be affirmed only through external means: it must be 'exciting'.

What pleases Americans about jazz is that jazz expresses the moment. But since for them the moment is abstract, they also want an abstract expression. They want noise, rhythms – nothing more. It may be that noise and rhythms are orchestrated with art and skill so that the present is indefinitely reborn from its death, but the meaning of the old jazz is lost. AE tells me that the most recent form of jazz, bebop, expresses this divergence even more clearly. Originally, bebop was hot jazz pushed to an extreme, an effort to express the quiver, the palpitation of life in its most fragile and feverish aspect. But from this inner fever whites – and blacks in their wake – made an entirely external tremor; the breathless rhythms survive, but they no longer have any meaning. Such a shift to abstraction is not limited to jazz. Strolling again through the art galleries and reading certain works by young writers, I've been struck by the general character of this phenomenon. Cubism and surrealism have also been emptied of their contents, with only the abstract scheme preserved. These formulas, which were living languages in Europe and whose life was destroyed by the movement itself, are re-encountered here, intact but embalmed. They are produced and reproduced mechanically without an awareness that they no longer have anything to say. In this country that's so ardently oriented toward concrete signs of civilisation, the word 'abstraction' is always on my lips. I must try to understand why.

12 April

Last night was the Broadway premiere of Chaplin's latest film, *Monsieur Verdoux*. There was quite a crowd, and no doubt there will be a crowd for several weeks. We go to the morning showing in order to get seats more easily. The reviews in all the conservative papers have been peevish. They denounce the film as anti-American, antisocial, amoral, etc. I would have been happy to find that it was good. But Chaplin has managed to create neither a man nor a myth; you get the impression he was intimidated by his boldness in spite of himself. Probably, too, it's difficult to shift from a spontaneous and primitive art to a conscious and classical one. I am reminded of a Dutch painter whose pictures I saw in Utrecht. He painted the portraits of town notables with crude but striking genius; he went on a trip to Italy and afterward produced nothing but deplorable imitations of Titian.

This evening we're going as a group to the Chinese theatre. It's located, of course, in the Chinese section, where I have dinner and stroll a bit with N. Chinatown is a much more closed community than Harlem. It has not only a culture that's different from American culture, but also an autonomous internal government. I don't know why it is said to be less authentic than the one in San Francisco; it seems much livelier to me. It's one of the few corners of New York where people stroll around, and I like strolling there myself, looking at the open markets where they sell spices, fruit pastry, shell dolls, spun glass, heaps of exotic sweets and cheap trinkets, which are much more amusing than the costly porcelain on Grant Street [in San Francisco]. The restaurants are caves guarded by dragons or pagodas lacquered red and gold; these beautiful colours, found in Chinese screens, enliven the drab streets and faded signs that share the poverty of the adjacent Bowery. At Chatham Square the Chinese and the tramps rub shoulders; at this crossroads, the elevated trains intersect, the iron structures become tangled up, and the whole square is a dark cavern with a black, metallic ceiling. The lights from a Chinese movie house gleam in the dark. Chinese films, I'm told, are copied from American productions and are very boring.

The theatre is not far from here. The hall is larger and the audience is more mixed than in San Francisco – there are many whites. And, seen from a distance, the show is not as striking. For scenery, instead of beautiful embroidered panels, there are backdrops painted in a realistic and ugly fashion. The actors perform like white actors, and neither their voices nor their gestures have a rhythm or style that makes knowledge of the plot superfluous. Perhaps we've stumbled onto some trivial modern comedy instead of an ancient drama. Perhaps the troupe has adapted itself to the mixed audience that comes to hear it and has renounced the rigours of tradition. In any case, we're bored and don't stay long. A woman friend who knows the actors a bit takes us backstage. We have time to admire the sumptuous costumes hanging in the cloakroom, along with the strange props, and we are fascinated to see the actors' faces up close with their red make-up.

After we have a drink in a Greenwich Village café, all our friends return home. It's still only eleven o'clock, and I decide to accept AE's invitation from yesterday to join him at a party at the home of some friends.

I don't know the people whose bell I'm ringing, but they're expecting me. The host, LW [Charles Harrison], is a fat, exuberant man with glasses who welcomes me in a tone of cordial challenge. He immediately attacks me on the subject of existentialism, but when he learns that I don't like *La Femme du boulanger* [*The Baker's Wife*, directed by Marcel Pagnol], which seems to so many Americans the last word in French cinema, he softens. He becomes openly friendly when I tell him that recently I liked Al Jolson. He shows me the French translation of a novel [*Generals Die in Bed*] that was published fifteen years ago and that I enjoyed, asking me what I think of the translator.

I don't have any thoughts on the subject, but I say that many of us in France liked the book. He blushes with pleasure – he is the author. He fills all the glasses with whiskey and swallows two, one after the other. Then he goes into his study to look for the manuscript of the book he's writing; he takes AE and his wife with him, and they're gone for five minutes. I chat with Mrs W, a small, dark-haired woman who is a high school teacher and seems much more cheerful, relaxed and lively than most Americans. There are several guests, among others a young man who is sleeping on the sofa and his wife, whose hair is pulled back and piled in a clump on the top of her head; she looks like she's sulking. When LW reappears, she walks up to him and declares coldly that she's leaving. This party is supposedly in honour of her birthday, and she finds it unacceptable that the host should disappear with other friends. I suppose she's jealous of VE [AE's wife]. Little by little she allows herself to be swayed by LW's friendly protests and stays a while longer, although still scowling. Mrs W tells me that such an incident is not unusual; American women have an overriding need for respect and attention, and if they feel they've been slighted, they owe it to themselves to show it. They don't indulge in passionate outbursts as Slavic women do, but their cold fury is just as dreaded, and it's one of the reasons men find them so tiresome.

Once this incident is over, we listen to jazz. Like all the intellectuals I know, the Ws have a magnificent phonograph and a huge collection of records of predominantly old jazz. Gradually, as the night wears on, everyone leaves except AE. Then LW shows me his manuscript. It's a satire on 'public relations', on an information agency that in principle is supposed to serve the interests of all citizens but whose information is highly selective. In fact, it's financed by businessmen and manufacturers, and with apparent but false impartiality, it invites the public to consume this or that product which the financial backers want to push on the market. For example, under the guise of public relations, doctors will launch a campaign declaring that beer is the richest and healthiest of foods; this is merely a veiled advertisement paid for by the beer manufacturers.

LW was more or less a communist in former times. He experienced a long period of psychosis, during which he was unable to write, and was cured by psychoanalysis. Today he lives as an individualist, and his attitude is primarily negative: he attacks American civilisation in satires and pamphlets. He despises the puritanical morality from which he is escaping, perhaps in part because he is of Jewish origin. He reproaches Americans for their hatred of the body. Posters and magazine advertisements are symptomatic, he says, and it's true. A dazzling young man with brilliantined hair tightly embraces a ravishing young girl in a gauzy dress; beneath the image is the caption: 'Are you sure you don't have body odour?' A young married couple in pyjamas frisks around beside their bed; they've just drunk a lemonade that's eased their constipation. In France, too, there are advertisements for deodorants and laxatives, but they don't pursue us so obsessively in the papers, the streets and the subways; they're more discreet. What is striking here is that they're used to evoke all the splendour and joy of the human body even as they highlight its infirmities. LW observes that the bathrooms in this country never have bidets (an observation that's the reverse of one made by Thomas Wolfe when recounting his stay in France in *Of Time and the River*). This is a sign that Americans, particularly American women, pretend to deny a certain part of their body, he declares. Besides, they're all frigid: you only have to see the kisses tolerated with scarcely a raised eyebrow by actresses in Hollywood films – kisses that would be irresistible to any normal woman.

LW speaks the way others play jazz, with a verve and a spirit that don't let up all night long, giving the best of himself to the moment. He is certainly the greatest virtuoso of the language I've met in America. But I notice that all the intellectuals I know talk in an animated way and discuss things passionately whenever they're given the chance. American muteness is certainly not an innate choice, but the result of numerous complexes: it is reinforced in everyone by the silence of all the others. Many people are happy when they can escape from it, and then they willingly let themselves go. Another observation seems important: LW's satiric truculence is exceptional, but this critical attitude is familiar to me – it's common to all my American friends. Yet one shouldn't be misled: there is a tradition of self-criticism in America, as there was not long ago in France. And the people who speak most harshly of the country here are not those who are least attached to it. The French who, in prosperous times, objected to jingoism were those most loyal to their conquered country. The Americans who attack a certain moral, political and economic position are showing that they insist on a destiny worthy of this great land where they are citizens; their demands and their lucidity are the highest forms of love. Neither LW nor AE nor NA would live anywhere but New York or Chicago; they have thrust their roots into this soil, and they expect harvests worthy of it. To label as anti-American books, films and statements that imbue Jefferson's ideal with a living reality – that is to mutilate America. The day America is forbidden to question itself, America will be no different from the totalitarian regimes it claims to oppose.

The sky grows light. We're sitting at the kitchen table and eating toast with orange marmalade while drinking tea. The window reveals a broad view of the Battery and the East River. It's the first time I've watched the dawn break in New York, and I'm moved by this new measure of our intimacy. But a more secret sign tells me that I'm really beginning to participate in America: I'm no longer dazzled by it or disappointed; I'm learning, like certain of its children, to love it sorrowfully.

13 April

I went to bed at seven a.m. At nine, N and I have a date with Richard Wright to attend a religious service in a Harlem church. The one he's chosen today is renowned for its spirituals and frequented by poor blacks. And although the ceremony is conducted with the same rituals as in the big middle-class church I visited two months ago, the atmosphere is much more vibrant.

Fearing that our presence here might seem shocking (although in northern churches blacks are very hospitable to visiting whites), Wright introduces himself and explains that we are French friends of his. We are seated in the second row, next to the choir in their long, grey robes. There are three groups of singers: one dressed in grey, another in brown and another in black. They wear square caps, and their outfit recalls that of English undergraduates. One choir has only men. The different groups sometimes sing separately, sometimes together. The voices are very beautiful, and in the tense silence of the audience, the spirituals seem singularly moving. There are mostly women in the pews, but also quite a few men. All are in their Sunday best, dressed with joyful fantasy: light suits, silk shirts, flowered hats, new dresses in soft colours. The attentive faces go from cheerfulness to laughter as moving songs or familiar speeches are offered. Old women go up to the dais to announce news of certain members of the community, to offer congratulations on some happy event, or to ask for money or help for this or that charitable enterprise. The pastor then speaks with the same goodwill. Today is his birthday, and the congregation offers him gifts and sings the ritual 'Happy Birthday' in his honour. He thanks them in that half-joking, half-serious tone that is the rule in America; he says that he already has six children and that he certainly hopes to have others, for, he declares, 'I am very sexy and my wife is too.' This good-humoured confidence prompts howls of delight, which he takes advantage of to enumerate the needs of the community and to ask the faithful to contribute as generously as possible. These churches are generally poor, the pastors are badly paid, and one of the chief resources is the Sunday collection, so it's natural that it should be surrounded by great solemnity. Women in white with blue sashes pass through the rows, plates in hand; offerings are put in directly or slipped into a small envelope made for this purpose. During this time the choirs sing a spiritual. Once the task is completed, the collectors file in front of the dais, holding the collection plate in one hand, with the other hand behind their backs, and stepping in rhythm to the music in what is really a dance step – a most astonishing moment.

Once again, the usual conversation resumes. Among others, the pastor indicates the presence of Richard Wright. He goes forward, speaks and is applauded. He introduces me as the citizen of a country that is unaware of racial segregation, and all the dark faces smile at me; I'm quite embarrassed when I must say a few words. Another spiritual is sung, and a new preacher stands before the audience. He's young, with an ardent face and a burning voice; his tone is entirely different from that of the pastor. Using modern images, he recovers the pathos and grandeur of the biblical style. The theme is mystical: above all, each man must seek out Jesus in order to see him, speak to him, and draw on his infinite riches. He expresses it more or less in these words: 'No excursion is successful, no sightseeing tour is worthwhile if you forget to see Jesus.' He speaks in a very marked, breathless rhythm that gathers speed by the minute, stressing his sentences by moving his feet, his hands and his whole body. Sweat runs down his face as his voice rises, chokes, breaks, dies away and begins again. It's a 'hot' improvisation; it's the most authentic jazz. He compares Jesus to all the treasures, all the beauties of the world, to its flora and fauna, its oceans, its monuments, its mountains, its plains and especially to those drugstores where all man's needs can be satisfied. And in a kind of trance, he again summons the faithful to go and see Jesus: 'Come, my brothers, come and see this travelling drugstore . . .' It's as if he were drumming up customers at the entrance to a fair booth. But the wonder here is Jesus, and the preacher's face is streaming with sweat, his whole body trembling as his head rolls back and forth.

Already, during the pastor's speech, the audience has shown its enthusiastic approval with exclamations and gestures, but now the orator's fever overwhelms them: 'Yes! That's right! We want Him!' They clap their hands, stamp their feet, roll their heads; a very respectable old woman madly shakes her big straw hat. The gestures and shouts are in rhythm with the speech, like a drummer backing up a trumpeter's solo. Yet from time to time, in one corner or another, a loud, unexpected cry bursts out; and there's one old black man who shouts as if his throat were being cut. The young singer beside us is silent, but tears are streaming down her cheeks. The preacher ekes out one more sentence, his voice breaks, and he falls back into the arms of two acolytes, who help him to an armchair as the strains of another spiritual rise in the church. Then the pastor makes a vibrant appeal to all the members of the congregation who have not yet become part of the community; he urges them to join without delay, as he walks up and down, holding his hand out to the faithful in a grand, sacred gesture. Everyone, together, chants his words of passionate appeal. I notice a young girl dressed in soft blue who has just stood up, very straight, her hands gripping the back of a chair; her lips are trembling and her little body is shaking in her joyous Sunday clothes. The pastor holds out his hand, the choir sings, and one after the other, hesitantly, eyes lowered, men and women come to sit on the pews at the foot of the dais. The young black girl in the blue dress is still trembling; something in her is struggling and fighting itself. She struggles for a whole quarter of an hour, and then, in a kind of cold trance, walks toward the pastor, who takes her by the hand.

This is not one of those extraordinary revivals I've often read about; those are increasingly rare, anyway. The younger generation distrusts the noisy hysterics of recent times. Also, whites have an interest in confining blacks to the arena of emotions in order to deny that they have any intellectual aptitude; today, blacks refuse to play that game. The upper classes are those with the greatest self-control, so much so that in the wealthy churches even spirituals have lost their place of honour. In poorer communities, behaviour is more spontaneous, but emotion is no longer systematically cultivated, even there. And that's what makes this ceremony so overwhelming to us: it is just an ordinary Sunday service, a weekly occurrence in the more than 160 churches of Harlem. The faithful have not taken leave of their senses but are simply being themselves. The wealth of feeling they express is something they possess in their daily lives. How wonderful it would be if the goal of these assemblies were to integrate that feeling into their earthly life instead of diverting it for the sake of a God who demands submission! What a moving symbol the outstretched hand of the pastor would be if it were an appeal to men for their own sake and not a false gesture! In black communities the church doesn't just play a religious role; it's also a sort of club where people are glad to meet, as much to show off their Sunday clothes, talk and laugh with friends, and find distraction from work and daily cares as to organise lectures, concerts and charitable endeavours, and to prove their solidarity. In all countries, all churches serve this function, but it is more important here than elsewhere, because black people have so little access to the life of general society, so few possibilities for action and expression. Just the fact of gathering to hope and pray together, to live collectively for a few feverish hours, helps them break their isolation and feel their strength. But apart from a few exceptions, the clergy here, as elsewhere, is of course allied to the powers that be, and all the more so as it needs the moral and financial support of whites. Religion is essentially exploited as a distraction. The pastors speak more eagerly of the other world than of this one, encouraging blacks to put their fate in God's hands; they preach a contempt for earthly goods and resignation. And yet, almost in spite of themselves, their sermons have immediate social resonance and help black people become conscious of their problems because they allude to the burning issues of justice and happiness. This is why many black intellectuals display a certain goodwill toward the Church, even as they deplore its submissive attitude.

We discuss these questions with Richard Wright while walking toward the subway entrance. In Harlem people look at this black man framed by two white women with curiosity but no ill will. However, in the subway the faces are less congenial, and when we get out around Fifty-ninth Street, an old woman asks me, 'What are you two doing with that Negro?' Even Americans who consort with blacks do it with a certain amount of caution. They readily welcome Wright because he's a famous writer. But I notice that in the one really 'high-class' house where he's admitted, only French, Jews, Japanese, Chinese and Hindus are invited with him. And I provoke obvious discomfort at this gathering when I report my impressions of the South.

To be sure, among liberal intellectuals there's no discrimination any more. After lunch we go with the Wrights to two parties given by white friends of his for whom there is no race question. The first is in Brooklyn, in a peaceful neighbourhood; it is shabby nowadays but charming in a provincial, old-fashioned way. There are trees along the streets, and, facing the Battery, which stands proudly across the water, the old hotels have rococo façades that transport us far from New York. I meet a professor from New York University who talks to me about John Dewey, the only philosopher known and recognised in America. We return to Manhattan at dusk. There's no excursion more beautiful than a trip across the Brooklyn Bridge when the lights are coming on in the city. The view we discover from the little apartment on Washington Square is another treat. The square is peaceful, like a provincial square, and all around it quiet houses shine with all their windows lit up. There's a birthday celebration, around a cake with ten layers, creamy and tasteless. Now that these parties have lost the attraction of novelty, I realise that for the most part they're as boring as a tea party in a French living room. Even whiskey doesn't liven them up. An important man – I don't know his credentials, but he considers himself important – makes an arrogant attack on France while talking to me: We are utterly decadent. Why did we allow ourselves to be beaten? Why are there so many communists in our country? He seems to think he's God the Father on Judgement Day. I've already heard this cutting voice and these insolent admonitions several times, and if I moved in certain circles, I know I'd hear them on a daily basis. The worst thing is that many French people agree with this attitude; our capitalists are creating active anti-French propaganda in America. Perhaps it's their servility that gives certain Americans permission to speak to a Frenchwoman about France in this accusatory tone. It's the tone German officers used when they occupied a village, saying, 'There, your politicians and your Jews have been taken away.'

14 April

Since the 'League for the Suppression of Vice' has attacked NG's novel as immoral, the matter is brought before the courts this morning. The trial takes place in a small courtroom on Fifty-seventh Street where they try minor civil suits. Any individual or association can sue an author for scandal in this way, and by invoking this right, the 'league' is proceeding as routinely as Father Bethléem when he publishes his bulletin. If the league wins, the matter becomes important; the incriminating work will then be judged by a court that can decide to censor it. If the league loses, as often happens, the book benefits from the additional publicity. There's a crowd in the courtroom when the debate begins around noon. All of NG's friends are there: the Wrights, AE and Farrell. NG is sitting in a box beside the judge, looking obstinate and childish. Standing before him, a gentleman with beautiful white hair, his face exuding virtue, questions him aggressively: Why has he written about homosexuality? Is he a homosexual? NG indicates that he's married. The league's representative is a little disconcerted, but he quickly regains his footing: Why does NG write? Who gave him the idea for it? Why does he use such words – this word, for example, and this one? 'Because they say what I wanted to say,' says the writer. 'It's an ordinary use of the words.' The level of the discussion is raised to questions of the realist aesthetic and artistic freedom. It's interrupted after an hour and will resume in the afternoon, but in the meantime we are going to lunch.

We settle into booths at a restaurant on Lexington. I'm sitting beside Farrell. He speaks to me at length about a subject he has developed in a number of articles – the lack of real freedom in American literature. There is such pressure on public opinion, he tells me, that in this domain, too, the democratic ideal is increasingly losing its truth. Trials like NG's are not very important: what matters are the more underhanded tyrannies. First of all, of course, publishers can refuse to publish a book, or once a book is published, they can kill it by stopping distribution. Conversely, if they decide to make a work a best-seller, however mediocre it is, they'll succeed through a barrage of publicity. Reviews, even in the papers and literary magazines, are little more than a disguised form of publicity: to a large extent, it's the publishers who finance all the journals, and they demand praise for the books they publish. The goal of reviews is to sell the reviewed book. Of course, it would be awkward to commend every work indiscriminately – the public wouldn't be taken in – so it's appropriate to introduce a few nuances, and even severity is allowed on occasion. But the articles' polite and complimentary tone is astounding when you're used to the harshness of French reviews.

We do not stay for the end of the trial. Even though it's beginning to rain, N and I are going on a tour of the Bronx. We take a quick look at the magnificent animals at the zoo, then we drift through the streets. The grand stage set of skyscrapers, so striking to the newcomer, is actually visible from only a few places in New York. In most neighbourhoods, the houses are only two or three storeys high, and they seem scarcely more rooted in the soil than the camps and settlements of the Far West; the walls are blackened with soot, the roads littered with garbage. From the elevated train, you can take it all in at a glance, across the Bronx,

Harlem and Manhattan – the monotonous, sordid sadness of the poor man's New York.

In the evening I give a lecture at Columbia and I have dinner with some professors and chat with students. At midnight I return with N to hear the trumpeter Sidney Bechet. One of his young white admirers is playing saxophone beside him, looking very proud and a little intimidated. I think of our friend, the little Italian, and hope he'll come north again. We dawdle until quite late in the bars along Broadway, because tomorrow N returns to Los Angeles and I'm leaving on a tour of colleges and universities.

15 April

I spend three days at Smith and Wellesley, sleeping in the white guest rooms that remind me of clinics or monasteries, and talking quite a lot with professors and students. The atmosphere at Smith is intimate and cheerful. Wellesley is more splendid with its large slate-blue lake, its trees and its medieval turrets. As at Vassar, the studies are serious (although the French scholarship students find them very superficial, and when American girls come to Paris, they are disconcerted by the difficulty of the exams in law, letters or political science). Only girls who did particularly well in high school are admitted. For those who don't want to work but whose social situation requires that they go to college, there are less demanding establishments. Near Wellesley I have seen one of the most aristocratic colleges, where they accept students who were rejected elsewhere, and the students lazily pursue their studies in almost luxurious comfort. They live in charming pavilions scattered around the countryside with hardly a care for anything but their appearance and their 'dates'. They have contempt for the Wellesley students, who are equally contemptuous of them. In the top colleges a much more democratic spirit prevails; for example, the sororities, about which the college girls at Smith speak to me so angrily, have been suppressed. They say these are stupid institutions that people want to join only because others are excluded. It's a cheap way of gaining superiority. The classic hazing to which the new members are subjected is brutal and idiotic. These clubs do nothing positive; their sole objective is their own existence, and their only rationale is snobbery. The girls express these opinions in a pure and rapid French, which proves that at least on certain points their knowledge is very solid.

The more I chat with these girls, the harder it is for me to form an opinion about them. Even more so because the colleges represent a certain kind of selectivity — all the girls are from rich or at least comfortable families. Although they belong to certain circles, from different regions, and despite their tendency to conformity, they are each individuals. At Wellesley I have seen upper-class students who seem as serious and profound as others appear frivolous. 'Even those who seem frivolous aren't always like that,' they tell me. 'You have to understand that, among us, frivolity has a certain snob appeal; we're afraid of seeming like bluestockings if we take our studies or ideas too seriously. But many students are interested in important questions; they just hide it because it's frowned upon. No, our first aim isn't to find a husband, and we won't be happy with a job that'll just keep us busy for a year or two. We want to do work that serves some purpose. And we want to see the world, to enrich ourselves intellectually.' Many of them repeat with conviction, 'We want to make ourselves useful.' They are preoccupied with economic and social problems, specialising in these fields and hoping to make careers out of them. They move me with their innocence and the ardour of their good intentions. Of course, they are an elite group, but in French high schools and universities, there are no longer many girls who sincerely hold such views. This desire for personal fulfilment doesn't come out of a need to compensate for anything — on the contrary, those who tell me this are the prettiest and the most charming. They add that it would be completely false to judge their generation by the elite colleges. At the more modest specialised schools or at the state universities, where it's much less expensive to study, the majority of students have no money and work much more seriously than they do here. They know they have only themselves to count on, and this gives them a more concrete independence. Here, independence is ordained, almost institutionalised. Students freely criticise the methods of the professors, who acknowledge their observations. But they often criticise for the pure pleasure of criticising, and they readily advance decisive or offbeat opinions in order to display a kind of individuality that they don't know how to embody concretely. These faults can be found in French young people, too, especially since they are more idle and conformist – the very assertion of originality can be a kind of conformism. Do the college girls like these superficial Edens in which they live? They are divided on this question. Many of them are enchanted by it and find their parents' homes boring and suffocating; they're afraid of leaving college. Others regret being cut off from the world and would prefer to live as French students do.

One evening I find myself in private conversation with an old French spinster who seems much more open-minded than her American colleagues. I question her about the students' sexual life: 'Is it true that they are so free and live such chaotic lives that, as I've heard, there are certain parts of the campus where you find piles of condoms?' She smiles: 'On campus, I don't know; sometimes in books . . .' According to some statistics, 50 per cent of college girls are virgins. But how do they come up with these statistics? 'It's possible,' she says, 'that virginity has become rather common in recent years; the young men are so afraid of being trapped by marriage that they leave their partners' reputations intact.' Besides, it's not a healthy way of life, and most of these girls are neurotic. For summer vacation last year, she took about fifteen students to France. She'd chosen them carefully from among the most balanced of the girls, yet there were scenes from the start. They would return in tears from their outings with young Frenchmen: after generously accepting and even initiating kissing, necking and petting – which, in America, didn't lead anywhere – they'd been totally astonished when their dates ignored the rules of the game and made open attempts on their virtue. Such loutish behaviour made them sob. The most interesting problem, it seems to me, is knowing at what point the sexual act (even a completed one) has consequences for them. Mademoiselle T tells me that despite the number and nature of their experiences, all these American girls remain innocent in a certain way; becoming a woman doesn't change them or mature them – it's as if it were an operation, in which they didn't participate. Clearly, these relations, which society tacitly condones and which occur with young men as naive as these young women, don't represent a real sexual initiation, and certainly not fulfilment. These are not the passionate relations of lovers but rather an extension of certain ambiguous childhood games. I imagine that the boldest of the girls remain rather puritanical and that in their search for pleasure the boys and the girls, by mutual agreement, make every effort to ward off all the mysterious agitations of sensuality.

Between lectures and conversations, I begin to discover New England. I am shown the old village of New Hartford, Connecticut, near Smith, where a great battle was fought between the English and the Americans during the Revolutionary War. They say that the tiny stream winding through the fields was the colour of blood. In such villages there are charming wooden houses, in grey or white, much more sombre than the romantic dwellings of the South. Some display a long-ago date above the front door; a few are even from the colonial period, and all reproduce that style. In the most beautiful ones, pink brick is combined with painted white wood. The most typical features are the two columns framing the stairs leading to the front door, the rectangular windowpane above the panelled door, and the little square panes of the façade. This general theme leads to many subtle variations.

The wooden churches, white and shining, surprise me; they would look like outhouses if it weren't for their charming belfries, which you might think were borrowed from a child's building-block set. The only drawback of these villages is that they are not built according to any plan: they have no unity; the houses are isolated from each other and scattered across an area that has no inherent form. There's only a vague background: neither the streets nor the squares have any individuality, and the empty space in the middle of the village is a kind of indeterminate fairground.

There are many of these villages around Wellesley, and this morning I am taken on a tour through the American past. It is a very blue spring day, flowering with yellow forsythias and pink and purple fruit trees. Not a leaf has appeared yet, only the flowers; it's an April without greenery, only pastels. Against this soft background bursts the glory of red maples with their syrupy sap. We follow narrow, winding roads with no other cars in sight, and suddenly we find ourselves at a crossroads where several cars are stopped. Behind these trees is Walden Pond, where Thoreau built his cabin a hundred years ago. We get out; I can never be blasé about such metamorphoses, and this one moves me and surprises me more than many others. The book of my youth, in the reds and blacks of the *NRF* [*Nouvelle Revue Française*, a monthly literary magazine and publisher of books], pictured a large, unspoiled slate-blue lake in the middle of the bare woods. I read *Walden* at the age when reading is magic. It's this same magic that, years later, wrests this place from the book's pages and breathes life into it – this place that I tried in vain to conjure up. Here's the way Thoreau himself describes it:

> The scenery of Walden is on a humble scale, and, though very beautiful, does not approach to grandeur . . . It is a clear and deep green well, half a mile long and a mile and three quarters in circumference, and contains about sixty-one and a half acres; a perennial spring in

the midst of pine and oak woods, without any visible inlet or outlet except by the clouds and evaporation. The surrounding hills rise abruptly from the water to the height of forty to eighty feet . . . They are exclusively woodland. All our Concord waters have two colors at least; one when viewed at a distance, and another, more proper, close at hand. The first depends more on the light, and follows the sky. In clear weather, in summer, they appear blue at a little distance, especially if agitated, and at a great distance all appear alike. In stormy weather they are sometimes of a dark slate-color . . . But looking directly down into our waters from a boat, they are seen to be of very different colors. Walden is blue at one time and green at another, even from the same point of view. Lying between the earth and the heavens, it partakes of the color of both. Viewed from a hilltop it reflects the color of the sky; but near at hand it is of a yellowish tint next the shore where you can see the sand, then a light green, which gradually deepens to a uniform dark green in the body of the pond. In some lights, viewed even from a hilltop, it is of a vivid green next the shore . . . It appears at a little distance of a darker blue than the sky itself; and at such a time, being on its surface, and looking with divided vision, so as to see the reflection, I have discerned a matchless and indescribable light blue, such as watered or changeable silks and sword blades suggest, more cerulean than the sky itself, alternating with the original dark green on the opposite sides of the waves, which last appeared but muddy in comparison. It is a vitreous greenish blue, as I remember it, like those patches of the winter sky seen through cloud vistas in the west before sundown . . .

The shore is composed of a belt of smooth rounded white stones like paving stones, excepting one or two short sand beaches, and is so steep that in many places a single leap will carry you into the water over your head; and were it not for its remarkable transparency, that would be the last to be seen of its bottom till it rose on the opposite side. Some think it is bottomless. It is nowhere muddy, and a casual observer would say there were no weeds at all in it.

[*Walden* (New York: New American Library, 1960), pp. 121–23]

I would very much like to see the cabin where Thoreau spent several years – it seems they've only just discovered the authentic spot after several errors – but we'd have to walk an hour through these forests, and we don't have the time. We go on to Concord, where he was born and where he spent the greater part of his life. We visit his house there. Thoreau is a great American historical figure, judging by the cars parked at the shore of his pond this beautiful morning and by the care with which his study, bedroom, living room and kitchen have been preserved. Every day, numerous tourists make a pilgrimage here to pay their respects. There is a Thoreau Association with thousands of members. The curious thing is that these people are brought together by the most varied – indeed, even contradictory – interests. Some like Thoreau the naturalist; others like Thoreau the abolitionist, the democrat, the apostle of freedom; others admire him as a certain type of humanist. The association concerns itself with camping and with historical projects about Thoreau's life. Each year it gives a large banquet and generally attempts to perpetuate and spread throughout the world the modern spirit of the man who's been called the American Saint Francis of Assisi.

Concord is one of the intellectual cradles of America. A mile from here, the first battle of the Revolutionary War took place. I'm shown the site, near one of Emerson's houses, and it seems made for such an unsophisticated battle. In the middle of large fields, there's a river with an island attached to the two banks by a bridge. Until recently it was a wooden bridge, but it has been replaced by a cement structure that outrages devotees of the past. Here the minutemen, those New Englanders sworn to answer the call to arms at any minute, dropped whatever they were doing and held King George's redcoats at bay. A bronze monument was erected for them: I know the image by heart, having seen it on dollar bills, posters, advertisements and proclamations; it's almost as famous as the head of the Republic in France. This is a statue meant for a public square, and it makes a striking contrast to the cheerful solitude of the fields, next to the burbling water. In Concord I see the wooden bridge and the river again in papier-mâché; little leaden redcoats are fleeing before the bold peasants, armed with rifles and scythes. The village has preserved its old eighteenth-century shops with their signs and their delicious colours. I'm told to notice, among other things, the blood-red colour of the taverns, so characteristic of the region. There's an old cemetery and, spaced less than a mile apart, the century-old dwellings of the gentle writers of the last century. Besides Thoreau's house, here is the house where Emerson lived lovingly with his second wife and wrote most of his books; here also is one of Nathaniel Hawthorne's houses, and one where Louisa May Alcott spent part of her childhood, dreaming of escape, crushed by the persuasive tyranny of her father, the clergyman, and bearing witness in her timid work to the limitations within which an American woman still managed to do something in those days. How far these peaceful avenues are from the skyscrapers and factories, from Wall Street, Hollywood, the adventurous deserts of the Far West, and the black slums of Jacksonville and Savannah!

We return by a different route, gaily flagged with the red catkins of maple trees and yellow forsythia bushes. We pass through other villages, and on the gravestones of an ancient cemetery I read the old biblical names of the Puritans: Sarah, Abraham, Abigail. They died well before the birth of the funeral home and of pin-up girls, Times Square, the Bowery, La Salle Street and Reno. These austere farmers and merchants had no inkling of the mysteries of finance or the prodigious dangers of the industrial age. Nor did Thoreau and Emerson understand its destructiveness. And yet this past which seems to have become so quickly outdated is present in every aspect of American life. In these forgotten little villages, the morality and ideology were forged that constitute the credo to which all of America adheres today. More than refrigerators and canned goods, this credo is what creates a profound national unity. This deceased Abigail casts her shadow over the Hollywood star, and around the languid and stagnant city of New Orleans the soul of old Abraham still wails across the cotton fields. Emerson and Damon Runyon belong to the same world. You cannot understand Chicago, Los Angeles or Houston if you forget that they are haunted by the troublesome, propitious, irritated or complacent ghosts of the old Puritans. If you want to find a way into the difficult heart of America, it's in Concord that you'll find the key to open the first gate.

18 April

The liberal press is indignant because the House of Representatives has just sent the Senate the most draconian legislation ever directed against the labour unions. The workers would be stripped of nearly every possible way of sustaining their claims. And, of course, the unions with communists or even former communists among their leadership would not be recognised. It's assumed that the Senate won't dare to pass this law without amending it.

I'm speaking at Harvard this evening, and Miss C, who is head of a little college in the area, has offered to drive me to Boston. She loves France, where she lived for a long time and, until recently, spent several months each year. She was born in Boston and seems to me a typical New England woman, from the same stock as Louisa May Alcott. In several of these older women who teach in the colleges, whether they're married or single, I've found an innocent and touching freshness, which has no equivalent in my French experience. The slightest emotion causes them to flush with anger; they sometimes choke up with timidity, and sometimes their eyes shine with childish enthusiasm. There's a joyous bird with bright feathers in their breast, beating its wings against the bars; it's never been free, and it never will be, but it's alive and fluttering. Miss C charms me especially. The existentialist philosophy seems a little pessimistic to her, a little sad; she believes in a vague benevolent God. But the idea of each man's individual responsibility in the world resonates deeply within her. An idealistic and generous democrat, she takes part in a number of charitable associations, anti-racist leagues, etc., but she's beginning to get discouraged, to think that good does not triumph by itself, that one can never do enough to ensure its triumph, that if one does not do enough, it's worthless. She doesn't like the 'Reds', and she hates violence. But faced with the threatening violence of the war, with the violence of poverty, of hunger (and, for example, going through a Boston suburb that's as dreary as all the outskirts of big cities), she feels lost. She no longer knows what she wants or doesn't want. 'There will have to be a crisis,' she says. 'Misery will have to become visible. Perhaps then we'll understand and we'll change. There's so much selfishness in this country!' I've heard this emotional wish expressed at other times by well-intentioned people who are confused. She tells me that she struggles to expand her young pupils' ideas. One day she invited a famous black professor to the college, and after his lecture, she entertained him at her table. 'If there are students who don't want to have lunch with us, that's fine,' she'd announced beforehand. Two little southerners who had always openly expressed their racist sentiments asked if, as a favour, they could join the table. The lecturer's words – proof of his intellectual and humane qualities – had affected them powerfully. Now at home with their families in Louisiana, they are fighting against racism as hard as they can. But Miss C knows very well that in this area, too, a few well-intentioned people are not enough.

The roads that lead to Boston are lined with large, bright yellow bushes, and we drive through parks where spring is timidly beginning to smile: in New England, spring awakens slowly. Miss C shows me the mayor of Boston's luxurious house set amid trees and lawns. He just spent a year in prison for extortion and fraud but then resumed his official post as head of the strictest town in all of America. That a man whom the newspapers daily refer to as a gangster should rule over this city, which stands for, among other things, the great Puritan dynasty of the Adams family, is one of those trivial facts that sums up the complexity of America.

Nowhere is the poetry of the American past as palpable as it is in the streets of old Boston, which are as narrow as those in a French village and are built in a pure, sober architectural style of red brick. The little square in the heart of Beacon Hill, surrounded by eighteenth-century houses, is more exquisitely proportioned than the Place des Vosges, and it extends into streets built in the same austere and noble style. Here and there one notices a beautiful violet windowpane, completely unexpected, whose secret has long since been lost. Time has not touched this aristocratic hill; nothing has changed in two hundred years in these monotonous, dignified streets. At the foot of the hill there are large avenues lined with houses that are not so old, but quiet and noble. In contrast, old monuments lost in the middle of modern thoroughfares are now no more than museum pieces cut off from their surroundings. We visit the library, which is known less for its rich collections than for the severity with which it censors reading. When Miss C wanted to consult a volume of *The Memoirs of Casanova* one day, her request and her credentials were scrutinised for a long time. Then she was taken into a room where, after receiving the book she wanted, she was locked in. After two hours someone came to find her and carefully deposited the volume back in its locked coffer.

We walk along the wharves where, among the narrow docks smelling of tar, the Boston Tea Party took place. The Revolutionary War began when Bostonians, rebelling against taxes, threw a whole cargo of English tea into the water. The wharves are made of wood and lined with dilapidated houses. Miss C confesses to me that she would have liked to live in one of these old frame buildings where they've installed studios and apartments, occupied primarily by artists, but she adds with a sigh that her sister dissuaded her from such an unreasonable project.

In any case, no one prevents her from choosing a restaurant for lunch today – this freedom makes her as happy as a schoolgirl. She takes me to the very end of the wooden pier, to a little lunchroom decorated with fishnets and candles stuck in bottles, as in the Far West. We eat chowder made with cream and fish, which is a regional dish. Through the window we see a bit of the sea and some boats.

I sink back into the past even more. We drive down the coast, heading south toward Plymouth, the beach where the first Puritans landed. I'm haunted by the image of Henry Adams, whose family gave the US several presidents and whose autobiography, published before the First World War, seems to Americans today to be one of the most important testimonies to their recent past. One of his grandfathers lived on Beacon Hill and the other in the village of Quincy, which we drive through. All these old villages look alike, with their charming houses scattered at random. My journey back in time is completed when I glimpse by the grey water the spot along the coast where the first New England colonists knelt in prayer.

Miss C is so happy to be taking this drive, as though it were my idea. At the slightest pretext she would have thanked me, as S did at Lone Pine. She wants to show me the north coast, too, and we make a date for another day. In Boston I meet some students, who drive me to Cambridge. We cross the broad, still river and walk through the campus area. They point out the girls' college, situated close to Harvard. 'They come here to marry us,' one of the boys says spitefully. After my lecture we have a discussion, but it's too brief. I will return to Boston, and we'll spend an evening talking. Tonight, I'm taking the plane back to New York. People take planes here the way we take suburban trains in France; the flight takes only one hour and costs the same as a berth or a seat in a Pullman car. I am beginning to get used to viewing distances of three hundred miles as absolutely trivial. But even so, I'm astonished to be in my bed at midnight after leaving Cambridge at ten o'clock.

19 April

In the morning paper I come across two small events that together seem significant. The black singer Paul Robeson was supposed to give a recital in Peoria; at the last minute, the concert was cancelled on the pretext that Robeson is a communist. The authorities insist that they didn't refuse to give him access to the hall because he's black but because he's a communist. Elsewhere, an amusing episode just reached its conclusion. Several weeks ago, a bus driver with a bus full of passengers travelling along some avenue got the bright idea to bypass all the stations and the terminal and to head out onto the highway amid his customers' panicked protests. He let them out in the end, then calmly continued on his way to Florida. When stopped and questioned, he cheerfully declared, 'That route was too monotonous. I've always wanted to see Florida. One fine morning, I said to myself, "Why not go to Florida?" So I went.' This driver has become a popular hero. Although he'd been fired, he went back to work yesterday amid ovations. He was interviewed, as well as photographed a hundred times, and in all the papers he's seen laughing through the windshield of the new bus he's just been given. Perhaps such a fantasy is conceivable only in New York; friends have told me that nothing similar could happen, for example, in Chicago. But even if they are incapable of doing it themselves, all Americans adore these uninhibited actions in which they see ready proof of their love of freedom. This driver is a 'character', an original who has openly demonstrated that individualism America is so proud of. And certainly in France he would never have been reinstated in his job. It's true that America is much more indulgent of sudden whims and impulses that do not seriously challenge its authority. I knew a pious and capable mother whose children were envied by all their little friends because they were allowed to climb trees, fight with one another, and stick their tongues out at their old teachers. When they grew up, all the daughters docilely married the husbands chosen for them and the sons entered careers approved by their parents. The pleasure and pride they found in their independence had made them even more submissive prey in their parents' hands. The bus driver would certainly laugh in the face of anyone who might doubt the freedom of American citizens. Paul Robeson, however, didn't want to do anything eccentric; he just wanted to sing.

'Our democracy is nothing more than a pseudo democracy,' a friend said to me this afternoon, as we were commenting on these incidents. 'The word "freedom" is devoid of all content. The individual has no more rights; he's at the mercy of arbitrary wills.' And indeed, people today invoke two principles successively and together, slipping from one to the other in a way that catches them in a fatal trap: 'The interests of each person take precedence over the interests of all,' they declare; and at the same time they assert, 'Everybody is free; even a coal miner is master in his own home.' Yet if a citizen is considered Red, he will be fired from the civil service in the name of the general interest; on the other hand, private employers will refuse to hire him: 'It's their right; everybody is free.' And the citizen also finds himself free, to be Red and to die of hunger. In the name of the first principle, the right to strike is restricted and labour unions are destroyed; in the name of the second, all sorts of private persecutions of racial minorities and political parties are authorised. And the sad truth is that the 'general interest' applies only to a 'private' category of citizens – those who profit from the ruling elite and who intend to go on profiting. And the others are free only to the extent that they submit, which is the most abstract of freedoms.

Someone tells me about an incident in which some of this duplicity is revealed. A Jewish captain wanted to go swimming in a pool in Baltimore; he was recognised as a Jew and barred from entering. He indignantly wrote to a newspaper; his printed letter provoked other letters of indignation, and these were printed too. But one correspondent objected: everyone seems to forget that the owner of the swimming pool has the right to admit only customers he wants to admit. The newspaper concluded, 'In this story we can admire the freedom the American citizen enjoys. The Jewish captain freely demanded admission to the pool, and they freely refused him. He freely wrote to the paper, which printed his letter and those of his supporters, as well as one that reflected a different attitude. This way, everybody exercised his freedom.'

It would be easy to conclude from this, as people sometimes do, that the democratic ideal in the USA is no more than a cynically exploited hypocritical lie. But this would not be entirely fair. This ideal, as expressed in the Declaration of Independence and as expressed each day through speeches and official documents, is more than empty chatter. Respect for the human being and for the principles that guarantee him his rights is deeply anchored in the heart of American citizens. A truly democratic climate prevails among them, and that is just what makes this country so attractive initially. A class hierarchy is not superimposed on inequalities of wealth. The average standard of living is high enough so that the existence of financial privilege doesn't create an inferiority complex; the rich American is not arrogant, and the poor American is not servile. In daily life, human relations are established on an equal footing; each person's pride in his title of American citizen creates an area of ready understanding. Each person can disguise the mediocrity of his fate by thinking that he participates in the life of a great nation. And each person recognises others as his fellow creatures and wants the dignity of man and of the American to be affirmed in his fellow creature just as it is in himself – hence the generosity, the benevolence, the atmosphere of friendship that is America's most endearing feature. And it is true, too, that once one is integrated into this society, one encounters only minimal constraint; for example, I was not asked once for my papers. And the fact that the bus driver's uninhibited behaviour was possible, and that many other such examples can be found, is not a trivial thing, after all. It would be false to call the taste for independence inauthentic – the sense of human dignity is manifest everywhere in numerous and striking ways. The truth is that every day there is an increasingly radical divorce between the ideal and the reality. Jefferson's idealism no longer suits life today, which is why there's such a large gap between theory and practice that one is tempted to say it's 'pure hypocrisy'. This gap does not come from a secret contempt for grand principles, allowing them to be sacrificed shamelessly for more practical concerns, but from the fact that in their obsolete form they no longer apply to modern life: the equality and freedom they permitted have been emptied of their meaning by the demands of the present situation.

Americans have never demanded an *actual* economic equality; they accept that there are different living standards, as long as every citizen has the *possibility* of rising from one level to another through his own efforts. But this is just where the deception begins. In pioneer times, when the land had no boundaries, when its resources hadn't been exploited and when the economy was truly anarchic, men did not impose limits on one another through the sole fact of their existence. Competition was truly free, and the words 'freedom' and 'equality' were not in conflict; an individual had his chance as long as he wasn't deprived of it by some specific act. Now, the New World is as fixed as the Old, society has lost its mobility, money is kept in a few hands and the worker's tasks are carefully defined. Opportunities, too, are limited. The individual does not begin with an open future; his place in the machinery defines the course of his whole life. Naturally, a few accidental successes fuel the cherished myth of the 'self-made man', but this is as deceptive as comparing a lottery ticket to a treasury bond: every ticket can win, but there is only a tiny percentage of winning tickets. Here, the equivocalness of the word 'chance' is exploited, for its precise statistical meaning is very different from the vague import it has for the individual bewitched by dubious promises. At a time when the economy is no longer individualistic, it's a lie to continue regarding every individual as a singular case: he has only the singularity of a number. Without knowing it, he is subject to the law of averages, like that stone Spinoza speaks of which thinks it is rolling voluntarily when in fact it is obeying the principle of inertia. This is what makes a man's 'participation' in the life of the country assume the guise of a lure. In fact, the destiny of the USA is not played out equally in each of its members: there is a class that governs in the belief that it is serving this entity 'America', yet the average American serves singular and concrete interests that are not his own. This means that freedom has no more concrete reality than equality. Of course, you can always believe you're free if you stay within your designated limits, and the whole cunning of the ruling elite is in knowing how to restrain its citizens without appearing to do so. But anyone who wanted to surpass these limits would run up against a wall. The middle-class citizen has no grip on the country's economic life and only a feeble influence on its political fate. The abundance of clothes, books, films, newspapers, etc., gives him the illusion of choice, but in fact he is passive. Many things conspire to make him resigned to this passivity. And among others, one has to reckon with that conservatism of Americans which students at Oberlin discussed with me one day — a conservatism that runs very deep despite the rapid progress in material and technical domains. The American credo seems to be the expression of a supreme law, at once natural and divine; it's apparently inscribed in eternity, and no one suspects that its earthly manifestation might have been modified. This is why one can say that Americans are both the most idealistic people in the world and the most pragmatic. They have such respect for their ideal that they have relegated it to an intangible heaven. By the same token, their realism escapes the bounds of morality, as we see by the ease with which these sincere humanists adopt the idea of war as soon as the opportunity seems warranted. The most determined idealist is also the most vulnerable as soon as someone explains to him, 'You have to take reality into account.' He cannot deny that, and since reality is not his province, he is prepared to accept all the experts' decisions. Instead of rigidly respecting an outdated law, which has become mere words, American morality must find a new and living meaning. A few handfuls of people are earnestly making this effort. But those who oppose it are more numerous and more powerful because the divorce between the too-distant heaven and the earth at hand allows them to exploit the earth to their profit.

I go to a big party at Piscator's this evening. Among the guests are Le Corbusier, Kurt Weill and Marc Connelly, the author of *The Green Pastures*, and so many important critics, musicians, writers and actors are pointed out to me that I don't know where to turn my head. But I'm saved from embarrassment by the arrival of the most illustrious of the Hollywood stars, Charlie Chaplin. From the moment he arrives, there's no question of anyone talking with anyone else. A circle forms around him, and he talks for three hours non-stop. N, who met him often in Hollywood, has described him to me in terms so precise that even as I see him with my own eyes, I don't learn much that's new. His hair is completely white, and in his ageing face, only the eyes and the smile remain young. He defends his film at great length with his usual long diatribes against society in general and America in particular. It is true that he was persecuted here in a rather hellish way. But these sweeping truisms don't entertain me very much. Sometimes Chaplin drops his prophetic tone and mimes his story; then he's Charlie again. He says that the American public wants people to face tragedy with cheerfulness and to bear even the worst catastrophes with kindness and initiative. He doesn't just say it, he acts it out – he acts out horror changing into laughter, and he juxtaposes the pin-up girl's grin with the tears of melodrama. Using his face and his whole body, he becomes an extraordinary and fascinating acrobat. But this first-class number doesn't last long. Once again, he speaks. We listen to him standing up; at most parties, people remain standing, which I find very tiring. The listeners fix broad, intelligent smiles on their lips and agree with him admiringly. Sometimes one of them, astonished by his own boldness, pretends to offer a subtle objection, but this is just a springboard that allows Chaplin to bounce even higher. There are only two women who stay well outside the circle, seated dejectedly in a corner: Chaplin's wife, who is pregnant as usual, and her friend. His wife is very much a brunette and is very beautiful in a violet dress with large gold earrings. The daughter of the playwright Eugene O'Neill, she had a brilliant youth; now she seems crushed by the weight of their conjugal glory. It seems that even in her husband's absence, she maintains the self-effacing and submissive attitude of an Arab wife. She couldn't have expected anything from him and surely married him for love, but it can't be very easy to be Chaplin's wife. He continues to speak – he's indefatigable – and the audience around him continues to smile. It is terrifying to think that he must repeat the same exercise several times a week. When at last he's sated with his own words, he goes off. I watch him leave with some regret: there is such charm in his smile and in his features, but I've witnessed only a mediocre performance, I haven't really seen Charlie Chaplin.

24 April

The Senate just voted to give aid to Greece by a count of sixty-seven to twenty-three.

My tour of the universities is coming to an end. Tuesday I spoke at Yale. Yesterday I set out for Princeton on a fine spring morning. The spring here is more moderate than the tempestuous orgies of the South, but more luxurious than a French April. In France there's a mixture of grass and meadows, of hedges and bushes shining with newly exposed flowers. Here, they burst out provocatively on leafless trees. Avalanches of violet clusters cover the skeletons of the Judas trees; the boughs of the magnolias bend beneath the weight of their fleshy blooms, as plump as fruit; the Japanese cherry trees and dogwoods glisten pink and white. There's no greenery; the attractive colours stand out sharply against the blue sky.

I'm driven through the countryside, with its broad, gentle horizons, to the little town [of Princeton], which has preserved a square and several streets in the pure colonial style. The hotel where we eat lunch is an old English inn in the gentle colours of a wild rose. Through the window, we can see the great lawns and rising buildings of the university. Flowers, grass and terraces dominate a vast area, giving this studious retreat the luxury of a royal residence. The medieval pomp of the dining hall and the sitting rooms is worthy of a refined prince. In the midst of the dignified furniture, paintings, tapestries and cupboards, it's odd to see young people in checked shirts, smoking, with their feet on the tables. American informality never displeases me, but why all these outdated splendours? I know the answer already. Without being like the English and agreeing to renounce the pleasures of informality, many of these students are nonetheless deliberate snobs; they like to find a reflection of their unique quality in their surroundings. The club system, which the Smith girls denounced with endearing indignation, prevails here more than at any other university, because this is one of the richest. Princeton is the only university in the North that remains faithful to southern traditions and strictly excludes students of colour. Many of the old colonial houses that grace the streets of Princeton are clubs: the students eat and sleep there, each personally elected to the group. New members are chosen because of wealth, family and social prestige; intellectual qualities count for nothing. When Wilson was president of Princeton University in 1902, he tried to force the students to live in common dormitories. The liberal professors supported him, but all the rich 'patrons' came out against him, and democracy at the university was overruled by the old tradition of the clubs. To defy these institutions, which only tend to create a new aristocracy in the midst of an already very aristocratic community, some evidently tried to establish a 'club for non-club members', but it was a failure. Yet the fact that the pariahs of this little society found no common ground, despite their feelings of inferiority, does not seem to me a trenchant argument in favour of the clubs.

I sleep in a house (ravishing, like all the Princeton houses) that belongs to a professor. Along with his wife, he welcomes me in the most charming way. Yet again, taking tea with them in the morning in the little gleaming dining room, I admire the great warmth and simplicity of American hospitality. How stiff we all would have been in France! Here, we are already friends, and I know that behind these pleasantries and these smiles, no malevolence, no second thoughts linger. Certain university professors seem more fossilised than our French fossils. But others preserve, at fifty or sixty, a childlike freshness – without a trace of pedantry or self-importance.

After a two-hour train ride I arrive in Philadelphia. The climate is very different from that of Princeton. The university is located in the heart of a big city. It isn't luxurious; it's almost poor – it's a typical state university. The tuition here is much less expensive and the professors much more poorly paid than in the great privately endowed institutions.

The day is devoted to historical pilgrimages. I visit Independence Hall, where troops of schoolchildren and pious tourists crowd around on guided tours. Despite the crowd, the place is impressive. They've kept the table, the old chairs, the inkwell and the feather pen exactly as they were on the day the USA was born. I see the great bell that rang out freedom when the Declaration of Independence was signed, the Liberty Bell; now it's cracked.

Through parks, hills and green valleys, on little twisting, overgrown roads, I'm driven to the famous site of Valley Forge. This is where, after losing Philadelphia, Washington camped through a long winter with a handful of men, whom cold and hunger claimed day after day; he dreaded an attack that would easily have annihilated his forces. No one knows by what miracle the English general passed up his chance and remained entrenched in Philadelphia like Hannibal at Capua. Several cannons with a provision of cannonballs have been placed in the field near a majestic triumphal arch. From a specially designed turret that rises above the treetops, you can see a vast plain with its farms, rivers and roads – the roads where Washington expected to see the enemy regiments approaching from one moment to the next. The house where he lived during this long, tragic interval has been piously preserved – each stool, each pot is in its place. I wonder if my companions are disturbed when they remember the hero who gave America to Americans and when they then think of the Greeks in Greece whom their dollars are going to 'aid'.*

We return to town through residential sections that, like those in all American cities, are lovely because of the greenery, trees, lawns and large areas of flowers. Specks of sunlight dance in the forsythia pushes. Before reaching the university, we ring the doorbell at the Barnes Foundation. Dr Barnes is a prodigiously wealthy former pharmacist who, over a period of ten years, amassed a collection of modern paintings that's supposed to be extraordinary. In New York I was advised to write him, asking for his permission to come and visit. But he's a misanthrope, and he particularly detests all people who have official functions in intellectual realms: professors, museum directors, etc. All the recommendations I could have mustered were judged to be dangerous, so I based my argument only on my desire to see such a rich and celebrated collection. He did not answer. Refusing access to his galleries is one of his greatest pleasures. Sometimes he subjects the supplicant to a test. A young sculptor asked to be admitted into the sanctuary and got no answer. But as he was preparing an exhibition of his work in New York, he received a note summoning him to come on the very day of his opening. He had to choose. He chose to see the Van Goghs, the Renoirs, the Cézannes, the Douanier Rousseaus.

---

* As part of the Marshall Plan, the United States aided the royalist regime, which was fighting communists.

And Dr Barnes was tricked, because the exhibition was actually delayed a few days. The foundation, standing at the back of a park, is a large, severe building; the windows and walls have bars. We ring the bell. After a long time, a watchman half-opens the door. Before we can say three words, he slips a card into our hands and slams the door. On the card a printed text explains that the museum is open only to 'students' who are enrolled in courses and lectures directed by Dr Barnes. There is nothing to do but turn around and go back to the university.

25 April

A night train takes me to Boston, where Miss C is waiting for me. We have a twinge of anxiety when a pompous lady, who is proud of living in one of the old houses on Beacon Hill, has doubts about coming with us. Finally, she sends us off on our own but phones an aristocratic country club to arrange for us to have lunch there. There's a lot of snobbery in this part of America.

Today we are heading north. I'm pleased to be spending another day in this temperate countryside, travelling through these old villages which I've almost never encountered in American literature and film; usually, they export very different, much flashier aspects of the country. Certain old villages, such as Marblehead, seem untouched since the eighteenth century; they have simply declined. Marblehead was a little town of prosperous ship owners with important dockyards, where the ships were built. The shipyards are dead, and prosperity has vanished, but all the old houses are standing with their little windows rimmed with red or violet. Arranged in tiers on a slope above the sea, they follow the line of the streets so closely that the village has an almost European quality.

Farther on, in a somewhat larger town [Salem], surrounded by new, modern neighbourhoods, we go to visit the house that Hawthorne described in his novel *The House of Seven Gables*. The plot unfolds in this dwelling, which belonged to one of his cousins; today it's a historic monument. It stands beside the water, at the very end of a quiet old street, and its complicated wooden architecture does indeed show off its seven gables. We enter. On this kind of excursion in France, you basically visit churches, cloisters, abbeys and now and then a fortified castle; our monuments have been bequeathed to us by the clergy and the nobility, rather than by the Third Estate. Here, the traveller is offered the old houses and shops of the middle class. We're shown the drawing rooms, the bedrooms, even the attics. All the furnishings, screens and porcelain strike Miss C as antique museum pieces. But I note, as I did in Concord or Charleston, that people lived with just such furniture at my grandfather's house. As in many New England houses, there is a hidden staircase that leads to a secret chamber: this is where they took refuge from the raids of outlaws who sometimes pillaged the countryside; this is also where they hid escaped slaves just before the Civil War, when northern abolitionists encouraged blacks to flee from their masters and offered them shelter. These Puritans, however, were not always humanists, full of sweetness and light. In many of these peaceful little villages, in the middle of the eighteenth century [actually, the late seventeenth], they put up wooden stakes for burning witches. I can easily imagine that in these pious colonies of sober houses and honest comfort they felt the need, from time to time, for violent distraction. A society that was obsessed with order and authority and that had enlisted God in its service had to defend itself bitterly against the dangerous mystique of individualism; distrust, foolishness, jealousy and boredom did the rest.

Here is one of the most astonishing stories from that time. Two children who were suffering from convulsions accused a woman with black eyes of having cast an evil spell on them. The community was suddenly panic-stricken and held a big trial, during which numerous people were accused. The children, who were probably eight or ten years old, sat in the middle of the court, and their faces were observed whenever a suspect entered. If they smiled, there was a strong presumption of innocence; if they fell into convulsions, the woman was immediately convicted of dealing with the devil. Beyond this, there was one sure way of escaping the flames: for the woman to acknowledge her crime. Her sincerity might seem questionable — but Satan forbade his real wives to denounce themselves, so those women who betrayed him could not be under his yoke; these mythomaniacs were sent home. As for those women who — out of scruples, pride or foolishness — insisted on denying their relations with the devil, they were burned.

It's noon when we arrive in Rockport. The sea is grey under a rainy sky. Wooden churches, blood-red taverns, old houses. Despite their similarities, these villages are never the same; they have as much individuality as those of France or Italy. This one is distinguished by its broad views of the surging ocean, by the rocks bristling along the coast, and especially by its little port where numerous artists vacation in the summer. Hanging on the cabin walls are slate-coloured fishing nets and bright red and blue buoys. The little houses themselves are painted in vivid tones; many are painting studios. There's a little theatre where they perform avant-garde pieces during the season. It's a less colourful St Tropez, a New England St Tropez. Miss C loves to spend her vacation here; in the small streets there's a prevailing liveliness that delights her. At the moment the streets are still empty; some workers are repairing a road; the curio shops, art galleries, and fabric and embroidery shops are in the process of renovating and setting up their window displays. They'll have to wait a month before the first customers arrive. Disdaining our reservation at the elegant club, Miss C takes me to a little restaurant that looks out onto the sea. Her freedom thrills her more than the 'chowder soup'. Leaving the coast, we return to Boston through the pleasant countryside, then through the dreary suburbs. It's raining quite hard. I say goodbye to Miss C and go back to work in my room.

26 April

After a day filled with a lecture and various conversations, I am going out this evening with some students from Harvard. It's a tradition on Saturday evening to wander through the city and into bars. Austere Boston comes alive tonight – on a large square with many bars and dance halls, there's a swarm of noisy young people. Some sailors stumble out of a café on the street corner, and there's another who's been thrown out on the sidewalk by the owner of a different establishment – you feel that Boston is a port. We sit down in a large smoke-filled room where a working-class crowd is dancing to the sound of a bad orchestra. Drinking beer, we talk late into the night. This, I think, is my last exchange with students, so I'm going to try to bring together my impressions of university life in America.

There are two kinds of universities in the USA. One kind, which is financed by the state – like the one in Philadelphia [the University of Pennsylvania] or New York University near Washington Square* – has only a very modest budget; its buildings are shabby, the professors are poorly paid, tuition is inexpensive, and the student body is chiefly made up of young people who need or truly want to be educated. Often, they hold down jobs at the same time in order to make a living. Unfortunately, because the salaries are so low, the most distinguished professors want to teach in the great private universities. Financed by wealthy patrons, enriched by gifts and bequests, these schools possess magnificent buildings and campuses. Their staff members are generously rewarded, and their prestige is beyond comparison to that of the public institutions. The cost of tuition at these schools is exorbitant, which adds still more to their allure. It's taken for granted that the most

---

* Because of their names, she has confused these private universities with public institutions like City College of New York, which were indeed much as she describes.

reputable scholars and men of letters teach at Yale, Princeton, Harvard and Columbia. So much so that this has led to a paradox: students who are motivated to study because of their social condition get only mediocre teaching, whereas the best and most brilliant instruction is offered to those who care least for intellectual values.

I am particularly struck by a remark by a Harvard student. Since I'm surprised by the contempt that so many of his comrades seem to have for intellectual values, he tells me, 'In Europe, students are intellectuals, but not here at home.' He flatters the European students; in France, too, in the law schools and medical schools at the Sorbonne, there are plenty of young men who are not intellectual at all. But the fact is, this comment is particularly true of the great American universities. They are filled with all the sons of good families who owe it to themselves to have a distinguished education, and for most of them it's just an elegant and fun-filled way to spend their youth. They congregate in clubs, form committees, and occupy themselves with these clubs and committees and with the university's internal organisation, which gives them the impression of independence and activity. They take some interest in sports and indulge in extensive drinking bouts. All the university organisations are supposed to be 'dry', but this doesn't influence anyone. In between, they take classes. But it is frowned upon to take your studies too seriously. It's not only in the clubs and fraternities that superiority in intelligence and education count for nothing and any obvious academic success must be avoided. The college girls at Wellesley spoke to me of this snobbism that is rife among them too, and it seems almost a caricature at Yale or Harvard. The young men want to be seen as gentlemen, not intellectuals; the two things seem incompatible to them. Serious studies suit only a few scholarship students. At final exams, there are five grades, A, B, C, D and E, which correspond more or less to our numbers: 20, 15, 10, 5, 0. The gentleman-scholar goes after the C, which is called the gentleman's C for that reason. In effect, an E or a D would be a failure; these lower grades would prove that you are incapable of reaching a goal that you've set for yourself. But a B or an A would be a sign of pedantry of the worst sort. Professor T, with whom I talked for a long time, told me that students frequently come to ask him, 'Just what do I have to read, how many lectures do I need to attend, and how much time must I devote to my degree to receive the gentleman's C?' And AE, who was a scholarship student at Yale, told me that to earn a little money, the scholarship students wrote theses for the wealthy students. During the last two months of the school year, they also offered lectures, in which they delivered the information needed for the exam in a predigested form. Prices differed, depending on whether the buyer wanted an A, a B or a C; the C was the most expensive. AE added that it was difficult to aim just right and not to earn too good a grade.

Of course, in spite of everything, there's an elite that studies in earnest. I mostly met students in French departments, and they do speak good French. I didn't stay anywhere long enough to assess either the value of the education offered by the professors or the level reached by the students. What they told me, and what I could feel, is that the teaching is very narrowly specialised. They turn out linguists, chemists, mathematicians and sociologists, but they do not form minds. To specialise in literature seems suspect: 'literary people' are considered strange aesthetes. They themselves derive a certain glory from this originality and isolate themselves in it; nothing disconcerts them more than the idea of 'committed' literature – they repudiate it. In their eyes, the domain of art, poetry and language is cut off from the rest of the world. Here, I re-encounter the tendency that struck me not so much among writers as among American intellectuals; moreover, it has deeper roots than the taste for specialization (I shall return to this subject). Philosophy is not at all the broadest discipline, as it is in Germany and in France; here, it is divided into completely independent branches – psychology, sociology and logic – which are treated like exact sciences and remain as narrowly self-enclosed as physics or chemistry. As for metaphysics, it hardly exists. Dewey's philosophy, which is the most generally recognised, is not a metaphysics or an ontology, and it even refuses to pose those kinds of problems. At Yale they are seriously interested in phenomenology and in various forms of existentialism, but this instance is nearly unique. Professor T — who is a European Jew, a philosopher and a physicist — tells me that he met with complete failure when he tried to initiate students into the methods of phenomenology, and also when he tried to explain to them the workings of Cartesian thought. Speculation seems useless, idle, to them, and nothing interests them less than the history of ideas; only practical results count.

Even in science they care little for demonstrations: the final formulas are good enough. T told me that one day, when he had to explain a difficult physical theory, he first stated the law and then set about proving it. He was politely interrupted: 'Don't go to all that trouble. We take your word for it.' The result of all this — at least in literary fields — is a clear-cut divorce between the university world and the living intellectual world. Contrary to what happens in France, where people complain that too many writers are or have been professors, here a professor is almost never also a writer. The majority of novelists have not gone to college. There is almost no connection between culture and life in general: that literature and philosophy should have political and human responsibilities is a surprising and even displeasing idea. In general, all these young people merely confirm the impression I had at Oberlin — they hardly dare to wish for anything, and they soothe their conscience by claiming that politics is a specialised field.

'When there is a war between America and Russia, which side will France be on?' I've often heard this question. It implies a fatalism that I find terrifying. Public opinion weighs heavily in America, and [the French philosopher] Alain's idea is truer here than elsewhere — being resigned to war is the first thing that makes it possible. Many add: 'Sure, war is a despicable thing, but if we don't wage war today, who can *guarantee* that Russia won't wage war when it is even stronger?' Propaganda for pre-emptive war makes headway among students as easily as among drugstore waitresses. I've seen only one veteran declare indignantly that he does not accept the idea of war at any price, in any circumstances – naturally he was labelled a Red. Even those who feel the most repugnance for such a tragic outcome consider it inevitable: 'A war would be absurd, unjust and criminal, but it will happen.' If you ask them, 'But if you think this way, why don't you try to do something about it?' you always get the same reply: 'We can do nothing.' This evening in Boston, P and D are indignant at the intervention in Greece and the anti-labour laws, but they do not even think of trying to find a way to make their protests heard. 'Look,' P tells me, 'my friend D must join his father's business, and I'm going to make a career in business, as well. You know that at the moment there is "the Red terror". If we flaunt left-wing opinions, they'll say we're Reds, and that would compromise our future.' This confession touches me with its naive sincerity; a young man from a prosperous French family would show more guile. But it's all the more shocking because P and D are men of good faith and good intentions. They are caught in a social machine from which it would take real heroism to free themselves. Their professors will not be the ones to preach courage; moreover, they have little influence and complain they are ignored. University professors have even less importance here than in France, but perhaps this is precisely because they don't seek to play the role of spiritual guide. This is a vicious circle: they have no part in the administration of the establishments where they teach, and they know that with one incautious word they could be easily dismissed; they can only serve the system with exemplary docility.

But the inertia I observed in Oberlin as well as in California and in the East cannot be explained simply by laziness and timidity. That is what's so disconcerting at first. Individually, these young people often seem quite gifted; there's no inner defect – it's the situation that paralyses them. They all are under the impression that America is too huge a machine with too intricate gears. An American told me, 'This country is like an enormous whale. It has a tiny brain – that's the East – and an endless body.' The tiny brain doesn't feel capable of commanding the crushing mass of flesh. For many reasons, a tradition of intellectual defeatism has been established in this world, so new and yet already so old. Myrdal describes it and analyses it quite penetratingly in his great work *An American Dilemma*. He writes, 'The political "do nothing" tendency is strong in present-day social sciences. It is, typically enough, developed as a general theory. The social scientists simply reflect the general mistrust of politics and legislation that is widespread among the educated classes of Americans . . . Fatalism in regard to *res publica* is a common disease of the democratic spirit which is on the way to becoming chronic.'

According to Myrdal, the source of this defeatism must be sought in Americans' puritanical and idealistic conception of the law – they believe it must be the emanation of a higher natural law. This idea is explained historically by the revolutionary origin of the USA, which rebelled against its subjection to England's fully established regime in the name of claims that sprang freely from people's hearts and ensured their triumph. In a sense, this conception of natural law reinforces the value of law in general by conferring upon it a higher dignity than that of an expedient, provisional institution. But, on the other hand, this idea authorises the challenging of any single law in the name of a higher morality determined by individual conscience. Here we find ourselves faced with the dramatic conflict Hegel describes when he speaks of the 'law of the heart': individual judgement challenges the universal order while attempting, in itself, to constitute a universal truth; but in the process, the very notion of universality is destroyed. Invoking the 'law of the heart' and drawing on the memory of the Revolutionary War, certain reactionary factions in America have refused on several occasions to submit to established legislation. Among other examples, there has been the failure of Reconstruction after the Civil War, the failure of the anti-trust laws (which were passed under pressure from farmers in the West and merely served capitalist ends) and the failure of Prohibition.

All these failures created real traumas in the American nation. In actuality, the failures often arose from laws that had been established in too theoretical a way, without serious regard for the possibilities of implementing them, as well as from poor administration. But the result has been a general defeatism, reflected in the slogan, 'state-ways cannot change folkways'. 'The American,' Myrdal continues, 'generally regards the politics and administration of his country and his community with indulgence and tolerance, as something for which he is not responsible; he does not look upon himself as a legislator and does not try to cooperate in organizing an agreeable social life. He is even inclined to dissociate himself from politics as something contemptible, and maintain outside the political arena the things he values. This is part of what Lord Bryce has called 'the fatalism of the "masses" in America. This non-participatory fatalism creates a vicious circle – it's both cause and effect.' It was the existence of this vicious circle that I, too, felt in the course of these conversations and that seemed so disheartening to me. No one can do anything because they all think nothing can be done; and fate triumphs when you believe in it.

Once you've understood the workings of this tragic circle, you can no longer feel indignant at the passivity of these young people or be surprised by it. But it seems even more pernicious because it will only gain strength and proliferate ad infinitum. Without knowing or wanting it, they weave the very nets in which they become entangled, and the world with them. Individually, they are not happy with this resignation. If the great drinking bouts the young indulge in are rites condoned by tradition, they also reveal an inner confusion and a need to escape. Yet young people's anxieties are not clearly formulated either.

One particularly intelligent and lucid young man at Yale said to me, 'We want to go to France, my friend and I, to discover what our problems are. We feel that we have them, but we don't even know what they are. How should we resolve them? From France, with some distance, I hope we will see things more clearly.' This young man, whose views were extremely left wing and who had quite forcefully discussed the connections between intellectual and political commitment, seemed like some sort of freak to all his friends. One of his friends added, 'No, we're not worried, but some of us are beginning to feel *a little uncomfortable*!' This feeling can be found especially among the young veterans who experienced Europe and the war, and it creates a vital new ferment in the heart of the universities. The government guarantees them scholarships that allow them to pursue their studies for free. Naturally, they often have very different backgrounds from those of students who owe the privilege of a higher education strictly to family wealth. In addition, they are coming to intellectual life from a vivid experience that has left a deep impression. They are more inclined than other students to ask questions and to try to think about their lives. Certain of these students have told me, 'We need a crisis; then things would change.' But this formula, which is meekly repeated by all well-intentioned Americans, is partly what's called lip service – vague words that no one really believes. In a more thoughtful and judicious way, another student objected, 'A crisis would only make the situation worse without arousing the political consciousness of the masses. We have already had crises, and nothing came of them. If a new one were to happen, it would be averted, and once it was averted, it would soon be forgotten. We're not even ready to learn our lessons.'

Through a lack of participation in society, these young people do not harbour any bold individual ambitions – first, because the one hardly ever happens without the other. To dream of making one's way in the world requires that the world be open, unstable, malleable. Americans still speak a great deal about their pioneer ancestors, for whom life was a constant act of creating the world, and they perpetuate the legend that the humblest immigrant can become president of the United States tomorrow. But by now, this time is past. The 'push to the top' that characterised American life, in which generations upon generations among the lower classes raised themselves up a rung in society, is almost complete. It was linked to the existence of open frontiers and an economy favourable to small businesses. Today, immigration has nearly stopped (8.7 per cent of Americans were born abroad in 1940 as opposed to 12.5 per cent in 1920). There is no uninhabited land left; agriculture is in a period of depression; and industry is so well organised that it takes enormous capital outlays to start any business – there is no opportunity in America for the self-made man any more. It's now a fixed, rigid universe where you can occupy only a pre-established place in the social hierarchy. In France, the young workers are in almost the same situation. They aren't offered any possibility of choice, but young, middle-class students can preserve the dream of doing something, of becoming someone. The world is open to them and constantly changing; the future is not foreclosed – it offers them individual opportunities. Here in America, personal ambition is still possible among the lower classes: the little New Orleans trumpet player who had such a passionate concern for his destiny was of humble origins. But in the higher spheres, from which the students at the great universities are recruited, an individual doesn't get any chance to invent his own projects.

Of course, in a sense this invention is always possible; in the most limited situation, freedom can be won. But this reconquest demands an inner revolution. And here we come to a second, deeper reason for American inertia: ambition, plans, self-promotion all presuppose a detachment from one's given situation, a return to the original sources of existence that everyone experiences within himself, a questioning similar to that which Descartes practiced in the realm of ideas. But such a shift is especially repugnant to the American conscience. I still think of that journalist who told me, 'Here, we don't pose questions; we resolve them.' Unfortunately, this witticism expresses an important truth. The taste for simple results and the disdain for the process that leads to them arise from the same prejudice. There are two reasons for this, and one is positive: the given world is marvellously rich, with an intoxicating abundance and perfection. Heidegger says that 'the world appears on the horizon of broken machinery', and here the machinery is not broken. The world, in its all-encompassing and disquieting presence, does not reveal its true character, nor that of the *subject*, which is its correlative. The individual is too busy with telephones, refrigerators and elevators, he is too invested in tools, to look above and beyond. The other reason is negative: the Puritan tradition and the sense of sin forbid a return to the original nakedness; the American is afraid of the dizzying void that the slightest question would carve around and within him.

Adolescence is precisely the passage from the given world of childhood to adult existence, where everything must be built and conquered – a passage that is often effected only through a difficult crisis. I think that the majority of adolescents in America do not make it; and this is what gives a certain truth to the otherwise superficial slogan 'Americans are just big children'. Their tragedy is precisely that they are *not* children, that they have adult responsibilities, an adult existence, but they continue to cling to a ready-made, opaque universe, like that of childhood. Conversely, American children are already little men: in one sense, childhood in this country is a golden age, yet at the same time it is hardly childhood – instead, it's an adult life on a smaller scale. And because the childhood world and the adult world are homogeneous, youth is not a privileged time; the individual doesn't question himself, form himself or choose himself any more during this time than another. This has many consequences, and I shall return to them later. Today, I wanted only to talk about youth. The impression I'm left with might be summed up this way – whereas in Europe every adolescent begins the world anew – whether in revolt, pride, eagerness or fear, whether timidly or impetuously – in America he simply fills the space assigned to him in a world that's external to him, a world that doesn't owe its existence to him. He spends his youth staying put, never knowing that it is man who is the measure of things, and not things that a priori impose limits on him. Perhaps the reason Americans remain so young until an advanced age is that they have never really been young.

29 April

Amid departures and returns, I have finally achieved what I've been so eagerly seeking for three months – I *am* in New York. At least that's how it feels. I've left the vicinity of Times Square; real New Yorkers don't live there any more than Parisians live near the Champs-Elysées. I've moved to Greenwich Village, to the Brevort Hotel, an old French hotel, the only one that extends a timid terrace onto the sidewalk in the summer. Nearly all my friends live in the neighbouring streets. In just a few steps I'm at the Wrights, and in the mornings I often go up to RC's place to discuss the translation of articles I'm writing. I meet people at the corner of Fifth Avenue, just as I do at Saint-Germain-des-Prés. 'I saw you passing beneath my window yesterday,' PB [Pearl Kazin Bell of *Harper's Bazaar*] tells me when we run into each other; and while I'm looking in the window of an antique shop, a Vassar student comes out of a bookstore to say hello. It's a real neighbourhood. I love walking in the Village. The women here wear flats and flannel trousers, and the men wear velvet jackets. Perhaps there's a little bohemian affectation in these outfits, but I prefer them to the feathers, spangles and oddly shaped hats you see uptown. If I want to find the swarming New York masses, I have to go only four blocks and there I am on Fourteenth Street, one of the most ear-splitting places in town, with its drugstores, dollar shops, bargain furriers, shoes, linens and candy – the fabulous opulence of the big department stores at a discount. Crowds jostle each other in the cafeterias and Automats, becoming more and more destitute the closer you get to the Bowery. In a large café I entered, there were only men – tramps. Most of them weren't drinking; they stood around, leaning on pillars, waiting for who knows what. If I want silence and calm, I go in the opposite direction toward the little streets below Washington Square. Lined with two- or three-storey houses, they are as peaceful as culs-de-sac; no one uses them except the residents. On Greenwich Avenue and on Eighth Street, it's moderately lively; you can stroll there as you stroll on rue Bonaparte or rue de Seine. I'm beginning to know the little shops one by one. There are many small bookstores where they sell rare books, antique shops and jewellery stores whose display windows are full of embossed silver and turquoise from Santa Fe. Here, you find treasures worthy of good days at the flea market: antique taffetas, cloaks, and odd blouses and dresses of the sort the women artists of Montparnasse used to like unearthing near the Porte de Clignancourt, not long ago. There are also wide studded belts, whimsical sandals, rugs, jackets and woven skirts from Mexico or Guatemala. It would be impossible to find these colourful and vividly beautiful objects in any uptown store. If I'm tired of walking, I sit down on one of the sunny benches in Washington Square: there are elderly women wistfully warming themselves, workers taking a rest, students – no doubt from the nearby university – studying or yawning. One can read as peacefully here as in the Jardin du Luxembourg.

On a damp Sunday afternoon the little streets were given over to children, and more than ever they seemed like the lanes of a private estate. No passers-by; the thick silence was broken only by the shouts of little boys hitting a ball with a bat or bouncing it against a wall with their fists. The older boys smoked and discussed things, leaning against the walls. It felt somehow indiscreet to be an adult passing through their territory. Yesterday at dusk, the Italian section was overflowing with street life. In the lit-up shops there was a riot of mortadella and prosciutto;

the housewives were chatting with their string bags on their arms, and the men were laughing in the little bars. From one street to the next, Greenwich Village is always changing, taking on different colours, depending on the days and hours – full of surprises. When I went to Professor JB's, I didn't expect to discover, behind his living room, a garden full of weeds, statues and old stones, just like the gardens you find behind old mansions in rue de Lille or rue de Beaune. There are many charming restaurants, as Italian as in Italy, as Spanish as in Spain – English, French or German. And in Bedford Street there's the only spot in New York where you can read and work during the day and discuss things all night long without arousing curiosity or disapproval – Chamby's. The walls are decorated with old book jackets, and there's no music, which promotes conversation. The room is square and utterly simple, with its little tables lined against the walls, but it has something so rare in America – atmosphere. It's a gathering place for journalists, in particular. The clientele is a little like the sort found in Montparnasse in recent times, but American-style – that is, better groomed. The women are a bit dishevelled, but the way their hair is washed and set is first-class, and their sloppy outfits are made of beautiful fabric. This luxury is discreet. Chamby's doesn't have the scent of money that poisons the uptown bars and restaurants; one doesn't come here to advertise a certain standard of living but simply because it feels good to be here. It's rare for Americans to experience this freedom of just feeling good anywhere; one always has the impression that thousands of invisible bonds paralyse them, that they don't allow themselves to invent anything new, that in choosing clothes, food or entertainment they refer to a checklist that no one would think of questioning. This is why, in contrast, an atmosphere of leisure, whimsy and relaxation seems so agreeable. You can eat hamburgers or grilled lobster here until five o'clock in the morning, drink whiskey, or watch faces. Sometimes you even recognise someone, and it's not unusual to chat.

On the other hand, the nightclubs displease me more than ever. Even when I hear Josh White again at Café Society, I realise that his boldness is constantly tempered by tact: he carefully sticks to terrain where a liberal audience will risk venturing. How could he do otherwise? He has a wife and three children, so he has to please the crowd. If he were really to bare his heart, he would have no recourse but to go shine shoes on the street corners. This need to please is what makes me uncomfortable. I know too well how deeply it's resented, even by the whites who are subject to it, whether they be musicians, singers, maître d's or restaurant waiters. For all those who smile for their supper, the customer is the enemy. But men who know that in addition their customers despise them, men who have been oppressed since birth and at every turn because of the colour of their skin – they are not smiling deep down. Yesterday evening I was at the Vanguard, the fashionable downtown club, with some French people and an American designer. There was an incredibly skilled black band, but how different this trio was from the one at Absinthe House! They mimicked the hot jazz style as spectacularly as the wrestlers in Houston feigned savagery and anger – and the lie was just as obvious. The white public stared in wonder; they wanted to participate in the mysteries of the black soul, to be caught up in the whirlwind of its primitive violence, to be shaken by its vibrant poetry. Well, they got what they wanted. The pianist jumped up and down on his stool, the guitarist and the bass player danced in place to a diabolical rhythm, and they all showed their teeth and rolled their eyes as if possessed. And all the white faces wore admiring and foolish grins.

Among the 'enlightened' whites in New York, there's a certain snobbery about black music and literature. Richard Wright eagerly tells the following anecdote:

A young man brings a manuscript to a publisher. 'A manuscript,' says the publisher. 'Did a Negro write it?'

'No,' says the young man. 'It's mine.'

'And you have no Negro blood?'

'No.'

'You're sure? Not a drop?'

'No, I'm sorry,' says the author.

'But I imagine it's a novel on the Negro question,' the publisher continues.

'No.'

'Well, surely one of the main characters is a Negro.'

The young man loses his composure: 'No, there isn't a single Negro in my book.'

'But in that case, what do you expect me to do?' says the publisher angrily.

This story has a double meaning; it also expresses the contempt in which literature is held: musicians and writers are never seen as anything but entertainers. And this is why blacks arouse such infatuation. The trio letting loose at the Vanguard knows this very well; I'm sure that among themselves they play in an entirely different way and that the pleasure of succeeding in a brilliant career is mingled with the pleasure of duping the public. Forgetting all the tragedies of racial discrimination – in the North they forget them rather easily – whites have opened their souls wide, and these appear soft and impressionable through the windows of their eyes, bathing innocently in the sophisticated music and the hatred.

The designer B is charming. He sleeps during the day, roams alone for hours at night through the clubs of Greenwich Village, and then goes home to work. He has talent and earns money; he's convinced that America is the country where artists have the best situation. Is there anywhere that pays better? This conversation is both the exact opposite and the perfect confirmation of the one I had with my painter friend CL when I arrived in New York.

'In Paris,' says B, 'my drawings often pleased people, but the prices I was offered were laughable compared with what I earn here.' I object that America is indeed generous with successful artists, but that others don't have their luck.

'But if they are great artists, they succeed and make money,' says B.

'Let's suppose they don't succeed.'

'Then they aren't great artists.'

There is something Hegelian in this reasoning: what is real is defined by what proves its reality. This is one American idea that I don't dream of disputing. Genius is confused with its expression, but is it the work done or the money earned that expresses that genius? This is where we're no longer in agreement. It always comes down to this paradox: the American is smitten with concrete reality, but the only manifestation of reality that he recognises is an entirely abstract sign – money. Other values are too difficult to appreciate. It's an agonising responsibility to judge whether a man has talent even though he hasn't achieved success yet; no one wants to take the risk; everyone would like to palm it off on others. The danger of such an attitude is that it shows no confidence in the future. With no interest in the past, Americans give no credit to the future. If you have talent, that's something; if you will have it, that's nothing. You have to have it today. The day you can say, 'I have it,' people will be interested in you. How you navigate between indifference and success is your business. If you have money, pay a publicity agent; if not, make out as best you can. In every field where the blossoming of a work takes time, sometimes involving the slow work of research, this doctrine is particularly sinister. It's true that in Paris, Modigliani committed suicide on account of poverty; I imagine that in New York he would not even have been able to live.

30 April

I feel too much like a New Yorker to resume my long morning outings. Now, instead of exploring voraciously, I roam through New York as if it were mine. I no longer enjoy everything indiscriminately – I choose. It's when I decline an invitation that

I feel most surely settled in my life here. I see only three or four friends, but very frequently. We always speak English; I read only American books. I end up thinking only in English, and at night this leads to nightmares in which I don't understand myself. During the day I sometimes have the painful impression that my level of intelligence has clearly dropped: my thoughts are very simple, and at the slightest difficulty I give up. I wonder if the immigrants who settle here suffer from the same deficiency; you have to master a language very well to be able to think freely. Perhaps their clumsiness in handling the American language helps them renounce their singularity and slip into the slots society has prepared for them. Contrary to what most people say, I find it easier to speak than to understand. When I speak, I choose the words myself, and I use only the ones I know. The people I talk to are more unpredictable. I notice that French people are much more sensitive than Americans to my deplorable accent. They attach great importance to how closely they're able to approximate an American accent. Americans, on the other hand, seem to regard these various degrees of imperfection with equal indifference; as long as you make yourself understood, it doesn't matter whether you speak quite badly or rather well.

Today I'm taking a walk with NA, who has come to New York on business.* He passed through town when he left for France as a GI and when he returned, but he doesn't know the city. Intellectuals and other people of modest means travel very little: a Chicagoan spends his life in Chicago; many people from Brooklyn have never seen Manhattan. I'm amused to see NA discover New York through the eyes of a man from Chicago. He's struck by the colourful laundry drying on the fire escapes, by the unexpected red façades in the dreary streets, by the whimsy of a bookshop or a little square, by the patina of a century-old house. The city seems rich with a weighty past and almost

* Actually, Simone de Beauvoir invited Algren to join her in New York at this point.

disconcertingly picturesque. The Bowery resembles West Madison Avenue, but it's only here in New York that the burlesque rubs shoulders with poverty. He stops in front of the tailor for fat gentlemen, the tattoo parlour and the place where they offer black butter as an aid to sore eyes. Chicago doesn't have this *Beggar's Opera* aspect.

We're going to tour the neighbourhood that Paul Morand [a French diplomat and writer who was a collaborationist] calls 'the ghetto' and that Americans call 'the East Side'. As we walk through the teeming streets, I feel transported to Central Europe. The grey houses, three or four storeys high with shutters and tarnished signs, remind me of certain places in Berlin in the old days. All along the sidewalk it's like one huge fair. Many of the shops are below street level, with stairs leading down to the stores; others are slightly elevated, and you climb three or four steps to reach them. They all extend into the streets with stalls featuring lingerie, stockings, socks, ties, shoes, scarves and cotton dresses – from north to south, east to west, for miles and miles. Buyers and sellers bargain vehemently; much of the merchandise is marked down, but it seems to be of good quality. Here and there, there's a dazzling display window with long satin or taffeta evening dresses in vivid colours, shimmering with sequins – rich dresses for poor women. I imagine that singers and hostesses at second-rate nightclubs come here to shop. In the more modest shop windows there's more genuine merriment: hand-painted ties decorated with horses and naked women, and I would like to know who buys those flowered underpants or those briefs with purple stripes. Behind one window, amid ladies in fur coats, there are two entirely naked mannequins: their wax faces are smiling, and below their rounded breasts, their bodies are as smooth as a head by de Chirico.

Once we come out of these lively streets, the broad avenues are deserted, the houses by the side of the road are too low and they are wretched-looking, the soil is muddy in the damp air – these are like the dreary roads that lead out of all big cities. We find the small streets again, full of pastry shops selling Jewish cakes, kosher delicatessens and bars where men drink alone – we're approaching the Bowery. We come out onto a street whose fantastic scenery seems like a set for a young girl's dream or an old bachelor's nightmare: in all the shops they're selling bridal gowns. To the right, to the left, for more than a mile, young girls smile under tulle veils crowned with orange blossoms. A lady in black delicately arranges a bride's train, like a mother putting the finishing touches on her daughter's dress on the morning of the wedding. This virginal street, which promises all the city's Cinderellas the kiss of Prince Charming and delightful transformations, opens onto the Bowery. Men without wives are standing in the rain, leaning on grey walls, or crouching on the steps of little stairways – ragged, hungry, lonely. When they cross this road, the white brides in satin dresses smile at them, but they don't look; they drift impassively through this lily-white triumph that's taking place in another world.

There is no Jewish section in Chicago, NA tells me. You don't find these Jewish theatres where Yiddish plays are performed. If a big building were insolent enough to post Yiddish inscriptions on its façade, its windows would soon be broken. Jews are tolerated only on the condition that they aren't too conspicuous. It's quite different in New York, and lovers of 'the real America' say that it's a 'Judaised' city. It's true that there are many very powerful Jews and that a great deal of finance and commerce is in their hands. This doesn't mean that anti-Semitism isn't widespread. On the contrary. The power and will to assimilate in the United States are so great that a mingling of Jewish blood often goes as unnoticed as German, Swedish, Indian or Irish ancestry; in the end, the melting pot produces Americans. As it happens – is this by chance? – most of the friends I've made in America have Jewish blood, and they seem perfectly assimilated to me. But I've heard evidence from several people that anti-Semitism, whether avowed or latent, is growing stronger in America each day. Dr T, who came here as a refugee seven years ago and who teaches in a great university, told me that anti-Semitism was remarkably widespread at Yale, Harvard, Princeton, etc., not only among the students but also among the professors. As for him, he has scarcely any contact with his 100 per cent American colleagues. At meals, for example, segregation is spontaneously established: he sits at the table near other refugees, 'foreigners' or 'Jews' like him. He told me that when a student asked him for a recommendation for a job as a headmaster at a prep school, he wrote sixteen letters, which he signed with his name and his title of professor at the University of X – all in vain. His secretary advised him, 'Give only your French credentials. That way they won't know you're a Jewish refugee.' He did it, and his letter of recommendation was immediately accepted.

LW told me an anecdote with certain curious implications. One day he was meeting some friends, several of whom were well-known Jews, and he invited along a young writer, L, a southerner, but one who professed the most liberal opinions. After a few whiskeys and under some forgotten pretext, L began to insult everyone there and even wanted to start fistfights. 'I'm blond and blue-eyed,' he said. 'We don't have the same blood.' And he made such anti-Semitic pronouncements that in the end they threw him out. Of course, he apologised the next day, but his reaction had disconcerted all his friends. They assumed that L, who had been raised in Georgia, must have fought long and hard to overcome his southern prejudice against blacks. In his book he is always careful to define his heroes' exact hair and skin colour; he is conscious of his light complexion. His anti-Semitism seems to be a kind of displacement. The relationship between Jews and blacks in the American consciousness in general, as well as in the actual interactions of the two groups, is a very interesting and complex question. The average Jew reacts to blacks just as any white person would. In certain pockets of Massachusetts and Connecticut (the heart of the real America), there are beaches reserved for Jews, who don't have the right to go swimming with Aryans; but the Jews in turn send their black domestics to swim at another beach. And given the gulf created by racial discrimination, to force Jews to associate with blacks would be a much worse insult than all the others directed at them. On their side, because of the fact that many of the whites they deal with – landlords and shopkeepers – are Jews, blacks are quick to be anti-Semitic. However, the fact is that both groups belong to minorities, and although their status is very different, they are both despised by the average American. This creates certain affinities between blacks and Jews. Even Jews who refuse to associate with blacks wish discrimination could be abolished – as long as it exists in the eyes of other whites. They play a prominent role in all the anti-racist leagues and campaigns. It's among blacks that they seek to escape from an American civilisation that is hostile to them: many of the white musicians who have successfully taken up black music are Jews. It is no accident that Mezzrow, who lived in Harlem after marrying a black woman and spent all his time with blacks, was Jewish.

This evening I go with my Spanish friends to a little music hall on Second Avenue, toward the end of Fiftieth Street. No one has ever mentioned this place to me, but I'm charmed by its façade – it looks like an old silent movie house or a travelling circus's tent. The lobby is decorated with colour posters of old movie stars: Clara Bow, Mary Pickford, George O'Brien, Lon Chaney. A large banner advertises silent films. At the back of the lobby there's a cool, darkened room with garden tables; the decor is vaguely evocative of trellises and arbours. There's a stage and a little screen on one side. You can have dinner, but there's only one dish on the menu: 'chicken in a basket', which is also called 'chicken in the rough'. It's a traditional southern dish. The fried chicken is cut into pieces and brought in a basket, on a bed of French fries. The ritual is to serve it 'without silverware', that is, without plate, fork or knife – you have to eat it with your fingers. Gradually, several customers arrive; everyone drinks beer. A woman sings; another dances. A magician skillfuly bungles every trick he promises the audience, but the disobedient objects have unexpected incarnations. The lights go out. There's an old Laurel and Hardy sketch, dating from that distant time when they didn't speak and were still funny. Another sketch retells the epic of the first railroad going to the Far West. The gags are naive, but I'm touched to rediscover on screen the Carson City locomotive with its tender loaded with wood, the rugged landscape, the passes, the precipices. My favourite part of the show is when, as at the Joyful 1900 nightclub in San Francisco, they project the verses of old songs and everyone joins in. These ballads are charming. And unlike the sophisticated decor of the 'international concession', this little music hall – as outdated as the Moulin de la Galette [a popular nineteenth-century Parisian dance hall depicted by Toulouse-Lautrec] – provides just the right atmosphere for them.

May

1 May

There is a lot of bustle this morning around Union Square: groups pass by; policemen stand about. A large crowd has gathered in the square, talking and waiting. It looks like something is about to happen. This is an impression I've never had before in New York, where it usually seems as though the gears of the machine keep grinding on forever. I'm invited to a party, so I never see the march. I'm told that it lasts a long time, without incident. I'm also told that the police, equipped with cameras, record the faces of the demonstrators as they pass by.

The party I go to takes place in a Greenwich Village studio belonging to an Annamite [Indochinese] friend of Richard Wright's who works at the UN. He also writes articles on gastronomy and world affairs. The last piece was entitled 'Mayonnaise and the Atomic Bomb'. He has personally prepared extraordinary sandwiches for the party. One of the windows looks out onto the rooftops, and we climb to the upper terrace via a complicated system of ladders and fire escapes. Our host tells us that he often comes up here to paint. The view is indeed pleasant; it's a view of the whole neighbourhood, including the low houses with their roofs and the peaceful streets. This spot is one of the oldest in the city, and it almost has the dignity of a provincial town.

There are many French people around the sumptuous buffet. Every time I see them in a group I feel a small shock, and then I look at Americans with new eyes. I experience the curious phenomenon Maurice Blanchot describes in *Le Paradoxe d'Aytré*: during my first days in America, everything struck me. I saw the richness of the drugstores and felt the kindness of Americans.

Now this background is familiar to me, and I see only the things that surprise or shock me. I need a contrast to grasp what charmed me so much at first, and what I would no doubt miss terribly in France. I realise this today because the contrast is provided. It must be said that, apart from some rare exceptions, the French in America embody all their country's faults and hardly any of its good qualities. Looking at them, I understand that one of the virtues of the Americans is that they are never vulgar. They have a spontaneous sense of human dignity that keeps them from seeking distinction; and by not seeking it, they have no notion of missing it – that aborted effort is specifically French. Nor do any Americans have that cultivated voice so dear to my compatriots in high places, that restrained, flat tone that reeks of correct spelling and the baccalaureate. In both high and low society, American voices remain natural, lively. When an American has nothing to say, he keeps quiet, he drinks. This silence can be depressing, but I prefer it to those elegant swirls, those verbal arabesques that unceasingly take flight and fall into the void like deceptive ghosts. And I also prefer wooden expressions to those tics of intelligence that agitate French faces.

What shocks me most deeply is to see French people so incapable of participating in the life of another country. Many even refuse to learn the language, like that waiter at the restaurant La Fayette who proudly told me the other day as I ordered in English: 'Madame, I don't speak English.' They don't try to mingle with Americans: they look down on them from the height of their millenary civilisation with a superiority complex, humiliating them. Or else they grovel at their feet, while consoling themselves deep down with that same blessed certainty of their own superior finesse and culture. They always admire or sneer from the outside. They don't realise that their own history is in the making here, a history that's also unfolding in China, in Russia, throughout the world, and they have the chance to discover one of its most striking aspects. Since they're here, this is where they should live their life; they no longer live it in France, as they aren't there. What makes all contact with them so awkward is that they no longer fit in anywhere.

I'm quite happy when I'm once again with my American friends, who live and struggle, hope and despair right here, without refuge or recourse. And I note once more that when they have something to say, they say it with more fire and passion than in any other country. I have dinner in an Italian restaurant with the Wrights, Farrell, AE and his wife, and LW and his wife. The entire meal is taken up by a political discussion, which is so heated that I have some difficulty following it. We ask a young, very nice journalist to join us; she has to be persuaded. Without her, we have an equal number of men and women, so she is embarrassed to be an 'extra woman' and feels superfluous. This reaction astonishes me. But I'm still more surprised when, in the middle of the meal, I see that her chair is empty; no one has paid special attention to her, so she has disappeared. This episode reminds me of the one I witnessed at LW's. And again, I'm assured that such behaviour is not unusual among women in this country.

Of course, *the* American woman is a myth. In America there are about eighty million individuals of the female sex. Even if I limit myself to my own experience, I've met all sorts. Some were simply good housewives, absorbed in caring for their husbands and children; others were dedicated teachers. B's husband is in delicate health, and it's her courageous work that enables them to live. I've met several women with real warmth, a uniquely feminine charm that European women might envy. And how can I compare that young writer with the homely, generous face (who was driven to alcoholism after her poor and troubled youth) with the beautiful, cold novelist who has already devoured three husbands and many lovers in the course of a cleverly managed career? Yet since everyone in America talks about it, especially men, there must be some truth to this myth. I'm often aware of referring to it myself.

In *Generation of Vipers*, Philip Wylie has brilliantly described 'Cinderella', the girl who expects Prince Charming to give her a mink coat (as necessary to feminine dignity as the detachable collar once was to the dignity of the French *bourgeoise*), and 'Mom', the middle-aged woman who subjects America to the reign of the matriarch. Appropriating her husband's chequebook, dominating her children, and demanding the most attentive respect from all men, the American woman is compared to the praying mantis that devours its male. The comparison is generally fair, but it must be properly understood.

Personally, on the strength of all these reports, I'd imagined that women here would surprise me with their independence. 'American woman', 'free woman' – the words seemed synonymous. At first, as I've said, their dress astonished me with its flagrantly feminine, almost sexual character. In the women's magazines here, more than in the French variety, I've read long articles on the art of husband hunting and catching a man. I've seen that college girls have little concern for anything but men and that the unmarried woman is much less respected here than in Europe. One evening I was invited to dinner by VD, a young woman about thirty years old who earns a decent living. She is pretty and intelligent, has friends and numerous relationships, and lives in a comfortable apartment in a good part of town. There was another friend – young, elegant and pretty – who also had an interesting career. Neither of them was married. For the first time in my life, a meal with women seemed to be a meal 'without men'. Despite the martinis, despite the good cheer, we were surrounded by a conspicuous absence. The apartment felt like a bachelor flat. Even while loudly congratulating herself on not being married, VD complained of her loneliness. Her friend said more frankly that she wanted a husband with all her heart. Both seemed obsessed by that empty place on their ring finger.

Their demanding, defiant attitude is proof that American women are not really on equal footing with men. They feel contemptuous, often with good reason, of the servility of Frenchwomen, who are always ready to smile at their men and humour them. But the tension with which they twist around on their pedestal conceals a similar weakness. In both cases, through docility or arbitrary demand, man remains king: he is essential, and woman is inessential. The praying mantis is the antithesis of the harem girl, but both depend on the male. The Hegelian dialectic of master and slave is also confirmed here – the woman who wants to be idolised is actually subject to her worshippers. Her whole life is consumed with catching the man and keeping him under her thumb. The assertion of independence is purely negative and therefore abstract. Once more, the word 'abstraction' comes to mind. True freedom comes about only through a positive project. Older women have told me that in their view, the earlier generation had more real freedom because feminism had not yet triumphed. It was still to be won; this was a concrete task. In that striving for liberation, freedom was achieved. Now, in certain economic arenas, there's still resistance to be overcome and territory to be conquered, but in general the battle has been won. Instead of surpassing the results gained by their elders, women today merely enjoy those results statically, which is a serious mistake, because an end is never justified except as a new point of departure. In Europe, women have understood much better that the moment to affirm themselves as women has passed. They try to prove their worth on a universal level, in politics, in the arts or sciences, or simply in their lives. This positive action makes the abstract attitude of defiance useless. Because she's unable to lose herself in an objective goal, the American woman stubbornly defends her superiorities, poorly concealing her inferiority complex. In truth, it's not her fault. She suffers from a situation shared by most of her fellow citizens. With the exception of big businessmen, powerful politicians, important engineers and a few rare individuals, Americans live in a closed world without finding a goal to aim for. I've spoken about this absence of any project in young students; it's just as true in the middle classes as among the rich – among manual labourers, employees and intellectuals.

And women are its special victims. Men are, on average, more fully occupied and have less time to realise that their lives keep turning in a purposeless circle; they are more settled in a world that for thousands of years has been fashioned by men. Satisfied with the place they occupy in the great nation they're so proud of, they vaguely hope that their routine work contributes to its destiny.

Woman is much less comfortable in this masculine world, where she has only recently been admitted as an equal. Unless a pressing objective tears her away from her concern about her condition, it is natural for her to twist and turn, with demands and refusals. The only way for her to overcome a weighty legacy of weakness and uncertainty would be to stop thinking about it. But then she would have to find absorbing goals outside herself. The ones she chooses are almost always inadequate. There are many women who write, but more often it's a way of earning money or a pastime analogous to the once-popular ladies' needlework, rather than a real vocation. In the careers they choose, women usually seek an affirmation of themselves through social success rather than through the accomplishment of an objective task. And most of them are deprived of even these resources. This inability to prove themselves concretely is a constant source of irritation, which, in their confusion, they readily turn against men.

The result is that relations between the sexes are a struggle. One thing that was immediately obvious to me when I came to America is that men and women don't like each other. Women can barely survive, except in relation to men. A Frenchwoman, a schoolteacher, told me that her colleagues are much nicer and kinder among themselves than they are in France; there's no meanness, jealousy or malice, and the women in this country aren't even aware of treachery and spite. But, on the other hand, American women have assured me that real, intimate, warm friendships between women are almost unknown. As for friendship between men and women, it doesn't exist either. Young men and women are not even pals; there's always some flirtation between them. Mrs C, a professor married to an Italian, told me that she didn't know any women, other than herself, who had real friendships with their husbands. This is partly because American men tend to be laconic, and in spite of everything, a minimum of conversation is necessary for friendship. But it's also because there is a mutual mistrust, a lack of generosity and a rancour that's often sexual in origin. It's commonplace for men in this country to say that women are frigid; for some, this almost becomes an *idée fixe*. But men also say as readily of one another that they are poor lovers; in this area they have an obvious inferiority complex in relation to both Europeans and blacks. The tragedy of the man or woman who can no longer live with a cold partner after discovering real passion in Europe is a stereotypical story. It's also said that only after taking refuge in alcohol will men and women consent to sexual adventures; then, they can bury them in the night of their conscience. 'This turns out to be quite expensive,' CI told me. 'It takes a lot of whiskeys to make a woman agreeably drunk, and if the dose is too strong, she's good for nothing but sleeping.' Americans detest prostitutes, but their legitimate wives fill them with a paralysing respect; they remain uncertain of their wives' erotic possibilities, and this doubt embarrasses and paralyses them even more. The wives feel frustrated, harbouring an equivalent doubt. And all these doubts and complexes create mutual rancour. I'd like to know which of the two partners begins this game of intimidation? Certainly, the women have their share of responsibility. The college girls, who are so outwardly pleasant, obviously have strong internal defences; it's possible that many never lower these barriers. In both sexes the influence of the Puritan background is often noticeable. But among women, there's also a social 'complex': their determination to rule and dominate their men must seem incompatible with giving themselves sexually. They accept the giddiness of alcohol, but they mistrust the insidious traps of sensuality.

Whether they really are frigid or whether this accusation

symbolically sums up all men's reproaches against them, American women do not seem like lovers, friends or companions. The men shut themselves up in their clubs, the women take refuge in theirs, and the relations between them consist of small vexations, small arguments and small triumphs. This basic enmity contributes to the widespread loneliness of people here. Lacking goals that would allow them to surpass the limits of their own lives, they don't even find in this life another being to whom they might devote it. You don't see lovers in the streets or couples entwined in the lanes of Central Park, lips joined. Besides, they speak of love in specialised, almost hygienic terms: an attractive woman is 'sexy', and you'd like to have a 'sexual affair' or 'sexual intercourse' with her. There is an acceptable rationale for sensuality, which is a surreptitious way of refusing it.

Two days ago I saw *Rome, Open City*. I can't think of a finer portrait of a woman than the one Anna Magnani gives in the film. She is all the more human, the more animalistic she is; that much freer, the more generously she gives herself, struggling beside the man she loves, living for him as he does for her and together for something outside themselves. Throughout the film, I was thinking, 'How different this woman is from the women I see here!' An American could never understand such a character. She is the perfect antithesis of Hollywood heroines and of the heroines who populate detective stories – whom the American woman likes to see as her ideal.

2 May

I went to the movies to see *Odd Man Out*, an English film with James Mason. Although it's radically different, I enjoyed it as much as I did *Rome, Open City* – with the same pleasure in seeing a film that wasn't American. I have certainly changed in three months: perhaps I've become a little American. In New York, at least, the success of foreign films is more and more striking.

Even *The Adventuress*, which I found quite childish, was considered the best film of the week. There's some justice in this critical attitude toward Hollywood. When I come out of an American film and walk in New York's streets, I'm indignant that their unpredictable, picturesque aspect, their poetry, their tragedy have never been expressed on screen. Marcel Carné would have shown us the blonde brides smiling in the mists of the Bowery; Grémillon would have captured the twilight falling on the ships of the East River, on the rusty ferryboats and the crates of fish. In a Chicago street at night, all along the sidewalks, tramps would be sitting in silence, and the bars where forgotten men seek refuge would be more astonishing than the stereotypical saloons of the Far West. 'In fifty years,' my friends tell me, 'all these things will have earned the right to be brought to the screen.' Probably to the degree that they no longer exist. You could count on one hand the landscapes used in movies: the deserts of the Far West, the beaches of Florida, the redwood forests and much more rarely an old southern plantation. But I've never seen the farms and villages of New England, the forests and bayous of Louisiana, the tobacco fields of Virginia, the abandoned pueblos of New Mexico, nor have I seen the suburbs of big cities or their real streets. Stereotypical stories unfold in a world that is really only two-dimensional; given the lack of atmosphere, everything looks flat. And yet New York need not envy Dublin, London or Paris. One might give Chicago or New Orleans as much presence as Rossellini gave Rome or as Carné gave Le Havre. Then, of course, you'd have to bring flesh-and-blood characters to life and make their stories human. At this rate you could put the Empire State Building into a bottle and make American movies into great art.

3 May

As in all big cities, people use a lot of drugs in New York. Cocaine, opium and heroin have a specialised clientele, but there's a mild stimulant that's commonly used, even though it's illegal – marijuana. Almost everywhere, especially in Harlem (their economic status leads many blacks into illegal drug trafficking), marijuana cigarettes are sold under the counter. Jazz musicians who need to maintain a high level of intensity for nights at a time use it readily. It hasn't been found to cause any physiological problems; the effect is almost like that of Benzedrine, and this substance seems to be less harmful than alcohol.

I am less interested in tasting marijuana itself than in being at one of the gatherings where it's smoked. No sooner have I stated my wish than it is granted; American willingness to oblige is truly inexhaustible. Z [Bernard Wolfe, or AE] is going to join some friends who are 'vipers', that is, habitual smokers; they are giving a party today. When he comes to pick me up this evening, he tells me that the gathering began in the middle of the afternoon: these sessions last a long time because marijuana seems to make time speed up. He himself has already smoked one cigarette, though nothing in his demeanour gives any hint of this. And he advises me to smoke one, too – a prudent step for a beginner, since it's impossible to tell how your stomach might react.

I'm astonished to find that Z is taking me into one of the largest hotels in New York. There is the characteristically respectable clientele in the lobby: old gentlemen in gold-rimmed spectacles, old ladies in flowered hats, all full of the decency and well-to-do morality of America. The elevator takes us to the fifth floor; we knock on the door. A circumspect voice asks, 'Who's there?' We give our names; the door is quickly opened and shut again. In the comfortable, overheated room, it smells like a hair salon, with a scent of violets or carnations, an odour of perfume. It's an odd group: a young man in pyjamas with girlish gestures; a blonde girl, her hair cut short, with the manners of a young boy; a magnificent black-haired woman with dark eyes; and a light-skinned black man who is, Z tells me, the most interesting person in the group. He is the master of the house, a dancer by profession, and he never goes out without a revolver in his pocket. The idea that a white man might insult him is so unbearable that he has decided that if it ever happens, he will kill the offending party and then himself. He seems to be smiling and relaxed.

They've all smoked already and are feeling high. They offer me a first cigarette: the taste is bitter, unpleasant. I don't feel anything. They tell me that I haven't swallowed the smoke; you have to inhale as though you were sucking on a straw. I inhale conscientiously; my throat burns. Everyone is looking at me: 'So?' Nothing. The young man in pyjamas carefully gathers up my ashes: no traces must be left. The blonde crushes a perfume-soaked paper against a light bulb and perfumes us one at a time; the smell of marijuana must also be masked. The black dancer gives me another cigarette. 'They cost a dollar apiece,' he tells me drily. All right. And I know you have to engage in a complicated strategy to get them. Even if the seller has lots of them in his pockets, he pretends that he must go to the other end of town to find them, so that he can charge more. I apply myself; I do my best. Nothing. The beautiful brunette is sprawled on the sofa, her head in her hands, with a desperate look on her face. 'I feel so happy,' she says. 'So insanely happy.' I'm curious about feeling such happiness. I persist – another cigarette. Always nothing. They tell me, 'Get up and walk around.' I get up and walk straight ahead. It seems that I ought to feel lifted up by angels: the others are floating, they tell me – they're flying. The dancer mimes this flight marvellously, and then he does a kind of 'slow-motion' number from the movies; he knows how to dance. He looks beatific. The brunette repeats 'so insanely happy', with her eyes full of tears. I try one more time, a last cigarette. All eyes are on me, critical and severe. I feel guilty; my throat is burning. I swallow all the smoke, and no angel bothers to lift me from the earth: I must not be susceptible to marijuana. I turn toward the bottle of bourbon. I think that now, for a long time, I'll dread even the lowliest cigarette.

5 May

I must leave at the end of the week. No sooner am I beginning to feel at home in New York than I have to go away. This idea makes me feverish, and I gobble everything up – I no longer sleep at all. As the anguish of departure sticks in my throat, I find it easier to drink than to eat. I live in a half-dream; perhaps the marijuana smoke insidiously slipped into my blood. From time to time during this trip, I've had moments of fatigue or confusion, but I've never acted so off-balance as today.

I'm often half-asleep when the telephone begins to ring at around nine in the morning. Today the sound wakes me with a start. A French voice apologises for disturbing me and stammers a name I don't take the trouble to listen to. It's obviously M, who under one pretext or another wakes me apologetically four times a week. He renews a lunch invitation that I've already refused. I hang up, after saying drily that I'll call him before I leave town. Ten minutes later, another ring; M's voice sounds gaily in my ears: 'Did I wake you up?' I suddenly panic: he wasn't the person who just called! Who was it then? I rack my brains in vain, and I can't excuse myself. Perhaps it was someone I really liked – how could I ever explain my coldness? I'm dogged by remorse all morning. Toward noon, vaguely surprised to find that I'm free for lunch, I telephone the Wrights and join them in a little restaurant. When I return to the hotel, there's a note from TB, a friend of N and IM's, whom I quite like and with whom I had a date: he's surprised that I didn't show up and asks if I can stop by at five o'clock and pick him up at his office. At five I'm in the lobby of the big building on Lexington Avenue, but I no longer remember the name of the publishing house he works for. In vain I question the black doorman: a building is like a small town; he doesn't know all the inhabitants. I stand rooted in front of the vast board that lists all the companies in the building alphabetically, but the list fills columns and columns, and I'm not even sure I'll recognise the name.

I'm about to leave in despair when TB is suddenly beside me. He guessed I was lost and came down to look for me.

We have a drink together, a moment of relaxation. But when I leave him around seven o'clock, I'm faced with a new worry: I am supposed to give a lecture this evening – in English, to make matters worse – but I don't remember the address. They gave it to me over the phone, but I didn't write it down. I try 214 East Fifty-second Street, on the off chance; it's a private house where, obviously, no one is expecting a lecture. I'm overtaken by a kind of fatalistic resignation, and I enter a little French restaurant on Third Avenue, thinking vaguely, 'Something will happen.' But at eight o'clock, I get worried again; the lecture is at 8:30. I try to telephone, but the people who know the location of my lecture have already left to get there. No one answers. New York is big; I'll hardly stumble into the right door at random. As I go back to my table, defeated, I glimpse CB and his wife at a table in the back. I rush toward them – I'm in luck. Indeed, they're on their way to listen to me speak. They give me a card with the address. At 8:30, I'm at my post.

Perhaps it would have been better to have gone to sleep early. I stayed up again at Chamby's with some friends, eating hamburgers and drinking whiskey until five in the morning.

6 May

A day in the country will not do me any harm. I'm happy to have been invited by the Hs [Jacqueline and David Hare]. I take a train that gets me to M at eleven in the morning; there, I'm told that the bus for Roxbury [Connecticut] doesn't leave until two o'clock. It's a beautiful day, and I'm delighted to spend three hours in a little American village for no special reason. It reminds me of the unexpected stops I made while travelling through France and gives me a feeling of intimacy with the country. The town is characteristically ugly, but there are trees in bloom and fresh lawns, and I love that there is such provincial peace on the outskirts of New York. The hotel where I have lunch is like a provincial town hall. The restaurant is on the second floor; it's decorated with frescoes and largely empty. My presence seems all the more gratuitous because no one is expecting me at any particular time. Besides, I don't know the Hs (I met them briefly three months ago), and they have no more reason to invite me than I to see them.

The bus takes me through a charming landscape where spring is as mild as in Ile-de-France: lots of water, lakes and rivers, undulating meadows, pale roads shaded by large trees, and flowers everywhere. Don't tell me there's no countryside in America, even if the meadows are infested with poison ivy. Besides, those big poisonous nettles don't scare everyone: many people are glad to be able to live in this fresh air. Even in this civilised part of the East, the magnificent expanse of space has survived modern civilisation: no train or even bus goes as far as Roxbury; when I get off the bus, I still have to take a taxi, for the village is lost in the hills. And it's not really a village – every house is lost in the middle of its fields and woods. In France, only wealthy landowners or poor shepherds enjoy such vast and joyful solitude; here, the humblest house reigns over a domain that extends as far as the eye can see. What empty spaces there are in America! Once again, I have the dizzying impression that I'm witnessing the childhood of the world.

SH is French; she paints [she is also André Breton's ex-wife]. Her husband has long been interested in the Indians' civilisation, and his house would be the envy of the residents of Santa Fe's Canyon Road. In the studio, where a wood fire is burning, there are Indian masks, dolls, beaded necklaces, jewellery, feathered headdresses, rugs, blankets, and pottery among flowers and branches. Nothing is excessive; everything is beautiful. On light wood shelves, there are old books – a vast library that H inherited from his parents and which anchors the new house in the old past. There are the complete works of Hawthorne,

George Meredith, Henry James and Thackeray – old American culture with its English roots. The beautiful New Mexican objects amid the New England flora, the weighty tradition of books between freshly painted walls – it's an apt synthesis of various charming aspects of America. And it's even more complete when the voice of Billie Holiday rises from the corner of the large rustic fireplace.

H is a sculptor – I saw a fine exhibition of his in New York. I take a quick look at his studio. I remember G's [Giacometti's] studio in Paris, in an overgrown garden: bits of plaster and other debris, stained walls, rain trickling through the ceiling, and G shivering in the winter. I don't think any American artist could work in such extreme poverty. In this vast, well-heated space, which is carefully lit, the contingency of the seasons and the caprices of the outside world have no place; everything is clean, scoured; everything has been anticipated and has its own place. There are minute tools and precision instruments, as if it were a clockmaker's studio. One expects the plans conceived by the brain to be executed with a strict exactitude, so it seems shocking when they are embodied in the crude form of something palpable. It would be ideal if the emptiness could be left to speak for itself. But H manipulates matter – it resists; he struggles, winning or losing. Despite the striking difference in equipment, I suppose that the same problems arise [for sculptors] here and in France. And undoubtedly the same problems confront men in general, whether they are using America's great new machinery or our old tools back home.

7 May

This morning S [Sweeney] comes to pick me up in his car. I'd known since the beginning of my stay that he'd agreed to sponsor one of my lectures. 'He's a very important man,' I was told twenty times by the Frenchman who introduced us at the

Saint-Régis bar and who was so full of the respect for importance exhibited by important Frenchmen, and even more by those who would like to be important, that he was choking with timidity. There are a few Americans who appreciate servility: S is not one of them, and he was visibly irritated. There was no indication in his manner that he attached the least importance to his importance; he was nothing more nor less than an ordinary man, cordial and lively. Of course, he soon displayed his cordiality in the most effective way through the meetings he arranged for me and the services he rendered. Thanks to him, I was able to see an old silent film with Douglas Fairbanks at the Museum of Modern Art, as well as the astonishing *Enoch Arden*, one of Griffith's first films. Today, S is taking me on a tour through Connecticut. His wife is driving the car, and their friend D [Marcel Duchamp] has come along. The car has a wooden chassis, and it's as large as a small bus; I've often seen these rustic models and thought they must be as slow as trucks, but they actually have excellent engines and can drive a family of ten children at eighty miles per hour.

Roxbury is one of the numerous artists' colonies around New York. We look for the house of the French painter T [Yves Tanguy], a neighbour of the Hs – which means he lives around twenty miles away. We get lost in the small lanes, where landmarks and signs are as sparse as in the Far West, before discovering the bright yellow wooden house. T offers us rum cocktails, as pink as raspberry syrup, and an excellent lunch. Soon afterward we leave him, for we have a long way to go. Not far from here is Alexander Calder's studio, with its flora and fauna of metal mobiles gently rustling; but we won't visit him because he is in New York today. The jewellery he creates is a badge of honour among women belonging to the 'avant-garde': I've seen gatherings where five out of five women were wearing it. I'm sorry not to get a glimpse of these treasures. But they take me into another art gallery, which is just as interesting. In the heart of a peaceful village of painted wooden houses, scattered on lawns with a stream running nearby, we find the house of Mrs D [Katherine Dreier]. In this retreat this eighty-year-old* woman of German descent has brought together Chinese porcelains, eighteenth-century curios, Spanish altarpieces and some of the most extraordinary works of modern art. Among the pieces are statues by Brancusi and Duchamp's famous painting on glass, *The Bride Stripped Bare by Her Bachelors, Even*, which was transported here from the Museum of Modern Art. It has been cracked in the course of its many travels, but the thin cracks in the glass harmonise with the overall design, adding to the truth of this strange object, poised on the border between the imaginary world and the real. Above the drawing-room door, Duchamp [who helped decorate the house] has done a painting on which he has glued a hand made of pink paper. He has also created a false window, which is a perfect imitation but on a reduced scale, and an elevator that looks so much like a real elevator that the old woman uses it to go from one floor to the other – you can lift yourself up by means of a pulley system. Mrs D asks what my earliest memory is from my past lives, and I'm too embarrassed to answer her.

A magnificent highway takes us to New York. Here and there we see a sign with the name of a town, and I suppose that down there, to our right, there are clusters of buildings. But we don't see a single house throughout the journey: only fields, woods, pines and, through clearings, the dazzling sea. It was this same landscape, seen through the ice of winter, that made me think of Canada when I left New York for the first time. There's nothing Nordic about it now – it's green and flowering. The suburbs of New York are charming, with their trim houses hidden in lavish gardens. To get back, we follow the banks of the Hudson, and for a long time we see the admirable George Washington Bridge in front of us. The sun is setting behind the Empire State Building, which is now as familiar to me as the Eiffel Tower; I leave and rediscover it each time with the same emotion. We follow the

---

* She was actually seventy at the time.

'drive' and enter a large tunnel: these multilevelled highways, these spiralling intersections, these underground routes that avoid all crossroads and allow maximum speed, overwhelm me with their complexity. The slightest error involves long detours. But Mrs S is used to these games and brings me to the Brevort without incident.

I have dinner with AE at the home of two of his friends on the staff of the magazine *View*. In their little apartment downtown, I once again meet SK [Harold Rosenberg] – poet, essayist and critic. It was at his place that I attended my first American party, but I was so bewildered then that I may well have been incapable of recognising him. An intense discussion on the question of action is under way, and it lasts well into the night. This subject is of great interest to me, since among young people at universities and New York intellectuals (not to mention those in the Far West or Santa Fe), I have consistently observed a penchant for inertia, which at first stunned me. By contrast, SK is stunned by what he calls our 'action complex'. He thinks Saint-Exupéry, Malraux and Koestler suffer from this malady, along with Camus and Sartre, to say nothing of Louis Aragon. Of course, he's not preaching a yogi's attitude. Throughout history, there have been moments when action has been possible. Lenin is an example of this. But today, the objective situation allows no effective individual intervention in France, or in America either. The will to action is now just a subjective attitude, a maladjusted attitude that begs to be psychoanalyzed – especially among intellectuals, given that, for the moment, they have no role to play. It's also noteworthy, he says, that the heroes of a Hemingway, like those of a Koestler, always define themselves as outsiders. In *For Whom the Bell Tolls*, Jordan doesn't even know exactly why he's on the side of the Spanish Reds. Similarly, in *Spanish Testament*, Koestler is merely a journalist, a witness. He describes the drama of Palestine from the outside, not being a Zionist himself. And in *Crusade without a Cross*, the main character is determined to join the war because of a childhood trauma, as he himself admits. I object that the theme of this last book is precisely that subjective and contingent spurs to action are not enough to explain a man, and that furthermore, he has the right to name his own motives freely. One can always choose to describe a man by his impulses, but this mechanistic view masks the truth that man perpetually strives beyond the given toward his own ends. Certainly, there is always a gap between the subjective truth and the objective reality of an action; every agent is also an actor, and he cannot know what kind of figure he is cutting in the world of other men through the role he is playing on his private stage. To the extent that this is what SK maintains, I agree. But I accuse him of sophism when he chooses to explain the committed intellectuals by their impulses, and his own attitude by an objective motive. We argue for a long time without convincing each other, of course. I would very much like to understand the complex of impulses and motives that underlies his own attitude.

Every intellectual I've met has been introduced to me by another one. It can't be said that they form a cohesive group – they don't all know each other – but they have common tendencies and values; they constitute *a* certain category, the only one I can speak about. In general, they're men of the far left who want a society without discrimination, class or boundaries. With only one exception, all were communists between 1930 and 1935, and later they each stopped being communists at different times. They subsequently developed in different directions. But except for Richard Wright, who because of his singular situation is and wants to be committed, they all profess a kind of pessimistic individualism today. I don't know enough about it to understand their attitude entirely, but this is more or less how I explain it.

First of all, I must say that their political development has a different meaning from that of a Frenchman who has turned away from the Communist Party. The communists are not an electoral party here; they have no real political existence – they're a diffuse group with rather vague boundaries, not a stable organism. People join and drop their membership much more easily here than in France: to declare that you are a communist does not represent the same type of commitment as it does at home, and to leave the movement is not such a serious act. Richard Wright, James Farrell and Nelson Algren belonged to the John Reed Club in Chicago, organised by the author of *Ten Days That Shook the World*, but it was a private club. To be a communist is almost a private attitude, a matter of personal opinion. I think it would be difficult to persuade Americans to accept a collective discipline if they were not in total spiritual agreement with it – their individualism goes too deep. All they need is an evolution in their thought to *discover*, almost without making any decision, that they are no longer communists. NA, for example, explained to me that he stopped being a communist because he couldn't see a reason to be one any more – that was enough for him. Acceptance and rejection are not, as with us, considered symmetrical attitudes, equally positive and meaningful: it's up to the communist to prove that his choice is well founded; it's not up to the person who remains neutral or becomes so again. Of course, there were nevertheless objective reasons for so many subjective fluctuations. The writers I mention only recently set their hopes on a social revolution because they wanted another America; they wanted concrete justice and equality. But the Moscow trials, the Stalinist dictatorship, weren't in keeping with their objectives at all – many repudiated Stalinism in 1936. Moreover, American communists do not have great prestige, even in the eyes of communists from other countries. They haven't managed to reach the working masses, their programme has never been revolutionary, and they're not effective or even very active. Today their actions are confined to pro-Russian propaganda, but there's almost no activity in the political, economic and social arenas. Beyond these objective reasons, everyone has more personal reasons – either impulses or motives, I don't know which. Besides, on the whole, today's communist intellectuals are a new team; the 1930–36 team has dissolved.

The paths that these intellectuals have followed since then are quite varied. Both the staff of the *Partisan Review* and Farrell were Trotskyites; the *Partisan Review* group ended by sliding toward the right and more or less making its peace with American imperialism. This shift was one of the reasons for the schism with *Politics*, which remains more faithful to the ideal of permanent revolution. Others have sought personal solutions. LW has confined himself to forceful satires, written and especially broadcast, against American civilisation. In his books, on the radio and in his personal life, NA is concerned with concrete social questions, such as juvenile crime. AE and SK are among those who most resolutely refuse to take action. AE sees martyrdom as almost the only possible outcome; he says that in the event of a Russo-American war, he'd become a conscientious objector, even if he would then be shot. SK has remained loyal to Marxist ideology, and he uses it to justify his own and his friends' current attitude – that in the present historical moment, there is no place for authentically revolutionary action in America; at this point in time, one must be resigned to a wait-and-see policy.

To discuss the objective truth of this statement, you'd have to question the philosophy of history as a whole; what interests me here is only the subjective aspect of the problem. Because, from my point of view, any conscious grasp of the predicament is a way of getting beyond it, I would like to know why American intellectuals have chosen this particular way of getting past it – namely, passivity. Surely it doesn't require much Marxist knowledge to see that the advent of a socialist state in the USA can't be expected tomorrow. If one rejects both the bureaucratic police state in Russia and American capitalism with its imperialist consequences, there's not much room for hope. But there is a flagrant difference between the behaviour of the French and Italians, on the one hand, and the Americans, on the other, in response to the same facts. This is because of the profound difference in the political traditions in these countries. The intense inner life of the parties, the connection between union life and political life, lets French citizens constantly participate in political movements:

each Frenchman sees himself as a historical agent. We know that nothing like this exists in America. Already, with regard to university students, I've pointed out the defeatism that weighs on the nation. There is a class that holds economic power, influences policy, handles a lot of business, forms projects, makes decisions and is entrepreneurial — it's called the Pullman class. In the age of the self-made man, this class was largely open, but with social barriers becoming more and more impenetrable, the lower classes no longer have much hope of reaching this level.

In any case, the intellectuals I've mentioned are not part of this class; they do not travel by Pullman, and it's not on the Pullman class that they hope to exert their influence. But, on the other hand, they don't find either an audience or any chance of support among the masses. Relations between French writers and the masses are far from satisfactory, but a decaying middle class, a lower middle class in disarray, and a hesitant working class constitute an accessible public. Richard Wright, for example, is struck by the prestige that certain writers enjoy in France today; whether they are famous or less well known, they carry some weight. In America such a relationship simply doesn't exist; writers are not popular, or if they are, it is only as entertainers. The women of the Pullman class, their primary readers, ask only to be amused; the rest of the nation ignores them. The writer is unable to have any meaningful effect on public opinion. Some young writers are so aware of this that they turn to radio; they don't think of books as a way of making their voices heard. One must also consider the economic controls on literature, which Farrell mentioned to me, and how opportunities are given only to neutral or conformist authors. Indeed, even if a writer manages to communicate his ideas to the masses, they're so inert, so deprived of any means of action, that he hasn't gained much. This passivity can be explained by the whole history of America. Immigration has led to a heterogeneity of cultures that is not conducive to collective consciousness. The existence of open frontiers and the opportunities offered to each citizen drew immigrants toward the realisation of individual goals, and social instability constantly pulled their leaders out of the lower classes. As a result, in today's rigidified society, the masses remain divided, inorganic, without any sense of solidarity – and therefore passive, impressionable. It's possible that the situation will change, but as it stands today, there's no hope for a writer to gather effective forces around him, simply because those effective forces don't exist. And for the same reason, he is not heard or listened to. In order to listen attentively, you have to have projects and expectations, things you want and things you don't want, and that is what's missing in the American people.

It's not true that ideas are held in contempt here. On the contrary, the average American is not in the least cynical, and an idea is not just a plaything to him: he is immediately prepared to extend it through action. But, conversely, if he's not disposed to action, he is closed to ideas. In France and Italy, ideas are more readily welcomed because they have fewer consequences. For Puritan consciences that make clear distinctions between Good and Evil, between True and False, ideas have consequences, but they are also avoided, or at least not eagerly welcomed. It seems to me that this is the essential reason for that difference in attitude that I mentioned: the French writer easily produces eddies and whirlwinds around him, and these results encourage him in an action that may be illusory, whereas the American does not disturb the frozen immutability he finds outside him. Rather than speaking in the desert, he keeps quiet or confines himself to whispering confidences to a small circle of friends. It would be presumptuous to decide which is the wiser course – the American's abstentions or our agitations.

8 May

Whatever the deeper reasons for the situation of American intellectuals, many of them certainly suffer as a result. LW told me spitefully the other day that French, Italian and English writers are jealous because each resents and envies the success of the other, but American writers detest one another because each sees in the other the image of his own failure and wretchedness. In part it's this bitterness, which turns into an inferiority complex, that prevents them from having bold aims and showing themselves worthy of a greater influence. Here, again, one finds the same vicious circle as among university professors. I've heard them deplore the fact that the League of [American] Writers has so persistently shown itself to be beneath its task. Its meetings are confined to questions of money and interest: How can we improve the distribution of books? How should the publisher advertise the publication of a book in a magazine? Discussions of ideas, if they ever occur, rarely rise above such themes as 'Is writing fun?' or 'Is writing partly pleasure?' Admittedly, our Société des Gens de Lettres, which is roughly equivalent to the league, doesn't have much influence either.

To change the atmosphere a little, Wright has the idea of inviting some foreign intellectuals who are passing through New York to get together this evening, and asking each of them for a brief account of the influence of American literature in their country. The evening begins with an excellent dinner, cocktails, wines and a very French menu at the lovely Algonquin Hotel. Then, an Argentinian, a Swede, an anti-Nazi German, an American who's lived a long time in China and I make our speeches in English, each with his national accent. The audience listening to us is older and dull; it's mostly women. A delegate from the state department, who wasn't invited by anybody, intervenes in a way that seems useless to all of us. Under the pretext of studying the 'influence' of American literature, he focuses strictly on the inroads that American books can and must make in foreign markets; you'd think it was a matter of selling cotton. He speaks with tender pity of poor little Europe without a roof over its head, without bread, heat or shoes, and the help that America must bring, the books it must send to nourish Europe spiritually. 'At a time when it's difficult to deliver any goods,' he says, 'we've flown a copy of the film *Gone with the Wind* into Poland. Some people reproach us for squandering resources, but perhaps, by watching this film, a handful of Poles have understood that a land of freedom still exists in the world.' 'It's miraculous,' Wright says to me, 'that the word "dollar" was never actually uttered. But better that all this was said by a member of the state department rather than by a writer.'

When I get home, I am perplexed as I go over these events in my mind. I'm supposed to leave New York in two days, but bad weather is delaying my departure. I hesitate. The other day NA suggested that I come back to see Chicago, and I've often been told that if you want to understand America, Chicago is just as important as New York. On the other hand, I'm happy here. I'm happy, but in a strange way: I'm beginning to feel ill at ease. I have a circle of friends and habits. When I stroll along Greenwich Avenue, when I sit on a bench in Washington Square, when I leaf through the *New Yorker* to find a movie schedule, I feel that my ghostly self has acquired a body.

This afternoon, AE's wife took me to see a dance rehearsal in an uptown studio: it was a futurist ballet, which will be performed a week from now for a very exclusive circle of people. The composer John Cage was at the piano. I liked the choreography, in which suppleness artfully imitates stiffness; I liked the beautiful, abstract props that the dancers solemnly carried in their hands, as well as the astonishing prowess of Merce Cunningham, the star of the troupe. But above all, I loved the intimacy of these hours of work in the heat of an early afternoon. The women wore torn and patched black tights, which seemed more beautiful to me than any costume created to beguile spectators. To be admitted backstage as an insider made me feel adopted by New York.

After a night of passionate discussion and jazz, I go for a walk with AE and LW along the East River. Dawn is breaking through the damp mist that shrouded the boats; the quay is deserted; a sailor is scrubbing down the deck of a big, gloomy ship; the outline of the Battery appears in the distance. One evening, when I was alone, I watched from the height of Tudor Square, leaning over a balustrade, as a huge round, red sun sank into the water. A few steps away, a man was leaning over the balustrade watching the same sun: I belonged to the city as much as he did. And yet, despite the comfort and the poetry of such impressions, they are only illusions. My friends have jobs and daily cares here. They have all the problems I've mentioned. I remain on the outside. When I discuss something, it's in order to understand, to know, but I'm not part of the game. Those dancers, tired and hot, who began again and again without a break, were living a real moment of their lives; they were risking themselves. I never risk anything. I remain a spectator. The more intimate I become with this world, the more I feel the need to find a real place here. Perhaps if I were staying longer, I would discover it. But nothing can be accomplished in ten days. New York is no longer a mirage that I must convert into a city of flesh and blood – it's a staggering reality; it has the opacity and resistance of reality. I shall receive nothing from it unless I give myself to it, and I would have to make a radical change in my life for this gift to be possible. To be a visitor, a traveller – that is my fate here. Tomorrow morning I'll reserve a seat on the plane to Chicago.

9 May

So this is my last evening in New York. I'm spending it in Harlem with AE and RW. We have dinner in a Chinese restaurant and ask a taxi to take us along the 'drive' that follows the East River. Transformed by the night, Brooklyn and Queens are glittering; the façades of the skyscrapers have become translucent, and the reds and greens of the neon signs deck the sky. This is the last time I'll see this fabulous landscape. Wright is in high spirits: he imitates a radio sports commentator at a baseball game and Mr

Anthony giving advice to troubled souls. When we stop, the driver says admiringly, 'He's quite a card, your friend,' and so as not to be outdone, he shows us how the windows in his car – the latest model – go up and down automatically.

In the first nightclub we enter, the band is playing that new jazz AE mentioned to me: bebop. Whites are in a hurry to distort what blacks invent, and blacks accept these deformations meekly. The musicians here are playing a kind of jazz that, instead of being in the New Orleans tradition like the original bebop, is merely the breathless, exasperated expression of New York's restlessness. The room is empty – it's the 'recession'. Or perhaps the public can't tolerate these rhythmic storms. To be honest, it's impossible to bear them for long, and we feel done in after half an hour. The second club is less deserted; the music there is less trying, and there are the additional attractions of singing and dancing. One number is a great success: an old Negress in a pink flannel bathrobe, with rollers in her hair and a nightcap, fat and down at the heel, sings and tells stories in a raucous voice. AE and RW assure me that she's very funny; but her songs and remarks, recited in a southern accent, with lots of allusions and double meanings, go right by me. The imitations amuse me, and I'm charmed by the character, but it's humiliating not to understand a single word.

We walk down Lenox Avenue, and since we're hungry, we go into a barbecue restaurant. I've seen signs for barbecue in every American town. Barbecued meat is simply meat cooked on a spit; this primitive technique is considered an amusing attraction in this country of electric stoves. We sit at a table of dark wood in a very small room where the spits turn on a grill behind a counter; chickens and pork cutlets are skewered on an iron rod. The walls are covered with photographs of boxers, dancers and black singers. There are many jocular inscriptions, as in all popular bars, but we're struck by one in particular: 'If you want your prayers answered, don't stay on your knees. Get up and holler!' We're in Harlem.

While eating pork chops and fries and drinking water – these modest places aren't licensed to sell alcohol – we naturally return to a discussion of the black question. Wright deplores, among other things, the kind of attraction toward blacks felt by many whites in the North, especially in New York. These whites define blacks as the antithesis of American civilisation. Magnificently gifted in music and dance, full of animal instincts (including an extraordinary sensuality), carefree, thoughtless, dreamers, poets, given to religious feeling, undisciplined, childish – that's the conventional image of blacks that these whites readily construct. And they 'are drawn to' blacks because they have projected onto them what they would like to be but are not. Those who feel the greatest fascination are people who feel most deeply deficient themselves. These 'nigger lovers', as southerners would call them, are for the most part embittered, ill, neurotic individuals, weaklings eaten up with a sense of inferiority. That Mezzrow should go to live in Harlem and systematically prefer blacks to whites can be attributed to this attitude. Wright finds this attitude pernicious because it tends to maintain the gulf between blacks and whites. The obvious differences between the two castes come from differences in their historical, economic, social and cultural situations, and these could – at least theoretically – be abolished. But this is a truth that white Americans, even the most benevolent ones, are reluctant to embrace.

11 May

From New York to Chicago, you fly over a plain that's even more monotonous than a desert; I sleep during the entire flight. As the time zone changes, I get confused by the differences between [Eastern] standard time and local time, so I don't know how many hours the journey takes: it seems as early in the morning when we arrive as it was when we left. I feel like I've been transported to Chicago by magic, and it's only by magic that I'll be able to leave.

Never before has a city enveloped me in such an impenetrable atmosphere; I feel more lost than on the day I arrived in America. I'm a prisoner. It's difficult to know where you are in these streets. They are cut at right angles, of course, and yet even on the map I've carefully provided myself with, they look quite jumbled; they do not alternate regularly with avenues, they often have names instead of numbers, and they dead-end in canals, vacant lots and railroads. I lose my way. The streets seem endless, even on the map.

New York is vast, but its street plan is clear, dictated by geographical necessities, and it's easy to form a single picture of it: the great rivers empty into the open sea, and to the north, the city ends precipitously at the Hudson, across from high cliffs. In Chicago you feel the pressure of infinite surrounding plains; it's a city that fills the land; even the lake, enclosing one side, allows no escape. From time to time, at the end of a long ride by tramway, train or elevated railroad, the buildings thin out, and it seems that the city is finally going to expire. Then it springs up again, even more vigorously; you've merely reached an old border, with new neighbourhoods built beyond. And beyond that there's yet another belt, and another farther on. But it's not only these exorbitant dimensions that give Chicago its density. Los Angeles is vast but porous. This town is made of a thick dough, without leavening. More than any city in the world, it reeks of humanity, and this is what makes its atmosphere so stifling and tragic. Neither nature nor the past can penetrate it, but in the absence of the picturesque, it possesses a dark poetry. Black is its colour – a proud, flashing colour like the facets of a block of anthracite. From north to south, east to west, the streets are crossed and inhabited by the metallic architecture of the elevated railroad, familiarly known as the El. This iron ceiling transforms the avenues into dark tunnels; beams shaken by the passing trains fill the air with groans that penetrate the houses: it's a great natural voice, like the wind in the forests. There are also viaducts, bridges and rails where trucks and whistling locomotives pass by, day and night.

The trams jolt noisily in the middle of the roads. Men's destinies are forged here in the din of metal and in the dust and soot. The dirt is so overwhelming that in the end it becomes invisible; soot from coal isn't dirty.

When you walk in the Loop on a sunny day, the shadows cast on the roadway harmonise so well with the night-coloured walls that you'd think these great fixed shadows were encrusted in the stones of the tall buildings. The blocks are split by narrow alleyways: to the right and the left, the walls are decorated with fire escapes, and they're so close together that a person on one side of the alley could join hands with someone on the opposite side. From the top to the bottom of these fissures, the shadows are filled with trembling dust. Located in the heart of the wealthy areas, these entanglements of night and metal already proclaim the hard and desolate life of the vast surrounding expanse. Far from the centre, among the brick cottages and wooden shacks, the darkness pales; unpaved alleys of packed dirt open out onto the paved streets, and there are dead ends and courtyards where trash cans overflowing with garbage spit their ashes into the wind – they're emptied only once a week. The wind raises whirlwinds of grey dust, blowing particles of straw and coal grit into your eyes, slapping your legs with old newspapers and greasy paper, and sometimes assaulting you with the sharp odours of something burning; as in New York, children amuse themselves by setting fire to the refuse. Yesterday, I walked for two hours in sandals on these sidewalks; despite my stockings, my feet became covered with a thick layer of soot. You need to walk with closed shoes and clean them four times a day.

Yet on the periphery of Chicago there's a smiling zone of blue. On this Sunday afternoon I come to rest beside the lake in the midst of vast green lawns. Beneath the sun, the water is pure silk and diamonds, and white sailboats glide back and forth – it has the serene luxury of the Côte d'Azur. On my left, in a haze of heat, stand the skyscrapers of Michigan Avenue. Nothing evokes poverty and its cast-offs. Many people are sitting on the grass in the sunshine, including well-behaved lovers who barely touch hands. Some young people have organised a baseball game on the lawn, and some children are hiding in the shrubs, pretending to be Indians preparing an ambush. I follow the crowd, which carries me toward a round building – an aquarium. There are hundreds of species of fish and thousands of visitors; they look at each other with mutual surprise. It's a leisurely spring day. Seagulls fly above the lake, and Chicago seems like a big, wealthy, cheerful city.

For me, New York nights were always magical; here, my throat is burning, I'm immersed in a suffocating atmosphere. I go out with NA and CL, a young woman who runs a bookstore near my hotel, and we wander a long time on Clark Street and State Street. Along with West Madison, these are Chicago's pleasure district. Luxury and poverty rub shoulders here with the most extraordinary familiarity. There are movie houses, restaurants, burlesque shows, cafés with musical entertainment, dance halls and endless bars. The elegant places are bathed in blue, violet or dark red lights, refined and gentle on the eyes. They are upholstered, soberly decorated and almost always three-quarters empty; they're good places to talk. Just next to these quiet, respectable spots are dives like the ones I saw on my first visit: noisy and swarming with drunks and tramps, with filthy wooden tables under strong lights. In all of them you find an attraction that's unique to Chicago – the dice girl. She stands behind a little table covered in green baize, with a dice box and paper within reach. The player stands facing her, chooses a number and rolls the dice; she marks down the points. On twenty-six rolls, you have to make your chosen number more than thirteen times in order to win a sum equivalent to what you've bet. This is a very rudimentary game, but it has the appeal that all games for money have, and the dice girl is never out of work. She's a popular type in Chicago, and she sometimes meets a tragic fate. It's not uncommon to read in the newspaper that a dice girl has been murdered; after all, she spends her nights on the edge of dangerous areas where the passion for gambling and eroticism run wild. In principle, other games of chance are prohibited, but in plenty of places the back room is a gambling den. I saw one yesterday that was quietly open beside the cloakroom. Women are not admitted, and you have to know one of the regulars to be introduced, but they are hardly clandestine spots. I suppose the police tolerate them in return for a fee.

'We won't go into this bar,' says NA. 'It's lost all its customers since the pianist was shot down by a bullet from a revolver.' Although the gangster era has passed, it seems that murder is still a rather frequent occurrence: there are settlings of accounts, private quarrels and petty local quarrels, not to mention assaults. 'In this bar,' NA says a little farther on, 'I saw one man attack another with a broken bottle. That's one weapon that frightens even the most courageous men. The other man fell through the front window — you have to be careful not to have a window at your back when you're in a brawl.' He points out the plainclothes policemen watching on the sidewalk; there are also many in uniform. This isn't a very quiet district.

We enter the bar, and it seems that the customers of the murdered pianist have moved on. It's like the one on West Madison: lots of tramps are sleeping with their heads on the tables, and beneath the 'No Dancing' sign, couples are dancing. A pretty young man laughingly caresses a fat dwarf, who is swooning repulsively on his shoulder. In the tumult of laughter, songs and the shrieks of fat women being tickled, the dice girl, very dignified, reads a book that's spread out before her on the gaming table. She's a plump blonde with fashionably curled hair, who is wearing three strands of heavy pearls around her neck. I look at the title of the book: *The Women of New Orleans*. We sit down at the counter. Signs on the mirrors say 'No Credit' in twenty joking ways. There are banknotes from every country and photographs of naked women: I notice, among others, some of naked young Japanese women — photos that GIs removed from the pockets of Japanese soldiers. The beggars beg, horribly unattractive couples embrace, drunks make speeches and stagger around, and sleepers groan. Poverty has ravaged all the faces, and vermin swarm beneath the clothes. Everywhere on the walls, there are fresh-faced images in drugstore colours of smiling American girls, healthy and cheerful, with well-brushed teeth and stomachs full of Quaker Oats and Coca-Cola.

12 May

All the states and cities in America have their pride and their local sensitivities. This morning, in the *Chicago Tribune*, I read a venomous article against a journalist from Los Angeles: he'd had the audacity to claim that snow had fallen in Chicago during the winter and that the climate here was harsh. In its editorial the *Chicago Tribune* replied sharply. As for snow, they said, only a few flakes had fallen; besides, our Los Angeles correspondent can guarantee that the air there is unhealthy, stifling, and that the city is enveloped in dank fogs for half the day. Behind this touchiness, I sense that certain interests are coming into play: every town is eager to attract as many visitors as possible, for tourism brings in a considerable number of customers and shoppers. You see brochures in which persuasive propaganda extols the beauty of Illinois. Certainly, there are also historic remains in New England and stunning landscapes in Florida, but 'Illinois offers lovers of history many places to visit and some of the most stunning panoramic views'. The press has a local character. Certainly, the *Chicago Tribune* and the *Chicago Sun* provide international coverage, but there's a whole side of them that's comparable to local French papers; reports on the weather, highways, crimes, accidents and city celebrations occupy entire columns. The photographs on the last page are almost always devoted to night-time or daytime views of the Loop; they may show back alleys with their garbage cans or, by contrast, parks and monuments. If a Chicagoan succeeds in politics or literature, he's proudly acclaimed as a native son – a 'local man' or 'local youth'. No one is interested in what's happening in New York. The vast majority of people are completely unaware of the great rival city.

Chicago is not a single city, however. More than any other American city, it consists of clusters of straggling villages, extending over a wide area and grouped around a commercial centre. The different neighbourhoods are much more closed off than in New York: the immigrants have not assimilated. Many speak only their national language, and they have national papers and develop a chauvinism that often leads to quarrels and brawls. The Irish and the Polish hate each other. NA tells me about an episode that illustrates the depth of this segregation. He made a special study of the Polish section, where he lives. Although he described the wretched life of his impoverished neighbours with total sympathy, the Polish newspaper attacked his book in 1941, accusing him of collaborating with German propaganda against unfortunate Poland and of being a Nazi agent. This is not in the least surprising, added the Polish critic, given that the author is of Swedish descent and Sweden is a traditional enemy of Poland. Chicago's Scandinavian newspaper praised the work passionately. But it mustn't be thought that the diversity of Chicago's population makes it particularly picturesque. Nothing resembles the Greek neighbourhood more than the Mexican one, and even the Chinese streets are not exotic: the shop windows have names and notices written in Chinese instead of in Polish or German, but nothing more. There are also many Japanese in Chicago. On the West Coast the Japanese were put in concentration camps during the war and regarded with hostility. Here, they are so well assimilated that they are considered as fully American as citizens of German descent, and many of them even fought in Europe as GIs.

When you leave the major avenues, you can find the peacefulness of a village just a quarter of an hour away from the Loop. There are corners that seem older than any street in New

York. At the doors of tobacco shops you can still see the painted wooden Indians that were used as signs in the nineteenth century, and in front of barber shops there are still poles with red-and-blue spirals. The dust that clouds the shop windows and covers the walls seems centuries old. Among other things, today I saw a little forgotten street beside an old train station where the rails were rusting. From time to time an empty tram went by. The little wooden houses had front porches, where people could sit savouring the sun or the softness of the evenings, and each had a tiny garden below street level: these were like the gardens in a French suburb, with the lawns ornamented with plaster statues, coloured spheres or little windmills made of varnished wood. There are hundreds and hundreds of streets that are just as silent, just as forsaken. Many have emerged at random, as needed, and their faded shacks are so worm-eaten that you could easily mistake them for poor hovels, though the interiors are often quite decent. I took the El, and for miles and miles I glided above areas the colour of mud, which were filled with these dreary houses planted in the hard earth. From time to time I could see a few tufts of grass in a vacant lot, a tree against a wooden fence. I've never been so moved by trees as by the ones in this dark city. They sprout up humbly among the garbage, the trash cans, the railway tracks, in backyards or at the corner of dead-end streets, but they're not tainted by the neighbourhood; instead, the green of their leaves is intensified. No Alpine pastures or tropical forests could produce so green a green. Older than the houses that they stand beside, they are the survivors of a major clearing, and they silently recall the existence of a non-human sovereignty. In an organised world in which contingency is always the reverse side of human will, in which all disorder takes on the face of misfortune, they have the nonchalance of natural things, and the sight of them soothes the heart.

In the evenings especially, a provincial poetry floats through the streets. At the corner of a dead-end street, children smoke and whisper about their plans. Sitting on their porches, women watch the city lights on the horizon. The groaning of the El shakes the silence; the foliage of a tree rustles; a cat rummages in a trash can: the slightest sound lingers. You feel far, far away from human ventures and follies, in the heart of a calmly ordered life that repeats itself day after day. Yet tomorrow morning you'll read in the paper that they found a corpse cut into pieces in one of these alleys, that two men slit each other's throats in a nearby bar, that a barkeeper was shot down with a revolver two steps away. The sweetness of Chicago nights is deceptive.

13 May

The journalist BS, whom I've met, told me that the percentage of crimes is no higher here than in Los Angeles or New York. Actually, it was little Washington that, in proportion to the size of its population, had the highest number of murders and robberies this year. But I suppose that Chicago is prouder of its criminals than other cities, because not a day goes by without the newspapers reporting some sensational drama. An old lady was murdered in broad daylight while she was shopping in a large grocery store; a fifteen-year-old boy strangled his little eleven-year-old friend; a young man suffocated his little niece, who had kissed him too tenderly. Money crimes or sex crimes – the reader is certain of finding his daily portion. This morning I read that a sexual predator was slain on the stairs of an apartment building while trying to force open the door where a sixteen-year-old high school girl was hiding; one of the tenants shot him with a revolver. He was a West Madison man. They printed his photograph. And he looked so similar to all those 'forgotten men', all those 'men without women' I saw wandering on the Bowery of Chicago, on the Bowery of New York, that my heart felt heavy.

This afternoon BS takes me to a 'police show'. The movies have already given me some idea of this ceremony, and it seems rather commonplace in the abstract, but it is gripping in reality. Three times a week, people who have lodged complaints of robbery, rape, fraud, burglary, etc. – without results – are invited to assemble in a room in the police court; criminals arrested in the last few days are then paraded before them for identification. The detainees are introduced in small groups and lined up on a platform against a wall, where they're measured against large horizontal lines. One after the other, they're questioned and asked to turn around, present themselves in profile, pose with and without hats, stand still and walk. I notice that many of them give the same address – West Madison Avenue. We begin with two dishevelled women with blotched and sagging faces who are accused of soliciting and robbery at the Palmer House. They lured the client into their room, drugged him, emptied his pockets and disappeared. I remember that the Palmer House seemed so respectable, and I wonder what good it does to have the old ladies who keep such a strict watch on the hallways. I also wonder, along with everybody else, what man with a little money in his pocket would be charmed by these poor creatures. The policeman who questions them says laughingly, 'They look better at night.'

He sits without pomp beside the platform, talking in a familiar tone and laughing frequently – it's all in the family. After the women, some blacks are brought in. After the name, age and address are taken down, the first question is: 'Why are you here?' And everyone answers, 'They *claim* that I was driving while drunk.' 'They *claim* that I broke into a shop window.' In any case, this isn't meant to be a proper interrogation; it's simply a 'show'. After the blacks come the whites. The whites and the blacks seem equally ill at ease, their voices hoarse, their lips trembling. Out of forty or so, there are scarcely three or four who answer articulately: a very handsome Indian with a proud face, an apprentice gangster who's quite young and insolent, and a hard-bitten type with a classic scarred face. The others are either afraid or ashamed. A pale little man with a bow tie nervously twists the button on his jacket, and before he opens his mouth, we're sure that he's a sexual pervert. He seems to be in great pain when he admits that his wife accuses him of having abused his eldest niece, and he protests with whitened lips. There are lots of automobile thefts, assault and battery charges, petty or grand thefts, and break-ins, as well as two murders. They also bring in two men handcuffed together, both white as a sheet, their trousers torn from thigh to ankle, their cheeks covered with scratches. They found themselves in prison this morning after celebrating someone's birthday last night, and they don't quite know what happened except that a window was smashed and they were injured by it. Despite the routine nature of the ceremony and the monotony of the offences, this sorry exhibition is striking because the physiognomies are often so marked that they seem to have been selected by design.

None of the accused is recognised by anyone present. It seems that the other day, two thieves identified each other, to the great joy of the police. The police show is not a public spectacle; one can come only by official summons or with a press pass.

In this same building they hear trials that would be referred to the court of summary jurisdiction in France. It seems a long way from the pomp of our French law courts. Neither the lawyers nor the judges wear robes here; only the usher in a gold-braided uniform thinks of himself as intimidating. I go into several courtrooms, and the routine seems very similar to that in France. Before one of the tribunals, there's a group of at least twenty-five men who were caught in a raid on a gambling house. They are released, one after the other, after a speedy interrogation. They leave with broad smiles, except for three of them, who are probably the owners of the gambling house.

In the evening, NA introduces me to MG, a black man from Chicago who has just written a very successful novel. It's the first novel by a black author that doesn't deal with the racial question; it takes place in Chicago's lower depths. We go to the north end of town, to a middle-class neighbourhood where the main street resembles all the main streets of America, and we have dinner in a restaurant that's decorated with stags' and boars' heads. After the meal, we go to a boxing match. There's a big crowd, even though seats cost a lot. The atmosphere in this neighbourhood hall is very similar to what you would find in France in the Central [presumably a boxing arena] on rue Saint-Denis, for example. We end the evening in the West Madison bars. I'm glad to see the literary cashier again, high on drugs and generously dispensing a little sleep to her wretched clients; I like her charitable bluntness. I watch the limping dancer, the child magician in a red silk turban, the drunks. It's easy to imagine them standing with their arms hanging at their sides, consigned to one of the cells painted with big black lines on the wall. Perhaps several of these men have already undergone this test and others will undergo it some day.

14 May

I continue to inform myself about Chicago's underside. This morning I visit the county prison with BS. This prison is not representative of the American penitentiary system: it's a model prison. The director has devoted all his Puritan philanthropy to it; but it is interesting in itself.

Of course, I need special authorisation to get in the door. They make me wait in a hall guarded by an armed policeman in a sentry box. Prison employees move around and deal with papers behind a thick barred grille; they are model prisoners who have managed to rise to these desirable positions. They don't seem much more caged in than ordinary bank employees, who are also separated from the rest of the world by a metal grille. After a moment, a policeman comes to find me. Any lipstick? Any cigarettes? To simplify matters, I leave my purse in the cloakroom. My guide opens a second door. Now I am in bright, scrubbed corridors patrolled by guards who are armed with revolvers. Through three layers of bars, I can see men at a distance, sitting in blue slacks and working at long tables. The window at the end of the corridor looks out onto a large square garden, where young men are digging in the ground and playing ball; these delinquents are under twenty-one and will serve no more than six months. Blacks and whites mix together; they are clean and even groomed, and they seem quite cheerful; you'd think it was a playground if not for the watchtower at the top of an unusually high wall.

They show us the room where prisoners receive visits from their families, as well as a kind of confessional booth, where they sit to confer with their lawyers, who are not admitted to the cells. I notice that all the clocks are stopped at noon and that none of the prisoners has a watch, so no precise time can be fixed for a riot or demonstration. An elevator takes us down to the basement: here is the laundry room, where linen is washed, disinfected and ironed in the steam-scented dampness. A number of prisoners are busy pressing their uniforms between two boards. Farther on, there's the kitchen, a huge tiled hall with enormous electric stoves where gargantuan pots are simmering. Well-supervised prisoners in immaculate white overalls are peeling mounds of potatoes and sorting beans. With wooden tables and tin plates, the refectory has the whiteness of a hospital. And so does the hospital. White-clad doctors examine patients with complicated instruments. I notice that in the men's section, blacks and whites lie side by side in the beds with no apparent segregation. Prisoners assigned to the kitchen, laundry and infirmary sleep in a large dormitory at the end of which there are several shelves with books. Not far away is the library, a classroom in which courses are given in the evenings and which is decorated with drawings and paintings done by the prisoners. A little farther on is the chapel, which is painted a tender toothpaste pink and decorated with gilt plaster – a chapel for nuns with childlike hearts. 'We have lovely services,' the guard says with conviction. He is proud of his prison, smugly commenting on everything. There's a little old man who has joined us on our tour, and he insists that every explanation be repeated three times. I sometimes have trouble understanding, also, and he asks me happily, 'Are you hard of hearing, too?' 'No,' I say, 'I'm a foreigner.' But I think he doesn't hear this, and he smiles at me in a conspiratorial way.

An elevator takes us to the second floor, to the women's section. I don't know why, but here blacks and whites are separated. I'm struck by the elegance of the prisoners; they all wear blue overalls, which they belt tightly at the waist, and the clients of Antoine would envy their magnificent hairdos. All of them are made up, with scarlet lips, although lipstick is strictly forbidden. They sew by hand or on machines; they tailor and mend: I've seen drearier workshops. But while I'm admiring this compulsory paradise, there are sudden, bone-chilling shrieks, followed by awful sounds of furniture being overturned – evidently coming from the drug addicts on the next floor. As we go up in the elevator, we hear more screams. A white-haired guard runs toward a door and opens it, revealing a large, bright cell with two beds. There's a young white woman, looking calm and bored, and a black woman sitting on the edge of her bed, twisting her arms and screaming, 'I can't go on! I'm going to die!' The guard cajoles her: they'll send for the doctor; he'll bring her relief right away. But she's not the one who began the uproar; it's another woman in a nearby room who overturned her bed, mattress, chairs and stools. In the corridor we pass the doctor with his bag. I think our visit was a godsend for the drug addict; normally, they would probably have tied her in a straitjacket until they thought she'd calmed down. Of course, drug addicts are not taken off their drugs from one day to the next – that would be murder – but the detox treatment is carried out with harshness.

We go down again. A metal door is opened for us, and we arrive in the section where the longest sentences are served. At the entrance to the corridor, behind the grille, a black man is standing still, his hands gripping the bars, his eyes staring. There is something strange about his stillness. The deaf old man has a sudden thought: 'He's condemned to death?' 'Yes,' says the guard. The old man looks at the black man for a long time: this is what he's come for; this promise of death fascinates him. We continue along the corridor. To our right, behind a grille, there are cells as narrow as boat cabins with two bunks, one above the other. In each cell, there is a sink with running water. Everything is meticulously clean; the sheets look as though they were changed this morning. Closed on our side, these cells open straight onto a corridor, which is flanked by another row of symmetrical cells; the prisoners can walk around and talk to each other. As long as his appeal is not rejected, the man condemned to death will remain here – one of these bunks is his. But instead of staying with his comrades, he's gone to the end of the corridor and is squeezing the bars of his cage between his hands. If his appeal is rejected, he will be transferred to the area reserved for the prisoners condemned to death.

We go down to that area. There are four cells side by side with a wall at the back and bars on three sides. They are rather large, each with a single bed, and dazzlingly white, but they are hermetically sealed. In front of them, there is a table where an armed guard sits day and night. For the moment, they are empty. To the right of the table, there's a complicated system of buttons and levers next to an iron curtain; on the other side of the curtain is the electric chair. Prisoners are led out to the chair this way, but the guard makes us go around to see it from the front. We come into the hall reserved for journalists and authorised police on execution days. Another iron curtain rises up, and behind a glass, like a dentist's chair exhibited for sale in a display window, is the chair, with its ingenious apparatus for holding the patient and bringing his blood to the boiling point in a minute and a half. There's a kind of mask for the face. The guard says to me proudly, 'You've never seen that? How do you do it in France, then?' I say that we have the guillotine. 'You still have the guillotine! Is that possible? But it's barbaric!' He is sincerely indignant: 'In a time like ours, to cut off heads!' At the same time, he's intrigued and asks lots of questions. Finally, since he has to go to Paris this year, he says with conviction, 'I'll go see that. I'd really be curious to see that!' He is obviously waiting for me to offer to be his guide. He again shows us the levers and buttons. 'When a condemned man is executed, there are four guards chosen to press four of these buttons. Only one kills the man, and no one knows which one, so no one really knows who has killed him.' This reminds me of the old custom of loading one rifle with blanks in a military firing squad; each soldier had one chance out of a dozen of keeping his hands clean. Here, each executioner has three chances out of four and can no doubt make peace with his nightmares. I'm pleased that there is no specialised executioner and that every guard is compelled to do his duty as executioner until the end. The guard escorts us toward the door and shakes his head: 'The guillotine!'

There are some states, California among others, that must speak with the same contempt of the old electric chair: they've adopted the more refined system of the gas chamber. In California they recently executed a woman, a fat, affectionate-looking gossip who had poisoned several husbands and lovers. She wore a flowered dress and a smile when she entered the little room where a comfortable armchair awaited her – without any ropes or electric panels. The condemned woman calmly settled down; they closed all the air vents, pressed some button, and it was all over in less than a minute. It's quicker and less intimidating than the electric chair, and they even claim that the condemned person dies in a kind of mild ecstasy. For my final edification, the guard launches into a grand defence of American philanthropy. 'In America,' he says, 'we're always ready to give someone a helping hand. And we include everyone – we even help our enemies. The Germans were our enemies, but now that's forgotten, and we're helping them as much as others.' We say goodbye. He does hope we'll go to see the guillotine together. I have to admit, there's nothing to criticise in such a beautiful prison, aside from the fact that it's a prison.

This afternoon CL has left her bookshop to join me on a walk through the streets of Chicago. On the edge of the black, Greek and Italian neighbourhoods, we discover, by chance, one of the biggest markets I've seen since the Djelma el Fna Square in Marrakech. It stretches for more than a mile along the pavement and sidewalks of a broad street. The sun is punishing, a midsummer sun, and dark Chicago has suddenly become an exotic village, hot and colourful, the way I'd imagined San Francisco would be. The men are wearing shirts of pale blue, delicate green, shrimp pink, salmon, mauve, sulphur yellow and indigo, and they let their shirts hang outside their trousers. Many women have knotted the ends of their white blouses above their navels, revealing a broad strip of midriff between skirt and bodice. There are many black faces, others olive, tan and white, often shaded by large straw hats. To the right, to the left, people in wooden stalls sell silk dressing gowns, shoes, cotton dresses, jewellery, blankets, little tables, lemons, hot dogs, scrap iron, furs – an astonishing mixture of junk and solid merchandise, a yard sale mixed with low-priced luxury. On the pavement small cars drive around selling ice cream, Coca-Cola and popcorn; in a glass cage the flickering flame of a little lamp heats the kernels and makes them pop. There's a tiny man in rags with the face of an Indian, wearing a big straw hat and with a hearing device fixed behind his dirty ear; he's telling fortunes with the help of a machine. The apparatus is very complicated, truly magical: on a moving cart there's a glass column full of liquid in which little dolls jump up and down. A customer approaches – a black woman with a naked midriff, who seems at once provocative, sceptical and intimidated. She puts her hand against the glass; the bottle-imps jump up and sink into the invisible depths of the instrument, which spits out a strip of pink paper on which the customer's fate is written. This mechanical apparatus in the service of magic, the hearing aid beneath the exotic hat, these juxtapositions give this market its unexpected character. It's an eighteenth-century fair in which drugstore products are sold amid the clamour of four or five radios. There's another charlatan worthy of the old Pont Neuf: he has twined a snake around his neck and is selling a black elixir that's supposed to be a cure-all, and he describes the fabulous properties of this universal panacea through a microphone. Another man specialises in headaches, curing them through a simple laying on of hands. He, too, pitches his sales talk through a microphone, and behind him there's a highly scientific anatomical drawing representing the human brain. There are shops on the sidewalks, often below street level, as in the Jewish neighbourhood in New York, and their merchandise spills out onto the pavement. Through an open door, I see a gypsy covered with scarves and veils in a darkened room; she's kneeling beside a basin, washing her linen. The radios blare, and each is playing a different tune.

On the street corner, some blacks are holding a religious meeting. The men are in ordinary clothes, but the women wear long black robes and veils edged in white, just like the nuns of certain orders. They are singing in chorus, and above their heads, a black family is sitting on a balcony lazily listening to them sing stirring spirituals. A little farther on, a black preacher is speaking passionately, and guitarists are playing jazz tunes on the edge of the sidewalk. Another black speaker with a red skullcap is gesticulating vehemently: he angrily singles out other preachers for preaching the God of the white man; in contrast, he is invoking the God of black people, and he exhorts his brothers to come to him and no one else. Sects that are openly against white people have arisen recently, but only a few. For the most part they are Islamic, worshipping the God of Muhammad, not the Christian God, and they look to the brown people of Asia Minor and Africa for the salvation of the black race. This preacher probably belongs to the 'Moors', which is not only a religious sect but also a small economic community with a harem. It includes two hundred blacks, mostly women, who live in one of the nearby slums. We listen, we look. Superstitions, science, religion, food, physical and spiritual remedies, rags, silks, popcorn, guitars, radios – what an extraordinary mix of all the civilisations and races that have existed throughout time and space. In the hands of merchants, preachers and charlatans, the snares sparkle and the street is full of the chatter of thousands of brightly feathered birds. Yet under the blue sky, the greyness of Chicago persists. At the end of the avenue that crosses the glowing bazaar, the pavement and light are the colour of water and dust.

15 May

This morning I visit a large psychiatric hospital. It's a model institute, unlike most such places in America. It's designed less for the treatment of patients than for scientific research. A very small number of subjects chosen from different hospitals have been gathered here because their cases are of special interest and because they provide choice research material for students in medicine, psychology, psychiatry, etc. The buildings, ten to twelve storeys high, surround large gardens; interns in blue smocks can be seen reading on the terraces in the sun. The woman doctor who serves as my guide shows me the big electric enclosures in which they treat paralytics: instead of raising their temperature by inoculating them with malaria,* as they used to do, they treat them externally with progressive electrification. I see the hydrotherapy basins, an 'iron lung', devices for rehabilitating the fingers and legs of patients with diseased spinal marrow, a number of operating rooms and surgical instruments. In more mysterious basements inhabited by herds of guinea pigs, rats, monkeys and dogs, I also see collected recordings of brain waves, endlessly varied according to the kind of illness. A tired-looking old lady is about to enter one of the rooms where they are going to chart her brain waves. The walls

---

* This reference to malaria is puzzling. Perhaps she is confused and means injections of Metrazol, which were once used to treat catatonic patients.

are decorated with parrots in brilliant, shiny colours, and this nursery cheerfulness seems quite ironic, but apparently these paintings have a soothing effect on the patients, who are often children. Unfortunately, I see only the shell of this beautiful hospital: you're not allowed to talk to the patients, and they are not exhibited on request — something I approve of but nonetheless regret. I get only a glimpse of a degenerate-looking adolescent sitting across from a doctor; he is taking a test, concentrating with excruciating determination, as though his life were at stake.

In the afternoon MG takes me through the black neighbourhoods. There are many such neighbourhoods in Chicago. Blacks have settled in the city since 1830, but it was during the slaughterhouse strikes of 1894 and 1904 that they began to pour in. There were still only a few of them, though, and they lived throughout the city, on the edge of the affluent white districts. Around 1915, when the war industries were booming, immigration sharply increased; during the same period, the city was expanding quickly, but blacks could not settle in the new neighbourhoods. The south side, which was the biggest black neighbourhood in 1910, expanded considerably, forming a narrow strip called the Black Belt. Other neighbourhoods also developed, but none within the city were open to blacks. As in New York, the growth of the black population, which increased sixfold during the First World War, led to stricter segregation. Even upper-class blacks, whose ancestors had lived in Chicago on an almost equal footing with their white neighbours, were now confined to black ghettos and were barely distinguished from the 'poor blacks' who had recently arrived from the South. Organisations were created to prevent white proprietors from selling or renting to blacks, and violence and threats were used to prevent blacks from gaining a foothold in white neighbourhoods. At Roosevelt's insistence, cheap housing was built primarily for blacks, who did indeed live in it, but this effort was insufficient. The constant migration of blacks from the South into the segregated areas that had been allotted to them led to the crowding of several families into an apartment meant for only one, the taking in of lodgers, the conversion of formerly spacious dwellings into tiny apartments – in short, to the creation of unsanitary conditions. All this helps explain the contrast, which strikes me today, between the mostly wretched exteriors of these apartment houses and their respectable interiors.

We walk along a broad avenue under the El's dark ceiling. To the right and the left are wooden houses with narrow stairways leading to tiny hovels. We climb up one of these stairways and go out onto a balcony where clothes are hung out to dry. We see a yard surrounded by a fence and other shacks with flat roofs. The towering architecture of the El dominates the landscape in this area: every house trembles as the trains pass by. Through an open door I see a small but very clean room. A little farther on, we explore another building, as picturesque, surprisingly, as those in southern France. It has three floors with terraces that are open to the wind and bordered by rooms on either side; a stairway as steep as a ladder runs past them, and I notice a sort of medieval hoist with ropes around a pulley going from the roof to the ground floor. In Italy and Spain, this crumbling apartment house would be full of sordid dens. Through glass doors I glimpse spare but well-kept interiors with refrigerators, linoleum, oilcloths and sometimes a radio. Of course, there are many poor families living in all the slums that give Chicago its dilapidated look, but with a housing crisis that's just as acute for white people, many people are forced to live in dwellings that are well below their general standard of living. The problem isn't a lack of space, though. From the upper terrace, leaning on a balustrade that encloses the galleries, you have a fine view of the Loop's skyscrapers and the indefinably grey, flat city. I notice the vast vacant lots that I've encountered as I've made my way through Chicago on foot and by subway. But the speculating on land, the high price of construction and the lack of capital all mean that lots are left vacant in the midst of the most overpopulated areas. We go back down, turn the corner of the avenue, and find ourselves in a more prosperous street, where the atmosphere reminds me of certain corners of New Orleans. The bungalows are less romantic, but the weeds, the spreading trees, the pink and blue shirts of the curly-haired children, and the indolent gait of the young men are reminiscent of the tropics. However, the fact that I can take a walk with a black man is proof positive that we are in the North.

You don't pass through Chicago without going to see a burlesque show. It seems that the great shows that attracted spectators by the thousands just two years ago no longer exist. On the other hand, between movie houses and bars, there are little theatres, something like cabarets, whose chief attraction is the ritual of the striptease. BS first takes me into a very modest club, where several couples, several families and one or two groups of men look at the dancers with the detached air I've observed in similar places in New Orleans. I would have readily concluded that no one enjoyed this sort of show any more, which would hardly have surprised me, because there is nothing more monotonous. However, the ambiance is completely different from that of the French Casino — these places always call themselves 'French Casino' or 'Paris Follies', just as we dub nude revues 'Broadway Follies' or 'New York Burlesques'. Here, the hall descends in tiers to the stage; it's carpeted in red and lit with that soft, glowing light that's one of Chicago's secrets. A master of ceremonies announces the artists with a good stock of obscene jokes, and the audience, drinking whiskey around little tables, seems to have heated up. There's a kind of walkway thrust into the middle of the room, and the girls sashay from the dais to the end of this proscenium amid applause and catcalls. They try to vary their styles. In general, the blondes appear in virginal and diaphanous dresses and preserve an air of startled modesty until the ultimate moment of complete nudity. Some brunettes wear ceremonial robes and assume various poses, a sphinx-like smile on their lips; others exude a cool licentiousness, and still others mimic animal passions. But it's always exactly the same game of zippers, panelled skirts, layers of brassieres abandoned one by one, and panties getting progressively scantier down to the triangle held by a simple silk cord that's called, for some unknown reason, a G-string, the name of one of the violin strings. With polished, depilated and powdered bodies, their nipples painted a bright red, these gorgeous creatures only rarely give the impression of being living flesh, despite some extraordinarily obscene shimmying. They make a pretty comfortable living, and it's less tiring than many other kinds of work, although there are several shows each day.

Since you usually have to drink in order to see the attractions, this is a rather expensive form of entertainment, even in the more modest clubs. Movie houses often alternate the film with several 'burlesque' numbers. And for the curious of very modest means, there are odd little dens that are usually swindles. I could not see them with my own eyes, because the cashier refused to let me enter (women are not admitted), but they were described to me as follows: The clients are brought into a bare room where nothing is happening; there are apparatuses installed in the wall, through which – for a nickel – you can see into the neighbouring room, where a girl begins to strip, following the traditional ritual. No sooner has she removed her gloves than the apparatus goes blank, and you have to put in another nickel to see a bit of thigh, another for a shoulder. A narrating voice keeps the onlookers in suspense, promising them more and more. When the show becomes enticing, they're told that for an extra fifty cents, they'll be able to go into another room, where they'll be regaled with truly sexy visions: what they're shown are some obscene dances. The attraction on the whole is the same as in the casinos, but I would have liked to have seen the audience.

16 May

I will not leave Chicago without also seeing the slaughterhouses. I know that from all over America, live animals flow into this great centre, and they are then sent back across the whole country in the form of canned or frozen meat. The slaughterhouses are quite far from the centre of town, and the elevated railway runs for miles and miles above a plain that's filled with corrals where the cattle are kept. From morning to night, they pour out of the trains that bring them from the West or the South, and cowboys on horseback guide the herds into the lanes of this enormous concentration camp. The smell of blood, gamy and rancid, drifts everywhere, even into the railway cars. When I climb down the station stairs, it catches in my throat, and even though I tried to harden my heart in advance, nausea sweeps over me with every breath. I haven't eaten lunch, and I ask where the restaurant is. I'm shown a large building that stands above wooden sheds; the restaurant is on the top floor. The place is filled from top to bottom with offices where typewriters are clacking away. The smell does not penetrate into this place. Here, the meat and blood are converted into abstract numbers that are written on clean paper in a carefully controlled environment. The offices of La Salle Street and Wall Street don't smell of oil and sweat either, but the gap that separates the world of profit from the world of work is more obvious here than elsewhere because the smell that infests the dungeon is so close at hand. From the windows, you see a whole town built of wood, market-like areas where the ground is covered with wet straw, wood shavings and trash, and you have a vague feeling that shady things are going on. Inside, everything is quite orderly and open. On the walls, there are photographs of cows and sheep glowing with health. You also see marvellous roast beefs and sliced hams pictured in mouth-watering, lying colours – reassuring images in which the triumph of man over nature is achieved.

I am going to witness the intermediate stage of the drama. After my meal, I ask what time the visit begins, and I'm told that a 'tour' is leaving in five minutes from a nearby building. I go down, walk through the stench, and then go up to an office where five or six people are waiting. The guide opens the door; it's as though we were going to visit a museum. But at the end of the long wooden gallery where the floor rises and falls in inclined planes, a sign warns us, 'Faint-hearted people should stay at the door.' Everyone goes in.

Slaughterhouses are private enterprises. There are large ones and modest ones; I think that this is one of the most extensive. Wooden platforms, built purposely for tourists, wind around the vast halls, halfway between the ground and the ceiling. From this elevated position, we can see the animals' agony and the human labour from a distance but in detail. Large numbered signs explain the different phases of the operations to us, like the road signs that recount American history or the posters that describe the monuments of Florence and Rome to the GIs – this country has a definite pedagogical streak. These large butchering factories have been described too many times for me to repeat it all here – the shrieking pigs, the spurting blood. Already by the fifth sign, the animals have been disembowelled, decapitated, scalded and are only pliable matter, like squared-off planks of wood. Before they are cut up, they spend twenty-four hours hanging from hooks in the huge refrigeration rooms. This seems to me more like a sacred rite than an operation with a useful purpose; it's the nightwatch before a battle, the initiation that transfigures a carnal being, rooted in nature and filled with murky discharges, into a human conquest that has its place and its role in society. The animal that just bellowed and spit its blood becomes a piece of food that a civilised individual can eat for nourishment with peace of mind. In the same way, marriage transforms a woman of the poisonous sex into a chaste wife. In the big open storerooms beside the refrigerators, hams rolled in cellophane have the colour of ripe corn or toasted bread; the crusty gold of the sausages has kept the purity of the flames, and the spell of flesh and blood has been conjured away. I would eat a piece of bacon without a second thought.

Even though the death of the cattle is less spectacularly ghastly than the sight of the pigs having their throats cut, and even though the animal is hidden behind a wooden fence when the executioner's mallet strikes its head, this enormous palace of butchery nevertheless makes the strongest impression. In the hot smell of blood, in the dull light of the hall where iron knives gleam, two dramas are superimposed: man against animals and men among themselves. It's no accident that the bloody arms carving up the carcasses are nearly all black arms under their red-stained gloves. Slaughterhouse work is arduous, and the history of the slaughterhouses is one of the darkest chapters in the history of American labour – a story of strikes and racial battles. In 1894 and 1904, blacks were used here as strikebreakers, which led the white workers to form an alliance against them and exclude them. During the First World War, when the bosses again had recourse to black workers, most of the unions refused to admit them as members, and a huge racial battle erupted in 1919. In 1921 blacks were again used as strikebreakers; the workers were defeated, and for ten years the unions played almost no effective role among the slaughterhouse workers. Since then, this game has continued: the bosses profit from the wretched situation of blacks, who are allowed to enter only a few professions and who are used systematically against union workers. This manoeuvre is unfortunate for both the white workers and the blacks themselves, who, identified as enemies, find themselves utterly dependent on their employers with no support among their own class.

I watch the cattle, felled by the mallet and still shuddering, roll through a trapdoor onto the tile floor. A hook grabs them and hoists them up, and an arm wielding a knife severs their artery and their life. They are decapitated and their legs draped in a large white cloth; carts carry away enormous blue entrails and buckets of foaming blood. Basins of water are emptied onto the tiles, and the metal gleams with murderous reflections against the red ground. This colossal slaughter is the visible tragedy, but it's only the symbol of another, crueller, deeper tragedy. In order to live, man consumes non-human lives, but he also feeds on the lives of other humans. It suddenly strikes me that the blades slicing the wounded meat, all this carnage of blood and steel, are there only to illuminate the awful meaning of that natural law to which we're inured from birth – man is an animal that eats.

This evening I'm going to explore the Italian neighbourhood, 'Little Italy', with NA and CL. We stroll through the Greek section and the Mexican section, where several curio shops remind me of Santa Fe. We stop at a street corner to watch a little carnival, one of those miniature amusement parks one finds so often in the crowded neighbourhoods of big cities. There are merry-go-rounds, shooting galleries, ice cream, airplanes – almost the same attractions as in our French fairs – and there's always a crowd. Americans love these mechanical and violent amusements. A little farther on, there's a magnificently lit shop window; fifty or so spectators are sitting on chairs, and two women wearing glasses, one dressed in pink, the other in blue, are singing and playing the harmonium. This is a religious meeting. We go in. On the walls there are edifying maxims and questions: 'When was the last time you wrote to your mother?' Most of the men who take refuge here are old tramps over sixty who clearly have no mothers any more. We're given hymnbooks with blue bookmarks. Everyone is standing and singing, or at least moving their lips. We stay only a moment and hand the pious volume to our neighbour as we leave; he shakes his head, with a complicitous wink. NA shows me one of the inscriptions on the wall: 'There will be dinner after the service.' This is why the meeting is such a success. Several hundred yards farther on, we observe another meeting taking place; here there's a man preaching instead of women singing. In front of the door a zealous disciple is distributing tracts. But we prefer to eat elsewhere.

We cross an intersection that's famous for the number of murders perpetrated there during the gangster era, when the Italians were particularly quick with their knives. And we enter a restaurant that's also a liquor store with an enticing collection of Chianti flasks. The tiled floor, the rough wooden tables, the dark-haired families chattering in Italian transport me to Rome. We're served red Chianti, giant pizzas and pastel-coloured spumoni. We return along little, wonderfully peaceful streets, where no cars or pedestrians pass by, where not a single streetlamp shines. We hear only the trees rustling in the wind and the shadows whispering on the porches of the bungalows. All around us we smell the green countryside and feel the roughness of bare earth under our feet. Only the sky above the dark pavement has the suspicious tinge of big city skies. There are many people in this huge and oppressive city who live as peacefully as those in a small village in Italy or France.

17 May

It's my last day in Chicago. I go to see the museum again in the morning, and the luxurious lake sparkling with the white sails of yachts. A young mulatto is sleeping in the sunny grass, his straw hat over his eyes. A greyish-blue mist dissolves the massive buildings of the Loop, and they seem to be cut adrift from the earth. But the blackness doesn't lose its grip; beside the harbour where the varnished boats slumber, on the banks of the smooth water, rise enormous heaps of coal and dust. These are depots furrowed with rails and, on them, train cars laden with black blocks. I cross an avenue where gleaming automobiles speed by; I walk down toward the canals and find myself in a strange subterranean world; here, underneath the roadway, the darkness is thicker than under the El. Lit by lamps, it's a real street with shops on the sidewalks and bars where neon signs glow at midday. My eyes are still dazzled by the sun and blue waters, and this bit of subterranean city makes me think of the old Metropolis. The street leads me back to the Loop, where I wander one last time.

I will miss Chicago. I haven't seen it at all in the same way that

I've seen New York, and that makes any comparison impossible. Instead of trying to get to know lots of people and places, I've preferred to profit from friendships that allowed me to know a single aspect in depth. My experience has been very limited. I didn't return to the 'nice neighbourhoods' that I glimpsed during my first visit; I didn't set foot in the elegant nightclubs; I didn't connect with the University of Chicago, which is one of the most interesting colleges, I've been told. But because I deliberately chose one point of view, I feel an intimacy with this city that I was unable to feel with New York. In any case, tomorrow it will be only a memory. In three days, all of America will be only a memory. My phantom slowly took on a bodily shape: I saw the blood flow in its veins, and I was happy when its heart was beating like a real human heart. Now, it's becoming disembodied with dizzying speed.

19 May

Two days of shopping and goodbyes. At GT's [William Phillip's] I have a laborious argument with Sydney Brock, a disciple of Dewey, about the philosophy of pragmatism and existentialism. At a party at DMD's [Dwight Macdonald's] place I meet several writers and say goodbye to most of my friends. At La Fayette, a restaurant where the marble tables make a sad effort to evoke a French café, I have a brief interview with Dos Passos, whom I knew in Paris. He rarely comes to New York; he lives very quietly in Provincetown in New England, where he is writing a book on the Jeffersonian period. He doesn't think war is imminent. 'I think they will be successful in keeping the conflict localised,' he tells me. 'Perhaps they'll fight in China – China is local, too.'

I go to declare the money I've earned these past four months and to pay the required taxes. In France this operation would have taken days of coming and going. Here, the business is transacted one-on-one, as always, and it's settled in half an hour. The official sitting across from me examines the sheet of paper I've submitted and asks me for my word of honour as verification – nothing more. Then he helps me deduct my expenses: transportation, secretarial help, receptions, hotels, laundry? He's the one who makes all these suggestions with touching enthusiasm. He deplores the fact that the total is not more substantial and that I still have to pay some taxes. Two imprints from the rubber stamp and I'm free to leave America.

I can leave. I'm going to leave. Evening falls on New York – my last evening. This country so often irritates me, and now I'm torn apart to be leaving. In the past few days, several people have asked me, 'Do you like America?' and I've gotten into the habit of answering, 'Half and half,' or, 'Fifty–fifty.' This mathematical evaluation doesn't mean much; it only reflects my hesitations. Hardly a day has passed that I haven't been dazzled by America; hardly a day that I haven't been disappointed. I don't know if I could be happy living here; I am sure I'll miss it passionately.

Columbus Circle, Broadway, Times Square. Four months have passed. It's the same crowd, taxis, cars, glimmering lights. The drugstores and the skyscrapers have lost none of their magic. I know why I love them. There's a fascinating mirage that spreads out across this civilisation of ease and abundance: the image of an existence that would not wear itself out just staying in place and would make every effort to forge ahead. Eating, moving around, getting dressed, all this is done effortlessly and efficiently – everything can begin after this. I feel such a dizzying attraction for America, where the memory of the pioneers is still recent and palpable, because it seems to be the realm of transcendence; compressed in time, magnificently expanded through space, its history is the creation of a world. This is what moves me about the skyscrapers: they proclaim that man is not a being who stagnates but one who is full of energy, expansion, conquest. And in the extravagant profusion of drugstores, there's a poetry as exciting as in a baroque church: man has caught the raw thing in the trap of his desires; he asserts the power of his imagination over matter. New York and Chicago reflect the existence of this demiurge of imperious dreams, and that's why they are the most human and exalted cities I know. There is no place here for the dreary wisdom of the petit bourgeois in carpet slippers whose only project, as expressed, for example, in the famous sonnet on happiness, 'is to stay at home and gently wait for death'. To devote yourself to such an expectation is already death. In this sense, Americans are fully alive: they live in the perspective not of death but of life. They are not satisfied with inertia; they judge a man by his acts: in order to be, you must do. The great metal bridges, the buildings, Grand Central Station, Park Avenue, the airports, the roads and the mines are the affirmation of this faith.

It will be hard for me to tear myself away from these grand visions of hope; yet I know their snares. In this country, too, life exhausts itself just to survive. 'I'm out by six o'clock in the morning,' a taxi driver was telling me at ten o'clock last night. 'You bet I want to get home.' I remember the rush for the ferryboat to New Jersey. All my friends have told me how hard the workdays are in this city of vast distances; in particular, women who have both a job and a household to maintain are worn out by the time evening comes. I've often seen them too exhausted to accept an invitation to go out or to take any pleasure in it. I've also learned that if people drink so much, it's not just out of habit; they need a strong kick at the end of the afternoon. And heart disease is the most common cause of death in New York.

That's not all. You have the exhilarating feeling that anything can begin here. But what, in fact, is beginning? What do people do with their time, with the money they earn? Of course, I don't know the ruling class that studies, invents, runs enterprises, struggles, but it constitutes only a small minority. The majority of Americans are like those I've rubbed shoulders with – they're content to let their lives go round in the same circle. They have neither the taste nor the understanding for collective life; nor are they concerned about their individual fates. This is the source of the sadness I've often felt around them; this world that's full of generous promise is crushing them, and its splendour soon seems sterile because there are no men to dominate it. All civilisations offer men an escape into 'the banality of daily life', but what is unique here is the degree to which this escape is systematically organised. Neither a person's education nor the setting in which he's raised is designed to reveal his inner life to him. He becomes conscious of himself not only as a body of flesh and blood but also as an organism that is protected and extended by an arsenal of mechanical devices. He goes up and down from one floor to the other by elevator; he travels around by subway, speaks on the telephone, writes on a typewriter, sweeps up with a vacuum cleaner. Interposed between food and his stomach are factories that make canned goods, refrigerators and electric stoves. Between his sexual desires and their satisfaction, there is a whole set of moral precepts and hygienic practices. Society hems him in from childhood. He learns to look outside himself, at others, for a model of behaviour; this is the source of what we call 'American conformism'. In fact, individuals are as different and as separate in the New World as in the Old World, but Americans more readily find ways of fleeing their singularity and avoiding the feeling of 'primal abandonment' – or perhaps they don't find an escape, but at least they look for it with more determination here. Like everyone else, they know boredom, dissatisfaction and doubt, but they try to rationalise their confusion by posing these as their 'problems'. Instead of drawing strength from solitude and trying to overcome it by examining it more thoroughly, they cling stubbornly to the given. They see the source of values and truth in things, not in themselves; their own presence is merely a chance occurrence to which they attach little importance. This is why they are interested in the net result, not in the mental effort that engenders it, like Professor T's students who didn't want to see the demonstration of a formula. Similarly, they think they can isolate the part from the whole, as evidenced by the preference for specialisation one finds in technology, the sciences and culture. In Hegelian terms, one can say that the negation of the subject leads to the triumph of understanding over Spirit – that is, the triumph of abstraction. And that's why in this country, which seems so doggedly turned toward the concrete, the word 'abstraction' has come so often to my lips. The object, erected as an idol, loses its human truth and becomes an abstraction because concrete reality envelops both object and subject. This is the paradox of all the positivisms, of all the pseudorealisms that turn away from man to affirm the thing – they miss the thing itself and attain only concepts.

Listening to their jazz, talking with them about it, I often felt that even the time they're living in is abstract. They respect the past, but as an embalmed monument; the idea of a living past integrated with the present is alien to them. They want to know only a present that's cut off from the flow of time, and the future they project is one that can be mechanically deduced from it, not one whose slow ripening or abrupt explosion implies unpredictable risks. They believe in the future of a bridge or an economic plan, not the future of an art or a revolution. Their time is the 'physicist's time', a pure exteriority that mirrors the exteriority of space. And because they reject duration, they also reject quality. It's not just for economic reasons that there is no 'craftsmanship' in America; even in the leisure activities of domestic life, they don't aim for superior quality: food is cooked and fruit is ripened as quickly as possible. In every area they rush for fear that the result will already be outdated the moment it's achieved. Cut off from the past and the future, the present has no thickness. Nothing is stranger to Americans than the idea of seeing the moment as a recapitulation of time, as a mirror of the eternal, and of anchoring themselves in it in order to grasp timeless truths or values. The contents of the moment seem to them as precarious as the moment itself. Because they don't acknowledge that truths and values *are evolving*, they don't know how to preserve them in the movement that surpasses them; they just deny them. History is a large cemetery here: men, works and ideas die almost as soon as they are born. And every individual existence has a taste of death: from minute to minute, the present is merely an honorary past. It must constantly be filled with the new to conceal the curse it carries within it. That's why Americans love speed, alcohol, film 'thrillings' and sensational news. They feverishly demand something more and, again, something more, never able to quell their restlessness. Yet here, as everywhere else, life repeats itself day after day, so people amuse themselves with gadgets, and lacking real projects, they cultivate hobbies. These manias allow them to pretend to take responsibility, by choice, for their daily habits. Sports, movies and comics all offer distractions. But in the end, people are always faced with what they wanted to escape: the arid basis of American life – boredom.

Boredom and solitude. It's been said a thousand times, and it's true: these people I rub shoulders with are alone. Because they are too eager to flee their original solitude, because they flee from themselves, they aren't truly in possession of themselves. So how can they give themselves? How can they receive? They are open and welcoming, they are capable of tenderness, passion, sentimentality and cordiality, but they rarely know how to build a deep love or a lasting friendship. They are far from heartless, yet their relations remain superficial or cold. They are far from lacking vitality, spirit and generosity, yet they don't know how to devote themselves to the project of their lives. The reason is always the same. To be Julien Sorel or Rastignac [the young, ambitious protagonists of Stendhal's *The Red and the Black* and Balzac's *Père Goriot*] demands self-possession, not a turning away from the self. There are few really ambitious people here. There is hero worship, which is rather capricious in itself, but for themselves, people desire little more than to rise one or two steps in the social hierarchy; furthermore, a young man eager to distinguish himself will wish to be distinguished as a citizen, not as a man. He will not dream of emerging beyond the given world, a dream symbolised by the tree in which Julien Sorel perches, the hill from which Rastignac surveys Paris so superbly. Such desires for grandeur are the source of plenty of disappointments and are often expressed in mean-spirited shortcomings that Americans know nothing about. Americans possess the virtues that are born of indifference to the self; they are not embittered, persecuted, malevolent, envious or egotistical, but they have no inner fire. Trying to lose themselves in the object, they find themselves without any object. They experience in another form the 'primal abandonment' that their civilisation pretends to mask from them. It's precisely this contrast between their secret fragility and their proud constructions that makes them so touching.

It seems to me that it's because of the abstract atmosphere in which they live that money takes on such inordinate importance here. These people are neither greedy nor mean. On the contrary, these are precisely the faults for which they reproach the French. They don't want money in order to amass a fortune; they're as ready to spend it on others as on themselves – giving is natural to them. Nor are they pleasure seekers, looking for a fortune to satisfy extravagant appetites. If money is the only goal for many people, it's because all other values have been reduced to this common denominator, the measure of all human accomplishments, though in fact it's only the abstract sign of true riches. Americans satisfy themselves with this empty symbol because they cannot generate and confirm concrete values. The truth is, they're not satisfied with it. Except for the high-flying capitalists, they are as embarrassed by their dollars as by their leisure time. I suppose this is one of the reasons American women are turned into idols – the dollar is too dreary a divinity. A man is sufficiently pleased to justify his work and his earnings by dedicating them to a being of flesh and blood. But the cult of the woman, like the cult of money, is only a substitute. The fate of the American man would be meaningful only if he succeeded in giving a concrete content to that abstract entity: his freedom. This is a sort of vicious circle, because in order to fill this empty freedom, he would have to change the political and social conditions in which he lives, and these are precisely what control his inertia. Of course, thousands and thousands of Americans are working to break this cycle. And of course, there are also thousands and thousands of Americans to whom my reflections here do not apply at all, or hardly at all. But inasmuch as generalisations are permitted, the great majority of Americans are victims of this mechanism. The flight from boredom and solitude traps them in solitude and boredom; by wanting to lose themselves in the world, they have lost their grip on it.

One of the things that's most striking to me is how much they hate questioning themselves and the world as it is. They need to believe that Good and Evil are clearly divided categories and that Good is or will be brought about easily. I've felt this since the beginning of my stay. But in the past few weeks I've had glaring confirmations of it. Among other things, I nearly created a scandal among the students at Columbia, Yale and Harvard when I spoke to them about the case of conscience posed in David Rousset's book *Les Jours de notre mort* [*The Days of Our Death*]. If some people in positions of responsibility could save the lives of two or three comrades in a deportation camp, what criteria should they use to make their selection? They stubbornly answered me, 'No one has the right to dispose of human lives,' or, 'What would give them the right to choose?' If I objected that not choosing would have meant saving no one, that any kind of positive act to spare two lives was more valuable than murderous abstention, they clammed up. I think that they themselves would have preferred to have let everyone perish rather than take such a burdensome initiative. Or, rather, they could not even *think* about a situation in which they would have been obliged *to take the side of Evil*. Here, they refuse to take that side, which is nonetheless the only way of fighting against it. People – even people of goodwill – refuse to articulate clearly the current conflict between justice and freedom, and the necessity of devising a compromise between these two ideas; they prefer to deny injustice and the lack of freedom. They don't want to admit that the complexity of various factors creates problems that go beyond all virtuous solutions. Evil is only a residue that we can progressively eliminate by making more rigorous use of intrinsically healthy institutions – this is the thinking of many idealistic souls. If this optimism seems too facile, they try to create a kind of artificial abscess, as it were, to localise the infections: the USSR, the embodiment of Evil, need only be annihilated to restore the reign of Good. All this explains how the very students who were so respectful of the human being could speak calmly of using atomic bombs against Russia.

If, as I reflect on these things, I again find so much to criticise, why do I feel, despite everything, so sad to leave? First of all, in European civilisation, in the French civilisation to which I am about to return, there is also much to criticise – different things, perhaps, but just as depressing. Our ways of being unhappy, of being inauthentic, are different from those of Americans – that's all. The judgements I've made on Americans during this trip are not pronounced with any sense of superiority. I see their deficiencies, but I don't forget ours. And inherent in what I like and what I loathe about this country is something fascinating: the enormous opportunities and risks America runs today and the world along with it. All human problems are posed here on a gigantic scale; and to a great degree, the solutions they find here will illuminate these problems, retrospectively, in a moving way or swallow them up in the night of indifference. Yes, I believe that this is what moves me so strongly at the moment of my departure: America is one of the pivotal points of the world, where the future of man is being played out. To 'like' America, to 'dislike' it – these words have no meaning. It is a battlefield, and you can only become passionate about the battle it is waging with itself, in which the stakes are beyond measure.

20 May

The Spanish moss and the springtime azaleas with their leaves shed by the autumnal rains, the lily-like brides at the street corner where the forgotten men beg, the stuffed coyotes, the bronze heroes, the ochre pueblos, the prefabricated houses scattered on the edge of the salt desert, the dark faces with hate-filled eyes, the varnished wood farmhouses in the shade of red maple trees, the laughing college girls, the cowboys in their rough boots . . . what bric-a-brac there is in the dusty attic where spiders are beginning to weave their webs.

Newfoundland. Shannon. Paris. It's daybreak at Orly. How old the customs officers look in their crumpled uniforms! They don't seem proud to be French citizens: there's a pleading look on their faces. They are too badly paid to have a puritanical respect for orders; they manage as best they can, holding a strange secret conference around an opulent piece of luggage. On the dreary avenue that leads toward Paris, people are poorly dressed; the women have undyed, untidy hair; the men have grey faces and look humiliated. The vegetables in the market are stunted. There's no taxi stand at the Invalides; at the edge of the sidewalk the travellers become irritated and begin to quarrel among themselves. It's grey outside. Paris seems numbed; the streets are dark and morose, the shop windows laughable. Over there in the night, a vast continent is sparkling. I'm going to have to become reacquainted with France and climb back into my own skin.

De Beauvoir's Itinerary

NEW YORK CITY

New York City: pp. 3–56
Vassar College (Poughkeepsie, New York): pp. 44–6
New York City: pp. 46–72

A TRIP SOUTH

Train to Washington DC, via New London, Connecticut: pp. 72–3
Washington DC: pp. 73–7
Lynchburg, Virginia: pp. 77–81

NEW YORK STATE

Rochester: pp. 81–3
Niagara Falls: pp. 83–7
Buffalo: pp. 83–4, 87–9

THE MIDWEST

Cleveland, Ohio: pp. 89–90
Oberlin, Ohio: pp. 90–2
Chicago, Illinois: pp. 92–101

THE WEST

Train across country to California: pp. 101–5

CALIFORNIA

Los Angeles: pp. 105–20

Ojai: pp. 120–5
Journey to San Francisco, via Monterey and Carmel: pp. 125–9
San Francisco: pp. 129–40
Sacramento: pp. 140–1
Journey to Reno, Nevada, via Placerville and Lake Tahoe: pp. 141–3

NEVADA

Reno: pp. 143–6
Journey to Lone Pine, California, via Carson City: pp. 146–9

CALIFORNIA

Lone Pine: pp. 149–52
Death Valley: pp. 152–5
Mojave Desert: p. 155

NEVADA

Las Vegas, Nevada: pp. 155–60
North to Boulder City: pp. 160–1
Journey to Los Angeles through the desert: pp. 161–4
Los Angeles: pp. 164–72

ARIZONA

Journey through Arizona to the Grand Canyon, via Williams: pp. 172–4
The Grand Canyon: pp. 174–8
Journey from Williams to Albuquerque, New Mexico: pp. 178–80

NEW MEXICO

Albuquerque: pp. 180–2
Santa Fe: pp. 182–7

Taos: pp. 187–91
Santa Fe: pp. 191–8
Journey through the desert to Texas: pp. 198–9

The South
Texas

Pecos: pp. 199–200
Journey deeper into Texas: pp. 200–1
San Antonio: pp. 201–7
Journey to Houston: pp. 207–10
Houston: pp. 210–14

The Deep South

Journey to New Orleans, Louisiana: pp. 214–16
New Orleans: pp. 217–28
Journey to Jacksonville, Florida, through Louisiana, Mississippi, Alabama and Florida: pp. 228–30
Savannah, Georgia: pp. 230–2
Charleston, South Carolina: pp. 245–7

Virginia

Richmond: pp. 247–8
Williamsburg: pp. 248–50

The East Coast

New York City: pp. 250–76
Smith and Wellesley colleges (Massachusetts): pp. 276–80
Concord, Massachusetts, and Walden Pond: pp. 280–5
Boston, Massachusetts: pp. 285–7
Harvard (Cambridge, Massachusetts): p. 287
New York City: pp. 288–94
Princeton, New Jersey: pp. 294–8

Journey to Boston, then north through Massachusetts via Marblehead, Salem, and Rockport: pp. 298–300
Boston: p. 300
New York City: pp. 311–35
Roxbury, Connecticut: pp. 335–9
New York City: pp. 339–50

Back to Chicago: pp. 350–78

New York City: pp. 378–80

VINTAGE CLASSICS

Vintage Classics is home to some of the greatest writers and thinkers from around the world and across the ages. Bringing you not just the books you already know and love, but new additions to your library, these are works to capture imaginations, inspire new perspectives and excite curiosity.

Renowned for our iconic red spines and bold, collectable design, Vintage Classics is an adventurous, ever-evolving list. We breathe new life into classic books for modern readers, publishing to reflect the world today, because we believe that our times can best be understood in conversation with the past.